A User-Friendly Look at the Good Book

the Bible FOR BLOCKHEADS

Douglas Connelly

S0-CFO-925

ZONDERVAN™

GRAND RAPIDS, MICHIGAN 49530

We want to hear from you. Please send your comments about this book to us in care of the address below. Thank you.

GRAND RAPIDS, MICHIGAN 49530

w w w . z o n d e r v a n . c o m

ZONDERVAN™

Requests for information should be addressed to:

Zondervan, Grand Rapids, Michigan 49530

Library of Congress Cataloging-in-Publication Data

Connelly, Douglas, 1949–
    The Bible for blockheads : a user-friendly look at the Good Book / Douglas Connelly.
        p. cm.
    Includes bibliographical references.
    ISBN 0-310-22267–2 (softcover)
    1. Bible Introductions. I. Title.
    BS475.2.C67 1999
    220.6'1—dc21   99-26110

Printed in the United States of America

Interior Design by Sherri L. Hoffman
Interior Illustrations by Patten Illustration

---

02 03 04 05 06 07 / ❖ DC/ 14 13 12 11 10

Contents

Part 7: Gospels

Part 8: History

Part 9: Letters

Welcome

The Bible makes us nervous. We know it's the "Good Book," but it can be intimidating. When we pick it up, we quickly find ourselves lost in its difficult names and churchy language. We may hear the Bible read once in a while, but we've concluded that it's out of our league.

This book will help. It is not a substitute for the Bible but an access code into an incredible book. Like the guidebook to a video game that seems impossible, my plan is to show you an easy way in. You'll be amazed at how much of the Bible you can grasp on your own with a few simple facts in your mental arsenal.

Suppose you find a letter blowing around on the street tomorrow morning. It probably won't mean a whole lot to you. But if you are told that the letter was written by a man to a friend or by a woman to her daughter, suddenly the letter takes on more significance. If you then discover that the man's friend is dying or that the woman's daughter is a runaway, the words may move you powerfully. Sometimes what will open your understanding to a section of the Bible is just knowing who wrote it and who first read it. Just a few words explaining what it's all about can make the Bible come alive.

This book is a guide to a great adventure. It assumes nothing except that you are ready to make the climb.

What You Will Find in This Book

After a couple chapters explaining what the Bible is and how best to start exploring it, you will find a short chapter on each of the sixty-six short books that make up the big book we call the Bible. I tell what each book is about, who the main players are, who wrote it and why— and then I leave it up to you to actually read that part of the Bible.

You will also find some special sections in each chapter. A chapter will contain several but not necessarily all of these:

- *Help File:* Fascinating facts about the book or author that will accelerate the learning curve.
- *Key Characters:* The main people connected with each biblical book.
- *Points 2 Remember:* Concise summaries of key points from each biblical book.
- *Download:* A verse or passage of Scripture to memorize.
- *Walking the Walk:* Suggestions for making what you have read more personal. Projects to explore or questions to consider.
- *Digging Deeper:* Resources to help you investigate further.

Other nuggets of information are scattered throughout the book:

- *Tool Time:* Practical insight into how to choose and use key resources to help you understand the Bible even better.
- *Footprints in the Sand:* Important discoveries in archaeology or history that shed light on the Bible.
- *People of the Bible:* Brief discussion of the main players on the stage of the biblical world.

The Bible: What's with It?

— Heads Up

➤ Discover how the Bible was written—and how it survived.
➤ Learn to find your way around quickly.
➤ Find out what role God played in the production of the Bible.

The word *Bible* means "the book." The Bible is one book, but it is also a collection of books. Sixty-six books were written over 1,600 years by at least forty different authors. You will find just about every kind of writing in the Bible—love letters, songs, historical records, diaries, visions of the future, genealogies, suicide notes. The Bible was the first book printed on a printing press, and it still outsells all other books in the marketplace. You can get the Bible on audio, on video, and online. It has been translated into more languages and has been quoted more and memorized more than any book in human history.

The Bible is divided into two main sections—the Old Testament and the New Testament. The Old Testament focuses on God's interaction with the people of Israel. The New Testament, written later, focuses on Jesus and his early followers called Christians. The word *testament* means "treaty or covenant," an agreement made between two people. God entered into a contract with the people of Israel in the Old Testament. God's new contract (in the *New* Testament) is made with anyone who will commit to following Jesus. In each testament the terms of the agreement are spelled out. The Bible is an instruction manual for people who want to do what pleases God.

The Old Testament

The first and longest major division of the Bible is called the Old Testament by Christians. (Jewish people refer to it as the Hebrew Bible.) Thirty-nine individual biblical books are included in the Old Testament. Some of the books are named for their author—like the book of Daniel. Daniel was a prophet, or spokesperson, for God who wrote that particular book. Some books are named for their main characters, who may or may not be the author. The book of Joshua is about a great leader named Joshua. The book of Esther is about a Jewish girl who became a courageous queen. Joshua probably was the author of his book. Esther probably was not the writer of the book about her.

Other Old Testament books get their names because of the story they tell. The book of Exodus, for example, tells the story of the nation of Israel's "exit" from Egypt. The books of Kings talk about (you guessed it) Israel's kings. Some books have unusual names that don't make much sense in English—Leviticus, Ecclesiastes, Psalms. (I've tried to give some explanation of these titles in the Help File section of each of these books.)

Originally the Old Testament was written in two languages. Most of it was written in Hebrew. Small sections of a few books were written in a language related to Hebrew called Aramaic.

Here's what Hebrew looks like in a modern Hebrew Bible:

> בְּרֵאשִׁית בָּרָא אֱלֹתִים אֵת הַשָּׁמַיִם וְאֵת הָאָרֶץ:
>
> In the beginning God created the heavens and the earth.

Hebrew is read from right to left (the opposite of English) and from the top line of the page to the bottom line (the same as English). The large blocky letters are the consonants (twenty-two in the Hebrew alphabet). The dots and small marks above or below the consonants are vowels or vowel "points." When the Old Testament was first composed, Hebrew was written with no vowels and no word divisions (mostly to conserve room on very expensive writing material). Word divisions were made about A.D. 100. Vowel marks were added in the ninth or tenth century A.D. to preserve the correct pronunciation of the ancient Hebrew language.

Hebrew is a very expressive language. It is a language suited to stories and poetry—exactly the forms found most often in the Old Testament.

The New Testament

The second main section of the Bible is the New Testament (twenty-seven biblical books). Just as in the Old Testament, some of these books are named for their author. The gospel of John, for example, is the story of Jesus (a gospel) written by one of Jesus' followers (John). Other books are named for their content. The book of Acts records the "acts," or deeds, of the early Christians. Many of the New Testament books are letters and are named for those who first read the letter. Ephesians, for example, is a letter sent to the Christians in the city of Ephesus. People living in the city of Corinth were called Corinthians—and we have two letters to the Corinthian Christians (1 and 2 Corinthians).

The New Testament was originally written in Greek. When the story of the New Testament opened, Rome ruled the world of Europe and North Africa, but the universal language of the Roman Empire was Greek, not Latin. The New Testament was written in "street Greek." It was not the difficult language of the scholars, but the everyday language of the people. Today it looks like this in a printed Greek New Testament:

Ἐν ἀρχῇ ἦν ὁ λόγος, καὶ ὁ λόγος ἦν πρὸς τὸν θεόν, καὶ θεός ἦν ὁ λόγος.

In the beginning was the Word, and the Word was with God, and the Word was God.

Greek is read from left to right just like English. While Hebrew is a poetic language, Greek is a very precise language. Its words and structure are more rigid than Hebrew. It is a great language for precise, clear communication.

A Survival Story

The original documents of the Bible have all disappeared, but copies of the originals have survived. We take making copies for granted. Every drugstore and post office has a twenty-five-cent copy machine. Before the printing press, however, every copy of a book or letter had to be made by hand. Some of the most respected people in society were scribes, those who could write or copy words. Think of how long it would take you to copy by hand even one book of the Bible or the latest John Grisham novel! People in the ancient world copied only the most important or treasured documents.

Hand-produced copies of the Hebrew Old Testament and the Greek New Testament are called *manuscripts*. Some of the manuscripts we possess are very old. We are confident that these manuscripts are accurate copies of the original writings because the Jews and later the Christians who copied the text took extreme care in their work. They were fanatics about accuracy!

So many copies (manuscripts) have survived that we can compare the places where minor discrepancies occur. Less than 1 percent of the accuracy of the New Testament text, for example, is seriously questioned. That is just one word out of every four thousand words. More significantly, none of the teachings of the Bible are affected by any variation in the text.

Over four thousand Greek manuscripts of the New Testament have survived. Compare that to some other ancient writings:

- Homer's *Iliad* has the most surviving copies of any other ancient document—643 manuscripts. Five percent of the text is questionable.
- Julius Caesar's *Gallic Wars* rests on only ten surviving copies.
- Tacitus wrote seventeen books of Roman history. Only four and one-half books survive in two copies.

Two of the oldest complete New Testament manuscripts that survive were copied about A.D. 350—some 250 years after the New Testament

THE EVIL BIBLE

In 1631 one enterprising group of printers produced a thousand copies of the Bible. There was just one little problem. One key word was missing from one of the Ten Commandments in Exodus 20. This Bible read: "Thou shalt commit adultery." The printers left out the word *not* and were fined thousands of dollars (three thousand English pounds). Their Bible became known as "The Adulterer's Bible."

was completed. In addition we have fragments of various New Testament books that can be dated 100 to 200 years earlier, to within 150 years of the writing of the New Testament. Other ancient writings don't even come close.

Scholars of the Greek dramatist Sophocles tell us that we have an accurate text of his seven surviving plays. But the manuscript upon which the text is based was copied more than 1,400 years after the poet's death.

The earliest surviving copies of the dialogues of Plato date from 1,300 years after their original writing.

We don't have the actual letter written to the Christians in Ephesus (our New Testament book of Ephesians), but we can put our confidence in the accuracy of the text we do have. The Bible has survived attacks from every direction. Dictators have tried to destroy it, critics have tried to shred it, skeptics have tried to ignore it, and enemies have tried to burn it, but it has survived them all.

Finding Your Way Around

Once Bibles began to be printed as books on a printing press (around A.D. 1550), chapters and verses were added to make it easier to find a specific text. Today we have a standard way of writing references to Bible verses. *John 1:12*, for example, means the *gospel of John* (the biblical book), *chapter 1* (the chapter is listed to the left of the colon), *verse 12* (the verse number is listed to the right of the colon). The Bible reference is the "address" of the verse in the Bible. You can pick up any Bible and find the gospel of John (the fourth book in the New Testament section). In the first chapter at verse number 12, you would read something like this:

> Yet to all who received him, to those who believed in his name, he gave the right to become children of God.

To refer to more than one verse, a dash is used to connect the first and last verses. *John 1:12–14* indicates the section of John, chapter 1, from verse 12 through verse 14. Individual verses in a chapter are separated by a comma. *John 1:12, 14* refers to John, chapter 1, verse 12 *and* verse 14. Sections of a book covering more than one chapter are also indicated by using a dash. *Acts 15:36–18:22* refers to the book of Acts, chapter 15, verse 36, *through* chapter 18, verse 22. Sometimes a Bible reference just includes the chapters of a book. *John 14–17* means the gospel of John, chapter 14 through chapter 17.

A few biblical books are just one chapter in length. A reference to those books mentions only the book name and verse number. *Jude 8* refers to the book of Jude, verse 8.

Occasionally a reference will be made to a small section of a verse rather than the whole verse. A lowercase "a" or "b" (and sometimes "c" if the verse is long) is used in the reference. *John 1:12a* refers to the first part of verse 12 in the gospel of John, chapter 1.

The Bible is also divided into paragraphs or stanzas of poetry. Different versions of the Bible have different ways of indicating those divisions. Sometimes the editors of a version of the Bible will insert section headings describing the content of a section or "passage" of Scripture. As you read and use your Bible more, you will become familiar with the "mechanics" of its layout. What is most important in your Bible, of course, is not the layout or size of the print or color of the cover. What is most important are the words of the Bible themselves.

But I Don't Speak Greek!

Down through the centuries, the Bible has been translated from Hebrew and Greek into other languages. A translation of the Bible is usually called a *version* of the Bible. The *Authorized Version* (AV; also

CHAPTER AND VERSE

The books of the Bible were not divided into chapters until the year 1214. Stephen Langton, who was England's leading clergyman, proposed chapter divisions that were adopted not only by the Christians but also by the Jews.

Verse divisions didn't appear until 1551. Robert Estienne, a French printer, decided to divide the chapters of the Bible into smaller sections. His son later wrote that Estienne had constructed the verse divisions while on a journey on horseback—which may explain why some of the verse divisions appear in such unexpected places!

The *New International Version* of the Bible is divided into 1,189 chapters and 31,086 verses. It contains 726,109 words—and a vocabulary of 14,462 words!

THE APOCRYPHA

Some Bibles have more than sixty-six books. Catholic Bibles, for example, have more than thirty-nine books in the Old Testament. Some Protestant Bibles include a separate section between the Old Testament and New Testament called the Apocrypha.

The fourteen or fifteen books of the Apocrypha (the word means "hidden") were written between 300 B.C. and A.D. 100. Jews and Protestant Christians do not accept these books as part of the Bible. The books are not connected directly to a prophet (authorized spokesperson for God), nor are the books quoted by the New Testament writers. The Roman Catholic Church does view the books of the Apocrypha as part of the Bible. Some Protestants (Anglicans and Lutherans) point to the value of these books as religious writings but do not put them on the same level as the books of the Bible. They believe the books can be read for enrichment but not as the basis for Christian teaching.

called the *King James Version* [KJV]) of the Bible is one of the most famous English translations. It was completed in 1611 and was the main version of the Bible used by Protestant, English-speaking Christians for more than three hundred years. But the English language has changed in the past four centuries, and the KJV has become more difficult to understand. In the mid-1900s several contemporary language English versions of the Bible were produced.

One popular English version is the *New American Standard Bible* (NASB for short). This very accurate translation converts the Hebrew and Greek text into English as directly as possible. The NASB was updated in 1998.

The *New International Version* (NIV) is the most widely used English version today. It translates the original languages accurately but in a more readable style than the NASB.

Other widely used versions in English are:

- *New Revised Standard Version* (NRSV)
- *New King James Version* (NKJV)
- *New American Bible* (NAB) (used by many Catholics)
- *Jerusalem Bible* (JB) (used by many Catholics)
- *The New Living Translation* (NLT)
- *The Contemporary English Version* (CET)

All versions or translations of the Bible attempt to express accurately the meaning of the original writings in a new language.

The best version for you to use is the one you will actually read! If you like and can understand the English of the KJV, fine. If you enjoy the NASB, plunge in. If you are new to the Bible or have never read the Bible much, the NIV is an excellent choice. That's the version I use throughout this guide.

Is the Good Book God's Book?

Christians look at the Bible as more than just a collection of ancient religious writings. The Bible is God's Word—God's truth written in human language. The Bible itself claims to originate with God, not with those who wrote it. One of Jesus' followers, Peter, wrote that the authors of the Bible "spoke from God as they were carried along by the Holy Spirit" (2 Peter 1:21). Paul, another New Testament writer, said, "All Scripture is God-breathed" (2 Timothy 3:16). Over four thousand times in various ways the Bible claims to be a record of what God said. The Bible speaks with God's authority and tells us the truth about God, about the world, and about ourselves.

DigginG DeEpeR

To learn more about how the Bible was written and preserved over the centuries, check out one of these books:

✗ Bruce, F. F. *The New Testament Documents: Are They Reliable?* Rev. ed. Downers Grove, IL: InterVarsity Press, 1984.

A defense of the reliability of the New Testament as an accurate record of real events.

✗ Ewert, David. *A General Introduction to the Bible: From Ancient Tablets to Modern Translations.* Grand Rapids: Zondervan, 1990.

A serious but readable account of how the Bible came to be.

✗ Hall, Terry. *How the Bible Became a Book.* Wheaton, IL: Victor Books, 1990.

A brief but interesting record of the history of the Bible.

God did use human authors to communicate his truth. The writers of the Bible were not robots, mindlessly recording the dictation of an inner voice. They wrote letters and historical summaries and wise sayings for people who lived in a particular culture at a specific time and place in history. But God guided what they wrote so that their writings communicated exactly what he wanted said. God still speaks to us in the Bible even though we live thousands of years later than the original writers and readers of the Bible.

You may not agree that the Bible is God's book. You may not even think that the Bible is true. It's okay to think that way. Clever arguments won't convince you differently, so don't expect any "pulpit pounding" from me! I encourage you to pursue your interest in the Bible at any level. What you will discover as you read is that the Bible can defend itself. God will begin to speak to your mind and your life when you least expect it.

Getting Started

— Heads Up —

➤ If you still think you can't understand the Bible, this chapter is for you.
➤ Find out how a bunch of ancient words still speak to us today.
➤ Discover some goof-proof ways to jump in.

This chapter should make your journey into the Bible a lot more fulfilling. Understanding the Bible is not difficult if you know how to read it. Some easy principles will jump-start the process.

Three Steps to Unlocking the Bible

First, let us look at three steps that will help unlock any Bible passage or book of the Bible you come to. Leave out one of these steps or mix them up, and all you'll get is frustration.

Step 1: What Does It Say?

The very first, most important thing you should do with the Bible is read it. People who think the Bible is mysterious have never read it. If you don't believe me, stop right here, find a Bible, and read the first chapter of the first book—Genesis. It's the Bible's account of the creation of the world. You won't find any really big words. (Well, "firmament" is big if you are reading from an older version of the Bible. Think "expanse" or "empty space.")

Most of the Bible can be understood if you just read it. Look for clues that answer basic questions: What people are involved in this story? What happens? How is God involved?

Remember that the writers communicated in different styles and through different forms of writing. You read a love letter differently than you read the phone book, don't you? The poetry of the Psalms in the Old Testament speaks to us differently than the tight arguments of one of Paul's New Testament letters. The sweeping story of Exodus will be read with different "rules" than the visions of Ezekiel.

Yes, you will encounter difficult passages and concepts sometimes, but there is so much you can understand. Remember that the difficult sections are difficult for everyone—including preachers and Sunday school teachers. Some passages in the Bible no one fully understands!

I will try to open the door to each biblical book for you, but don't use this book as a substitute for the Bible. What I say should just provide access for your own reading.

Step 2: What Does It Mean?

Once you have a grasp of what a biblical passage or book says, the next step is to ask questions. The Bible is never embarrassed by questions! If you are reading a gospel (an account of Jesus' life) and you read about some event in Jesus' life, ask *why* Jesus did what he did. In the gospel of John, chapter 2, Jesus went into the Jewish temple in Jerusalem and chased the animal sellers and money exchangers out. The story is not hard to understand. But what was the temple, and why was it important to Jesus? Who were these money exchangers? Why did their transactions make Jesus so angry? What results came from Jesus' actions that day?

To answer these questions, we usually have to go outside the passage we are reading. Sometimes just reading further in the story gives us the insight we need. For example, later in John's story of Jesus, we learn that Jesus' actions in John 2 aroused the hostility of the people in charge of the temple. Their profit margin was seriously decreased that day, and they blamed Jesus.

Sometimes our questions about one passage in the Bible are answered by reading other sections. In the Old Testament books of Leviticus and 2 Samuel, we learn that Israel's temple was to be a place where the people focused on worship to God, not a place where commerce was conducted and where poor people were ripped off. Jesus was reclaiming the temple for its intended purpose.

Other resources can help us answer our biblical questions too. A *Bible dictionary,* for example, will tell us about the temple and its place in Israel's worship. A *commentary* in which a scholar looks carefully at the original language in which the passage was written as well as the cultural background of the story can provide additional insight. Study notes in a good *study Bible* will also help us understand some of the cultural settings or will make sense of a figure of speech or unusual word.

As valuable as these resources are, they never take the place of the Bible itself. Always read the passage for yourself. You will gain far greater insight from reading the Bible passage than you will ever gain just from reading what other people say about the passage.

Step 3: So What?

After you have worked through the first two steps, you are ready to ask another question of the biblical passage or book you are reading: So what? What is in this passage for me? How does this make a difference in my life? This is when you take inventory of your life.

Understanding what a passage in the Bible says is important, but it is not enough. Asking good questions and finding the answers so you understand fully what a passage means are interesting pursuits, but they won't make a drastic difference in your life. The Bible was written to change us. The passage you read and studied may have commands in it that God wants you to obey or promises you need to hold on to in a difficult time. The passage might lay out an example for you to follow (or not to follow). If the passage has taught you something about God, how will you respond to God in the light of what you have learned? If the passage has exposed something you are not doing in your relationship with your mate or your friends, what changes will you make?

Sometimes the application of a verse or passage is very clear. For example, you will read this in Ephesians 4:29:

> Do not let any unwholesome talk come out of your mouths, but only what is helpful for building others up.

Easy to read. Easy to understand. But think back right now over what you have said in the last twenty-four hours to other people—your kids, your coworkers, your spouse, your boss, the guy on the highway. Have you been *practicing* the command of Ephesians 4:29? It does very little good to know what the verse says or even where to find it in the Bible if we aren't *doing* it.

At other times the application of a passage is not as direct. Take the story in John 2 of Jesus chasing the money exchangers and animal sellers out of the temple. Should we go to church next Sunday armed with a whip ready to drive out anyone selling tickets to a Christian concert or taking orders for Girl Scout cookies? I don't think so! But it might mean that the primary focus of our time in church should be to lift up and honor God, not to raise money for the new gymnasium. It might also mean that we should concentrate fully on what we are singing and saying to God in worship instead of thinking about our next business deal or the afternoon football game.

The application step is the painful part of the process! Once we understand what the Bible says, we have to line up our lives and see how we measure up. We can't change the Bible! All we can do is change ourselves—or just ignore what the Bible says.

Picking a Plan

You can approach the Bible from any one of its entry points.

The Whole Elephant Approach

How do you eat an elephant? One bite at a time. You may want to start at the beginning of the Bible and work through each book in order. If you have some knowledge of the Bible but have never really studied it, this is a great way to expose yourself to all that the Bible says. You can also use this approach to work your way through just the New Testament before you tackle the Old Testament.

Steps in the process:

1. Read the chapter in this *Blockheads* guide about each biblical book—Genesis, for example. You will get a helpful overview of the book and some suggestions on what transitions and main characters to watch for.
2. Read the biblical book. You may want to do it in one or two long sessions, or you may find it easier to read a few chapters a day. If you get bogged down or tired of a particular book, move on to the next one. You can always come back to a hard one.

3. Keep a journal handy (a small spiral notebook will do) to record your progress and to jot down significant thoughts and insights. The journal is for your eyes only, so make it personal. I've written all kinds of things in mine—prayers, key verses, regrets, resolutions. Think of it as a spiritual diary. On some days you will write the date and the passage you read and nothing else. On other days you might fill pages.

4. Use the notes in your study Bible to help you with any difficult passages, but don't try to do an in-depth study of every verse. Get the big picture instead. Focus on the grand sweep of the book.

5. When you have finished reading a biblical book, come back to the chapter in the *Blockheads* guide and read through it again. Respond to the points in the Walking the Walk section. Add any of your own key insights to the Points 2 Remember section.

6. Move on to the next book and repeat the process. One bite down—sixty-five to go!

The Jesus First Approach

If you haven't had much exposure to the Bible, the best entry point is with the story of Jesus. The gospel of Mark (second book in the New Testament) is where to start.

DiGGinG DeEpeR

If you want to know more about how to interpret and apply the Bible, one of these books will help.

✗ Hendricks, Howard, and William Hendricks. *Living by the Book.* Chicago: Moody Press, 1991.

A very helpful book with practical steps to guide you in your study of the Bible.

✗ Kuhatschek, Jack. *Taking the Guesswork Out of Applying the Bible.* Downers Grove, IL: InterVarsity Press, 1990.

This book will show you how the principles and promises of the Bible apply to your life.

Steps in the process:

1. Read the *Blockheads* chapter on the gospel of Mark (p. 0308). This will give you a basic introduction to what the book is about.
2. Read Mark's gospel. Don't get discouraged if you come upon something you don't understand. Just keep reading. You might want to read the gospel twice—the first time straight through, the second time more slowly. Study Bible notes will help you with difficult words or concepts.
3. Come back to the *Blockheads* guide and work through the Walking the Walk section. (You have already done the first project!) Use your journal to record your response to the book. What parts of the story were most interesting? What parts were hardest to believe?
4. Move from Mark to the next stage in the biblical story—the book of Acts (the fifth book of the New Testament). The book of Acts tells us what happened after Jesus rose from the dead. Follow the same steps that you followed in reading Mark.
5. After Acts, try these books:

   Romans: Understand the Christian faith.
   Colossians: Find out who Jesus really is.
   James: Get practical instruction for daily living.
   Genesis: See how it all began.

The Wal-Mart Approach

Some people just like to walk up and down the aisles and pick out what they want. Be my guest! Jump in anywhere in this book and choose any section of Scripture that interests you. The *Blockheads* chapter will give you a map to follow through Job or Proverbs or Hebrews. Then launch out on your own exploration. You might want to read the biblical book first and then come back and read what I have to say. It's okay! There are no rules in this process.

I've said enough to get you started. Just do it!

TOOL TiMe

Study Bibles

The best tool for learning about the Bible is—a Bible! But one stop at your local Waldenbooks will leave you dizzy with choices. First, there are at least a dozen different translations of the Bible. Then you discover that each translation comes in several different formats. Reduced to simplest terms, you will find four "kinds" of Bibles for sale.

Text: The most basic Bible is one with just the words of Scripture in it. No study notes, no charts or outlines—just the text. Sometimes a text Bible is the best Bible for reading because there isn't much to distract you from what the Bible actually says. Text Bibles are relatively inexpensive too.

Devotional: Many Bibles are designed to help you grow stronger in your faith. These Bibles have sections that give practical encouragement for living as a Christian. They are usually focused on a particular interest group—the *Men's Bible,* the *Women's Bible,* the *Couple's Bible,* the *African-American Heritage Bible.* Everyone has a Bible! The words of the Bible are not altered, but devotional material is added on the side to make the Bible's message more personal. Devotional Bibles are a good choice for daily reading and for personal growth. Their disadvantage is that some readers will focus more on the devotional message than on the words of the Bible itself.

Reference: A reference Bible has the text of the Bible, but it also includes other helps to assist you in learning the Bible. You will find cross-references, for example. Along the margins or in the center of each page, other Bible references are printed. As you read a verse, you can look in the cross-reference section and find other Bible verses that give you additional insight on a person or event or biblical theme. A reference Bible usually has maps of Bible lands in the back and a small index for locating verses on similar topics. Reference Bibles typically try to help you compare one Bible verse with other Bible verses. You are left to draw your own conclusions from the words of the Bible itself.

Study: A good study Bible is a wonderful tool for learning the Bible. You can carry a whole library of information with you in one book. A study Bible has everything a reference Bible has—the words of the Bible, cross-references, maps, indexes, and charts—plus a lot more. Study notes on each page explain important words, give insight to difficult verses, provide historical or cultural background on a passage, or point to other Bible passages that shed light on the one you are reading. Introductions and outlines of each biblical book will help you understand the author and setting of that particular book. Most study Bibles also include helpful charts and maps to give you a visual overview of biblical material. Take the time to read the introduction to your study Bible so you learn how to use the resources it provides to the fullest.

When you choose a study Bible, look first for the translation of the text that you want. Most study Bibles are built around four main translations—the *New International Version,* the *New American Standard Version,* the *Authorized* or *King James Version,* and the *New King James Version.* Each translation has several study Bibles available. Sometimes the study notes are written by one person. The *Ryrie Study Bible* produced by Moody Press has study material written by Dr. Charles Ryrie, a well-known Bible teacher from Dallas Theological Seminary. The *Scofield Study Bible* was one of the first study Bibles. It was designed and written by C. I. Scofield, a prominent Bible teacher of the early twentieth century.

WHAT ARE THESE WORDS IN RED?

In the New Testament section of many Bibles you will see some of the words printed in red, especially in the first four books, the Gospels. The editors of that Bible have used red ink to highlight the actual words spoken by Jesus. You will find more red ink in the early chapters of the book of Revelation where Jesus speaks directly to seven churches.

My favorite study Bible is the *NIV Study Bible* produced by Zondervan Bible Publishers. It was written and edited by several respected Christian scholars, and it has been widely used since its publication in 1984. The study notes are consistently helpful, and it is filled with well-designed charts, maps, and diagrams.

Talk to other people and find out what study Bibles they are using. Ask them what they like and what they don't like. A spiritual mentor or pastor can give you some direction too. Look at several Bibles before you invest in one. A good study Bible will provide you with abundant help and insight for years.

SAMPLE PAGE FROM *THE NIV STUDY BIBLE*

Editor's summary

Cross-reference (other verses in the Bible on the same subject)

Words of the Bible

Chapter number

Verse number

Study Notes (explanation and background to help you understand the Bible)

Charts and Maps

1359 | **JONAH 1:8**

Jonah Flees From the LORD

1 The word of the LORD came to Jonah[a] son of Amittai:[b] [2]"Go to the great city of Nineveh[c] and preach against it, because its wickedness has come up before me."

[3]But Jonah ran[d] away from the LORD and headed for Tarshish.[e] He went down to Joppa,[f] where he found a ship bound for that port. After paying the fare, he went aboard and sailed for Tarshish to flee from the LORD.[g]

[4]Then the LORD sent a great wind on the sea, and such a violent storm arose that the ship threatened to break up.[h] [5]All the sailors were afraid and each cried out to his own god. And they threw the cargo into the sea to lighten the ship.[i]

But Jonah had gone below deck, where he lay down and fell into a deep sleep. [6]The captain went to him and said, "How can you sleep? Get up and call[j] on your god! Maybe he will take notice of us, and we will not perish."[k]

[7]Then the sailors said to each other, "Come, let us cast lots to find out who is responsible for this calamity."[l] They cast lots and the lot fell on Jonah.[m]

[8]So they asked him, "Tell us, who is responsible for making all this trouble for

1:1
a Mt 12:39-41; 16:4;
Lk 11:29-32
b 2Ki 14:25
1:2
c S Ge 10:11;
S Na 1:1
1:3
d Ps 139:7
e S Ge 10:4
f S Jos 19:46;
Ac 9:36,43
g S Ex 4:13;
S Jer 20:9;
S Am 3:8
1:4
h Ps 107:23-26

1:5
i Ac 27:18-19
1:6 j Jnh 3:8
k S Ps 107:28
1:7 l Nu 32:23;
Jos 7:10-18; S 1Sa 14:42 m S Pr 16:33

1:1 *The word of the LORD came.* See 3:1; a common phrase used to indicate the divine source of the prophet's revelation (see, e.g., 1Ki 17:8; Jer 1:2,4; Hos 1:1; Joel 1:1; Hag 1:1,3; Zec 1:1,7). *Jonah.* See Introduction: Title; Author.

1:2 *great city.* See 3:2; 4:11; see also note on 3:3. According to Ge 10:11–12, it was first built by Nimrod (perhaps along with Rehoboth Ir, Calah and Resen) and was traditionally known as the "great city." About 700 B.C. Sennacherib made it the capital of Assyria, which it remained until its fall in 612 (see Introduction to Nahum: Background). Nineveh is over 500 miles from Gath Hepher, Jonah's hometown. *its wickedness has come up.* Cf. Sodom and Gomorrah (Ge 18:20–21). Except for the violence (3:8) of Nineveh, her "evil ways" (3:8,10) are not described in Jonah. Nahum later states that Nineveh's sins included plotting evil against the Lord (Na 1:11), cruelty and plundering in war (Na 2:12–13; 3:1,19), prostitution and witchcraft (Na 3:4) and commercial exploitation (Na 3:16).

1:3 *ran away.* The reason is found in 4:2. The futility of trying to run away from the Lord is acknowledged in Ps 139:7,9–10. *Tarshish.* Perhaps the city of Tartessus in southwest Spain, a Phoenician mining colony near Gibraltar. By heading in the opposite direction from Nineveh, to

what seemed like the end of the world, Jonah intended to escape his divinely appointed task.

1:4–5 Although Jonah's mission was to bring God's warning of impending judgment to the pagan world, his refusal to go to Nineveh brings these pagan sailors into peril.

1:4 *the LORD sent a great wind.* God's sovereign working in Jonah's mission is evident at several other points also: the fish (v. 17), the release of Jonah (2:10), the vine (4:6), the worm (4:7) and the wind (4:8).

1:5 *his own god.* Apparently the sailors, who may have come from various ports, worshiped several pagan gods.

1:6 *The captain went to him.* The pagan captain's concern for everyone on board contrasts with the believing prophet's refusal to carry God's warning to Nineveh.

1:7 *let us cast lots.* The casting of lots was a custom widely practiced in the ancient Near East. The precise method is unclear, though it appears that, for the most part, sticks or marked pebbles were drawn from a receptacle into which they had been "cast." *lot fell on Jonah.* By the lot of judgment the Lord exposed the guilty one (cf. Jos 7:14–26; 1Sa 14:38–44; Pr 16:33).

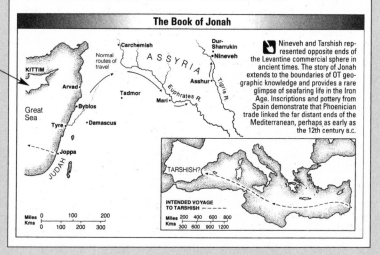

The Book of Jonah

Nineveh and Tarshish represented opposite ends of the Levantine commercial sphere in ancient times. The story of Jonah extends to the boundaries of OT geographic knowledge and provides a rare glimpse of seafaring life in the Iron Age. Inscriptions and pottery from Spain demonstrate that Phoenician trade linked the far distant ends of the Mediterranean, perhaps as early as the 12th century B.C.

Part 1

FOUNDATIONS

The first five books of the Bible are the foundation on which the whole Bible rests. Every major theme of the Bible has its beginning in these books.

The books of Genesis, Exodus, Leviticus, Numbers, and Deuteronomy are called the Pentateuch (*pen-ta-tuke*). The word is a combination of two Greek words meaning "five" and "scrolls" or "tools." The writers of the Bible referred to these books as the "Book of the Law" (Joshua 1:8), "the Law of Moses" (1 Kings 2:3), "the Law of God" (Nehemiah 10:28), or simply "the Law" (Ezra 10:3). The books are filled with God's commands and instructions for the Old Testament nation of Israel.

The Jews use the word *Torah* to describe these five books. Torah includes the idea of "law," but it is a broader term meaning "teaching" or "instruction." Within the Torah we find God's teaching on how human life began and how the nation of Israel began. The Torah also explains the presence and power of evil in our world and tells how people who have done evil can find forgiveness and hope.

Most of the Pentateuch is narrative, stories about God's people. These are the foundational stories of the Bible. What happened to Adam and Eve and to Abraham and to Moses and the people of Israel at the Red Sea echoes throughout the rest of the Old Testament and beyond into the New. We are still affected today by what happened way back then!

The books of the Law are fairly easy to read and understand. As you read, you will learn a lot about God and how God works in our world and in people's lives. You will see yourself in many of these stories too— not doing exactly the things the biblical people did, but struggling, failing, succeeding, and learning to love God the same way they did.

Christians and Jews have traditionally viewed Moses as the author of these books. Some scholars have tried to sort out several "sources" for these books and say that a later editor managed to weave the parts together to form the books we have today. However, both the internal evidence (statements made in the books themselves) and the external evidence (facts we can learn from the culture and history of Moses' time) strongly support the authorship of Moses. It is obvious that later biblical writers added a few important things (the account of Moses' death in Deuteronomy 34, for example), but the essential material in these books came from God through his servant Moses.

Genesis

➤ Find out how our universe began—and how evil invaded.

➤ See how God intervenes to turn bad news into good news.

➤ Follow the fortunes of one family as they try to obey the Lord.

Key Characters

Adam and Eve: the first human beings; they were tempted by Satan to disobey God and paid a big price (Genesis 2–3)

Noah: a good guy who built a big boat (an ark) and saved his family and two of every kind of animal from destruction in the Flood (Genesis 6–9)

Abraham: the physical and spiritual "father" of the people of Israel; an idol worshiper who came to believe in the one true God and was directed by God to a new land (Genesis 12–25)

Isaac: Abraham's son who inherited God's blessing (Genesis 26–27)

Jacob: Abraham's grandson, Isaac's son; God changed Jacob's name to Israel; his sons became the source of the clans, or tribes, that made up the nation of Israel (Genesis 28–35)

Joseph: One of Jacob's sons who was sold into slavery by his brothers; he eventually rose to great power in Egypt and saved his family from starvation (Genesis 37–50)

The book of Genesis takes us back to our roots. Everything of significance starts in Genesis: life, the human race, marriage, the family, languages, civil government, technology, farming. A few not-so-good things first appear in Genesis too: murder, adultery, rape, theft, slavery.

Everything begins in Genesis except God. In the very first verse of the book, when time began ("in the beginning"), God already existed. The Bible does not argue the existence of God; it just declares that God is. He is the source from which the universe came into being. Space, planets, animal and plant life, and human life were brought into existence by God's power. We may disagree over the *method* God used for creating our world and the life in it, but the Bible leaves no doubt about the *source* of all we see. "In the beginning God created the heavens and the earth."

Back to the Beginning

The book of Genesis is easy to read and easy to understand. You can skip the long genealogies in chapters 10 and 36, but the rest of the book is a very compelling story. The book divides into two sections: the story of the human race and the history of the Hebrew race.

The Story of the Human Race (Genesis 1-11)

The first eleven chapters of Genesis cover the time from creation to the scattering of various people groups throughout the world. The focus in these chapters is on four key events: the Creation, the disobedience of Adam and Eve, the Flood, and the scattering of the people.

Creation (Chapters 1–2)

God fashioned and filled the world as a place of incredible beauty. The world was made as a dwelling for human beings. Adam and Eve were given the responsibility of caring for the paradise in which they lived.

Disobedience (Chapters 3–5)

God instructed Adam and Eve not to eat the fruit of just one tree in the Garden of Eden. God did not want robots worshiping him. He wanted Adam and Eve to obey his commands willingly. He wanted the worship of intelligent beings who had made a deliberate, joyful choice to do what pleased him. Satan, God's adversary, wanted Adam and Eve to fail God's test, so he tempted Eve to disobey God's instruction about the tree. Adam and Eve (and all their descendants) now had a "bent" toward evil. Human beings became basically sinful. Sin separated Adam and Eve from God, and that separation is pictured by their expulsion from the garden. God promised that some day he would take

HELP FILE

GENESIS

The name of the book, Genesis, comes from the Greek translation of the Hebrew Old Testament. In the Hebrew Bible the title of this book is the first word of the text, *Bereshith*, which means "in the beginning."

The human author of Genesis was probably Moses, the great leader of Israel introduced in Exodus, the next book of the Bible. There is no direct statement naming Moses as the author, but Christians and Jews have traditionally attributed the first five books of the Bible to Moses.

Genesis 1:26

Then God said, "Let us make man in our image, in our likeness, and let them rule over the fish of the sea and the birds of the air, over the livestock, over all the earth, and over all the creatures that move along the ground."

the initiative to restore human beings to a place of friendship with him. The rest of the Bible is "salvation history"—the story of how God willingly suffered the penalty for human sin and made it possible for human beings to be in his presence forever.

God's warning to Adam and Eve that disobedience would ultimately bring death was dramatically demonstrated when Cain murdered his brother Abel. Death also claimed one after another of Adam and Eve's descendants.

Flood (Chapters 6–9)

The human race became more numerous over time, but they did not become more obedient to God. Human desires and actions became more and more evil. Eventually only one family was faithful to God. God told Noah to build an ark, a wooden barge, big enough to hold animals, food, and Noah's family. The Flood destroyed all human life except for the eight people in the ark.

Scattering (Chapters 10–11)

God told the descendants of Noah to fill the earth. Instead, they decided to stay together and build a city as a demonstration of their own power. God confused their languages, and they were forced to move out into the world. From that early scattering, the racial and ethnic groups of the human race emerged.

As you read the early chapters of Genesis, you will probably wonder if these events really happened or if they are just myths—attempts to explain things that can't be explained, like where the world came from or why evil exists. Jesus took these chapters as an accurate account of real events. He referred to Adam and Eve as real people and to creation as a real event (Matthew 19:4–6; Mark 10:6–9). Jesus also spoke of Noah as a real person who survived a literal flood (Matthew 24:37–38).

The History of the Hebrew Race (Genesis 12–50)

Genesis 1–11 covers a very long span of time. Genesis 12–50 covers about three hundred years of time. In the first part of the book the focus was on events. In the second part the focus is on people—four key individuals. God selected one family and began to work out his plan and program through them.

Abraham (Chapters 12–25)

Abraham was born about 2165 B.C. in the city of Ur, near the convergence of the Tigris and Euphrates rivers in modern-day Iraq. God called Abraham to leave his city and to go to a new place. God didn't tell Abraham where he was going, so Abraham had to trust God. Eventually God led him to the land of Canaan, where God promised two things to Abraham: a multitude of descendants and possession of the land around him. There were only two problems—(1) Abraham had no children, and (2) Canaanites already lived in the land. Those may have been problems for Abraham, but they weren't problems for God! Abraham had to keep trusting God's promises, because a son wasn't born to his wife, Sarah, until Abraham was a hundred years old and Sarah was ninety! They laughed when God told them they would have a child, and their son, "Laughter" (Isaac), was born nine months later.

You will read some intriguing stories about Abraham in these chapters. Some will surprise you and some will disappoint you. At one point God asks Abraham to sacrifice his own son—and Abraham obeys! In the

A BIBLICAL STANDOUT

Three world religions trace their spiritual roots back to Abraham. (1) Judaism views him as the great father of the Jewish people and as the recipient of God's original promises. (2) Christians see Abraham as a model of faith, which is a foundational principle of Christian belief. The apostle Paul wrote in the New Testament: "Those who believe are children of Abraham" (Galatians 3:7). (3) The religion of Islam points to Abraham as a true "Muslim" (one who submits to God). Islam traces its spiritual heritage to Abraham through his son Ishmael.

Abraham is called the "friend of God" three times in the Bible (2 Chronicles 20:7; Isaiah 41:8; James 2:23). He is referred to by name 233 times in the Old Testament and 74 times in the New.

Points 2 Remember

☑ Genesis is the book of beginnings.

☑ Adam and Eve failed God's test and suffered separation from God. The rest of the Bible is the story of God reaching out to rescue and restore human beings to friendship with him.

☑ God began to work out his plan for humanity through one family. Abraham, Isaac, Jacob, and Jacob's sons are the fathers of the nation of Israel.

end Abraham emerges as a man of great faith, a man who believed God even when God's promises seemed like impossible dreams. Abraham became a great model for following generations of what it means to have confidence in God.

Isaac (Chapters 26–27)

Of all the biblical patriarchs (great fathers), we know the least about Isaac. We do know that his wife, Rebekah, bore him twin sons, Esau and Jacob. As the two boys grew up, Esau (the oldest) became Isaac's favorite and Jacob became Rebekah's favorite. Jacob deceived his father (with Rebekah's help) and received Isaac's blessing. In that culture the blessing conferred the right of ownership over all the family's possessions.

Poor Isaac never seemed to be in charge of anything! He was always overshadowed by his distinguished father (Abraham), his clever son (Jacob), or his controlling wife (Rebekah). But twice God reaffirmed to Isaac the promises he had made to Abraham (Genesis 26:2–3, 23–24). Isaac was an important link in God's plan for his people.

Jacob (Chapters 28–36)

When Jacob's deception of his father was exposed, he packed his bags and left home. He went to find a wife among Abraham's relatives, who lived four hundred miles away in Haran. There he fell in love with a woman named Rachel. But Jacob met his match in Rachel's conniving father, Laban. Jacob was tricked into marrying Leah, Rachel's older (and less attractive) sister. Then he married Rachel too. Both Leah and Rachel gave Jacob a servant woman through whom to produce children. Eventually Jacob had twelve sons and (we assume) several daughters. Jacob's deceitful nature changed over time, and God gave him a new name. Jacob ("deceiver") became Israel ("he struggles with

God"). God also repeated to Jacob the promises he had made to Abraham and to Isaac: a great nation would come from their lineage, and God would give them the land of Canaan (Genesis 35:9–13).

In time Jacob's sons became the heads of twelve extended families (called clans or tribes). These clans of Jacob became the people of Israel. God chose the descendants of Abraham through Isaac and Jacob to be the people of his promise. They would receive the fulfillment of all that God had said. It would be through these descendants of Israel that God would bring a deliverer who would reverse the separation from God caused by Adam and Eve's sin.

Joseph (Chapters 37–50)

Jacob had twelve sons, but he favored one son, Joseph, above all the others. Maybe it was because Joseph was the son of his wife Rachel. Whatever the reason, it didn't set very well with the other eleven. Joseph's brothers took the opportunity one day to get rid of their little

DiGGinG DeEpeR

✗ Baldwin, Joyce. *The Message of Genesis 12–50.* The Bible Speaks Today series. Downers Grove, IL: InterVarsity Press, 1986.

A helpful guide through the stories of the patriarchs.

✗ Ross, Allen. *Creation and Blessing.* Grand Rapids: Baker, 1988.

An in-depth but very readable explanation of Genesis.

Resources on Abraham and Joseph:

✗ Dobson, Edward. *Abraham: The Lord Will Provide.* Grand Rapids: Revell, 1993.

✗ Swindoll, Charles. *Joseph.* Dallas: Word, 1999.

Excellent video productions of biblical stories from Genesis have been produced by Turner Broadcasting and are available to rent or purchase. They are worth a look! The videos *Abraham, Jacob,* and *Joseph* are available from Turner Pictures Worldwide, distributed by Warner Alliance Home Video.

JESUS IN GENESIS

In the book of Genesis we get our first glimpses of God's promised deliverer, someone who would reverse the tragic consequences of human sin.

In Genesis 3:15 God told Adam and Eve that a person would come from the seed of the woman who would crush the serpent's head. Christians believe that prediction was fulfilled when Jesus died on the cross and rose from the dead and thereby crushed Satan and his power. God also said that, in crushing the serpent, the seed of the woman would suffer a bruised heel. When Jesus delivered the final blow to Satan, he suffered a fatal blow to himself—his death on the cross as the payment of our penalty.

In Genesis 22 Abraham was asked by God to sacrifice his son Isaac. Abraham's willingness to offer his own son pictured God's willingness to give his Son, Jesus, as a sacrifice for sin. In the Abraham story, God provided a ram in place of Isaac. In the Bible's story, God provided Jesus to die in our place. He suffered what we deserved.

brother, but God used even their evil to bring about good. Joseph was sold to some traders who took him to Egypt as a slave. Through an amazing series of events, Joseph rose to great power in Egypt and saved his family from starvation during a famine. Joseph was reunited with his brothers and father as the entire family of Israel moved to Egypt under Joseph's protection and care. Because of his faithfulness to God, Joseph received a double portion of God's blessing. Joseph's two sons, Ephraim and Manasseh, became fathers of tribes in Israel. Genesis ends with Joseph's death in Egypt in about 1805 B.C.

The Rest of the Story

Three themes from the book of Genesis weave themselves through the rest of the Bible.

1. *We are created by God.* The universe and all that fills it was made to display God's power and majesty—and human beings are creation's crowning glory!
2. *We have all been marked by sin and disobedience to God.* Adam and Eve's bent toward disobedience was passed on to all generations that followed. Thus, every human being has a tendency toward sin. We find it easier to do wrong than to do right! Our

choice to do wrong (even once) confirms the separation between us and God.

3. *God has taken the initiative to restore his friendship with us.* We can never erase the penalty of sin by our good deeds or religious efforts. God himself has provided the payment for our rebellion against him. In time he sent a Redeemer, a deliverer, to restore us to friendship with God. The Redeemer's name is Jesus.

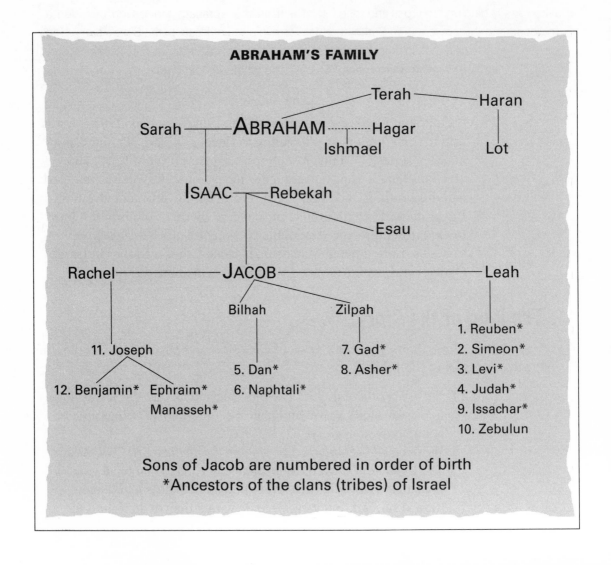

ABRAHAM'S FAMILY

Sons of Jacob are numbered in order of birth
*Ancestors of the clans (tribes) of Israel

Walking the Walk

1. How do you explain the presence of evil in our world? What insight has the book of Genesis given you about that issue?

2. Do you think you have ever done something wrong or sinful? How do you think God will handle the wrong you have done?

3. Explore your own spiritual "roots." Think about the people who have guided you on your spiritual pilgrimage. If you have never expressed your appreciation for their impact on your life, this is a good time to write them a letter or give them a call.

Exodus

➤ Read the incredible story of Israel's great escape from Egypt.

➤ Follow Moses as he confronts Pharaoh with God's ten plagues, leads the Israelites in an edge-of-your-seat chase scene, and guides thousands of people across the Red Sea on dry ground.

➤ Learn that God makes the rules!

The story of Exodus has inspired generations of oppressed people throughout the ages. The great cry of the human spirit is for freedom, and Exodus speaks powerfully to that longing. As you read the book, you will see God deliver his people from bondage and unify them as a nation. Genesis was the story of humanity's failure; Exodus is the story of God rushing to our rescue.

Genesis ended with Jacob and his family moving from Canaan to the land of Egypt. Jacob's son Joseph had become a powerful ruler in Egypt, and he had settled his father's family in the fertile delta of the Nile River. As the years passed, Jacob's family prospered and grew. When a change in political administration came, the Egyptians began to look at Israel, not as honored guests, but as a threat. Joseph and his deliverance of Egypt had been forgotten long before. The new rulers needed workers, cheap labor to enrich the kingdom. Four hundred years after Egypt had welcomed the tiny band of Israel, they decided to make slaves out of them.

But the people of Israel continued to expand until the ruler of Egypt, the pharaoh, feared that the Israelites might some day be a security threat and ordered male babies to be thrown into the Nile. One Hebrew mother hid her baby boy for a while, but when it became too difficult to hide him, she put her baby in a waterproof basket and set him

Key Characters

Moses: the man who led the people of Israel out of slavery in Egypt

Aaron: Moses' older brother and spokesman to Pharaoh

Miriam: Moses' sister

Pharaoh: the Egyptian ruler; he was considered by the Egyptians to be a god, and he governed with absolute authority

among the reeds along the bank of the Nile near the place where Pharaoh's daughter came to bathe. Pharaoh's daughter saw the basket among the reeds and sent her slave girl to get it. Upon opening the basket and seeing the Hebrew baby crying, she felt sorry for him and arranged with the baby's sister, who had been watching at a distance and had now appeared, to find a Hebrew woman—Moses' birth mother—to nurse him. Pharaoh's daughter named the baby Moses, which means "to draw out." She probably believed he was destined to be the next Pharaoh.

A Murderer Makes Good

The human hero of the book of Exodus is none other than the basket-boy, Moses. His life divides very neatly into three parts, each forty years long.

HELP FILE

EXODUS

The title Exodus comes from the Greek translation of the Hebrew Old Testament. The word means "to go out" or "departure"—Israel's *departure* from Egypt.

Two dates have been proposed for Israel's exodus from Egypt—an "early" date and a "late" date. Lengthy books have been written about the issue, but the arguments are fairly simple. The early date view is based on 1 Kings 6:1, which says that the Exodus occurred 480 years before Solomon began building the temple in Jerusalem. Solomon began the temple project in 966 B.C., which would make 1446 B.C. the date of the Exodus. Under this scheme the pharaoh of the Exodus was Amenhotep II, who ruled from 1450 to 1425 B.C.

The late-date view is based on Exodus 1:11, which says that the Israelite slaves built the cities of Pithom and Rameses. Egyptian records suggest that the Pharaoh Rameses II named the city after himself. Rameses II ruled from 1290 to 1224 B.C. According to this view, the Exodus took place about 1282 B.C. Those who propose a late date have to take the 480 years of 1 Kings 6:1 as a symbolic number representing twelve generations of forty years each.

No Egyptian ruler is mentioned by name in Exodus. Rather, the title Pharaoh is used, which means "great house." The pharaoh was considered to be the intermediary between the gods and the people.

Moses lived his first forty years thinking he was somebody important. After all, he grew up in Pharaoh's house and was trained at Nile State University. He was on his way to the top! But he never forgot his roots, and in time he came to believe that *he* was to be the deliverer of his people. He started his new career by killing an Egyptian who was beating a Hebrew slave. His treasonous sympathies were exposed, and he ran for his life.

Moses spent the second forty years of his life realizing he was a nobody. He ran from Egypt into the Sinai desert and married into a family of shepherds. He worked for his father-in-law herding sheep! One day while kicking along in the wilderness Moses saw a bush on fire. As he approached, God spoke to Moses from within the bush and commissioned him to do exactly what Moses feared most—go back to Egypt. What excuses would you have used? Moses came up with a bunch, but God still insisted.

In the last forty years of his life, Moses learned that God can make somebody out of a nobody. Moses didn't do anything spiritually significant until he was eighty years old! That might give a few of us some hope! But the road to freedom for God's people would not be easy.

God Delivers His People (Exodus 1–18)

Moses stood before the Pharaoh of Egypt and demanded the release of the people of Israel—and Pharaoh said, "No way!" So God sent plagues on Egypt—ten of them:

1. The Nile River was turned to blood.
2. Frogs covered the land.
3. Gnats flew in like dust.

GOD'S NAME

When Moses asked God his name, God said, "I AM WHO I AM" (Exodus 3:14). God was to be known to his people as "I AM." The phrase "I AM" became the basis for the Hebrew name "Yahweh," sometimes translated "Jehovah" or in the New International Version as "LORD." Other Hebrew names for God were Elohim (= "God") or Adonai (= "Lord"). Yahweh or LORD was God's covenant name, God's personal name. The New Testament writers transferred that name to Jesus. He is the *Lord,* Jesus Christ.

4. Biting flies inflicted discomfort on the people.
5. Domestic animals died.
6. People broke out in painful boils.
7. Hail and lightning destroyed crops.
8. Locusts ate whatever vegetation was left.
9. Darkness covered Egypt for three days.
10. The firstborn child in every Egyptian household died.

With each plague Pharaoh promised Israel's release. When the plague was lifted, however, Pharaoh changed his mind.

The Israelites were protected from the last plague because they killed a lamb and spread the lamb's blood on the doorframes of their houses. God promised that when the last plague came, he would "pass over" every house with blood on the door. The Jewish celebration of Passover is a reminder of God's great deliverance of his people.

The pharaoh finally agreed to let the Israelites go. So about two million people left! They headed toward the Sinai wilderness but soon came to the Red Sea. To make matters worse, Pharaoh's army was pursuing them from behind. In a powerful miracle, God parted the water of the Red Sea and the people of Israel crossed on dry ground. The Egyptian army pursued them only to be drowned by the returning water.

Israel's escape from Egypt and their deliverance at the Red Sea became the defining event of the Old Testament. Centuries later, if a biblical writer wanted to appeal to irrefutable evidence of God's power

PASSOVER

Jews throughout the world celebrate Passover or seder with a meal of symbolic foods like *matzah* (unleavened bread) and bitter herbs (usually horseradish, to evoke the tears of bondage). Since the destruction of the Jerusalem temple in A.D. 70, no lambs are sacrificed because in Jewish tradition the temple was the only proper place for sacrifices. Other meats are substituted for the Passover lamb. Several questions are asked during the ritual meal, and the answers recount the deliverance of Israel from slavery in Egypt. Since the Holocaust and the formation of the state of Israel in 1948, Passover has also become a celebration of the miraculous survival of the Jewish people.

and faithfulness to his people, the writer would point to the miraculous crossing of the Red Sea.

God Dwells with His People (Exodus 19-40)

The Israelites crossed the wilderness to the place where God had spoken with Moses at the burning bush. This time the whole mountain was on fire, covered with smoke and clouds. The people were so afraid they begged Moses to go up and talk with God.

The Law

Moses came back down from the mountain with two things. First, God gave Moses the Law. These were the "rules" under which God's people were to live. God's Law was summarized in the principles called the Ten Commandments. They introduced a more detailed code of law in Exodus 20–24. The Law is expanded further in the next book of the Bible, Leviticus.

People who lived in the Old Testament era were not made right before God by keeping the Law. For one thing, no one could do it! But it has never been God's plan to rescue anyone from sin's penalty through a system of rule-keeping. God's plan has always been a plan of grace. God provides for us what we do not deserve and can never earn. So men and women in the Old Testament received forgiveness and new life when they *believed* God's promises. They did not keep the rules in order to be accepted by God. They kept the Law as an act of love and devotion to God, who had delivered them from sin's bondage.

God entered into an agreement with Israel at Mount Sinai. The covenant, or treaty, was that God would be their God and they would be his people. When

Points 2 Remember

- ☑ Exodus is the story of God's rescue of his people from slavery in Egypt and the agreement made between God and Israel at Mount Sinai.

- ☑ The Ten Commandments (Exodus 20) were the basic principles of God's Law.

- ☑ Sacrifices were required for removing the penalties for disobedience and sin. A substitute suffered the judgment that the sinner deserved.

- ☑ The Tent of Meeting, or tabernacle, became the center of Israel's worship of the Lord. Almost five hundred years later King Solomon would build a permanent sanctuary in Jerusalem called the temple.

The Ten Commandments
Selected Verses from Exodus 20:3 – 17

1. **You shall have no other gods before me.**
2. **You shall not make for yourself an idol in the form of anything in heaven above or on the earth beneath or in the waters below. You shall not bow down to them or worship them.**
3. **You shall not misuse the name of the Lᴏʀᴅ your God.**
4. **Remember the Sabbath day by keeping it holy.**
5. **Honor your father and your mother.**
6. **You shall not murder.**
7. **You shall not commit adultery.**
8. **You shall not steal.**
9. **You shall not give false testimony.**
10. **You shall not covet . . . anything that belongs to your neighbor.**

Moses read the Book of the Covenant to the people of Israel, they said, "We will do everything the Lᴏʀᴅ has said; we will obey" (Exodus 24:7). The Sinai covenant, or the Mosaic (= through Moses) covenant, was the foundation upon which the rest of the Old Testament rested. When the people disobeyed God's Law or broke the agreement by worshiping false gods, they suffered severe consequences. The Law was only set aside when Jesus fulfilled the Law's demands and made a *new* covenant through his death and resurrection.

The Tent of Meeting

The second thing Moses received from God was a set of detailed instructions for building the tabernacle, the Tent of Meeting. The tabernacle was the place where God and his people would meet. The tabernacle did not contain God—the entire universe cannot do that. But the tabernacle was a visible reminder to Israel of God's presence and protection. It was also the center of Israel's worship to God.

The tabernacle itself was a portable tent surrounded by a curtained courtyard and filled with certain articles of furniture. The outer courtyard was where animal sacrifices were made. God wanted each worshiper to be

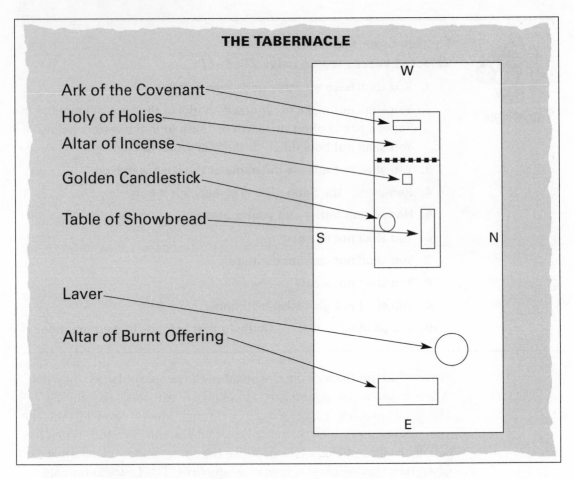

THE TABERNACLE

Ark of the Covenant
Holy of Holies
Altar of Incense
Golden Candlestick
Table of Showbread
Laver
Altar of Burnt Offering

W
S
N
E

impressed with a vivid reminder of the consequences of sin before a pure God, so an animal was sacrificed as the substitute for the sinning person. The sinner deserved the penalty, but a sacrificial animal died in the sinner's place. Various parts of the animal were then burned on the large altar in the courtyard. The blood of the animal was poured next to the altar or sprinkled on the corners of the altar. The other piece of furniture in the courtyard was a large basin where the priests of Israel washed the blood from their hands and robes.

Only one family in all the clans of Israel could enter the actual tent that sat in the courtyard. The direct descendants of Aaron, Moses' brother, were chosen by God to be the priests in Israel. They acted as the go-betweens, representing God to the people and representing the people before God. The tent itself was divided into two sections. The larger section was called the Holy Place. The word *holy* means "set apart, reserved." It was a place reserved for the worship of a holy God, a God set apart from sin and impurity. In the Holy Place, a lampstand stood on the left, a table filled with bread (representing the twelve clans or tribes of Israel) stood on the right, and a small gold altar stood in the center. Twice each day hot coals were placed on the small altar and incense (wood chips saturated with perfume) was sprinkled over the coals. The smoke that rose up symbolized the prayers of God's people rising up to the Lord.

Only one member of the priestly family could enter the inner room of the tabernacle. This room was called the Most Holy Place. Once a year, on a special day of repentance, the high priest, the oldest direct male descendant of Aaron, took a bowl of blood and went behind the heavy curtain that separated the Most Holy Place from the Holy Place. One piece of furniture stood in the center of this small room—a chest called the ark of the covenant or ark of the Testimony. Inside the box were the stone tablets inscribed with God's Law. The cover of the box was solid gold, and two gold angels spread their wings over it. The

Digging Deeper

✗ Cole, R. Alan. *Exodus: An Introduction and Commentary.* Tyndale Old Testament Commentary series. Downers Grove, IL: InterVarsity Press, 1973.

A brief but helpful explanation of Exodus.

For a study of Moses, check out:

✗ Baker, Don. *The God of Second Chances.* Wheaton, IL: Victor Books, 1991.

Turner Broadcasting has produced an outstanding video presentation of Moses' life available to rent or purchase. *Moses: The Bible Collection* is available from Turner Home Entertainment, distributed by Warner Alliance Home Video.

Lots of good studies on the Ten Commandments are available, such as:

✗ Hughes, R. Kent. *Disciplines of Grace.* Wheaton, IL: Crossway Books, 1993.

✗ Peel, Bill, and Kathy Peel. *Where Is Moses When We Need Him? Teaching Your Kids the Ten Values That Matter Most.* Nashville: Broadman and Holman, 1995.

priest sprinkled the blood over the box as a sacrifice for his own sins and for the nation's sins. As the blood of the sacrifice was sprinkled, God forgave his people, and the covenant relationship was restored.

After Moses finished building the tabernacle, the brilliant light of God's presence, the glory of the Lord, came down and rested over the ark of the covenant. God was dwelling with his people.

> Then the cloud covered the Tent of Meeting, and the glory of the LORD filled the tabernacle....
>
> In all the travels of the Israelites, whenever the cloud lifted from above the tabernacle, they would set out; but if the cloud did not lift, they did not set out—until the day it lifted. So the cloud of the LORD was over the tabernacle by day, and fire was in the cloud by night, in the sight of all the house of Israel during all their travels. (Exodus 40:34, 36–38)

Walking the Walk

1. How does your own spiritual journey parallel the story in Exodus? What was it like before you came to believe in the Lord? When was the turning point? What was it like after the Lord came into your experience?

2. What excuses have you used to avoid doing what God has impressed you to do? Do they sound anything like Moses' excuses in Exodus 3–4?

3. Think about the person who has been a "Moses" in your life, the person who has been your spiritual leader or hero. Did that person ever fail? How did you respond to his or her failure?

4. If your moral life were evaluated on the basis of the Ten Commandments, what grade would be on your report card for each one of the ten?

TOOL TIME

Commentaries

The Bible has been studied since it was first written. Christians still want to understand its message and apply biblical principles to their lives. In any well-stocked Christian bookstore, you will find dozens of books written by people trying to explain the Bible or a particular book of the Bible. The writers make "comments" on the text (the actual words of the Bible), and the books they produce are called "commentaries."

The men and women who write commentaries are serious students of the Bible. Many of them have learned the original languages in which the Bible was written and have studied the culture in which particular biblical books emerged. In some cases, they have devoted many years to the study of one biblical book or section of the Bible. In addition the commentators have thought deeply about the message of the biblical writers and the importance and relevance of that message for today.

Commentaries help us because they do a lot of the research for us. They bring insights from the languages and the historical setting that we don't have the time or the training to explore on our own. They help us understand difficult passages or bring in other passages of Scripture that shed light on the text. God often uses their words of insight from a passage to bring change in our lives.

For all these reasons, commentaries are great tools—with one word of caution. A commentary is no substitute for reading the Bible itself. Sometimes the writer of a commentary will deviate from what the Bible clearly says. The source of authority for Christian belief and behavior is the Bible, not a particular person's interpretation of the Bible. If you think a writer is on the wrong track, don't be intimidated. Let the Bible speak first.

Commentaries fall into several categories.

Technical/scholarly commentaries are detailed, in-depth explorations of a biblical book that provide a wealth of material, which may take you months to dig out. We need scholarly studies, but if you aren't a scholar, you may want to wait a while before you bite into one of these.

Expositional commentaries attempt to explain the biblical text so that the average serious reader can understand what is being said. The art of *exposition* is the ability to "expose" the meaning of a passage without overwhelming the reader with technical arguments and dozens of footnotes. Most of the commentaries I recommend in this book fall into the expositional category.

Devotional commentaries focus primarily on applying what the Bible says to our lives today. These commentaries usually just hit the high points of a biblical book. The writers focus on passages that are easy to understand and apply in a practical way. The disadvantage of many devotional commentaries is that you aren't prompted to interact with the biblical text very much. You might come away thinking you understand the book of Deuteronomy when in reality you understand only a very few verses.

When you decide to focus on one book of the Bible for your personal study, a good commentary can be an immense help. Read the biblical text first, then read the commentary. If you have study notes in your Bible or a second commentary on the passage, compare what each writer says. Then come back to the words of the Bible and compare the comments with what you read in the passage. It is always helpful to keep a journal handy to write down key verses or personal insights or steps you can take to respond obediently to what the Bible says.

If you have never carefully studied through a biblical book, start with a short book or a gospel (Matthew, Mark, Luke, or John). Set aside time on a regular basis for reading and study. The Bible will begin to come alive in your mind and life.

Before You Buy

Before you buy a commentary, look through it. Read a few pages. Can you follow the author's explanation? Is it too technical for you right now—or too elementary? Ask your pastor or a trusted Bible teacher for suggested commentaries on particular books. You will begin to add valuable tools, one by one, to your study library.

One- or Two-Volume Commentaries on the Whole Bible. The comments on each verse or passage are brief. These commentaries can be helpful, but a good study Bible gives you just about as much help.

The Bible Knowledge Commentary. 2 vols. Wheaton, IL: Victor Books, 1985.
　Written by professors from Dallas Theological Seminary. Reliable but brief.

The New Bible Commentary. Downers Grove, IL: InterVarsity Press.

Multivolume Commentaries on the Bible. A different author writes the comments on each book. One book may be dull reading and the next one may be fascinating, but the writers are accurate and their remarks are dependable. The best set is:

The Expositor's Bible Commentary. 12 vols./CD-ROM. Grand Rapids: Zondervan, 1999.

Zondervan NIV Bible Commentary. 2 vols. Grand Rapids: Zondervan, 1994.
　An abridgment of the larger *Expositor's Bible Commentary;* an excellent first choice!

In the Digging Deeper section of each chapter I recommend individual commentaries that I have found helpful. They will give you a good place to start.

Leviticus

— **Heads Up** —

➤ Take a look at Israel's how-to worship manual.

➤ Examine the Old Testament law code and find out why it's so important.

➤ What about this "eye for an eye" stuff?

Leviticus used to be the first book of the Bible Jewish children studied in synagogue school. In the modern world, it tends to be the last part of the Bible anyone looks at seriously. You probably know a verse from Leviticus and don't even realize it. Leviticus 19:18 says, "Love your neighbor as yourself." You thought that came from Jesus, didn't you? He was just quoting Leviticus.

Leviticus may seem like dry and difficult reading, but there's a good reason for that. The book was never designed to be interesting to *us*. When God had Moses write down all the laws and ceremonies in Leviticus, he was not writing to Christians living two thousand years after Jesus was born. God wrote this book to Israelites who worshiped in a portable tent and who came to God through animal sacrifices. Christians do not need Leviticus to find access to God. But to an Old Testament Israelite, this book was very important. If the only way you could come to God was through the blood of a sacrifice, you would want to know how to do it.

Key Characters

Moses: Israel's leader and lawgiver who received all these laws and instructions from God

Aaron: Moses' older brother who was chosen by God to be the priest in charge of implementing God's instructions to his people

The book of Leviticus is a record of the laws and rituals the people of Israel were to follow if they wanted to live in harmony with the Lord. Because they were God's own people, their lives were to be different from the lives of the people who lived around them. These laws and regulations and sacred days set the Israelites apart. They were to be a holy people. The word *holy* means "set apart." God's people were to be set apart *from* sin and evil and set apart *to* God. Holiness, or holy living, has to incorporate both aspects—we *will not* do what God has said is wrong and we *will* do what God has said is right.

Christians no longer follow the rules of Leviticus, but holy living before God is still important. That's what we learn in Leviticus. Five times in the book God says to be holy because he is holy (11:44, 45; 19:2; 20:7, 26). The same admonition is repeated several times in the New Testament (1 Peter 1:16; cf. Romans 12:1; 1 Corinthians 3:17; 1 Peter 2:9). God expects holiness from his people—separation from what is wrong and separation toward what is right and good and true and pure.

Finding the Path

The title Leviticus means "concerning the Levites." One of the clans (extended families) that made up the nation of Israel was the clan descended from Jacob's son Levi. God chose the clan, or tribe, of Levi to oversee God's worship in Israel. Within the large clan of Levi, God selected one family to be the priests in Israel. The direct descendants of Aaron, Moses' brother, were responsible to offer sacrifices to God and to conduct the worship ceremonies in the tabernacle. One further distinction was made. The oldest direct descendant of Aaron was called the *high* priest in Israel. So all Levites were responsible for some aspect of the worship of God. One family of Levites was set apart as priests and one priest was set apart as the high priest.

Leviticus was the instruction book for the Levites—and for all the people of Israel. God very carefully set down exactly how the rituals of worship were to be carried out. But there's more here than just a bunch of church rules. Obedience to God involved every

DoWNLoAd

Leviticus 26:3, 11–12

"If you follow my decrees and are careful to obey my commands, . . . I will put my dwelling place among you, and I will not abhor you. I will walk among you and be your God, and you will be my people."

aspect of life. God gave Israel dietary regulations—certain foods were "clean"; other foods were "unclean." God gave Israel directions for handling all kinds of issues: sickness, health, marriage, shoplifting, menstruation, planting, harvesting, animal care, acne—just about every issue of life was touched somewhere in Leviticus. These were not just "helpful hints for happy living." This was God's Law.

The book itself divides into two sections. Here are the highlights.

Sacrifice: The Way to God (Leviticus 1–17)

Offerings and Sacrifices (Chapters 1–7)

The worship of God in the Old Testament centered on five basic offerings.

1. *The burnt offering (1:3–17; 6:8–13).* A voluntary offering given to God as an expression of praise and submission to him. The entire animal was burned up on the altar.
2. *The grain offering (2:1–16; 6:14–23).* A voluntary offering given as thanks to God for his goodness and provision.
3. *The peace offering (3:1–17; 7:11–36).* A voluntary offering expressing appreciation to God and to others for the joy of their friendship. The animal was eaten by the worshiper and family or friends.
4. *The sin offering (4:1–5:13; 6:24–30).* Anyone guilty of unintentional sin or wrong was required to make this sacrifice.
5. *The guilt offering (5:14–6:7; 7:1–7).* This sacrifice was required from anyone guilty of breaking the law of God.

These animal sacrifices removed God's anger against sin and restored the friendship between God and the repentant person. Of course, true worship

Points 2 Remember

☑ Leviticus is an instruction book to Old Testament Israel about sacrifices and rituals for worship and God's regulations for daily life.

☑ Christians today are not under the regulations of the Old Testament law. We live under a new arrangement because Jesus died as the ultimate and final sacrifice for human sin.

☑ God expects his people to be holy—set apart from evil and fully devoted to what is good.

THE DAY OF ATONEMENT

The Day of Atonement (or Yom Kippur in Hebrew) is still observed by Jewish people. Animal sacrifices are no longer made, but it is a day when each person seriously reflects on his or her life and repents for any failures or wrong. In response, Jews believe that God wipes the slate of their lives clean and they face a new year determined to do good.

came from a heart of love and submission to God. Simply going through the motions of offering the proper animal as a sacrifice was not enough. God looked at a person's inner attitude.

The Day of Atonement (Chapter 16)

The most sacred day of the year in Israel's worship was the Day of Atonement. On that day the high priest offered sacrifices to God for the sins of the nation. The ritual centered around two goats. One goat was killed and its blood was taken into the innermost room of the tabernacle. The high priest sprinkled the blood over the ark of the covenant. The blood "covered" Israel's sin and guilt for breaking God's law. Atonement was made. The penalty for Israel's sin was paid by the death of a substitute. The high priest then put his hands on the head of the second goat, confessing the sins of the nation, and finally released that goat into the wilderness. The goat pictured God's removal of the guilt of sin from his people.

DiggiNG DeEpeR

✗ Harrison, R. K. *Leviticus: An Introduction and Commentary*. Tyndale Old Testament Commentary series. Downers Grove, IL: InterVarsity Press, 1980.

A reliable guide through the book.

An excellent chapter on how Christians should interpret and apply the laws of Israel can be found in:

✗ Fee, Gordon, and Douglas Stuart. *How to Read the Bible for All It's Worth*. Grand Rapids: Zondervan, 1982, 135–48.

AN EYE FOR AN EYE

Yes, the idea of "an eye for an eye, a tooth for a tooth" really is in the Bible. The Old Testament law required that punishment was to be carried out in exact measure to a crime.

> "If anyone injures his neighbor, whatever he has done must be done to him: fracture for fracture, eye for eye, tooth for tooth. As he has injured the other, so he is to be injured." (Leviticus 24:19–20)

When we read this passage it seems vindictive and unchristian. Politicians would label it "mean spirited"! Actually the principle made the Law of God apply equally to everyone in Israel. A rich person or powerful ruler could not "get off" with a lighter sentence than a poor person for the same crime. On the other hand, the poor could not plunder the rich either. The injured party received only what was fair. You couldn't sue for two teeth if you had only lost one! Personal injury lawyers must have had a rough time in Israel.

Jesus took this rule one step further:

> "You have heard that it was said, 'Eye for eye, and tooth for tooth.' But I tell you, Do not resist an evil person. If someone strikes you on the right cheek, turn to him the other also." (Matthew 5:38–39)

Separation: Our Walk *Before* God (Leviticus 18–27)

The Sacred Days (Chapters 23–25)

God established eight key festivals and sacred observances for Israel.

Weekly: The Sabbath (The seventh day [Saturday] was a day for worship and rest.)

Yearly: Passover / Feast of Unleavened Bread / Firstfruits (spring; eight days)

Feast of Weeks / Pentecost (summer; one day)

Feast of Trumpets [Rosh Hashanah] (fall; one day)

Day of Atonement [Yom Kippur] (fall; one day)

Feast of Tabernacles / Ingathering (fall; seven days)

Every seven years: Sabbath year (No crops were planted; the Lord provided for his people's needs.)

Every fifty years: Jubilee year (A "sabbath" of Sabbath years was observed, debts were forgiven, land was restored to its original owners, indentured servants were released.)

How Does This Help Me?

I come away from Leviticus thankful that we aren't under all these regulations and rules anymore! Leviticus was designed to become obsolete. All the sacrifices pointed to the one final sacrifice of Jesus Christ on the cross. Jesus did not destroy the law. He fulfilled it. After Jesus' death and resurrection, the law with its rituals and rules was set aside. Jesus' sacrifice did not have to be repeated. It was made once and has eternal effect. We don't need an earthly priest to bring us into God's presence either. Those who have believed in Jesus have a High Priest already in heaven, Jesus himself. We can come confidently to God because Jesus has opened the way.

That doesn't mean, however, that we don't need Leviticus! It is still the Word of God even if these commands are not given directly to us. Two vital lessons ought to stay with us from this book.

1. *God is holy.* He is absolutely separate from sin, and he hasn't changed since he spoke to Moses on Mount Sinai.
2. *God expects his people to be holy.* We have all the resources we need to live lives that are pleasing to God. We don't have long lists of regulations, but we have the Bible and God's Spirit to guide us. God's people are called to be different from the people around us who don't have a relationship with the Lord—not weird, not condemning, not offensive—but different, reserved for God, set apart for him.

Walking the Walk

1. As you think about your own faith commitment to the Lord, do you see it as a "Sunday only" thing, or does it affect every aspect of your life?

2. What difference should your relationship with Christ make in:
   Your marriage or friendships?
   Your career or student life?
   Your entertainment choices?

3. Sometimes other people try to impose their spiritual convictions or rules on us as if they were God's rules. How should you respond to people who want you to live under their "law"?

Numbers

— Heads Up —

➤ Spend forty years on the road with the people of Israel.

➤ Learn how God provided food, water, and protection for the trip.

➤ Watch Moses make a bronze snake to rescue Israel from destruction.

Some people avoid the book of Numbers because they think it has something to do with math! Don't panic—no story problems at the end. Instead, the book of Numbers traces the travels of the people of Israel from Mount Sinai (where they received God's law) to the edge of the land of Canaan. God had promised the land to Abraham more than five hundred years earlier. Numbers also records one of the worst spiritual disasters to ever come upon God's people—and a whole generation of people died without seeing the fulfillment of God's promise. (The book gets its name, by the way, from two census reports, or counting of the people, recorded in chapter 1 and chapter 26.)

As you read the book of Numbers, you will discover that the writer switches back and forth from story (narrative) to God's rules for his people (law). As new situations arose in Israel's experience, God gave them his direction and expanded his law.

Key Characters

Moses: Israel's (usually) patient leader

Aaron: Israel's leading priest; Moses' brother

Eleazar: Aaron's son and his successor as high priest

Joshua and Caleb: two of the spies sent into the land of Canaan

Balaam: a sorcerer hired to put a curse on Israel

Phase 1: From Mount Sinai to the Land of Promise (Numbers 1–12)

In the first ten chapters of Numbers, the clans, or tribes, of Israel were organized and counted. More than two million people were camped at Mount Sinai. God cared for his people by preserving their clothes and shoes (no Mount Sinai Wal-Mart) and by providing water to drink and manna for food.

MANNA

Manna was a white flake-like food that covered the ground every morning (except on the Sabbath day) during Israel's forty years in the wilderness. The people of Israel gathered the manna and used it to make bread or boiled it as a hot food. Manna was similar to frost or a small coriander seed. It tasted like cakes or bread made with olive oil (Numbers 11:7–8). Several attempts have been made to explain manna and where it came from, but the Bible simply says that God provided it for his people. In Psalm 78:24–25, manna is called "the grain of heaven" and "the bread of angels." The people of Israel just called it "manna," which means "what is it?"

The camp was organized around the tabernacle, or Tent of Meeting. Three clans camped on each of the four sides of the worship complex. The leaders of Israel's worship, the tribe of Levi, camped closest to the tabernacle.

Eleven months and five days after Israel's arrival at Mount Sinai, the cloud that stood over the tabernacle as the sign of God's presence with his people rose up and began to move. That was the signal for Israel to pack their belongings for another transition. The people had been organized, the priests had been set apart as God's servants, the law had been given, and the place of worship had been constructed. Now God was moving his people north to Canaan, to the Promised Land.

Points 2 Remember

☑ Numbers is the story of Israel's journey from Mount Sinai to the edge of Canaan.

☑ Because of their unwillingness to follow the Lord's direction into the land of promise, the entire population of Israel over twenty years old died in the wilderness during forty years of wandering.

Phase 2: Refusal to Enter the Land (Numbers 13–14)

God led Israel to Kadesh Barnea, an oasis on the southern edge of Canaan. Moses selected twelve men to go into the land and check things out. They came back after forty days with an interesting report. They all agreed that the land was beautiful and productive. They all said the cities were strong and well-protected. They all testified that giants lived in the land! They were divided, however, on what to do next.

Ten of the spies said, "We can't do it. We'll never defeat these people." Two of the spies, Joshua and Caleb, had a very different perspective.

> Then Caleb silenced the people before Moses and said, "We should go up and take possession of the land, for we can certainly do it."

> But the men who had gone up with him said, "We can't attack those people; they are stronger than we are.". . .

> All the Israelites grumbled against Moses and Aaron, and the whole assembly said to them, "If only we had died in Egypt! Or in this desert! Why is the LORD bringing us to this land only to let us fall by the sword? Our wives and children will be taken as plunder. Wouldn't it be better for us to go back to Egypt?" And they said to each other, "We should choose a leader and go back to Egypt."

> Then Moses and Aaron fell facedown in front of the whole Israelite assembly gathered there. Joshua son of Nun and Caleb son of Jephunneh, who were among those who had explored the land, tore their clothes and said to the entire Israelite assembly, "The land we passed through and explored is exceedingly good. If the LORD is pleased with us, he will lead us into that land, a land flowing with milk and honey, and will give it to us. Only do not rebel against the LORD. And do not be afraid of the people of the land, because we will swallow them up. Their protection is gone, but the LORD is with us. Do not be afraid of them."

> But the whole assembly talked about stoning them. (13:30–31; 14:2–10)

The people of Israel, in very democratic fashion, took a vote—and the "No" votes won! God's judgment was quick. Since the people refused to believe his promise to give them the land, they would wander in the desert areas of Sinai for a total of forty years. Furthermore, the whole

---

Numbers 6:24 – 26

"The LORD bless you and keep you;
the LORD make his face shine upon you and be gracious to you;
the LORD turn his face toward you and give you peace."

DOWNLOAD

---

generation who refused to follow the Lord would die in the wilderness. Everyone who was twenty years old or older when the Israelites left Mount Sinai would be buried in the desert rather than in Canaan. Only two exceptions were made. Joshua and Caleb, the two courageous spies, would live in the Promised Land.

Phase 3: Wandering in the Wilderness (Numbers 15–36)

At that point, Israel began a thirty-eight-year period of wandering (forty years total from when they left Egypt). Their experience is referred to as wandering, but mostly it was camping. God was simply waiting for the unbelieving generation to die. Every day at least eighty-five people died. Every funeral was a vivid reminder of their disobedience to God.

Very little is recorded about these years in the wilderness. It is not a particularly bright time in Israel's story. The years were marked by complaining, rebellion, judgment, and death. Twice God threatened to wipe out the whole nation and start over, but each time Moses intervened and God spared his people.

You will read some interesting things in these chapters, however.

God told Moses to speak to a rock, and when he did, God provided water from the rock for the people. Another time Moses hit the rock in anger. Water still came out, but God judged Israel's leader: Moses would not enter the land of Canaan. Moses was brokenhearted, but God never removed the consequences of Moses' disobedience. (Read Numbers 20:1–13.)

The people of Israel had to detour around the territory of the Edomites, and the trip was a rough one. The people complained

DiggiNG DeEpeR

X   Wenham, Gordon. *Numbers: An Introduction and Commentary.* Tyndale Old Testament Commentary series. Downers Grove, IL: InterVarsity Press, 1981.

A very helpful guide through Numbers.

again about the food, and God sent poisonous snakes into the camp. God then told Moses to make a snake out of bronze and put it on a pole. Anyone who was bitten could look at the snake and instantly be healed. (Read Numbers 21:4–9.)

Near the end of the forty years of wandering, the Israelites camped on the plains of Moab on the east side of the Jordan River. The king of Moab hired a pagan psychic named Balaam to put a curse on Israel. When Balaam tried to curse Israel, "the Spirit of God came upon him" (24:2), and he blessed Israel instead! Balaam *did* find a way to bring judgment on Israel. He advised the Moabite king to send Moabite women into Israel's camp. The women invited the Israelites to worship Baal (a false god) with them. Their "worship" involved sexual immorality and sacrifice to an idol. God sent a plague to punish his people, and 24,000 died. (Read Numbers 22–25. Balaam's own judgment came in Numbers 31:8.)

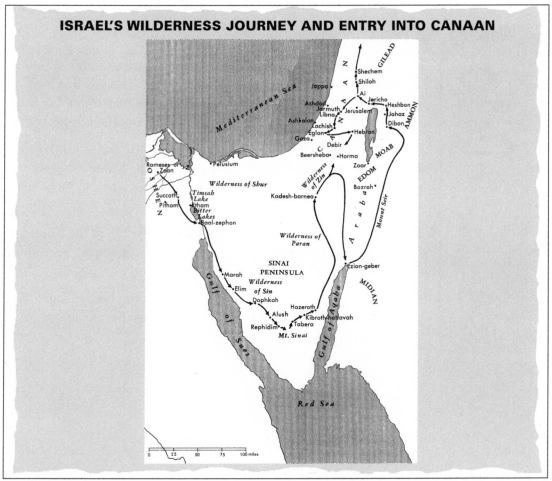

ISRAEL'S WILDERNESS JOURNEY AND ENTRY INTO CANAAN

Standing on the Brink

This generation of God's people missed an incredible opportunity! They had seen God deliver them from Egypt. They had walked across the Red Sea on dry ground. They had heard God's voice at Mount Sinai. Then they had stood on the threshold of the land. But because of their fear and lack of trust in God, they drew back and missed God's blessing. We remember them for their failure, not their faith.

I wonder if we do the same thing. We come to the brink of seeing God do some great things in our families or in our churches but draw back in fear. I wonder what future generations will remember about us. Will they see us as men and women who courageously followed the Lord— or will we be remembered as the generation who *could have seen* God work but who stepped back in unbelief?

Walking the Walk

1. Think about a "wilderness" experience in your own life, a time when you seemed to wander from God or when you lived out the consequences of a bad decision. In a journal or notebook, write about that experience and try to pull out the lessons you learned along the way.

2. What are you most likely to complain about? When are you most prone to complain? What can you do to cultivate a more patient or thankful spirit?

3. Draw a "map" of your own spiritual journey. Fill in the camp-sites along the way and the people who had an impact on you for good or for evil.

4. How do you want to be remembered by your children and grandchildren? What do you need to change in your life to strengthen your legacy to them?

Deuteronomy

— Heads Up —

➤ Listen to Moses' last words to his people.

➤ Stand in awe as Moses speaks to a new generation about God's great power.

➤ Discover the blessings of obeying God and the disaster of disobeying.

The nation of Israel's long years of wilderness traveling were almost at an end. They were camping on the east side of the Jordan River on the plains of Moab, poised to enter the land God had promised to their ancestor Abraham. Moses, Israel's leader, knew that he would not enter the land with his people. So before his death, Moses gathered the people around him and reviewed God's great and powerful ways.

The book of Deuteronomy is a collection of well-constructed, strikingly illustrated messages to Israel. Moses told the story of Israel's escape from Egypt and God's provision over the last forty years. He repeated the essential teachings of the law and he challenged the people to trust God for the future. As a faithful parent or a compassionate pastor, Moses passed the spiritual torch to a new generation.

A Leader's Farewell

Most of the people who listened to Moses had never known any other spiritual leader. Only some of the oldest Israelites would have remembered the days of slavery in Egypt and God's miraculous rescue. Their parents and grandparents had pledged allegiance to the Lord and obedience to God's law at Mount Sinai nearly forty years earlier. Moses wisely realized that the new generation could not survive on secondhand faith. The next generation had to claim the Lord God as their own. So Moses led them in a renewal of the agreement, or covenant, made between God and his people. God had not changed over the forty years in the wilderness,

Key Characters

Moses: Israel's leader giving his farewell address to the nation

Joshua: Moses' assistant who succeeded him as leader of God's people

65

but each generation was responsible for recommitting themselves in love and obedience to the Lord.

Each of the three speeches recorded in Deuteronomy had a different focus. Moses looked back to Israel's past, he looked around at Israel's present, and he looked ahead to Israel's future.

Moses' First Message: What God Has Done in the Past (Deuteronomy 1:1 – 4:43)

Moses first reminded Israel of God's rescue of his people from the bondage of Egypt and his protection during the difficult years in the wilderness. Moses wanted to impress the new generation with God's faithfulness in spite of their parents' unwillingness to enter the land of Canaan as God had instructed. He wanted his listeners to respond to God differently than their parents had responded.

Moses' Second Message: What God Expects in the Present (Deuteronomy 4:44 – 26:19)

Moses then reviewed the law of God and applied its principles to the new circumstances under which the people would live. Every area of life was touched by God's commands and instruction. Moses used several key words and phrases again and again to drive home the

HELP FiLe

AN OFT-QUOTED BOOK

Deuteronomy is quoted in seventeen of the twenty-seven books in the New Testament. More than eighty quotations or allusions to Deuteronomy appear in the New Testament.

Jesus quoted from Deuteronomy more than from any other book of the Old Testament. You can read some of his quotes in Matthew 4:4, 7, 10; 22:37; Mark 7:10; 10:19.

The title Deuteronomy comes from the Greek translation of the Bible and means "second law." It is not a different law but a faithful repetition and amplification of the law God gave to Moses on Mount Sinai nearly forty years earlier.

Points 2 Remember

☑ Deuteronomy is a collection of Moses' final words to Israel before his death. He passed the spiritual torch to a new generation.

☑ The language and teaching recorded in Deuteronomy echoed down through the rest of the Old Testament. Each new generation was drawn back to their own renewal of the covenant with God.

☑ People in every generation need to commit themselves to faith in the Lord and loyalty to his Word. You can't ride into heaven on your parents' faith!

importance of the people's responsibility to follow the Lord joyfully and obediently. Look for these words as you read these chapters. Mark them. Remember them.

"Love": The response God looks for in his people is love for him.

"Hear": Moses repeatedly called God's people to listen to the voice of the Lord—not just to hear his words, but to obey what God said.

"Fear the Lord": To fear God does not mean to shrink in a corner, afraid that God will smack you! It means to take God seriously, to respect his authority as the Lord.

Other crucial words or phrases: "Serve the LORD"; "Hold fast to the LORD"; "Walk in all the ways of the LORD"; "Do what is right in the eyes of the LORD"; "Keep the commands/decrees/laws." We get the point! God desires fully committed followers.

Moses' words became part of the national heritage of Israel for hundreds of years after they were spoken. The later writers and prophets used the same phrases over and over to remind their own generation of their responsibility to follow the Lord with the same intensity and devotion.

Deuteronomy 6:4-5

Hear, O Israel: The LORD our God, the LORD is one. Love the LORD your God with all your heart and with all your soul and with all your strength.

DownLoad

Moses' Third Message: What God Will Do in the Future (Deuteronomy 27:1 – 34:12)

Moses brought his farewell speeches to a close by looking to the future. In a series of blessings and curses, Moses gave the people a solemn warning about what would happen if they refused to take their covenant promises seriously. A promise to God can't be blown off without serious consequences. Obedience to the Lord would bring blessing, long life, and possession of the Promised Land. Disobedience would bring disaster.

The book of Deuteronomy ends with the death of Moses. God took his servant up on a high hill and let him see the land God had promised to Abraham. Then Moses died, and God buried him. He was 120 years old, yet his eyesight had not failed and his physical energy was undiminished. No prophet like Moses would come on the scene again until Jesus, the prophet of the new covenant, came to Israel. Moses was a *servant* in the household of God, but Jesus was a *son* over the household. Jesus would lead a new exodus of God's people, liberating them from the power of sin and death.

The people of Israel grieved thirty days for Moses, but then their grieving ended. They had a new leader, Joshua, and a new adventure ahead. God had given the land of Canaan to their ancestors, but that generation had not been courageous enough to take the land—and they had paid a big price. This generation would be different; they would fully follow the Lord.

Digging Deeper

✗ Brown, Raymond. *The Message of Deuteronomy: Not by Bread Alone.* The Bible Speaks Today series. Downers Grove, IL: InterVarsity Press, 1993.

An excellent guide.

✗ Craigie, P. C. *The Book of Deuteronomy.* New International Commentary on the Old Testament. Grand Rapids: Eerdmans, 1976.

A more thorough and detailed study of Deuteronomy. Wonderfully insightful.

HOW THE OLD TESTAMENT FITS TOGETHER:
Exodus and Conquest

	Crossing the Red Sea	Wilderness Wandering	Moses Dies	Joshua Dies
Genesis	Exodus	Numbers	Joshua	Judges

Leviticus
(Summary of the Law)

Deuteronomy
(Sermons from Moses)

Ruth

Walking the Walk

1. You can develop a personal book of Deuteronomy by working through the same progression Moses worked through—looking at the past, examining the present, and anticipating the future.

2. Think back over God's work in your own life from the time when you entered into a relationship with him to the present. Record the times God has sustained you in sorrow or difficulty, the blessings he has brought into your life, and the people he has used to encourage or help you. As you remember God's faithfulness in the past, take the opportunity to thank him for each evidence of his provision.

3. Renew your loyalty to God by expressing your love for him in a creative way. You may want to do it in a prayer of worship or by composing a song that tells God why you appreciate and love him. You may also want to express your devotion to God in a testimony before your family or friends.

4. Set spiritual goals for the next year. What areas of your life or character do you want to see God change? What specific steps can you take to be obedient to God in those areas? Share your goals with a friend who will pray for you and hold you accountable.

Part 2

STORY

Almost half the Bible is narrative—stories about men and women, kingdoms and nations, rulers and slaves. What makes the Bible unique is that it records God's story. It is a magnificent story filled with hundreds of characters, intriguing plots, and astonishing miracles—all focused on God and on his work in the world.

The Bible's story is a true story—an accurate, reliable record of real events and real people—history from God's perspective. It does not contain myths or fairy tales. No story composed purely from the human mind can begin to compare with the power and impact of biblical narrative. Not every page is spellbinding, of course, and sometimes the plot is complex. Many times we wish more details had been included. But no matter how often we read these passages or how long we reflect on their significance, the biblical story is never exhausted of its compelling insights.

The next twelve books of the Old Testament are books of history—not dry-as-dust history, but history embedded in the story of God's people. The family of Abraham, Isaac, and Jacob had escaped the slavery of Egypt and had come to the land God had promised their ancestors. The Bible then tells the story of Israel's life in the land and the ultimate loss and restoration of that land. One thousand years of time pass before us as we turn the pages of these twelve books.

Remember as you read that these are not just stories pieced together about people who lived long ago. These are stories about what God did in the lives of those people. God is the hero of the story! Men and women live and die, kingdoms rise and fall, hundreds of years pass in a few pages sometimes, but behind it all, God stands as the leading character in all the stories.

What's Here for Me?

If you read the Old Testament as ancient history, you have missed the point. God moved prophets and historians to record this story as one means of instructing us in how to live our lives to please the Lord. The accounts recorded in the Old Testament don't usually teach spiritual principles directly; rather, they teach by example. On one level we are reading about Ruth or King David or Elijah the prophet, but on another level we are seeing how they obeyed God (or disobeyed) and what results their actions produced in their lives.

The Old Testament characters and the nation of Israel as a whole become illustrations of what the Bible teaches us directly in other places. When David committed adultery with Bathsheba (2 Samuel 11), the storyteller did not say, "Adultery is wrong." That statement was made in the Law, in the Ten Commandments (Exodus 20:14). The narrative in 2 Samuel illustrates the consequences of disobeying God's command. We are expected to make the application to our own lives as we read and reflect on the biblical story.

So as you read the story of God's people, think about what God is saying through the story to you today. Keep in mind that none of these Old Testament stories is about you directly. God does not intend us to do exactly the same things the Bible characters did. The men and women of the Bible are good sometimes, evil many times, wise on occasion, foolish on more occasions. We have the privilege of watching their lives and learning from their example. As you see God at work in history, you will gain a new understanding and a new appreciation for how he works in your life.

Joshua

➤ Follow the career of one of Israel's great generals.
➤ See city walls fall down and the sun stand still.
➤ Discover how Israel conquered the land God had promised to them.

I don't know of a biblical book that has more excitement per square inch than Joshua. Within a few pages, spies are hidden and narrowly escape with their lives, the waters of the Jordan River are pushed back, celestial beings appear, the walls of a city crumble, treachery is exposed, a great general stirs his armies to battle, and the sun stands still! Move over, Tom Clancy and Steven Spielberg!

The book is named after its main character. Joshua in the Hebrew language of the Old Testament means "the Lord saves." Translated in the Greek language of the New Testament, the name Joshua becomes Jesus, "the Lord saves." The book is an account of the conquest of the land of Canaan drawn from the battle diaries of Israel's five-star field general, Joshua.

Joshua began life as a slave in Egypt. When God delivered the people of Israel from bondage, Joshua became Moses' assistant. Moses instilled confident faith in Joshua and a deep respect for God's Word. When Moses was about to die, God spoke to his people and appointed Joshua as Moses' successor. Joshua's book opens with Moses' death and Joshua's challenge from the Lord.

"Moses my servant is dead. Now then, you and all these people, get ready to cross the Jordan River into the land I am about to give to them—to the Israelites. I will give you every place where you set

Key Characters

Joshua: Israel's military and political leader; born a slave in Egypt, he became a man of courage and commitment to God

Rahab: a prostitute in the city of Jericho who hid two Israelite spies; she later was rescued from the destruction of the city (Joshua 2:1–21; 6:22–25)

Achan: an Israelite soldier who disobeyed God and paid the ultimate price (Joshua 7)

your foot, as I promised Moses. . . . As I was with Moses, so I will be with you; I will never leave you nor forsake you.

"Be strong and courageous, because you will lead these people to inherit the land I swore to their forefathers to give them. Be strong and very courageous. Be careful to obey all the law my servant Moses gave you; do not turn from it to the right or to the left, that you may be successful wherever you go." (1:2–3, 5–7)

When the Promised Land Is Enemy Territory

I see several themes in those opening verses that are woven throughout the rest of the book.

- Possession of the land God promised to the descendants of Abraham, Isaac, and Jacob:

    "I will give you every place where you set your foot." (1:3)

God had promised the land to Abraham five hundred years earlier and had repeated the promise to every generation. Now the time to claim the promise had come.

- The responsibility of the people to act on God's promise:

    "Be strong and very courageous." (1:7)

God had given them the land, but they had to act in faith and courage to occupy it.

- The absolute necessity of obedience to God's voice:

    "Be careful to obey." (1:7)

DOWNLOAd

Joshua 1:8 – 9

"**Do not let this Book of the Law depart from your mouth; meditate on it day and night, so that you may be careful to do everything written in it. Then you will be prosperous and successful. Have I not commanded you? Be strong and courageous. Do not be terrified; do not be discouraged, for the LORD your God will be with you wherever you go.**"

Victory would come as Joshua and the people of Israel followed God's instruction.

After the opening challenge, the book divides into two sections.

Conquering the Land (Joshua 2 – 12)

The conquest of Canaan involved overcoming several obstacles. The first was the Jordan River. Israel was camped on the east side of the Jordan; the heart of the land God had given them was on the west side of the Jordan. Just to make it difficult, the river was at flood stage. No transport vessels or cargo planes were available, so God had to make a way. Following God's instructions, priests carried the sacred ark of the covenant down to the river. When their sandals touched the water, the river was suddenly and miraculously dammed up. A wall of water began to form on one side while the rest of the water flowed on to the south. A wide road of riverbed opened in front of the people of Israel, and they walked across on dry ground.

The next obstacle was a walled city. Jericho was a strategic city in Joshua's strategy for conquering the land of Canaan. It guarded the way into the center of the territory. God's plan for taking the city was simple. March around the city once a day for six days. On the seventh day, march around seven times and then shout—and the walls will fall down. Yeah, right! Even though they may have thought it sounded foolish, they obeyed, and God kept his promise. Jericho fell—literally!

Digging Deeper

✗ Hess, Richard. *Joshua: An Introduction and Commentary*. Tyndale Old Testament Commentary series. Downers Grove, IL: InterVarsity Press, 1996.

A thorough explanation of Joshua; very easy to follow.

✗ Wiersbe, Warren. *Be Strong*. Colorado Springs, CO: Chariot Victor Publishing, 1993.

A brief but practical guide through the book.

HOW CAN GOD DO THAT?

God ordered Joshua and the people of Israel to completely destroy the Canaanites. Men, women, children, and animals were all to be killed. How can a God of love command such cruelty from his own people? The brutality of Joshua's book has led some readers to call the God of the Old Testament a "bully"—or worse!

The Bible gives two reasons for the destruction of the Canaanites. First, the people of Israel at that time and place were the instruments God used to bring his judgment on the Canaanites. The wickedness of the Canaanites had reached such a level that God would no longer tolerate it. God did not give Israel blanket permission to do the same to any nation they encountered at any time. His commands were limited to this particular situation. Furthermore, God did not have a double standard when it came to sin.

The Israelite Achan took items from Jericho that God told him not to take, and his whole family was destroyed.

The second reason the Bible gives for the complete destruction of the Canaanites is that Israel was to establish a pure worship of God in the land. God knew that the immoral worship and pagan gods of Canaan would become a snare to his people unless they were cleansed from the land. Israel failed to remove the Canaanites completely and, as a result, frequently fell into idolatry and disobedience to God.

Those who think the God of the Old Testament is too harsh should look again at the God of the New Testament. His perfect character has never changed. God is a God of love, but he is also a God of holiness and justice and even anger.

God had told the people of Israel that they were to keep none of the plunder from Jericho, but an Israelite soldier named Achan took some silver, some gold, and a really cool cloak. He hid these things in his tent and thought no one would ever know. But this one man's disobedience to God brought defeat to the entire nation at the very next town on the conquest map. Sin against God was the next obstacle to be overcome, and it wasn't a pleasant sight.

After the conquest of Jericho, the Israelite armies pushed into the center of Canaan. With the Canaanite forces divided, they could turn first to the south and fight a decisive battle at Gibeon. The next step was to sweep to the north, where victory was secured at the battles near Merom and Hazor. The Canaanite armies were defeated; the main cities had been conquered or destroyed; the land was securely in Israelite hands.

Points 2 Remember

☑ Joshua was the leader of Israel's conquest of the land of Canaan. Until his last breath, he urged God's people to fully follow the Lord.

☑ God's promises and God's power never diminish the importance of our obedience. He expects us to be strong and courageous!

Possessing the Land (Joshua 13 – 24)

In the second part of the book, Israel settled into their new home. Joshua divided the land among the clans of Israel and set boundaries between them. The final mop-up operation was left to each clan. The book ends with a powerful farewell address from the great man himself.

"Now fear the LORD and serve him with all faithfulness. Throw away the gods your forefathers worshiped beyond the River and in Egypt, and serve the LORD. But if serving the LORD seems undesirable to you, then choose for yourselves this day whom you will serve, whether the gods your forefathers served beyond the River, or the gods of the Amorites, in whose land you are living. But as for me and my household, we will serve the LORD." (24:14–15)

Still Claiming God's Promises

Joshua casts a long shadow down through Israel's history. He impacted a whole generation for the Lord and continues to stand as a compelling example of a person who served God courageously. We feel kind of puny next to a man of his spiritual caliber. It helps to remember that Joshua's God is the same today as he was back then. We aren't called to wage war on Canaanites, but we still face powerful enemies. The strongholds of evil and injustice seem as invincible as Jericho's walls. The weapons we use today seem foolish to the world—prayer, the message of Jesus, humility, sacrifice, servanthood, obedience to God. Those weapons may seem weak and ineffective, but under God's direction and in the arsenal of courageous people, those weapons can send the enemy into full retreat and bring a nation to repentance and faith. God is still the same. The weapons of spiritual warfare are still available. What seems to be lacking are the courageous people.

PEOPLE of the BiBLE _____

THE CANAANITES

The people known as the Canaanites came from several regions of the ancient world and settled in the eastern Mediterranean around 2000 B.C. The groups spoke different languages and had various ethnic heritages, but if they lived in the land of Canaan, they were called Canaanites. By the time Joshua led Israel into the land, the Canaanites had developed a system of small city-states, each with its own king. We would think the cities were tiny today, but they were strongly fortified with thick walls.

The Canaanites were farmers and traders. Those who lived near the Mediterranean Sea sent their merchant ships to Egypt, Crete, and Greece. The Canaanites were also excellent artisans, working with pottery, masonry, metal, and wood. The alphabet (a written symbol representing each spoken sound in a language) began among the Canaanites.

Canaanite religion centered around many gods and goddesses. Some of their deities—Baal, Dagon, Asherah, and Astarte—appear often in the Old Testament. Their worship involved animal (and possibly human) sacrifices. Both male and female cult prostitutes played a large part in their fertility festivals. Canaanite religion and worship are pictured in the Bible as disgusting to the Lord. God commanded the Israelites to destroy the Canaanites "on account of the wickedness of these nations" (Deuteronomy 9:4–5). Some Canaanite practices were especially repulsive to God—practices such as burning their sons and daughters in fire to their gods (Deuteronomy 12:31). Because God's command to destroy the Canaanites was never fully carried out, the people of Israel often followed their Canaanite neighbors in immoral and idolatrous worship.

Walking the Walk

1. One weapon of our warfare is God's Word. It can penetrate a person's strongest defenses and move the loudest critic to faith. The Word is most effective when we know it and use it in our witness to others. A great way to start making God's Word a permanent part of your life is by memorizing Joshua 1:8–9!

2. If you aren't interested in reading all the details about how the land was divided up, skip chapters 12–22 but don't miss Joshua 1–11 and 23–24. What qualities in Joshua's character impress you the most? Which quality needs the most cultivation in your own life?

Judges

➤ Read some of the most exciting stories in the Bible.

➤ Witness the death of a great leader—and the downfall of a nation.

➤ Discover the sad consequences of failing to follow the Lord.

When we think of a judge, most of us picture a person in a black robe presiding over a courtroom. A judge in the Bible, however, is more like a military commander, a patriotic leader who rises up in a time of national crisis and stirs God's people to throw off the tyranny of an oppressor. That fact alone will help you make a lot of sense out of the book of the Bible called Judges.

Another fact to keep in mind as you read this book is that a cycle of events happens over and over. Different people grab the headlines and different outside nations get involved, but essentially the same old story repeats itself again and again. The cycle begins when the people of Israel forget about their loyalty to the Lord God of Israel and worship the gods of their Canaanite neighbors. They leave the true God for idols of wood and stone. In his love for his wandering people, God brings chastening into their lives. He allows a foreign power, usually one of the nations living near Israel's borders, to attack his people and oppress them. Sometimes the enemies simply raid Israel's territory; more often they bring the nation or some part of the nation into bondage. They oppress God's people and bring them to the point where they cry out to God for help. When God sees their willingness to return to him, he raises up a deliverer, a judge. The judge leads the people in a military uprising and the invaders are driven out of the land of Israel. A time of peace usually follows as the judge becomes the civil leader in Israel and guides the people in the path

Key Characters

Ehud: a left-handed assassin (Judges 3:12–30)

Deborah: Israel's only female judge (Judges 4–5)

Gideon: a cowardly farmer who became a courageous general (Judges 6–8)

Samson: a he-man with a "she" weakness (Judges 13–16)

Delilah: Samson's deceitful girlfriend

of obedience to the Lord. But soon after the judge dies, the people begin to forget their promises to God, and the gods of the people around them become attractive again. The sad cycle starts another turn. At least seven revolutions of that same, tired process can be traced in the book of Judges.

The third fact that will help you make sense of this book isn't recorded until the end, but you sense it all the way through the story. The days of the judges as a whole were days of moral and spiritual chaos—or, as the writer of the book puts it: "Everyone did what was right in his own eyes" (21:25 NASB). Judges traces the downward course of a society that loosens its grip on God's truth. The nation suffers wave after wave of destruction and loss. Fortunately, we also meet some people who served God faithfully in the middle of spiritual disaster. These men and women not only survived, they flourished!

THE JUDGES OF ISRAEL

JUDGE	DATES AND YEARS OF JUDGESHIP		OPPRESSOR	REFERENCE IN JUDGES
1. Othniel	1367–1327	(40 years)	Mesopotamians	3:8–11
2. Ehud	1309–1229	(80 years)	Moabites	3:12–30
3. Shamgar	?	(10 years)	Philistines	3:31
4. Deborah	1209–1169	(40 years)	Canaanites	4:2–5:31
5. Gideon	1162–1122	(40 years)	Midianites	6:1–8:35
6. Tola	1119–1096	(23 years)	?	10:1–2
7. Jair	1119–1097	(22 years)	?	10:3–6
8. Jephthah	1078–1072	(6 years)	Ammonites	10:7–12:7
9. Ibzan	?	(8 years)	Ammonites	12:8–10
10. Elon	?	(10 years)	Ammonites	12:11–12
11. Abdon	?	(7 years)	Ammonites	12:13–15
12. Samson	1075–1055	(20 years)	Philistines	13:1–16:31

☑ The judges of the Old Testament were military leaders who were used by God to end Israel's oppression by foreign nations.

☑ The book of Judges is a record of the cycle of Israel's disobedience, their enslavement by an enemy, and their deliverance by God's power.

☑ Even when we fail, God remains faithful to his promises and to his people.

A Sad Story—Again and Again

The book of Judges picks up the story of Israel's spiritual pilgrimage where the book of Joshua ends—and carries us along for almost 350 years! During those years, Israel existed as a loose confederation of tribes or clans. They had no central government and no human king. Their king was the Lord, and his Word was the law. What united the clans of Israel was their worship of God and their loyalty to him as Ruler.

That system worked pretty well when the people maintained their faith and obedience to God. But when they began to worship the gods of the Canaanites, their unity began to crumble. After Joshua's death a new generation came on the scene "who knew neither the LORD nor what he had done for Israel" (2:10). In the span of one generation, loyalty to God dissolved.

Deterioration (Judges 1:1–3:6)

The book opens with the sad chronicle of Israel's failure to drive the Canaanites from the land God had given them. Joshua's military campaigns had secured the land, but each tribe was responsible to finish

DownLoad

Judges 5:2–3

"When the princes in Israel take the lead,
    when the people willingly offer themselves—praise the LORD!
Hear this, you kings! Listen, you rulers!
    I will sing to the LORD, I will sing;
    I will make music to the LORD, the God of Israel."

the job in its particular territory. The problem was that no one carried through. Over and over we read that Israel did not drive out the remaining inhabitants (1:21, 27, 28, 29, 30, 31, 33). Instead of removing the spiritual cancer from their land, the Israelites caught the disease. Soon God's people were ensnared in idolatry and pagan worship. That started the cycle of failure and deliverance that marks the book.

Deliverance (Judges 3:7 – 16:31)

Seven cycles of departure from the Lord, oppression by an enemy, and deliverance by a judge fill the heart of the book of Judges. Some of the greatest Bible stories come from these chapters: Samson and his downfall with Delilah (16:4–22), Gideon's courageous rout of the Midianites (7:1–25), and left-handed Ehud's attack on fat King Eglon (3:12–30). Thirteen judges are mentioned in the book, twelve men and one woman. Four more judges are found in the book of 1 Samuel (Eli, Samuel, Joel, and Abijah). Some of the accounts of the judges' exploits are extensive; some are frustratingly brief. Gideon receives one hundred verses of coverage; Shamgar gets one.

Decline (Judges 17:1 – 21:25)

The book closes with several examples of the severe moral decay in Israel during this 350-year span of time. The people of Israel, on more than one occasion, were guilty of more degrading things than the worst of their pagan neighbors.

DiggiNG DeEpeR

✗ Wilcock, Michael. *The Message of Judges: Grace Abounding.* The Bible Speaks Today series. Downers Grove, IL: InterVarsity Press, 1992.

A serious but readable commentary on Judges.

When We Fail, God Stands Firm

The dramatic contrast in Judges is between the disobedient people of Israel and the faithful God of Israel. The people continually break their promises; God continually keeps his. After the opening record of each tribe's failure to drive out the Canaanites, God promises, "I will never break my covenant with you" (2:1). I wouldn't have said that! If I had been betrayed, ignored, and deserted like God had been, I would have checked out of the relationship. But God stood true to his word. The Lord is the ultimate promise keeper!

You might read Judges and think of it as just so much ancient history. Our modern world seems far removed from three-thousand-year-old events in Palestine. But if you look more closely, you will see that our culture is headed down the same path of moral and spiritual decay. When we stop long enough to even think about our behavior, we don't ask, "Does *God* say this is good and right?" We ask, "Does it feel okay to *me?*" The book of Judges speaks with a powerful voice to a society on the skids.

How the judges survived or failed in their culture gives us insight into the options we have in ours. It's possible to be like Samson, to be seduced by the attractions of power or a bigger paycheck or an immoral lifestyle. When we try to stand on our own in a society without standards, we soon collapse. The other option is to see ourselves as weak men and women who can be made strong as we trust in God and walk in obedience to him.

The declining culture of Judges is mirrored in our culture, but God is the same today as he was then. He is still faithful to his promises and faithful to his people. You might feel oppressed by the declining circumstances in which you have to live every day. Your work situation or marriage or home life or health might be dreadful. But God stands ready to empower you to live obediently and courageously in the most difficult circumstances.

The book of Judges says that as a test God allowed pockets of Canaanite culture to survive in the land after Joshua's victory. "I will use them to test Israel and see whether they will keep the way of the LORD and walk in it" (2:22). That may explain why you are in the workplace you are in right now or why you live in the neighborhood you live in. God has you there for a purpose. Israel failed God's test. Our success or failure depends on our willingness to faithfully follow the Lord.

Walking the Walk

1. Judges says more about the Holy Spirit than any other Old Testament book. God's Spirit transforms men and women far beyond their own capabilities. As you read the book, mark the places where the Holy Spirit is mentioned. What does the Spirit do in those he comes upon?

2. What are some ways God might work today to bring a society or nation in moral decline back to the place of faith and obedience to him? How can you be involved in that process?

3. Who is your favorite judge in the book of Judges? Why did you pick that person? Write out some specific ways that you are like that person—and then some ways you want to become more like him or her.

Ruth

➤ Be captivated by an interracial love story.

➤ Discover helpful hints for getting along with your mother-in-law.

➤ Explore how to live honorably before the Lord and your community.

Weddings bring us to church at the weirdest times—like 1:00 on a Saturday afternoon or 6:30 on a Friday evening. We come because we love to love—and we love to see people in love.

It might surprise you to know that tucked into the pages of the Bible is one of the most captivating love stories ever written. I never get tired of reading it. The story of Ruth is the story of the love of a daughter-in-law for a mother-in-law. It's the story of the love of a rich man for a poor, outcast woman. It's the story of the love of God for ordinary people like us.

The book of Ruth is the only book in the Old Testament whose main character is a Gentile (a non-Jewish person). Ruth was a Moabite woman who ultimately married an Israelite man, Boaz. So it's the story of an interracial marriage that shows us the boundlessness of God's love.

Key Characters

Naomi: an Israelite woman; Ruth's mother-in-law

Ruth: a Moabite woman who married Naomi's son; she became an ancestor of King David and of Jesus

Orpah: a Moabite woman who married Naomi's *other* son

Boaz: an Israelite man who fell in love with Ruth

The book of Ruth is a true story, a video clip in the long saga of God's people. The story opens "in the days when the judges ruled" (1:1). Most likely the events in the book took place during the time of peace that followed Gideon's victory over the Midianite oppressors of Israel. It was a time of peace but not necessarily a time of plenty. A famine struck the land, and at least one family made the decision to leave Israel and move to Moab, a land to the east of Israel. The people of Moab worshiped false gods and usually lined up against the people of Israel. But on this occasion a desperate family found refuge in Moab. Elimelech and Naomi and their two boys settled in and soon became part of the community—so much so that the boys fell in love and married Moabite women.

But tragedy struck again when first Elimelech and then both sons died. Naomi was left with her two daughters-in-law, Orpah and Ruth.

Walking the Walk

1. Since the book of Ruth is short, why not put this book aside and read the biblical story. Try to enter into Ruth's experiences. It might help to record with one- or two-word summaries how you might feel in similar circumstances. How would you respond to the death of your spouse? What would it be like to move into a new culture surrounded by people who viewed you with suspicion? What emotions must Ruth have experienced as she waited to see the outcome of Boaz's proposal?

2. Think about the social and emotional barriers you put up in your own life. Are you hesitant to love another person because of a past hurt? How willing are you to reach beyond racial or ethnic or religious boundaries to demonstrate care and compassion and even friendship to people who may feel isolated? Look for opportunities to open yourself to relationships beyond the comfort zone of your current friends.

3. Share Ruth's story with someone you know. Tell that person how much you enjoyed reading it, and buy him or her a Bible (or lend yours) if he or she doesn't already have one. Enthusiasm is contagious!

Getting Along with Your Mother-in-Law

Naomi decided to return to her hometown in Israel. The famine was long over, and shirttail relatives would help her. But three mouths to feed seemed overwhelming. So Naomi urged her Moabite daughters to stay in their homeland. "Get married again, have kids, enjoy life," she told them. Orpah took her advice and headed back to Moab, but Ruth was drawn by a deeper bond than just her love for Naomi. She made

Points 2 Remember

☑ The book of Ruth is the story of the love between a daughter-in-law and her mother-in-law and between a Jewish man and a non-Jewish woman.

☑ Ruth is a picture of all of us who were separated from God's blessing and in great need. Boaz is a picture of our kinsman-redeemer, Jesus Christ, who willingly paid the supreme price to bring us into a close relationship with him.

☑ Ruth's commitment to Naomi went beyond emotional attachment. Ruth had come to believe in the true and living God of Israel. By God's grace she became part of the ancestry of Jesus Christ.

one of the most incredible commitments found anywhere in Scripture. Ruth said to Naomi:

"Where you go I will go, and where you stay I will stay. Your people will be my people and your God my God. Where you die I will die, and there I will be buried. May the LORD deal with me, be it ever so severely, if anything but death separates you and me." (1:16–17)

What a radical shift! Not only was Ruth expressing her love to Naomi, but she was claiming Naomi's people in Israel as her own. More significantly, she renounced the gods of Moab and put her trust in the Lord God of Israel!

Naomi and Ruth returned to Bethlehem in the territory of Judah. They had each other but not much more. They were forced by their need to rely on Israel's welfare program for food. Actually it was a "workfare" program. God had instructed the farmers that when harvesttime came they were to leave the corners of their fields uncut. Any poor person was free to cut the grain left standing and use it to feed his or her family. But even if a person was too poor to own a knife or sickle to cut the grain, he or she didn't go hungry.

Ruth 1:16

"Where you go I will go, and where you stay I will stay. Your people will be my people and your God my God."

DownLoad

A SHOE ON THE WRONG FOOT

An understanding of the culture and customs of ancient Israel helps us make sense of what happens in many parts of the Old Testament. Archaeologists, historians, anthropologists, and language experts all make a contribution. Commentaries, Bible dictionaries, and books on Bible backgrounds are valuable sources of information on the cultural setting of Scripture.

For example, even though Boaz was a close relative of Ruth through Naomi's husband, Elimelech, one other man in Bethlehem was a *closer* relative. Technically he had the first opportunity to "redeem" Ruth and Naomi out of poverty by purchasing Elimelech's property and marrying Ruth. When Boaz confronted the man with his responsibility, the other kinsman declined and transferred the right to Boaz. We would have shaken hands on the agreement or signed a contract. These men traded shoes!

Giving away one's shoe had come to symbolize the transfer of land ownership in that culture. If land was sold or the rights to buy the land were transferred, a shoe was exchanged in front of witnesses to validate the transaction. (I wonder if the man ever got his shoe back!)

With the "Nike exchange" out of the way, Boaz immediately promised to redeem Elimelech's land and marry Ruth.

The harvesters were instructed not to pick up stalks of grain they dropped or even a bundle of grain stalks inadvertently left behind. These "gleanings" were left for the poor to pick up.

(The specific commands about food for the poor can be found in Leviticus 19:9–10 and Deuteronomy 24:19–22.)

A Cold Night on the Threshing Floor

It so happened that, when Ruth went out to pick up the gleanings, she came to the fields of Boaz—and Boaz took immediate notice! He made sure she had enough food for lunch, told his servants to provide water for her, and even gave her extra grain to take home. In terms of cultural love signals, Boaz hit a grand slam!

Naomi put the final piece of the puzzle in place when she told Ruth to put on her best robe, spritz on some knock-'em-dead perfume, and go down to the threshing floor and lie down at sleeping Boaz's feet. Huh? Why not just go up to Boaz and say, "Listen, I love you, you love me, let's get married!" In the culture of ancient Israel, the custom when you were in need was to seek the help of a close relative—a kinsman-redeemer. Boaz was related to Naomi's deceased husband, Elimelech, so Ruth turned to him for help.

She went down to the area where the grain was prepared for storage, and she watched from the shadows until everyone was asleep. Then she quietly uncovered Boaz's feet, laid down, and waited. In the middle of the night, Boaz woke up because his feet were cold. As he sat up to cover his feet, he found a woman there—and not just any woman; it was Ruth! (By the way, if you are having trouble getting your husband's attention, uncover his feet some cold night and wait!)

Ruth asked Boaz to spread his robe over her and to act as her kinsman-redeemer. Basically she proposed to him and he accepted. The next morning in front of the elders of the city, Boaz asserted his right to take Ruth under his care as his wife. From that marriage a child was born who would be the grandfather of David, Israel's greatest king. Ultimately, from the same family line, Jesus was born. God honored Ruth's faith and courage by making her an ancestor of Israel's promised Redeemer.

Digging Deeper

✗   Atkinson, David. *The Message of Ruth.* The Bible Speaks Today series. Downers Grove, IL: InterVarsity Press, 1983.

A detailed commentary on the story of Ruth.

✗   Hayford, Jack. *A New Time and Place: Ruth's Journey of Faith.* Sisters, OR: Multnomah, 1997.

An explanation of Ruth's story with practical application of its truth to our lives today.

FAMINE OR FEAST?

The famine that forced Naomi and her family to seek refuge in Moab was not the only famine recorded in the Bible.

- A famine caused Jacob's sons to go to Egypt to buy grain, where they eventually were reunited with their brother Joseph (Genesis 41:53–57).
- Elijah the prophet prayed that God would withhold rain from Israel because of the nation's sin, and famine resulted (1 Kings 17).
- When the Babylonians besieged Jerusalem, famine swept the city (2 Kings 25:1–3).
- A famine in Palestine in the time of the New Testament was predicted by the prophet Agabus (Acts 11:28).
- The book of Revelation pictures "famine" as one of the four horsemen that stalks the earth just before Jesus' return (6:5–8).

The Bible also records some great feasts!

- Samson's wedding feast was ruined by a riddle (Judges 14:10–18).
- Solomon held a feast at the dedication of the temple in Jerusalem (1 Kings 8:65).
- Belshazzar held a feast at which God wrote his judgment on the palace wall (Daniel 5).
- Jesus told the story of a father's feast for his returning runaway son (Luke 15:23).
- God will hold a marriage feast in his future kingdom (Revelation 19:9).
- The book of Revelation gives an account of a gruesome feast for the birds after a great battle in the future (19:17–18).

1 Samuel

Heads Up

➤ Find out how Israel got a king—and lived to regret it!

➤ Meet King Saul—he makes great promises but doesn't carry through.

➤ Marvel over David's killing a giant with one well-aimed stone.

The lives of three men overlap and interweave through the book of 1 Samuel:

- Samuel, the last judge in Israel
- Saul, the first king of Israel
- David, the young successor to Saul

Key Characters

Samuel: a judge and prophet in Israel; God's man on the scene

Eli: the priest who raised Samuel but couldn't control his own sons

Hannah: Samuel's mom

Hophni and Phinehas: Eli's wicked sons

Saul: a tall man from the clan of Benjamin who was chosen to be Israel's first king

David: a young shepherd boy chosen by God to be the *next* king of Israel

Goliath: a giant hit man hired by Israel's enemies to intimidate Saul's army

Jonathan: Saul's son and David's best friend

The characters enter the drama, interact with each other, and move on. Above the stage and overshadowing every event is God. This is not simply the *political* history of ancient Israel; it is also a *prophetic* history. We see events on earth from God's perspective. Hidden motives are made clear. The masks people wear to cover their real desires and thoughts are removed. Normally we only get to see external events and actions. In God's view we see much more.

As 1 Samuel opens, we are in the last years of the judges in Israel, a time when the nation had no central government. The clans of Israel lived together in a loose confederation, but each clan pursued its own self-interests. Israel's neighbors exploited any sign of weakness as an opportunity to raid or oppress God's people. Spiritually the people of Israel had begun to drift from the Lord. Their religious leaders were compromising, their worship had degenerated into superstition, their loyalty to God's law was sporadic. Most of the people were convinced that a human king could solve all their problems. They found out that the wrong king only made problems worse.

Samuel, Israel's Last Judge (1 Samuel 1–8)

Samuel was dedicated to the Lord before he was born. His mother, Hannah, promised God that if he gave her a son, she would give him back to God to serve in the tent of worship, the tabernacle. The priests of Israel at the time were Eli and Eli's two bad boys. Eli's sons thought nothing of changing God's clear instructions about animal sacrifices to fit their own whims. They thought nothing of committing open immorality in the tabernacle. God's judgment came when Eli's sons were killed in battle and the ark of the covenant (a sacred box that symbolized God's presence in Israel) was taken by Israel's enemies. When Eli heard the news, he fell off his chair and died.

Samuel governed in Israel until he was more than ninety years old. When Samuel was old, the people of Israel came to him with a request. They wanted a king—not an invisible king ruling from heaven, but a human king, a king like the nations around them had. Samuel warned Israel that a king would bring new burdens and new

HELP FILE

"TWIN" BOOKS

First and Second Samuel are the first set of "twin" books in the Bible. Their titles are written as 1 Samuel and 2 Samuel (older versions of the Bible use Roman numerals—I Samuel and II Samuel), but the books are referred to as *"First* Samuel" and *"Second* Samuel" (not *"One* Samuel" and *"Two* Samuel"). You will encounter several other pairs of books both in the Old Testament and in the New.

Biblical books were often titled according to the first person of importance in the book. First Samuel gets its name from the man Samuel who appears early in its story.

Originally the two books of Samuel were one book. When the Hebrew Old Testament was translated into Greek (about 200 B.C.), the long book was separated into two shorter books.

Points 2 Remember

☑ Three lives are interwoven in 1 Samuel—those of Samuel, Saul, and David. Their stories show Israel's transition from a confederation of clans to a nation ruled by a powerful king.

☑ God may be rejected, but he cannot be removed. He rules over his world and accomplishes what he desires.

☑ Integrity on the inside is far more important than an impressive appearance on the outside.

taxes, but the people persisted. Samuel reminded them that the Lord was their king, but still they insisted on their own way. God told Samuel to give them what they wanted. Be careful what you ask God for! Sometimes he gives it to us and we regret the day he did.

Saul, Israel's First King (1 Samuel 9–15)

Israel's first king makes his entrance in chapter 9. Saul was a very impressive man to look at. He looked like the perfect king. He started well too. The Spirit of the Lord came on him, and godly advisors helped him. A few military victories raised his approval ratings even higher. But success came too fast and too easily. Saul began to think that a leader's moral integrity didn't matter.

In chapter 13 we see Saul's first act of disobedience to God. His armies were ready for battle, but Samuel had told Saul that offerings to God needed to be made before the battle began. Saul was ready but Samuel was late, so Saul offered the sacrifices. Big mistake! He had good excuses for his disobedience, just as most of us can find someone or something else to blame for our failures, but his decline had begun.

Time after time God gave direction to Saul and Saul refused to fully obey. When Saul was confronted with his sin, he didn't repent—he

1 Samuel 16:7

"The Lord does not look at the things man looks at. Man looks at the outward appearance, but the Lord looks at the heart."

DOWNLOAD

argued. Finally, Samuel pronounced God's judgment: "The LORD has rejected you as king over Israel!" (15:26).

David, Israel's Greatest King (1 Samuel 16 – 31)

Chapter 16 tells of the choosing of a new king, but the kingdom would not be his for nearly twenty years. David was a young teenager stuck with the job of watching his father's sheep. He wasn't much to look at, but God saw into his inner being and found integrity and faith.

One of the greatest stories in the Bible is David's confrontation with Goliath in chapter 17. This giant of a man (a little over nine feet tall!) challenged Israel to a winner-take-all battle. One warrior from Israel would fight Goliath. If Israel's champion won, the enemies of Israel would serve them. If Goliath won, Israel would submit to bondage. No place was quieter after Goliath's challenge than the Israelite camp. Young David, on a food-supply mission to his brothers, heard Goliath's words and took him with a sling and a stone—and the power of God. David said to Goliath,

> "You come against me with sword and spear and javelin, but I come against you in the name of the LORD Almighty, the God of the armies of Israel, whom you have defied." (17:45)

David's victory over Goliath made him an instant national hero. It also made Saul jealous of the young upstart. Saul tried (unsuccessfully) to take David's life at least twice. Finally, David had to run. For fourteen years David eluded Saul's manhunt by living in the desert area southwest of Jerusalem. At first David was all alone, but more and more men began to join him until he had a fairly large army. David never fought Saul, however. He knew that God would put him on the throne of Israel in God's own time.

DigginG DeEpeR

✗ Barber, Cyril. *The Books of Samuel.* Vol. 1. Neptune, NJ: Loizeaux, 1994.

A thorough and practical explanation of 1 Samuel.

A Tragic End

First Samuel closes with Saul's death. In still another battle with the Philistines, Saul's three sons were killed and Saul was mortally wounded. Fearing torture from his enemies, Saul ended his life by falling on his own sword. Saul started well, but he didn't fully obey the Lord. His life ended in tragedy.

God's hand is seen on every page of 1 Samuel. God rules and overrules to work out his plan perfectly. That is one of the lessons we need to carry away from this book. God can be rejected, but he cannot be removed. By demanding a human king, Israel had rejected the Lord, but they had not removed him from control. He still ruled over his people.

Saul chose his own way too. Saul's obsession was his image. Rather than being concerned with how God evaluated his life, he wanted to look good to those around him. In that respect, Saul would fit perfectly into our modern culture. We want to look good—buff bodies, attractive spouses, knockout cars—but we think very little about what God sees as he examines our hearts. Saul had it all, but when the pressure was on, he chose to disobey God and compromise his integrity. Even in his death he trusted only in himself and not in God.

THE PHILISTINES

The entire book of 1 Samuel is played out against a backdrop of oppression and attack on Israel by the Philistines *(fill-a-steens)*. The people of Philistia lived west of Israel between the border of Judah and the Mediterranean Sea. Five main cities made up the Philistine confederation: Gath, Ashdod, Ashkelon, Gaza, and Ekron. The Philistines were ruled by five lords or governors, one for each of the five cities.

Originally the Philistines came to the eastern Mediterranean as part of the migration of "Sea People" from the area of ancient Crete. They arrived about 1200 B.C. and conquered the original Canaanite inhabitants of the region. Rather than imposing their own culture, however, the Philistines absorbed most of the Canaanite culture. The Philistines were Israel's main enemy during the period of the judges and the early kingdom. David finally subdued them in the early years of his reign.

The Philistines were not an unusually tall people, although Goliath and his four brothers were certainly "giants" (1 Chronicles 20:4–8). Think of the salary a nine-foot champion could pull down in the NBA!

Walking the Walk

1. Who is the "king" in your life? Who rules?

2. Which of these people have you submitted to as king at times:

   Your boss?

   Your friend or spouse?

   Your own desires?

   The opinion of others?

3. In what ways do you see yourself in Saul? How are you different from Saul?

4. List one or two situations in which you find it easy to disobey God. What can you do now to avoid or prepare for those situations in the future? To whom will you make yourself accountable for obedience to God?

2 Samuel

— Heads Up

➤ Watch as a great ruler rises to power, falls into sexual sin, and then faces the consequences in his life.

➤ Discover God's promise to David that his descendants would rule over Israel forever.

Imagine having a book of the Bible all about *you!* For hundreds of years people in every culture and on every continent would read about your fame, your great successes, and even your failures. Israel's great King David is the central character in 2 Samuel. David gets a lot of press in the Bible. In fact, sixty-two chapters of Scripture tell his story—more than any other Old Testament personality. The influential leader Joseph has fourteen chapters; the prophet Daniel, twelve; the prophet Elijah, less than ten. In addition David is referred to fifty-nine times in the New Testament, more often than Abraham or Isaiah. God wanted us to know that David had some very significant things to teach us.

First Samuel centers on Samuel, Saul, and the early years of David's life—115 years go by as you turn its pages. Second Samuel spans only forty years. It opens with David's coronation as king; it ends with David as an old man passing the kingdom on to his son Solomon.

Key Characters

David: Israel's greatest king

Bathsheba: David's next-door neighbor—and fatal attraction

Nathan: God's prophet and David's chief advisor

Absalom: David's son who rose in rebellion against his father (2 Samuel 13–18)

Tracing a Great Man's Career

Political leaders today follow the popularity polls very closely. The book of 2 Samuel traces a different approval rating. David's integrity before God rises, levels off, and then begins a steady decline. The turning point comes at midlife for David. He should have been leading his armies. Instead, he was lounging on the rooftop with too much time on his hands.

A SPECTACULAR PROMISE

God made an unconditional promise in 2 Samuel 7. It is one of the great agreements (or covenants) in the Bible between God and his people. God promised David that his descendants would reign over Israel forever.

God's prophet, Nathan, spoke as God's voice:

> "'The LORD declares to you that the LORD himself will establish a house for you: When your days are over and you rest with your fathers, I will raise up your off-spring to succeed you, who will come from your own body, and I will establish his kingdom. He is the one who will build a house for my Name [the temple], and I will establish the throne of his kingdom forever. . . . Your house and your kingdom will endure forever before me; your throne will be established forever.'"
> (2 Samuel 7:11–13, 16)

The responsibility to keep that promise did not rest on David or on David's descendants. The promise rested fully on God—and God kept his word! David's descendants ruled over the kingdom (or a portion of it) for almost four hundred years. Even when the people of Israel were dominated by outside powers and had no king, God kept his hand on David's family. Eventually Jesus was born in the royal line of David, and he inherited all of David's authority. Jesus had no children, but he didn't need to pass on the kingdom. He lives forever as God's anointed King! His kingdom will never end.

Triumph (2 Samuel 1–10)

The opening chapters find David on the rise. He was crowned first as king over his own clan of Judah. For seven and a half years he reigned in Hebron. Then he captured Jerusalem from the Jebusites and united the whole kingdom under his authority. David reigned over all Israel for thirty-three more years.

These chapters tell a story of incredible victory. David never experienced military defeat in the first years of his reign. He extended the borders of Israel and subdued enemies on every side.

> The LORD gave David victory wherever he went. (8:6)

David prospered because he set his heart to honor God. Even when God said no to David's request to build a permanent temple in Jerusalem for God's worship, David responded in humility and obedience.

Points 2 Remember

- ☑ Second Samuel is the story of David's forty-year reign as king over Israel. It is also the story of David's failure and the consequences that failure brought into his life.

- ☑ Prosperity and comfort often make us more vulnerable to personal failure unless there is whole-hearted dependence on the Lord.

- ☑ When we confess our sin, God will always forgive, but the scars of sin remain.

Tragedy (2 Samuel 11–12)

Men and women at the pinnacle of professional or public success are often the most vulnerable to personal failure. At the height of his power, David took his eyes off the Lord and they fell on a beautiful woman.

In the spring, at the time when kings go off to war, David sent Joab out with the king's men and the whole Israelite army. . . . But David remained in Jerusalem.

One evening David got up from his bed and walked around on the roof of the palace. From the roof he saw a woman bathing. The woman was very beautiful. (11:1–2)

The woman David saw was Bathsheba, the wife of one of his most trusted friends. His desire and Bathsheba's consent led to immorality. When Bathsheba became pregnant, David manipulated a cover-up that ultimately resulted in the death of Bathsheba's husband.

Between chapter 11 and chapter 12 one year elapses without a comment. David seemed the same, but inwardly his heart was growing hard. Finally, God sent the prophet Nathan to point his finger at David and to reveal David's sin. David confessed his failure, but the consequences still came. God told David that the sword of strife would never leave David's house.

Trouble (2 Samuel 13–24)

Here is the list of consequences that pummeled David's life:

The child conceived with Bathsheba got sick and died.

David's son Amnon raped his half-sister and then was murdered.

Absalom, another son, rose up in rebellion and drove David from Jerusalem. Absalom eventually was killed, and David collapsed in grief.

David in disobedience to God took a census of the people to see how strong his nation had become. God struck Israel with a plague and 70,000 people died.

By the opening of the next biblical book (1 Kings), David is old and senile, and another son, Adonijah, is attempting to take the throne by force.

Cultivating a Heart for God

The Bible pictures its heroes with stunning honesty. In times of adversity and trial, David walked close to the Lord. What tripped him up was prosperity. When we reach the comfort zone in life, it seems easier to forget the Lord. Maybe that's why God keeps so many of us in crisis situations! We stay closer to him.

David's sin is never swept under the carpet but, looking back, we can also sense the abundance of God's grace to David. In all the New Testament references to David, his sin with Bathsheba and his conspiracy to murder her husband are never mentioned. David's sin was recorded for all future generations to read, but God's forgiveness is forever.

DiGGinG DeEpeR

✗ Baldwin, Joyce. *1 and 2 Samuel: An Introduction and Commentary.* Tyndale Old Testament Commentary series. Downers Grove, IL: InterVarsity Press, 1988.

An excellent study of these two books.

A helpful study on David's life is:

✗ Swindoll, Charles. *David: A Man of Passion and Destiny.* Dallas: Word, 1997.

If you want to do some personal Bible study on David's life and example, try Jack Kuhatschek's Bible study guide *David* in the LifeGuide series published by InterVarsity Press.

Walking the Walk

1. As you read chapters 11 and 12 of 2 Samuel, be sure to read Psalm 51—David's confession of his sin to God—and Psalm 32—David's joy over God's forgiveness. These praise poems will help you understand why David was called a man after God's heart (1 Samuel 13:14).

2. Evaluate your own life situation. Are you in a time of crisis or comfort? Do you sense a daily reliance on God for wisdom and strength, or would self-sufficient better describe your everyday life?

3. What steps could David have taken to keep himself more dependent on God and more accountable to others? Your answer might give you insight into how to preserve your own integrity or to regain integrity you have compromised.

1 and 2 Kings

Heads Up

➤ Follow the reign of wise King Solomon.

➤ Watch the nation divide—the north breaks away from the south.

➤ See two kings ruling two kingdoms and both headed for disaster.

First and Second Kings are a jumble of weird names and bloody revolts. The books record the slide of the kingdom of Israel from wealth and influence to poverty and obscurity. The people commissioned to bring the light of God's truth to the world become more and more like the world around them. At times pagan idols and the immoral worship of false gods replaced the Lord and the law in Israel. If it weren't for the faithfulness of a few true followers of the Lord and occasional brief times of spiritual renewal, it might seem like God had simply given up on his people. But God is true to his promises even when his people turn their backs on him.

These books cover 385 years of Israel's history—from 970 B.C., when David's son Solomon was crowned king, to 586 B.C., when the city of Jerusalem was destroyed by the Babylonian army. First Kings covers the first 115 years; 2 Kings the last 270 years. First Kings opens at the

HELP FILE

TWO LONG BOOKS

This is another set of paired books in the Bible. The titles are written 1 Kings and 2 Kings (or I Kings and II Kings), but the books are referred to as "*First* Kings" and "*Second* Kings." Originally 1 and 2 Kings were one long book. They were divided for convenience. So now we have *two* long books!

A Jewish tradition names the prophet Jeremiah as the primary author and compiler of these books, but we don't know for sure who wrote them.

height of Israel's power; 2 Kings closes as the remaining survivors of David's great kingdom are marched off in chains. The building of God's temple in the early chapters of 1 Kings is followed by the burning of the temple in the last chapters of 2 Kings.

The Kingdom United (1 Kings 1–11)

First Kings picks up where 2 Samuel left off. King David is old and dying. As one of his last official acts, David chooses Solomon to succeed him, and that choice is approved by God.

Solomon is a study in contrasts. As a young man, Solomon followed God with his whole heart. Shortly after Solomon's coronation as king, God came to Solomon and offered him whatever he wanted. What would you ask for if God gave you a blank check? Solomon asked for wisdom to rule God's people well. Because God was pleased with Solomon's choice, God threw in everything else as a bonus—wealth, long life, fame, influence. Solomon started brilliantly!

Solomon was a songwriter, a naturalist, a judge, a poet, and an architect. People came from all over the known world to seek Solomon's wisdom. (You can explore some of Solomon's wise teaching in the biblical book of Proverbs.)

Chapters 5–8 of 1 Kings describe the building of the temple, a permanent house for the worship of the Lord. Solomon prayed one of the greatest prayers in the Bible (chapter 8) as he dedicated the temple to God.

Unfortunately, some cracks in Solomon's character began to appear at the time of his greatest power and influence. He made alliances with other nations instead of trusting the Lord to protect his people. Many of those alliances were secured by exchanging daughters with foreign kings. The foreign king married Solomon's daughter, and Solomon

DoWNloAd

1 Kings 8:56–57

"Praise be to the Lord, who has given rest to his people Israel just as he promised. Not one word has failed of all the good promises he gave through his servant Moses. May the Lord our God be with us as he was with our fathers; may he never leave us nor forsake us."

married the daughter of the foreign king as a treaty wife. Foreign women moved into Solomon's palace and brought their idols and pagan gods with them. In time Solomon allowed temples to be built for the worship of these gods, and it wasn't long until Solomon was going to church with his wives. His heart was turned away from fully following the Lord.

Solomon's later years were marked by compromise, disobedience, and turmoil. Solomon pursued every avenue he could think of to find satisfaction and happiness—and every one was a dead-end street. (He described his fruitless search in the biblical book of Ecclesiastes.) In his old age, Solomon turned back to God but soon died. The golden years of Israel's kingdom came to an end with his death.

The Kingdom Divided (1 Kings 12 – 22)

An undisciplined father produced an undisciplined son. Solomon's successor, Rehoboam, had been given every luxury growing up, and he wanted even more when he became king. The leaders of the clans of Israel gathered to crown Rehoboam as king, but there was rumbling in the ranks. The ten northern clans demanded tax relief. They couldn't continue to meet the heavy demands placed on them by the king. In a move only the stupidest political advisor would suggest, Rehoboam told them that he would increase his demands, not lessen them.

The ten tribes in the north refused to acknowledge Rehoboam as king and split off from the united nation. The disastrous split that took place that day was never mended. From this point on the nation was divided. Suddenly there were two kingdoms and two kings. As you read you will notice that it becomes far more difficult to follow what is happening. A few basic facts will help you keep your bearings.

The ten northern clans that split away were now called Israel. (Yes, it is confusing. The whole nation was called "Israel"; now only part of it is called Israel.) The northern kingdom is also called "Ephraim" (the name of the clan that took the leadership in pulling away) or "Samaria" (the city that eventually became the capital of the northern kingdom).

The southern two tribes (Benjamin and Judah) were simply called Judah (mostly because Judah was a larger and more influential tribe than Benjamin). The capital remained in Jerusalem.

The northern kingdom, Israel, lasted 209 years—from 931 B.C. when the division began to 722 B.C. when the nation was conquered by the Assyrians. The people of the northern kingdom were then scattered throughout the Assyrian Empire. Israel was ruled by twenty kings from several different dynasties (or ruling families). *All* the kings of Israel were evil and refused to follow the Lord. Seven Israelite kings were assassinated; one committed suicide.

FOOtpRiNts
in the SanD

We have learned a lot about the god Baal and his worship in the ancient world from a large collection of epic literature discovered at Ras Shamra, an area in modern-day Syria. The city of Ras Shamra was originally named Ugarit. Many of the texts discovered there are written in an old Canaanite language now called Ugaritic. The mythological stories of Baal and various other gods and goddesses have given biblical scholars a new window on the language, culture, and beliefs of the people who lived around the Old Testament Israelites. (You can read some of these myths in Michael Coogan's book *Stories from Ancient Canaan* [Philadelphia: Westminster Press, 1978].)

Key Characters in 1 Kings

Jeroboam

(First king of northern kingdom; reign 931–910 B.C.; 1 Kings 12:25–14:20)

Early in his reign Jeroboam committed an act that sealed Israel's spiritual doom. Every king in the north followed Jeroboam in this and no one ever reversed it. Jeroboam did not want his people going down to Jerusalem in the southern kingdom of Judah to worship the Lord in the temple. So he set up two new worship centers in Israel (much more convenient!). He made priests out of people not qualified to be priests, and he changed Israel's holy days. Worst of all, he put golden bulls in Israel's new worship centers as "helpful aids to worship." God was nauseated by all of it.

Ahab

(King of Israel; reign 874–853 B.C.; 1 Kings 16:29–33; 20:1–22:40)

Ahab ruled Israel during one of its most prosperous times. Ahab not only continued in the way of Jeroboam's sin—he made it far worse. Ahab married a Phoenician princess named Jezebel and invited her to bring her main god, Baal, into Israel as the supreme god! Ahab and Jezebel eventually died under the judgment of God.

Elijah

(Prophet of God in Israel; ministry 870–850 B.C.; 1 Kings 17–19, 21; 2 Kings 2:1–11)

Ahab and Jezebel had to contend with a fiery prophet named Elijah. Elijah appeared in Ahab's palace one day and announced that no more rain would fall on Israel until he said it would. Imagine the impudence of this hick from the hills of Israel! But for three and a half years no rain fell. Finally, Elijah challenged the prophets of the god Baal to a contest of the gods on Mount Carmel. It's a spectacular story! (You can read it in 1 Kings 18:16–40.) Elijah spoke for God for about twenty years in Israel. In the end he was taken to heaven in a whirlwind of fire.

The southern kingdom, Judah, lasted 345 years. It was conquered in 586 B.C. by the Babylonians. Judah had nineteen kings (and one queen), all descendants of King David. In Judah's history only eight kings were good—Asa, Jehoshaphat, Joash, Amaziah, Uzziah, Jotham, Hezekiah, and Josiah. The others led God's people into idolatry and false worship.

One other significant fact will help you make sense of these books. The author talks about events in the northern kingdom of Israel for a while. Then he backs up in time and switches to the southern kingdom of Judah for a while. Then he goes back and picks up Israel's story for a few more kings—only to switch again to Judah a few pages later. If you keep the kingdoms straight, you will understand a lot more of what is going on.

The Kingdom Destroyed (2 Kings 1–25)

The same dreary story of decline and spiritual decay is picked up in
2 Kings. In chapters 1–17 the focus is primarily on the northern kingdom (although various kings of Judah are also discussed). Everything
came crashing down for Israel when the Assyrian army crushed the last
remnants of the northern clans in 722 B.C.

> The king of Assyria invaded the entire land, marched against Samaria,
> and laid siege to it for three years. In the ninth year of Hoshea [Israel's
> king], the king of Assyria captured Samaria and deported the Israelites
> to Assyria. . . .
>
> All this took place because the Israelites had sinned against the LORD
> their God, who had brought them up out of Egypt from under the
> power of Pharaoh king of Egypt. They worshiped other gods and fol-
> lowed the practices of the nations the LORD had driven out before
> them, as well as the practices that the kings of Israel had introduced.
> (2 Kings 17:5–8)

For all practical purposes the ten tribes of the northern kingdom were
absorbed into the Assyrian Empire. The Assyrians were a particularly
cruel nation. Their approach to captive peoples was to disperse the few
survivors into various areas of the empire far from their homeland.
Organized rebellion was impossible under those conditions, and that's

DiggiNG DeEpeR

✗ Wallace, Ronald. *Readings in First Kings*. Grand Rapids: Eerdmans, 1995.

Wallace has broken the book into sixteen sections for personal or group study.

✗ Wiseman, Donald. *1 and 2 Kings: An Introduction and Commentary*. Tyndale
Old Testament Commentary series. Downers Grove, IL: InterVarsity Press, 1993.

A thorough and serious study of these books.

If you would like to study more about God's prophet Elijah check out:

✗ Roper, David. *Elijah: A Man Like Us*. Grand Rapids: Discovery House, 1997.

A personal, practical look at Elijah's impact plus good questions for further reflection.

Key Characters in 2 Kings

Elisha

(Prophet of God in Israel; ministry 853–797
   B.C.; 2 Kings 2:1–8:15)

Elisha was Elijah's successor. He (like Elijah)
   was empowered by God to perform amazing miracles—a dead boy was revived to
   life, a man's leprosy was healed, and an
   iron axhead floated!

Hezekiah

(Godly king of Judah; reign 728–715 B.C.;
   2 Kings 18–20)

Hezekiah was one of the most faithful kings
   ever to rule over the kingdom of Judah. He
   reopened the temple of God (which Ahaz,
   his father, had closed) and he reestablished the true worship of the Lord in
   Judah. Many people who were loyal to the
   Lord in the northern kingdom of Israel
   migrated south to Judah during Hezekiah's
   reign. The prophet Isaiah played a prominent role in Hezekiah's kingdom. Hezekiah
   made a dramatic appeal to the Lord for
   protection from the Assyrian army, and
   God destroyed 185,000 Assyrians in one
   night!

Josiah

(Godly king of Judah; reign 640–609 B.C.;
   2 Kings 22:1–23:30)

Josiah began to seek the Lord when he was
   very young, and he led one of the greatest
   spiritual renewals in the history of God's
   people. A copy of the Law was discovered,
   and it was reestablished as the basis for
   Judah's society. The pagan idols were
   removed from the land along with the
   sacred groves devoted to pagan worship.
   Josiah was killed in a battle in 609 B.C.

Nebuchadnezzar

(Ruler of Babylonian Empire; 605–562 B.C.)

Nebuchadnezzar led the armies of Babylon
   against tiny Judah three times. The last
   time his troops destroyed the city. Nebuchadnezzar built the Babylonian Empire
   into a world power. He also created a magnificent palace in the city of Babylon. At the
   height of his power and pride, Nebuchadnezzar was humbled by God. Ultimately, he
   came to acknowledge the Lord as the only
   true God. (You can read this surprising
   story in the book of Daniel, chapter 4.)

the way the Assyrians liked it. (For more on the Assyrians, see People
of the Bible: The Assyrians, p. 252.)

The Assyrians harassed the southern kingdom of Judah for a while and
tried to conquer it, but God's intervention prevented Judah from being
destroyed. (The story of Judah's deliverance is in 2 Kings 19.)

Chapters 18–25 of 2 Kings focus on the last remaining part of David's
great kingdom, the kingdom of Judah. Some of Judah's godliest kings
ruled during these years—and some of Judah's worst kings! By the
beginning of the sixth century B.C., a new world power had come on
the scene. The Babylonians had overthrown the Assyrians and had

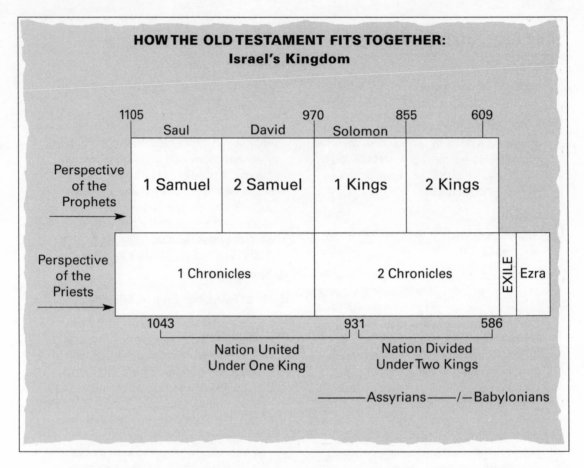

HOW THE OLD TESTAMENT FITS TOGETHER:
Israel's Kingdom

	1105		970	855	609
	Saul	David	Solomon		

Perspective of the Prophets →

| 1 Samuel | 2 Samuel | 1 Kings | 2 Kings |

Perspective of the Priests →

| 1 Chronicles | 2 Chronicles | EXILE | Ezra |

1043   931   586

Nation United Under One King

Nation Divided Under Two Kings

————Assyrians————/—Babylonians

reconquered most of Assyria's empire. In 605 B.C. the Babylonian king, Nebuchadnezzar, led his armies against Judah and forced Judah to accept Babylonian control. Nebuchadnezzar took a group of talented young men back to Babylon with him. One of those men was Daniel, a man who would eventually become God's spokesman to the Babylonian kings.

A few years after the initial conquest, Jehoiachin, the king of Judah, joined Egypt in a rebellion against Babylonian authority. Nebuchadnezzar and his armies returned and forced a heavier toll on God's people. Ten thousand Judahites were taken to Babylon, and the temple was stripped of its gold and silver. King Jehoiachin was also taken into exile, and his uncle, Zedekiah, was installed as a puppet king in Judah.

Foolishly, Zedekiah rebelled once more, and Nebuchadnezzar had had enough. This time (586 B.C.) the city of Jerusalem was destroyed. The temple of God and all the houses were burned. The city walls were reduced to rubble. The people who survived the siege and final attack were marched off into exile. Unlike the Assyrians, the Babylonians allowed captive people to live together. The exiled Judahites were settled six miles south of Babylon and were given land and tools to build houses and farms and marketplaces. Within a few years they had settled in. For fifty more years, God's people lived in Babylon—and prospered! They prospered so well that, when another new empire pushed the Babylonians aside and the new king said the Judahites could return to Jerusalem, very few were willing to go. But that's the next part of the story. . . .

Walking the Walk

1. One profitable way to study the book of Kings is to read your own life experience into the lives of the people in the story. Evaluate your obedience (or disobedience) to God in comparison to godly King Josiah or perverse King Ahab. Thinking about how Elijah stood for God in a society on the skids will give you insight into how you can make the same impact on your society.

2. If the book of "20th Kings" was being written today, how would God evaluate the moral character of our five most recent national leaders? How would God evaluate the last twenty years of our nation's moral direction?

1 and 2 Chronicles

Heads Up

➤ Explore a unique perspective on Israel's history.

➤ Read "the rest of the story" about some of Judah's kings.

➤ Join with God's people as they experience spiritual renewal.

The books of Chronicles seem to be the Bible's version of summer reruns. When you turn from 2 Kings to 1 Chronicles, you get the feeling that what you are reading you have read somewhere before. Second Kings ends with the destruction of Jerusalem and the exile of God's people in Babylon. Then you turn the page and read: "Adam, Seth, Enosh." You go clear back to Genesis and (apparently) start over! Before you grab the remote and turn to something else, there are some things you need to know about these books.

A Unique Perspective

The Chronicles do repeat a lot of information from other books. In fact, about half the material is taken virtually word for word from other books. What sets Chronicles apart is that the author looks at Israel's history from a new perspective. He covers some of the same ground but with new facts and a fresh approach.

Key Characters

David: Israel's second king

Solomon: David's son, successor and wisest of Israel's kings

Hezekiah: a godly king in Judah who led his people in spiritual renewal

Josiah: a king who as a very young man turned the people of Judah back to the Lord

All the evidence suggests that 1 and 2 Chronicles were written after the exile in Babylon had ended. Some of God's people had returned to Jerusalem, the temple had been rebuilt, and the walls of the city had been restored. Only one part of the great nation of Israel was still intact. The southern kingdom of Judah had survived; the northern kingdom of Israel had not. Therefore, as the author (we'll call him "the chronicler") retold the story of God's people, his focus was on Judah. Israel in the north is hardly mentioned in Chronicles. The center of

Points 2 Remember

- ☑ The books of Chronicles are a review of the story of Israel's kingdom with an emphasis on the rewards of living obediently before God.

- ☑ The chronicler wants us to see our own lives reflected in the lives of the kings he tells us about.

- ☑ The books were written to encourage the people returning to Jerusalem from exile in Babylon. David's throne and kingdom may have been gone, but David's God was still in control.

attention was the line of kings that God promised to bless—the descendants of King David who ruled in Judah. The kings in the north had not been from David's family, so they were ignored.

This focus on David's descendants is the unique *historical* perspective of Chronicles, but a unique *spiritual* perspective also comes into play. The chronicler was a priest, a leader in the worship of God. As a priest and preacher, he was very concerned about moral and spiritual instruction. The chronicler didn't just record history—he drew spiritual lessons from the events of history. When he wrote about Judah's good, godly kings, he emphasized their good deeds and their obedience to God. When he wrote about King David, for example, no mention was made of David's sin with Bathsheba or the murder of Bathsheba's husband or the rebellion of David's son, Absalom. The chronicler put the stress on David's godly character. He wasn't trying to cover up David's sin. The account in 2 Samuel was available for anyone to read. He was focusing the reader's attention on obedience to God and the importance of following that example in our lives.

HELP FILE

THE THIRD PAIR

This is the third set of paired books in the Old Testament. The titles are written 1 Chronicles and 2 Chronicles (or I Chronicles and II Chronicles) but they are referred to as "*First* Chronicles" and "*Second* Chronicles."

According to the Jewish Talmud, Ezra the priest wrote the books of Chronicles. No author is named in the books themselves.

The sins of Judah's kings weren't always avoided as the chronicler compiled his book. We are told in 2 Chronicles 26 about the sin of King Uzziah even though 2 Kings never mentions it. Uzziah was filled with pride and tried to enter God's temple to offer incense to God, something only a priest in Israel was supposed to do. God struck Uzziah with leprosy because of his sin. But even Uzziah's failure became an opportunity to teach a spiritual lesson about the consequences of disobedience to God.

DiggiNG DeEpeR

✗ Wilcock, Michael. *The Message of Chronicles.* The Bible Speaks Today series. Downers Grove, IL: InterVarsity Press, 1987.

A thorough study of these books with plenty of practical insight for today.

The chronicler was very interested in the temple and sacrifices and prayer. He put a high priority on the proper worship of God. In Samuel and Kings we have history from the viewpoint of God's prophets. Elijah and Elisha, for example, are very prominent in Kings. In Chronicles we have history from the viewpoint of the priests who led God's people in worship. Elijah is mentioned only once in Chronicles; Elisha not at all.

The books of Chronicles then are a review of Israel's history with an emphasis on living obediently before God and worshiping him with reverence. The chronicler gives us the same stories that we find in the books of Samuel and Kings, but he adds some things the other writers leave out. He gives us accurate history but from a unique perspective.

WHAT ABOUT SOME HARMONY?

If you would like to read everything the books of Samuel, Kings, and Chronicles have to say about each king in order, one approach is to flip back and forth between the books and try not to miss anything. An easier method is to buy a "harmony" of these books. Each biblical passage that talks about David, for example, is printed in the order in which it happened. In another section, the reign of evil King Manasseh is described from the perspective of both 2 Kings and 2 Chronicles. The passages are printed side by side for easy comparison.

The best harmony of these books is edited by James D. Newsome, *A Synoptic Harmony of Samuel, Kings, and Chronicles* (Grand Rapids: Baker, 1986).

A Map for the Journey

First Chronicles has two main sections:

In chapters 1–9 the chronicler traces the family tree of David from Adam through Abraham, Isaac, Jacob, and Judah. It's not much fun to read, but it establishes the credentials for the line of kings that descended from David.

Chapters 10–29 focus entirely on David and on his reign as king over Israel.

Second Chronicles also divides into two parts:

Chapters 1–9 give us an account of Solomon's reign.

Chapters 10–36 trace the decline of David's kingdom from the division of the nation under Solomon's son Rehoboam to Judah's exile in Babylon.

The story in the books of Chronicles is easier to follow than the story in Kings. There's not so much jumping back and forth from northern kingdom to southern kingdom. Chronicles is also more interesting. We get deeper insight into the character of each king, and we see more practical relevance for our own lives. So skip the long genealogy in 1 Chronicles 1–9 and plunge in. You just might find yourself carried away by the story. You might also find your life changed by the very personal truths you discover.

FOOtPRiNts in the SanD

In 1988 a museum in Israel paid a Jerusalem antiquities dealer $550,000 for a small (one-and-one-half-inch) ivory carving of a pomegranate. The museum directors paid that price because they believe the piece was a decorative tip from a priest's staff in ancient Israel. The Hebrew inscription on the piece read: "Belonging to the temp[le of Yahwe]h, holy to the priests." The letters in brackets represent the best guess of scholars, since the ivory is chipped away. *Yahweh* is the name of the Lord in Hebrew.

2 Chronicles 7:14

"If my people, who are called by my name, will humble themselves and pray and seek my face and turn from their wicked ways, then will I hear from heaven and will forgive their sin and will heal their land."

DOWNLOAD

Walking the Walk

1. As you read Chronicles (particularly 2 Chronicles), watch for occasional outbursts of great spiritual renewal among God's people. These times of renewal or revival drew the people back to obedience and love for God. God used faithful leaders to spark revival at least five times:

   Revival under Asa: 2 Chronicles 15
   Revival under Jehoshaphat: 2 Chronicles 20:1–19
   Revival under Joash: 2 Chronicles 24:1–14
   Revival under Hezekiah: 2 Chronicles 29
   Revival under Josiah: 2 Chronicles 34

2. Each revival required costly and courageous commitment from the leader and from God's people. That is still the requirement for revival! Spiritual renewal in our hearts, in our churches, and in our nation will come only when God's leaders set the course and when God's people turn in humility to the Lord.

Ezra

➤ See how a restored nation emerges out of the ashes and rubble of destruction.

➤ Discover how one person can make a difference in the workplace or in a nation.

The book of Ezra is about survivors—men and women who survived Judah's exile in Babylon. Their parents and grandparents had survived the destruction of the city of Jerusalem and the march in chains to Babylon. The people in Ezra's story survived a different challenge. They survived in the prosperity of Babylon and willingly sacrificed convenience and comfort to return to the city of their fathers—or at least to what was left of the city.

Key Characters

Ezra: a priest who led the second return of exiled Jews to Jerusalem

Joshua: a priest who lived earlier than Ezra; one of the leaders of the first return of exiles to Jerusalem

Zerubbabel: the governor and political leader in Jerusalem after the first group of exiles returned

Cyrus: the Persian ruler who originally gave the exiled Jews permission to return to their homeland

Artaxerxes: a later Persian ruler who gave Ezra permission to take a second group of Jews back to Jerusalem

When the Jews first arrived in exile in Babylon, they had to work hard just to stay alive. But over the decades they settled in. In fact, they prospered in the land of their captivity. When the Babylonian Empire collapsed under the attack of the Persians from the east, the Jews were thriving. The Persian ruler, Cyrus, gave his permission for the people of Israel to return to Jerusalem. They could rebuild God's temple and revive the worship of the Lord. Jerusalem had been deserted for fifty years, and the walls and buildings had been leveled. Not many volunteered to go back, but those who did were pioneers.

The Big Picture

To get the whole story of what happened after Judah's exile in Babylon, we have to cut the book of Ezra in half. In Ezra 1–6 Ezra describes the

Points 2 Remember

☑ Ezra's book tells the story of the first and second returns of Jews from Babylon after they were released from captivity. Ezra led the second group and restored God's law to a place of authority over the people.

☑ Ezra was a man deeply committed to understanding God's truth and passionate about communicating it to others.

first return of Jews from Babylon to Jerusalem—a return that happened before Ezra was even born. It took place in 536 B.C. under the leadership of Joshua the priest and Zerubbabel the governor. About 50,000 people made the journey with them. The main priority of those who returned was the rebuilding of the temple of the Lord. In 516 B.C. the new temple was finally completed. (For more insight on the first return from Babylon, see the books of Haggai and Zechariah in part 6: Prophets.)

Between chapters 6 and 7 of Ezra's book, there is a fifty-eight-year gap. (You might want to write that in the margin of your Bible at that point.) During that gap of time the events of the book of Esther took place. The second section of Ezra describes the return of the second group of Jews from Babylon to Jerusalem. The date of Ezra's return is 458 B.C.

HELP FILE

EZRA

Ezra was a priest in Israel and as such was responsible for systematically teaching God's law and overseeing the worship of the people — responsibilities Ezra took very seriously.

In early Hebrew manuscripts Ezra and Nehemiah were combined as one book. Early Christian writers referred to the books as 1 Ezra (or Esdras) and 2 Ezra.

Sixty-seven verses of Ezra (4:8–6:18; 7:12–26) are written in Aramaic rather than Hebrew. The two languages are related, but Aramaic was the international language of trade and communication in the Persian Empire and soon became the common language of the Jews.

(Flip to the chart on page 122 to see how these books of the Old Testament fit together.)

Artaxerxes (*ar-ta-**zurk**-sees*), the Persian king, appointed Ezra as his personal representative to the Jews in Jerusalem. He also repeated an earlier Persian decree allowing any Jew in Babylon to return to Jerusalem. In a final act of help, the king opened the royal treasury to finance Ezra's trip.

Ezra returned to Jerusalem accompanied by six thousand Jews and with enormous gifts of gold and silver to use in the worship of the Lord. They made the three-and-a-half-month trip without a military escort but reported, "The hand of our God was on us, and he protected us from enemies and bandits along the way" (8:31). Ezra's priority was to restore the law of God as the basis for the Jewish community.

Ezra was followed fourteen years later (in 444 B.C.) by Nehemiah, who brought a third group of Jews to their homeland. Ezra was still in Jerusalem teaching God's Word. Nehemiah sparked the reconstruction of the walls of the city. One hundred fifty years after Jerusalem was

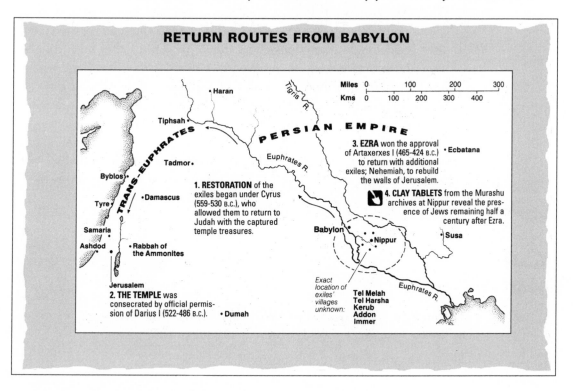

RETURN ROUTES FROM BABYLON

Haran

Tiphsah

TRANS-EUPHRATES

PERSIAN EMPIRE

Tadmor

Byblos

Euphrates R.

Tigris R.

Miles 0   100   200   300
Kms 0   100   200   300   400

3. EZRA won the approval of Artaxerxes I (465-424 B.C.) to return with additional exiles; Nehemiah, to rebuild the walls of Jerusalem.

Ecbatana

Tyre

Damascus

1. RESTORATION of the exiles began under Cyrus (559-530 B.C.), who allowed them to return to Judah with the captured temple treasures.

4. CLAY TABLETS from the Murashu archives at Nippur reveal the presence of Jews remaining half a century after Ezra.

Samaria

Ashdod

Rabbah of the Ammonites

Babylon

Nippur

Susa

Jerusalem

2. THE TEMPLE was consecrated by official permission of Darius I (522-486 B.C.).

Dumah

Exact location of exiles' villages unknown:

Tel Melah
Tel Harsha
Kerub
Addon
Immer

Euphrates R.

LEADERS ON THEIR KNEES

Three prayers by three great leaders of the Jews can be found in Daniel 9, Ezra 9, and Nehemiah 9.

Daniel confessed the sins of his people and asked God to remember his promises to allow them to return from exile (Daniel 9:4–19).

Ezra also prayed a prayer of national confession and asked God to forgive their disobedience to the law (Ezra 9:6–15).

In Nehemiah the Levites (worship leaders along with the priests) led the people in a public prayer remembering God's great works and asking for God's blessing (Nehemiah 9:5–37).

crushed, the temple, the law, and the community were finally restored to their place of prominence and security in the land God had given to their ancestors.

A Powerful Impact

Whenever God wants to do a great work, he raises up a man or woman who is committed to the Word of God. Ezra was that man in the years after Judah's exile. Ezra doesn't get much press today, but he certainly hasn't been overlooked among the Jews. It is possible that Ezra compiled and wrote the books of 1 and 2 Chronicles along with his own book and possibly the book of Nehemiah. The Talmud, a compilation of Jewish laws and traditions, had this to say about Ezra: "When the law had been forgotten in Israel, Ezra came up from Babylon and established it." He was a man devoted to God and to God's truth recorded in Scripture. Here is a one-sentence spiritual biography of the man.

DiGGiNG DeEPeR

✗   Kidner, Derek. "Ezra" in *Ezra and Nehemiah*. Tyndale Old Testament Commentary series. Downers Grove, IL: InterVarsity Press, 1979.

A detailed but easy to follow explanation of Ezra's book.

Ezra had devoted himself to the study and observance of the Law of the LORD, and to teaching its decrees and laws in Israel. (7:10)

That short verse exposes the secret of Ezra's impact on his culture and his world. He had a very precise goal for his life—he "devoted himself to the study" of God's law. He made a firm decision to make God's Word the top priority of his life. What's your life objective? The options are limitless. A Christian can have many good objectives in life. So where does reading and understanding the Bible rank in your list?

Ezra wasn't content, however, just to study the Bible; he was also committed to obedience. He had a passion to read, but it was matched by performance on the street and in the business world. The Bible wasn't given just to fill our minds. It was given to change the way we live.

PEOPLE of the BIBLE

THE PERSIANS

The last world empire to cross the pages of the Old Testament was the Persian Empire. You will also hear it called the Medo-Persian Empire since it started as a partnership between the Medes and the Persians. Eventually the more numerous Persians became dominant.

The Persians lived east of the old Assyrian and Babylonian centers of power. Both Assyria and Babylon had conquered and oppressed the Persians. When Babylon's power began to weaken, the Persians rose up in rebellion. They first became independent of Babylon and then crushed their old overlords. The Persian armies conquered the city of Babylon in 539 B.C. and quickly asserted their authority over the entire region of southwest Asia.

The Persians governed their empire more compassionately than the Babylonians. They allowed people who had been uprooted by pre-vious empires to return to their homelands. All the subject people had to do was maintain loyalty to the Persian rulers and pay their taxes.

The Persians are best known in world history for their attempt to conquer Greece under King Xerxes (the king of the book of Esther). The heroic defense of the Greek peninsula and the defeat of the massive Persian army have become legendary.

The religion of the Persians was Zoroastrianism, a belief in two gods, one good and one bad, who continually battled for dominance.

The Persian Empire eventually became the Parthian Empire (in New Testament times). In the early eighth century A.D. the heart of the Persian Empire was conquered by Arab armies and became part of the early Islamic empires.

For more information about the Persians, check out Edwin Yamauchi, *Persia and the Bible* (Grand Rapids: Baker, 1990).

Beyond learning it and obeying it, Ezra had a desire to teach God's Word to other people. It didn't matter if it was a handful of children in a Sunday school class or a couple's Bible study or a series of messages to hundreds of people. Ezra burned with the desire to communicate God's truth.

No wonder we read three times that God's hand was on Ezra! Ezra invested time in study, he modeled obedience in his life, and he touched people with his teaching. Maybe that's why we don't hear much about him. He's too intimidating! Maybe that's why we have so few men and women who are making a significant impact for God in the corporate offices or in the halls of government or in television production meetings—because there are so few Ezras around.

Walking the Walk

1. Ezra loved lists—but they don't make the most captivating reading. To get the essential story of Ezra, skip the lists in chapter 2 (verses 1–67), chapter 8 (1–14), and chapter 10 (18–44).

2. Think about the opportunities you have to communicate God's truth to others. How faithfully do you instruct your own children? How well do you prepare for a class or Bible study group? How willing are you to share God's perspective with a friend?

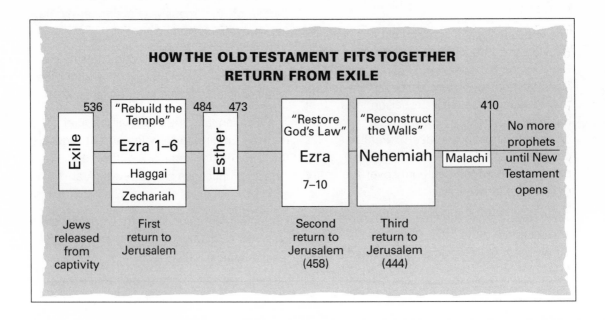

HOW THE OLD TESTAMENT FITS TOGETHER
RETURN FROM EXILE

536	"Rebuild the Temple" Ezra 1–6 Haggai Zechariah	484 473 Esther	"Restore God's Law" Ezra 7–10	"Reconstruct the Walls" Nehemiah	Malachi	410 No more prophets until New Testament opens
Exile						

Jews released from captivity — First return to Jerusalem — Second return to Jerusalem (458) — Third return to Jerusalem (444)

3. Examine your own pattern of Bible study. If it's just hit-and-miss, begin to set aside a regular time for reading and investigation. Schedule it in or it won't get done. Think you are already too busy? Think through your priorities again. Suggestions on how to get started in a regular study can be found in the Getting Started section of this book (pp. 18–23).

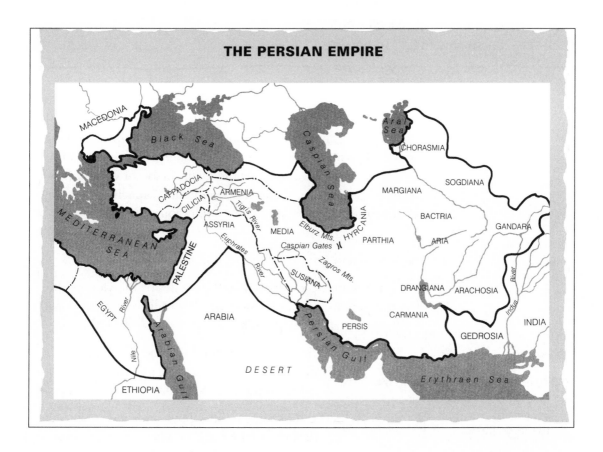

THE PERSIAN EMPIRE

Nehemiah

➤ See how one man takes on an impossible task and succeeds.

➤ Discover what makes a great leader.

➤ Learn how to handle opposition.

Nehemiah was a man on a mission! He was moved by God to do an incredible task in the midst of impossible circumstances—and he did it for God's glory. Nehemiah's book is especially helpful to those of us who are in positions of leadership. If you are a parent or a business executive or a shop foreman or the chairperson of your child's parent-teacher association, if you function in any capacity of leadership or ever aspire to leadership, Nehemiah's journal will help you be a great leader.

Nehemiah's book and Ezra's book share the same background.

The city of Jerusalem was destroyed by the armies of Babylon in 586 B.C. The temple of God was burned, the city walls were torn down, and the population was deported to Babylon.

In 539 B.C. a new empire arose. The Persians defeated the Babylonians, and the Persian king released the Jews to return to their homeland.

The first return of the Jews (in 536 B.C.) is described in Ezra 1–6. The early pioneers rebuilt the temple of God.

The second wave of returnees came in 458 B.C. under Ezra's leadership (Ezra 7–10).

Ezra reestablished the law of God as the basis of Israel's society.

Nehemiah led a third return of Jews from Babylon in 444 B.C. His return sparked the reconstruc-

Key Characters

Nehemiah: a Jewish advisor to the Persian king; he was the motivating leader who inspired the Jews to rebuild the walls of Jerusalem

Artaxerxes: the Persian king who gave Nehemiah permission to rebuild Jerusalem's walls

Sanballat: leader of the opposition to Nehemiah's plan

Ezra: a Jewish priest who had returned to Jerusalem fourteen years before Nehemiah's trip

tion of the walls of the city. Almost 150 years after the walls were torn down, they were rebuilt. What had been a source of humiliation and shame to God's people now became a sign of God's blessing.

Following One Man's Career

Nehemiah wore three different hats in the book he wrote; he had to play three distinct roles to see the work finished.

Nehemiah, the Cupbearer (Nehemiah 1:1 – 2:8)

As the book opens, the walls of Jerusalem are piles of rubble. Nehemiah is eight hundred miles east of Jerusalem in the city of Susa, one of the Persian capitals. His job description is in chapter one, verse 11—"I was cupbearer to the king." The title "cupbearer" doesn't sound very impressive. It makes me think of a dishwasher. In the ancient world, however, it was a powerful position. The cupbearer tasted the king's food and wine to be sure it wasn't poisoned. He was the king's personal aide. All appointments to see the king were made through and approved by the cupbearer. Nehemiah controlled who got to see the king and who didn't. He was the head of the Secret Service, the chief of staff, and the king's most trusted friend. Nehemiah was powerful, influential, wealthy, highly respected—and godly.

When Nehemiah heard that Jerusalem's walls were still broken down and that the people were in distress, his heart ached for the reputation of the Lord. The city of Jerusalem in the Old Testament was a reflection of the majesty and splendor of God, but a city without walls displayed very little glory.

Digging Deeper

✗ Kidner, Derek. "Nehemiah" in *Ezra and Nehemiah*. Tyndale Old Testament Commentary series. Downers Grove, IL: InterVarsity Press, 1979.

All the details of the book are explained—along with plenty of practical insights.

✗ Swindoll, Charles. *Hand Me Another Brick*. Nashville: Thomas Nelson, 1985.

A warm, witty examination of Nehemiah's impact on his world and on ours.

When the opportunity came, Nehemiah asked his boss for an extended leave and headed toward a city he had never seen except in his vision of the work God had given him to do.

Nehemiah, the Builder (Nehemiah 2:9 – 7:73)

Nehemiah exchanged his robes of influence for jeans, a tool belt, and a hard hat. He surveyed the scene, called the people together, and galvanized them to do the work. He was doing a great work for God—and you wouldn't believe the opposition he had to face! It came at three crucial times, at exactly the times you and I face opposition to whatever God compels us to do.

The first wave of opposition came before the project ever got started. The people of Jerusalem said, "Let's start rebuilding"; the opponents said, "It can't be done." The minute fresh enthusiasm for God's work is generated, someone will be ready to throw cold water on it. Nehemiah's response was not to buckle under or to send the project back to some committee for more study. He said, "The God of heaven will give us success."

The second outbreak of opposition came halfway through the project (4:6–8). The enemy comes at midterms in that college class and says, "You'll never make it." Nehemiah had a very practical response to this opposition too. He prayed—and posted a guard (4:9).

The third time of attack was just before the wall was done. When only a few more stones needed to be put in place, the fiercest opposition arose. This time the critics ignored the wall and focused on the leader. Nehemiah responded to each barrage and kept praying. Eleven times in thirteen chapters Nehemiah is pictured praying.

The project came in ahead of schedule and below budget! In fifty-two days the wall was completed. The enemies faded because they realized the work

Nehemiah 8:10

"This day is sacred to our Lord. Do not grieve, for the joy of the Lord is your strength."

Download

Points 2 Remember

☑ Nehemiah was a leader who gave vision and direction to the people of Jerusalem so that the city walls were rebuilt.

☑ Opposition will always come against those who are committed to doing a great work. Don't be surprised by it!

☑ A successful leader learns to rely on a great God.

had been done under the blessing of God (6:15–16).

Nehemiah, the Governor (Nehemiah 8:1 – 13:31)

In the last part of the book, Nehemiah stepped into the background. Ezra brought out the book of the Law of Moses and read it to the people. A great spiritual renewal followed. New promises were made; new commitments to obedience were signed; prayers and shouts of praise rose up to the God of Israel. Nehemiah was the civil leader, but he joined with Ezra and the religious leaders to promote justice and obedience to God. His memoirs close as we would expect—with prayer: "Remember me with favor, O my God" (13:31).

They Said It Couldn't Be Done

What impresses me the most about Nehemiah's story is that the people who were in trouble when the story opened are the same ones who finished the wall. There wasn't an infusion of new people who did the work. No construction company accompanied Nehemiah from Susa. The demoralized, discouraged people Nehemiah found when he rode into the city were motivated to do the job.

What made the difference was leadership. A leader arose with vision and courage, and the leader brought the people to a new level of accomplishment. That is still how God works. There has never been a group, a family, a team, a business, or a congregation that has done anything of significance in any arena that did not have at its center a person or a small cluster of people who embodied a vision and who infused the vision in others. A good leader raises any group from mediocrity to greatness.

The same journey the Jews made can be made today by those who are facing a failing marriage. Your marriage can go from despair to restoration with the help of your God. A friendship that is deteriorating, a church in decline, a business stuck in neutral can be turned around. We have a God who can infuse the least likely person with great vision *if* that man or woman is willing to trust him. Our world desperately needs people courageous enough to step up to that challenge.

Walking the Walk

1. As you read Nehemiah's book, keep your journal open. Write down the principles you see that will help you be a better leader and respond more effectively to problems and opposition. Begin to integrate the principles into your workplace or leadership responsibilities. You might find your leadership transformed!

2. Evaluate the place of prayer in your professional/work life. Nehemiah's prayers were never a distraction from his job; they were quick, private, pointed but essential. Once he asked God for wisdom, he believed that God had given it, and he acted on it.

3. Ask God to lead you to someone who can be a spiritual mentor to you, someone you can turn to for wise advice and mature judgment. Cultivate that relationship—and then look for someone you can mentor and help.

Esther

➤ See how a young Jewish woman becomes queen of Persia.

➤ Watch as one evil political leader tries to exterminate an entire nation.

➤ Find out how God intervenes to rescue the Jews.

The book of Esther tells the story of a Jewish woman who coura-geously saved her people from destruction. The book bothers some people, however, because it doesn't seem very religious. There's no mention of the Law of Moses or sacrifices or the temple. In the middle of a crisis the Jewish people fast (stop eating food) and weep, but nothing is said about prayer to God. What is strangest of all, God's name never appears in the book. So how can a book like that be in the Bible?

The story of Esther is a captivating illustration of one of God's greatest works. God sometimes intervenes in human history through a powerful miracle or a direct spoken command. Usually, however, God guides human history indirectly. God works to bring about what he desires through people, through human decisions, through what appear to be normal situations. Theologians call it God's *providence*. In the shadows of human history and in the backdrop of our lives stands a powerful God who is work-ing out all things according to his desire and plan. No event, no circumstance, no incident no matter how small is outside the knowledge and control of God. That is what the book of Esther shows us. God sees to it that his desires and goals are fulfilled despite humanity's best attempts at thwarting his program.

Key Characters

Esther: a Jewish woman who becomes queen beside King Xerxes

Xerxes (also called **Ahasuerus**): king of the Persian Empire from 485–465 B.C.

Haman: Persian official who tries to wipe out the Jewish people

Mordecai: Esther's relative and an official in the Persian government

What's a Nice Jewish Girl Like You Doing in a Palace Like This?

The story of Esther does not begin with Esther. It begins with a Persian king. His name in Hebrew was Ahasuerus (*a-has-yoo-err-us*), but he is known in most history books by his Greek name, Xerxes (*zurk-sees*). Xerxes was the fourth king of the vast Persian Empire and reigned from 485–465 B.C. One day, after seven days of feasting and drinking, Xerxes ordered his queen, Vashti, to come to the banquet hall and display her beauty to the men gathered there. When Vashti refused, the king exploded! Vashti was sent into exile.

In time, however, the king began to miss Vashti. He had a harem of women for his sexual pleasure, but now began to think about bringing Vashti back. In desperation, the king's officials who had engineered Vashti's exile came up with a great plan. They would search the empire for the most beautiful young women. The one who most pleased the king would become the new queen. We aren't sure how many young women were brought to the palace, but one of them was named Esther—and she knocked the king's socks off!

Two other characters have a prominent place in Esther's story. The first is Mordecai, Esther's relative, who had raised Esther as his own child. The second is Haman, a Persian bureaucrat in Xerxes' government. He had such a powerful position that people bowed to him as he walked by. Everyone bowed except one Jew—Mordecai. Haman was so con-

HELP FILE

ESTHER

The events of the book of Esther took place around 473 B.C. A group of Jews had moved back to Jerusalem from exile in Babylon more than fifty years earlier, but most of the Jews still lived in Babylon or in other cities in Persia.

The author of the book is unknown, but obviously it was someone familiar with Persian customs and government figures. It could have been Mordecai or someone who had access to Mordecai directly and to Mordecai's journal (9:20).

The longest verse in the Bible is found in Esther 8:9.

Points 2 Remember

☑ The book of Esther is the story of one woman's courageous action that resulted in the deliverance of her people from annihilation.

☑ Even though God's name is not mentioned in the book, God is not absent. He is working behind the scenes to preserve his people and to keep his promises.

sumed with rage at Mordecai's refusal to bow to him that he plotted to have the entire Jewish population of the empire killed. He even got Xerxes to sign an irrevocable law ordering that the Jews be killed. When Mordecai heard about the plot, he went to Esther and urged her to make an appeal to Xerxes to protect the Jews. At first Esther was hesitant. She had kept her Jewishness a secret. But Mordecai reminded her that if the Jewish people were slaughtered, she would die too.

In a plot that challenges the most intriguing action thriller, Esther exposed Haman's evil plan, and the Jews survived.

So What's the Point?

If Haman's plan to exterminate the Jews had succeeded, not only would Esther and Mordecai have died, but the people descended from Abraham, Isaac, and Jacob would have disappeared. Virtually every Jew in the world at that time lived within the boundaries of the Persian Empire. God had promised, however, that the people of

HISSING IN THE SYNAGOGUE

The Jews celebrated their deliverance from Haman's evil plot by inaugurating the Feast of Purim. Purim became part of the cycle of Jewish festivals still celebrated today. Every year the book of Esther is read to remind Jewish people of their unique history of survival down through the centuries. They also make the reading fun! The reader in the syn-agogue can use different voices for the characters or even put on different hats to picture them. Every time Haman's name is pronounced, the people boo or hiss or stamp their feet. Children are given noise-makers to rattle or horns to blow. People laugh, babies wail, but Haman's name is "blotted out"!

Esther 4:14

"Who knows but that you have come to royal position for such a time as this?"

Israel would survive even the worst attacks. God had also promised that a Deliverer, a Messiah, would come from Israel who would bring great blessing on the world. If Haman had succeeded, we would not celebrate Christmas, because Jesus never would have been born. His human ancestors would have been wiped out! If Haman had succeeded, God would have failed to keep his promises. So God worked through Esther's courage, through normal circumstances, through the unfolding events in Xerxes' kingdom to bring about deliverance for the Jewish people.

What was true of Israel then is still true today. People and nations may forget God's promises, but God does not forget. So the book of Esther is not just about a Jewish girl who makes it to the top and valiantly tries to save herself and her people. It is also about a God who is faithful to his promises and who exercises dominion over his world in order to keep his word.

DiggiNG DeEpeR

✗ Baldwin, Joyce. *Esther: An Introduction and Commentary.* Tyndale Old Testament Commentary series. Downers Grove, IL: InterVarsity Press, 1984.

A serious and helpful discussion of each passage in Esther.

✗ Swindoll, Charles. *Esther.* Dallas: Word, 1997.

An extended retelling of Esther's story with practical encouragement for today.

Walking the Walk

1. The story of Esther (especially chapters 5–7) can easily be adapted for a group reading or a dramatic presentation. Spring-board from the story and talk about how God has been faithful to keep his promises to you.

2. Think about how God has worked in your life and in your family's experience to guide you or protect you. Usually we can look back at a difficult time and see how God directed one event after another to bring about what he desired. You may want to write out some of the experiences of God's providence and care in a journal. Reread what you have written when you go through another challenging time or when God seems far away.

3. Just as God brought Esther to her place in the Persian Empire "for such a time as this" (4:14), you have been given a sphere of influence in which to live fully for the Lord. In what specific ways can you courageously bring an influence for good into your particular world?

Part 3

DRAMA

Some issues are hard to talk about. The minute a philosopher or historian tries to unravel a human tragedy like the Holocaust, for example, we realize how difficult it is to explain an event that defies explanation. Reading *The Diary of Anne Frank*, however, puts a human face on the tragedy of the Holocaust. Suddenly we can talk about the unexplainable in terms of one life.

The book of Job allows us to talk about human suffering in terms of one life. We listen to an ancient conversation about the unexplainable problem of why we must experience pain and loss. We enter this biblical "chat room" as visitors, not as direct participants, but the questions that are raised are the same ones we ask in the darkness of despair. Why is this happening? Why now? Why me?

Job puts a human face on suffering and pain. He asks God the questions we are usually too afraid to ask. His friends say things out loud that we only think about when we see other people struggling.

The drama of Job helps us think about the unthinkable and forces us to examine how much we really trust God. We panic when the stock market drops a few hundred points. What would we do if we, like Job, literally lost everything?

Job

— Heads Up —

➤ Ponder the question, "Why do bad things happen to good people?"
➤ Witness a cosmic contest between God and Satan.
➤ Listen to Job's friends as they give him plenty of (bad) advice.

I got a phone call not long ago that a friend of mine had been rushed to the hospital. I arrived at the emergency room a few minutes later only to discover that my friend had already died. He was a young man. His wife and daughters were suddenly left behind; his parents and brother were plunged into grief.

Key Characters

Job (rhymes with *robe*): a good man who suffered incredible loss and personal pain

Satan: originally created as an angel of great power, Satan was filled with pride and rebelled against God; in this book Satan tries to get Job to abandon his faith

Eliphaz: the oldest and (supposedly) the wisest of Job's friends

Bildad: another FOJ (friend of Job)

Zophar: the third friend—and the harshest

Elihu: a young man who listened to the debate between Job and his friends and then came up with some explanations of his own (Job 32–37)

Where is God when we need him most? One of the oldest books in the Bible helps us sort out the problem of human suffering. We don't get all the answers we would like, but we begin to see some glimpses of light in the darkness of our pain. The story of Job is not a book of theory. Job talks about suffering from the perspective of a sufferer. He had been there.

What makes this book unique is that we get to look behind the scenes of Job's suffering and see how God fits into our experience of pain and sorrow. We see how Satan fits in too! We don't read the book of Job simply to cry along with him. We read it to help us understand our own suffering and to learn how to comfort others who are in pain.

Biblical Shakespeare

The book of Job is really a magnificent drama. Scenes open and close; actors enter and leave; special effects usher us into heaven or into the middle of a raging storm. Unlike fast-paced modern drama, the actors' lines in Job sometimes turn into long speeches, but you can't read this book without being moved. The horror of Job's suffering, the passion of each of the speakers, and the sense of frustration, anger, and pain that boil to the surface all draw us into the story. We start arguing with Job or his friends or even with God.

Job asked God the hard questions that we are afraid to ask. He asked his questions persistently and powerfully—and then refused to take God's silence for an answer. As one interpreter puts it, "He refused to let God off the hook."

HELP FILE

WAS JOB FOR REAL?

Some people who have studied this biblical story deny that Job ever lived. To them the story is just that—a story, a work of fiction. They admit that it is a great dramatic poem and even a literary masterpiece but say that it is no more historically true than Homer's *Iliad*.

Several factors point in the opposite direction, however. The author of Job certainly wrote this narrative as a true account. The prophet Ezekiel, living hundreds of years after the events of the book took place, listed Job along with Noah and Daniel as well-known models of right living (Ezekiel 14:14, 20). In the New Testament, James pointed to Job as a real person who exhibited incredible patience under pressure (James 5:11). Even God characterized Job as a man unlike any other person on earth in his desire to live correctly (Job 1:8).

No one knows for certain who wrote the book of Job. One ancient tradition says that Moses wrote the book. Other suggestions have been Solomon or even Ezra. Most likely Job himself recorded the original account (except for the verses at the end about his own death), which then passed down through his family until it came into the possession of the people of Israel. Moses, or perhaps Solomon, then translated the book into Hebrew, and it was recognized as truth revealed by God for the instruction and encouragement of his people.

The Law of Moses is never mentioned in the book, nor are the people of Israel. The setting of the book seems to be the time of Abraham (around 2100 B.C.). Job was apparently a non-Israelite who had come to believe in the true God.

ANGELS? WHAT NEXT — MERMAIDS?

The Bible has a lot to say about angels. A Bible concordance will help you find more than two hundred references to angels. Jesus and every New Testament writer referred to angels as real beings who are actively involved in the affairs of our world.

Angels are divided into two distinct groups. Holy angels serve God and God's people as guardians and messengers. Evil angels or demons serve Satan. Originally Satan was a brilliant, powerful angel who served God, but he chose a path of rebellion and pride rather than obedience to the Lord. Satan decided to attempt to set up his own kingdom in opposition to God's kingdom.

As this incident in Job makes clear, however, Satan is not equal with God. Far from it! Satan operates under God's control. For a while Satan is allowed to have power, but God's judgment on him is certain.

Act 1: It Only Gets Worse (Job 1–2)

As the curtain opens, Job enters the scene as a man of integrity and fabulous wealth. His ten children are all grown, but a close family bond still remains. From everything we are told, Job had done nothing to deserve the suffering that was about to break over him. When tragedy strikes, we usually ask, "What did I do to deserve this? There must be some failure in my life that brought this loss or pain or sickness."

Sometimes pain does come as a consequence of our own wrong choices. But suffering may come simply because we live in a world marked by evil or because God is testing us to bring us to stronger faith in him—or because God wants to teach Satan a lesson!

As the lights dim on Job's earthly scene, we are ushered into heaven. We learn something from these opening scenes in Job that we don't find anywhere else in the Bible. Satan is required to appear before God, and God expects (and gets) a regular report on his activities.

> One day the angels came to present themselves before the LORD, and Satan also came with them. (Job 1:6)

Notice that God brought up Job's name, not Satan. God challenged Satan by asking, "Have you considered my servant Job?" Satan shot back that, of course, he had looked Job over, but God had put a wall of protection around Job. Everything Job touched turned to gold. Who

P⊙ints 2 Remember

☑ The book of Job is a drama that explores human suffering through the experience of one person.

☑ The grueling discussion between Job and his friends ultimately ends in frustration. Only insight from God can provide any meaningful understanding of why we experience pain and loss. But God doesn't always explain himself to us. He asks us to trust him when it seems like we have no answers.

☑ We come away from the book of Job with a deeper knowledge of and trust in God and with fewer quick, easy answers to the problem of pain.

wouldn't serve God for those kind of capital gains!

God gave Satan permission to take everything Job had, but Satan could not touch Job's body. Almost before the lights came up again on the earthly scene, tragedy struck. In four swift, cruel blows, Satan took it all away—wealth, servants, retirement fund, and worst of all, Job's ten children. Job's response was not to sink into despair. He wept and tore his clothes in agony, but instead of complaining, instead of blaming God, he said:

"Naked I came from my mother's womb,
    and naked I will depart.
The LORD gave and the LORD has taken away;
    may the name of the LORD be praised."

In all this, Job did not sin by charging God with wrongdoing. (Job 1:21–22)

Job recognized that God was the one ultimately responsible for what happened to him. He did not say, "The Lord gave and *Satan* has taken away." He said, "The Lord gave (as it was his right to do) and now the Lord has taken away (also his right). In it all I will speak well of the Lord's character." Job stood beside ten fresh graves and did not blame God.

The scene shifts to heaven again where God confronted Satan with Job's faith. Satan had been wrong. Job served God out of love for God, not just for the "perks." But Satan was ready for the challenge. His claim was simple: Job still had his health. Touch his body, and he would abandon his faith in the Lord.

On earth disaster struck again. Job was afflicted with a painful, disfiguring disease. His own wife counseled him to "curse God and die" (Job 2:9). Then some of Job's friends showed up. News of Job's calamity spread fast over the ancient Internet! When the friends saw Job, they couldn't believe their eyes. They were so sure he was at death's door that they sat down to wait for the funeral. But, as one hour flowed into another and as one day became seven days, their compassion for Job faded and their anger grew.

Act 2: With Friends Like These (Job 3–37)

The silence was finally broken when Job cried out in despair. He wondered why he had ever been born. Given a choice, Job would have chosen death over the incredible pain he was experiencing. When Job's cry ended, the three friends, Eliphaz, Bildad, and Zophar, began their analysis of the situation. A cycle of dialogue takes up most of the book of Job. Eloquent Eliphaz gave his opinion on Job's condition first, and Job answered by speaking not only to Eliphaz but also to God. Brutal Bildad then spoke with his pat answers and pious precepts, and again Job

DiGGinG DeEpeR

✗ Lawson, Steven J. *When All Hell Breaks Loose: Surprising Insights from the Life of Job.* Colorado Springs, CO: NavPress, 1993.

Filled with helpful applications of Job's suffering to the pain we experience. Lawson adds some humor too!

✗ Peterson, Eugene. *Job: Led by Suffering to the Heart of God.* Colorado Springs, CO: NavPress, 1996.

A poet's paraphrase of the poetry of Job; part of Peterson's whole Bible work, *The Message.* Be sure to read his perceptive introduction to the book.

✗ Zuck, Roy. *Job.* Everyman's Bible Commentary. Chicago: Moody Press, 1978.

A concise commentary that will guide you through the intricacies of the arguments of the book of Job.

Job 19:25 – 27

"I know that my Redeemer lives,
    and that in the end he will stand upon the earth.
And after my skin has been destroyed,
    yet in my flesh I will see God;
I myself will see him
    with my own eyes — I, and not another.
How my heart yearns within me!"

responded. Zealous Zophar was the bluntest of the friends, and he got the bluntest response from Job—and the cycle started all over again.

The central issue of the debate was: What had Job done to deserve such suffering? Job maintained that, while he was a sinner like everyone else, he had done nothing so evil as to deserve such harsh treatment from God. The friends believed that Job was a secret sinner, a man who had done unbelievable evil. That was the only way they could explain his unbelievable pain. Both sides called on God to speak. The three friends wanted God to expose Job's sins while Job wanted God to affirm his innocence. The only problem was that God wasn't talking!

The silence of God is an issue every suffering Christian has struggled with. When we are in pain or sick or grieving over a loss, we want God to tell us *why* this has happened—or at least assure us that he is still with us.

The dialogue between Job and his friends ended in frustrated silence. Everything had been said and nothing had been resolved. If we learn anything from this long debate, we learn that we need more than our own human perspective on suffering. Attempts to explain suffering that leave God out bring us only to frustration and despair.

Act 3: God Breaks His Silence (Job 38 – 41)

When Job and his friends fell silent, God finally spoke. But he didn't say what either side wanted to hear! Instead of explaining Job's suffering, God brought Job and his friends (and us) to a new awareness of his majesty and awesome power. In spite of what Job felt or thought, God was in control of Job's situation. Job was not alone. God was uncovering levels of pride in Job that could only be exposed and removed by the experiences he went through. The same God who controlled the universe and who cared for the natural world was intimately involved with Job's pain. God had a goal in mind all along. What he asked Job to do was trust him.

Epilogue: It Finally Gets Better (Job 42)

In the end, Job's fortunes and family were restored to him. God didn't answer all of Job's questions. He won't answer all of ours either. But Job came out of the fire of testing with a heart humble enough to trust God even in the darkest night of despair.

We will probably never know the ultimate answers to suffering in this life: why our friends get cancer and die, why our children die, why God's people suffer. No answer is given—except that God has the right to do what he does and that he always does what is right. Sometimes that is all we have to cling to.

Walking the Walk

1. Read the book of Job in a contemporary translation or para-phrase. Enlist some friends to read the various "parts" in the drama. Reading the words out loud or hearing them spoken adds to your appreciation of their passionate meaning.

2. Write down the facts about your own faith in God and what you believe about his love and care for you. In a time of suffering or tragedy, review those facts and let the Holy Spirit comfort you as you trust in God's promises.

3. Think about Job's friends the next time you go to a hospital or funeral home. We usually bring the most comfort when we speak the fewest words. An arm around the shoulder, a kiss, gentle tears of sorrow, or a humble prayer can do more to heal a broken heart than volumes of words.

4. Explore the possibility of volunteering for hospice care or in a nursing home. Reading to the blind or sitting with someone who is dying are visible expressions of the love of Christ for those who are hurting.

TOOL TiMe

Concordances

I wish I could remember the episode of the television sitcom *Seinfeld* when Cosmo Kramer bragged about the "Mackinaw peaches." If I had a *Seinfeld* concordance, I could find out! I would look up "Mackinaw" or "peaches" in the alphabetical listing of key words and it would tell me the episode number and how many minutes into the program the reference first occurred. A CD-ROM concordance might even provide a short video clip.

A Bible concordance works the same way. It lists all (or almost all) of the words of the Bible in alphabetical order along with the references to where each occurrence of the word can be found. Computer concordance programs will "look up" the verses for you and let you read the full reference. For example, here are all the places in the Bible where the word *leviathan* can be found (leviathan is a name for a large sea creature): Job 3:8; 41:1; Psalms 74:14; 104:26; Isaiah 27:1 (twice).

So What Good Is It?

You can use a concordance to help you find the reference for a verse if you can only remember a few key words and can't remember where the verse is found in the Bible. By looking up a key word, you can locate the reference.

A concordance also helps you study a theme or particular word throughout the Bible. If you look up and read all the references to "angel" or "angels," for example, you will gain a broad picture of what the Bible teaches about angels. Or you may want to know where else in

Scripture the name Satan appears. A concordance will list all the occurrences of the name.

Some study Bibles include a partial concordance as a study help. You can purchase a fairly complete concordance in a small size book or an exhaustive (every word) concordance in a large volume. Bible study computer programs also include a concordance. Be sure the concordance you buy corresponds with the version or translation of the Bible you regularly use.

Recommended Resources:

The NIV Complete Concordance. Edited by Edward Goodrick and John R. Kohlenberger III. Grand Rapids: Zondervan, 1981.

The NIV Study Bible Basic Library CD-ROM contains, along with other features, the *NIV Complete Concordance* and the *KJV Cruden's Concordance.* Grand Rapids: Zondervan.

JAAZANIAH
2Ki 25: 23 *J* the son of the Maacathite,
Jer 35: 3 So I went to get *J* son of Jeremiah,
     40: 8 and *J* the son of the Maacathite,
Eze 8: 11 and *J* the son of Shaphan was standing
     11: 1 I saw among them *J* son of Azzur

JAAZANIAH
1Ch 24: 26 The son of *J*: Beno
     24: 27 The sons of Merari: from *J*: Beno,

JAAZIEL
1Ch 15: 18 Zechariah, *J*, Shemiramoth, Jehiel,

JABAL
Ge 4: 20 birth to *J*; he was the father

JABBOK
Ge 32: 22 and crossed the ford of the *J.*
Nu 21: 24 land from the Arnon to the *J,*
Dt 2: 37 the land along the course of the *J*
    3: 16 and out to the *J* River,
Jos 12: 2 of the gorge—to the *J* River
Jg 11: 13 land from the Arnon to the *J,*
    11: 22 all of it from the Arnon to the *J*

JACKALS (JACKAL)
Job 30: 29 I have become a brother of *j,*
Ps 44: 19 us and made us a haunt for *j*
    63: 10 and become food for *j.*
Isa 13: 21 *j* will fill her houses;
    13: 22 *j* in her luxurious palaces.
    34:13 She will become a haunt for *j,*
    35: 7 In the haunts where *j* once lay,
    43: 20 the *j* and the owls,
Jer 9: 11 a haunt of *j;*
    10: 22 a haunt of *j.*
    14: 6   and pant like *j*
    49: 33 "Hazor will become a haunt of *j,*
    51: 37 a haunt of *j,*
La 4: 3 Even *j* offer their beasts
    5: 18 with *j* prowling over it.
Eze 13: 4 O Israel, are like *j* among ruins.
Mal 1: 3 left his inheritance to the desert *j.*"

JACOB (JACOB'S)
Ge 25: 26 so he was named *J.*
    25: 27 while *J* was a quiet man,
    25: 28 loved Esau, but Rebekah loved *J.*
    25: 29 when *J* was cooking some stew,

Part 4

WORSHIP

The word *worship* makes most of us think of long church services and boring sermons. But worship focuses first on the person who is worshiped. We go to church under the impression that we are the audience and the performers are up on the stage. In reality God is the audience, and he doesn't just watch what goes on up front. He looks at each person's heart. What pleases him is genuine, sincere worship—at church or anywhere else we happen to be!

Worship means "to announce someone's worth." When we worship, we speak about God's worth. We praise his character and his work, his majesty, his power, his grace, his love. Everything about God is worthy of our adoration. That's where the psalms come in! These poems help us put into words the feelings we have for God. When we gather together for worship, we can sing or speak or shout praise to God. (Yes, even shouting is encouraged in the psalms!) In our own personal worship, we can express joy or thankfulness or sorrow or even disappointment to God. In the times when we can't find the strength to pray or don't know how to pray, the psalms give us words to express our pain or our happiness.

The focus of worship is God—but worship also requires a worshiper. As we use the psalms to express our joy or despair or fear, we learn new truths about God and his care for us. The psalms touch us deeply and move us closer to God.

Psalms

── Heads Up ──

➤ Listen to powerful words from great poets.
➤ Explore the full range of human emotion.
➤ Find comfort and encouragement for life's struggles.

When you open the book of Psalms, you are opening the songbook and prayer book of the Old Testament. You are also opening one of the most read and most loved books of the Bible. The psalms have dried more tears, comforted more hearts, covered more hurts, and soothed more sorrows than any other part of the Bible. They have also been turned to more, quoted more, and memorized more than any other part.

The book is a collection of 150 poems. Each chapter (each psalm) stands on its own and is not necessarily connected with the psalm before or after it. The psalms are not dry sermons or lectures on philosophy. They are passionate expressions of love and devotion to God. They are songs of the human heart lifted up to God. Every human emotion—from great joy to bitter despair—is expressed somewhere in these chapters.

Digging Deeper

✗ Kidner, Derek. *Psalms 1–72* and *Psalms 73–150.* Tyndale Old Testament Commentary series. Downers Grove, IL: InterVarsity Press, 1973, 1975.

Brief but very helpful comments on each psalm.

✗ Longman, Tremper. *How to Read the Psalms.* Downers Grove, IL: InterVarsity Press, 1988.

A warm, insightful introduction to the book of Psalms.

In the Hebrew Bible the book of Psalms is called *Tehillim,* meaning "praises." Not every psalm is a praise psalm, but the main theme of the book is praise to God. In the Greek language of the New Testament, the book was called *Psalms,* meaning "a poem sung to musical accompaniment." The psalms originally were sung—biblical karaoke! God enjoys it when his praises are not only spoken in words, but also sung in songs.

Some of the psalms were sung by the choir in the temple. Some were very personal songs sung by one person to God. Occasionally a notation was added to a psalm listing the instruments that best accompanied that particular song. Christians in the time of the New Testament and in many churches today sing the psalms as part of their worship.

A Map for the Journey

Most books of the Bible have only one author. The book of Psalms was written by many authors over a long period of time in a wide variety of

HELP FILE

THE 'SALMS

Each of the psalms (pronounced *salms;* the *p* is silent) stands alone. As a collection or book, they are referred to as plural, such as, "In *Psalms* we find every human emotion expressed." When referring to a single psalm, we use the singular form: "I was reading *Psalm* 34," not "I was reading *Psalms* 34." You will also hear the entire book referred to as the "Psalter."

According to the notations attached to the psalms, seventy-three were written by David. Two others are credited to him in the writings of the New Testament.

Peter in Acts 4:25–26 says that David wrote Psalm 2; Hebrews 4:7 says that David wrote Psalm 95.

Only Isaiah is quoted more often than the book of Psalms in the New Testament.

The Bible's longest chapter (Psalm 119) and shortest chapter (Psalm 117) are found in this book.

The middle verse of the Bible is Psalm 118:8:

It is better to take refuge in the LORD than to trust in man.

JESUS IN THE PSALMS

Many of the psalms made predictions about God's promised Messiah, Jesus. Here are some of the specific predictions and the fulfillment of each in the New Testament.

Jesus would be forsaken by God in the time of his greatest need (Psalm 22:1; Matthew 27:46).

He would be scorned and mocked (Psalm 22:7–8; Luke 23:35).

His hands and feet would be pierced (Psalm 22:16; John 20:25, 27).

Others would gamble for his clothes (Psalm 22:18; Matthew 27:35).

None of Jesus' bones would be broken (Psalm 34:20; John 19:32–33, 36).

He would be betrayed by a friend (Psalm 41:9; Luke 22:47).

He would be rejected by Israel's leaders (Psalm 118:22; Matthew 21:42–44).

Zeal for God's house would consume him (Psalm 69:9; John 2:17).

His body would not decay in a tomb (Psalm 16:10; Acts 2:27).

His reign as king will never end (Psalm 45:6–7; Hebrews 1:8).

Jesus, the Messiah, was God the Son (Psalm 110:1; Matthew 22:41–46).

He would conquer all enemies (Psalm 110:1; Acts 2:34–35).

situations. Each psalm was written individually; later they were collected into one book. The book of Psalms is sometimes called "The Psalms of David" but only half of the psalms were written by Israel's great King David. Twelve of the psalms were written by Asaph, a priest who directed the music ministry in the temple. Ten of the psalms were written by the sons of Korah, a group of singers and composers. Other authors were Solomon, Moses, and two disciples of Ezra named Heman and Ethan. No author is given for fifty of the psalms.

The dates of the psalms span a thousand years—from Moses at the time of Israel's escape from Egypt to members of the Jewish community returning with Ezra the priest from exile in Babylon. The psalms were collected in five stages during Israel's history, so we have five divisions or volumes in one long biblical book.

A brief explanation of the author and the circumstances that prompted the writing of a psalm often appears above the text of the psalm itself. Those lines are called the "superscription" (what is written above). The superscription of Psalm 50, for example, just gives us the author's name:

Psalm 50

A psalm of Asaph.

Then the poem itself begins with verse 1: "The Mighty One, God, the LORD...."

The superscription of Psalm 51 tells us much more:

Psalm 51

For the director of music. A psalm of David.

When the prophet Nathan came to him after David

had committed adultery with Bathsheba.

We know from those lines that David wrote the psalm. We also know when and why he wrote it! David's sin with Bathsheba had just been exposed by God's prophet Nathan. (You can read the story in 2 Samuel 11–12.) David wrote this psalm as a cry of confession before God.

Points 2 Remember

☑ The book of Psalms is a collection of 150 poems written by various authors throughout Israel's history. Half of the psalms were written by King David.

☑ Every human emotion finds expression in the psalms. They are passionate songs and prayers lifted up to God.

☑ Whatever emotional condition we find ourselves in, the psalms will touch our lives.

Not every psalm has a superscription, but don't ignore the ones we have. They give us insight into the setting and spirit of the psalm. Psalm 51 becomes a powerful expression of our own hearts when we have failed and need God's forgiveness.

Haunted by Emily Dickinson

The most dreaded assignments in high school English always seemed to center around poetry. Most of us still get nervous near a poem. But don't be put off by the poetry of the psalms! Most of it is easy to grasp, and all of it will resound in your own experience.

Biblical poetry does not rhyme—not in Hebrew in which it was written nor in

English. What marks this poetry is its use of two or three lines of text to fully express one idea. The technical term is *parallelism*, that is, two lines run parallel to one idea. The writers did that to give the idea more time to sink in. If we don't get it the first time, maybe a slightly different perspective the second time will make it stay with us.

Sometimes the lines express the *same* idea.

> The heavens declare the glory of God;
> the skies proclaim the work of his hands. (Psalm 19:1)

Two lines can express *opposite* views of the same idea too.

> For the LORD watches over the way of the righteous,
> but the way of the wicked will perish. (Psalm 1:6)

DOWNLOAD

Psalm 23

The LORD is my shepherd, I shall not be in want.
    He makes me lie down in green pastures,
he leads me beside quiet waters,
    he restores my soul.
He guides me in paths of righteousness
    for his name's sake.
Even though I walk
    through the valley of the shadow of death,
I will fear no evil,
    for you are with me;
your rod and your staff
    they comfort me.

You prepare a table before me
    in the presence of my enemies.
You anoint my head with oil;
    my cup overflows.
Surely goodness and love will follow me
    all the days of my life,
and I will dwell in the house of the LORD
    forever.

Two lines can even *expand* one idea.

> How can a young man keep his way pure?
> By living according to your [God's] word. (Psalm 119:9)

The imagery of the psalms is drawn from ancient Palestine, of course, not the modern world. But the images are so powerful and so vivid that people from every culture and climate over the last three thousand years have been comforted and challenged by these wonderful poems.

Stylin' Through the Psalms

Since the psalms were written with such passion and emotion, try to revive the emotional style as you read each psalm. You will gain some help with that from the superscription and the circumstances that prompted the psalm. More help will come from the words and style of the psalm itself.

There are several styles or kinds of psalms.

Praise psalms focus on exalting the Lord's character or the Lord's work. It is common in praise psalms to read the word, "Hallelujah" (which is Hebrew for "praise the Lord").
Examples: Psalms 48, 92, 96, 103, 113

Lament psalms are sad songs of despair or sorrow. Usually the psalmist (that's what the writer of the psalm is called) is asking God to deliver or rescue him. He may even be frustrated with God. As you read the lament psalms, try to enter into the emotion of the writer. Groan with him.
Examples: Psalms 17, 32, 42, 55, 83, 102, 120

Wisdom psalms talk about how God wants us to live our lives. These psalms point out the wisdom of following God's truth and the foolishness of relying on a purely human perspective.
Examples: Psalms 1, 9, 19, 50, 119, 128

Kingship psalms focus on the human king, but they also look beyond him to the true King of Israel, the Lord God.
Examples: Psalms 20, 21, 47, 98

Temple psalms were songs used in the formal worship of Israel. Psalms 120 through 134 were called "songs of ascents." They were sung as God's people gathered for the great sacred festivals of the Old Testament and as they "ascended" from the lower elevations to the city of Jerusalem.

What an amazing variety of songs Israel sang to God!

Songs of the Heart

The psalms touch our lives wherever we are emotionally—and they work instantly to bring relief. When we are discouraged, the psalms lift us up. When we are lonely or confused, these songs bring assurance to our spirits. When we are afraid, they put their arms around us and encourage us. When we are bursting with joy, they give expression to our happiness.

The psalms also provide profound insight into our own lives. Our masks are pulled away, our pious words fall flat, our true feelings are open before God. That honesty and transparency in God's presence are what draw us back to these chapters over and over. When we are at our most vulnerable, God begins to work to calm us and change us.

The psalms deserve serious, repeated, reflective reading. Once you've tasted their goodness, you will never get enough.

Walking the Walk

1. Select one style of psalm from the previous page and read the examples that are listed. What words and themes are repeated? Try to express the emotion and passion of one of the psalms as you read it out loud. (Probably not in a crowded elevator!)

2. Write a psalm of your own that expresses the emotional condition of your own life right now. As you reflect on God's involvement (or noninvolvement) in your situation, what feelings and words come to mind? Pray or sing the psalm back to God—and then listen patiently for God's response.

3. If you have a favorite psalm, memorize a section of it. (If you've never memorized Psalm 23, that's a good place to start.) When you are sitting in traffic or waiting at the doctor's office, meditate on the psalm and let it draw your attention to the Lord.

WHERE TO TURN IN THE PSALMS

Attack—25:16–21; 30:1–5; 37; 57; 109:21–31; 126; 143

Comfort—23; 73:25–28; 91; 102:1–12, 19–20; 130

Disappointment—55; 62:1–8

Discouragement/Depression—16; 34; 42; 43:5; 55:22–23; 103:1–6

Divorce—25

Doubt—8; 146

Fear—23; 27; 46; 91

Feeling far from God—42:5–11; 139:1–18, 23–24

Finances—37:16, 25–29; 49:10–13, 20

Growing old—37:23–29

Guidance from God—15; 23; 73:23–26

Guilt—19:12–14; 103:8–19

Help—5; 46; 57; 86; 121; 142

Hope—25:21; 31:23–24

Insecurity—73:21–26; 108:1–5

Joy—30:4–5, 11–12

Justice—10; 75; 94

Loneliness—23; 25:16–18; 40:17; 42; 68:4–6

Oppression/Harassment—9:9–10; 12:5–7; 103:1–6

Parenting—127; 128

Patience—13; 37:1–10; 40:1–5

Politics—2; 33:10–22; 146:3–8

Praise—47; 100; 145; 147; 150

Prayer—34:4–8; 145:18–19

Pride—131

Rejection—38

Repentance—19:12–14; 32; 40; 51

Rest—91

Retirement—90; 145

Sickness/Suffering—31:9–10; 109:21–31; 119:153–160; 121

Strength—46; 138

Temptation—19:12–14; 141

Tiredness—3:5–6; 62:1–8; 91

Trust in God—25; 31:1–5; 37:3–6; 46:1–3; 112; 143

Words—12; 19:14; 34:12–14

Worry—25; 112:1–8

Part 5

WISDOM

Wisdom in the Bible has very little to do with college degrees or graduating with honors. From a biblical perspective, wisdom is the ability to live skillfully. A wise person lives a life marked by passionate obedience to God, devotion to family, integrity in the workplace, and concern for others. Wisdom permeates every layer of our existence from handling our money to raising our children to driving on the freeway.

The wise teachers of Israel were as concerned about earth as they were about heaven. Living well, living skillfully, does not come to us naturally. We all need mentors, role models, teachers to help us develop wisdom. In the pages of Scripture some of the wisest minds of the ages point us in the right direction. We learn from their words and from their example. Some of the best instruction comes from those who have walked down the *wrong* path and have come back to warn us about the dangers.

The only prerequisite for entrance into the Bible's school of wisdom is a humble, teachable spirit. The cleverest people don't like these wisdom books very much because the ideas seem old-fashioned. We've been conditioned to look for the newest, slickest techniques to make our way in the world. But the men and women who want to be wise and not just clever come to these books to be instructed, mentored by people who have deep, practical insights to share.

In a world full of sales pitches for the wrong way, these books show us how to live the good life by pointing us in the right way. Wisdom doesn't come easily; we have to search for it, work for it, and most of all, want it. But the reward is worth it!

> How much better to get wisdom than gold,
>   to choose understanding rather than silver! (Proverbs 16:16)

Proverbs

➤ Discover the secrets of living wisely and well.

➤ Meet some very successful people who want to help you succeed.

The book of Proverbs is a collection of . . . well, proverbs! Proverbs are wise sayings written by wise teachers for people like us who want to become wise.

Proverbs will give us practical, down-to-earth insight into how we can skillfully raise our children, honor our parents, pursue our careers, use words well, make peace with our enemies, and treat our friends with kindness. We sometimes think that serving God happens only when we go to church or help feed hungry people. Proverbs lets us know that a well-managed life patterned after God's instruction also honors God. In fact, if we have minds full of information but lives that dishonor God, we are called fools.

Who Is the Wise Guy Who Wrote This?

Most of the proverbs were originally spoken by Solomon, one of the great kings of Israel. Solomon gained his wisdom from several sources. Some came from the instruction of his father, David, and his mother, Bathsheba (Proverbs 1:8; 4:3–4; 6:20). Jewish tradition says that Solomon was tutored by a prophet of God named Nathan. So some of Solomon's wisdom came from a wise teacher.

Key Characters

Solomon: the third king of Israel—and a very wise man

Agur and Lemuel: more wise teachers who wrote sections of Proverbs

What set Solomon apart from everyone else, however, was the gift of wisdom he received from the Lord. As a young man, God gave Solomon a blank check. He told Solomon to ask for anything and God would grant it to him. If your mind is already scrolling through everything you might ask for, you know how Solomon felt. In the end Solomon

Points 2 Remember

- ☑ Proverbs is a collection of wise sayings and practical principles that point the way to a well-managed life.

- ☑ Proverbs are guidelines for wise living, not ironclad promises. Leave room for exceptions to the rule.

- ☑ Wisdom begins with a healthy respect for God. When we take God seriously, we also take his Word seriously. God is honored by a life lived skillfully.

- ☑ The book of Proverbs has been called "compressed experience." You can't read it once and suddenly find yourself wise! Reading a proverb takes only a few seconds; living a proverb takes a lifetime.

asked God for wisdom to rule the nation with skill. Wise choice! Because God was pleased with Solomon's choice, he gave him wisdom—plus riches and honor and long life—all the things he could have asked for but didn't.

When Solomon sat down to write the book of Proverbs, he opened with an extended discussion of what wisdom is and why we should seek after it (Proverbs 1–9). Solomon wanted the generations of those who would read his book to pursue the art of skillful living with passion and energy. Living wisely is not for wimps! It is one of life's great adventures.

Solomon spoke 3,000 proverbs (1 Kings 4:32). About 300 of these are collected in Proverbs 10:1–22:16. Added to Solomon's "top 300" are the "sayings of the wise" (22:17–24:34). When King Hezekiah ruled in Jerusalem 250 years or so after Solomon died, 130 more of Solomon's proverbs were added to the official collection (25:1–29:27), along with the words of the teachers Agur (chapter 30), Lemuel (31:1–9), and the unknown author of the poem about a virtuous woman (31:10–31).

How to Spot a Proverb

A proverb is a short, wise statement that gives us insight into some aspect of human experience. Three distinctive marks identify a proverb.

DoWNloAd

Proverbs 4:7 - 8

Wisdom is supreme; therefore get wisdom.
    Though it cost all you have, get understanding.
Esteem her, and she will exalt you;
    embrace her, and she will honor you.

A proverb is brief. The best proverbs give us the most wisdom in the fewest words. Proverbs stick in our minds because they are short and to the point.

A proverb is instructive. They speak to real situations we face every day. Proverbs are not hard to understand; the challenge is to live them out.

A proverb often paints a vivid picture. Many proverbs use imagery and comparisons to get their point across. "As a door turns on its hinges, so a sluggard [lazy person] turns on his bed" (26:14).

A proverb is a probability, not a promise. Some people have been discouraged because they have claimed a biblical proverb as a guaranteed promise from God. Then when there is an exception to the rule,

DigginG DeEpeR

✗ Kidner, Derek. *Proverbs: An Introduction and Commentary.* Tyndale Old Testament Commentary series. Downers Grove, IL: InterVarsity Press, 1968.

Kidner gives some suggestive topical studies plus helpful verse-by-verse commentary.

✗ Sailler, Ronald, and David Wyrtzen. *The Practice of Wisdom: A Topical Guide to Proverbs.* Chicago: Moody Press, 1992.

These authors have done the work of gathering relevant proverbs under a whole range of topics: alcohol, death, finances, laziness, and many others. A very helpful guide to further investigation.

the person thinks God has failed. That is a misuse of the proverbs. They are guidelines for wise living, but they make room for exceptions to the rule.

Here's one example: Proverbs 16:7 says, "When a man's ways are pleasing to the LORD, he makes even his enemies live at peace with him." In general that is true, but it's not always true. The Bible is full of men and women who were faithful to God but were hunted and hounded and even killed by their enemies. You may be living obediently to God yet be under attack right now. Has God failed to keep his promise in Proverbs 16:7? No way! In general that proverb is true, but leave room for the exception.

Walking the Walk

1. Acquaint yourself with some of the key sections of Proverbs.

    Proverbs 2:1–11   Finding wisdom
    Proverbs 8:1–36   Wisdom's song
    Proverbs 31:10–31   A woman of excellence

2. Since Proverbs has 31 chapters, you can start on the first day of next month and read one chapter a day over the course of the month. As you read, pick out one principle that you will seek to apply that day. Write it down on a card or sticky note and remind yourself to look for opportunities to demonstrate wisdom.

3. Ask a trusted friend to evaluate your life honestly. Ask the friend to point out areas of strength and areas where you fall short. Listen to your friend carefully and humbly. Then determine to work on the weak areas by reading through the book of Proverbs and marking or copying out all the verses that apply to that particular area. For example, if your words are abusive or unkind, check out every verse that talks about the tongue or words. Draw principles from the verses and ask God to help you become wise in areas that until now have been blind spots.

SEARCHING FOR SILVER

In his opening remarks, Solomon challenges his readers to look for wisdom as if it were silver and to search for it as if it were hidden treasure (Proverbs 2:4). So here is a field guide to a few mining expeditions in Proverbs. Check out the verses and apply the principles you discover to your own life. It won't take long for other people to notice the new direction your life has taken!

Work: 6:6–11; 10:4–5; 13:11; 14:23; 22:29; 23:4; 28:19

Lying: 6:16–19; 10:18; 12:19, 22; 13:5; 19:5; 20:17; 21:6

Political Leaders: 14:34–35; 16:12–13; 19:12; 20:28; 21:1; 23:1–3; 28:15–16; 29:2

Parents and Children: 1:8–9; 4:1–6; 6:20–24; 10:1; 15:5; 17:25; 22:6; 23:22–25; 29:15

Anger: 14:17, 29; 15:1; 16:32; 17:14; 19:19; 21:23; 22:24–25; 29:22

Ecclesiastes

— Heads Up —

➤ If you've ever asked, "What's the point?" this book is for you!

➤ Sit in on an interview with the richest, most powerful, yet most frustrated person of his day.

➤ Read how the author boils all of life down to basic principles.

The book of Ecclesiastes is the journal of a man who tried everything the world has to offer and found it all empty. He's the guy who bails out of his life as a hardworking, faithfully married family man to buy a Corvette and date women twenty years younger than he is. He's got the money and the energy to do it all! But he ends up depressed, disillusioned, and close to despair.

Fortunately, our friend wrote memoirs of his journey. He launched into his own "excellent adventure" with high hopes but finished up on a dead-end street. Nothing he saw, discovered, experienced, or accomplished tamed the longing in his spirit for fulfillment or satisfaction.

The first words of his book let you know how the story ends:

> "Meaningless! Meaningless!"
> says the Teacher.

HELP FILE

GETTING A HANDLE ON ECCLESIASTES

The author of this book calls himself "the Teacher." The original Hebrew word, *qoheleth,* meant "one who speaks to an assembly." Sometimes you will hear the writer or the book referred to as *Qoheleth* *(ko-**hay**-leth).* The title Ecclesiastes comes from the Greek word for "The Teacher" or "The Preacher" (another possible meaning). We get our English term *ecclesiastical* from the same Greek word.

Points 2 Remember

☑ Ecclesiastes is the journal of a man who pursued every conceivable avenue to find personal satisfaction. Because he left God out of his quest, however, he ultimately found life "under the sun" meaningless.

☑ This book does not teach us much about God; it shows us instead the futility of life without him.

> "Utterly meaningless!
>   Everything is meaningless." (1:2)

If This Is My Midlife Crisis, It's a Good One!

The writer of this book never identifies himself by name. He simply calls himself "the Teacher, son of David, king in Jerusalem" (1:1). Traditionally great King Solomon has been fingered as the author. The wealth expended, the creative energy required, and the restless longing of his heart all point to Solomon as the likely man on a quest.

If Solomon did write Ecclesiastes, he had a major part in the production of three biblical books. He likely wrote the *Song of Songs* (or Song of Solomon) in his young years as a reflection on his first love. He wrote *Proverbs* in his mature years as he passed on his wisdom to his children and to his nation. And he wrote *Ecclesiastes* at the end of his life, after years of spiritual decline and frustrated searching. He was not calling us to follow him in his search. Far from it! Solomon wanted us to learn what to avoid as we walk with him through some wasted years of his life.

The list of activities and avenues Solomon pursued in his quest for fulfillment is pretty impressive. Maybe you have tried (or are trying) some of the same paths. The shocking truth is that Solomon did far more than any of us will ever succeed in doing and found the end to be totally empty.

Academic Accomplishments

Solomon pursued every source of wisdom and knowledge available to him. He had every academic and honorary degree imaginable. His resumé was beyond impressive. But in the end he felt like he was "chasing after the wind" because

with much wisdom comes much sorrow;
    the more knowledge, the more grief. (1:17–18)

Sensual Pleasure

The next avenue of fulfillment Solomon tried was pleasure in all its forms and at all costs: comedy clubs, bigger and better houses, the fastest vehicles, a massive staff of servants to meet every need, all the latest toys, sexual excitement, musical concerts, and drop-dead art collections. He had the cash to finance anything his mind could conceive! But it all turned to ashes, dust in the wind.

Work

Serious work captured Solomon for a while too. He was at the top of the corporate ladder. But as he sat down in his penthouse office, he wrote,

When I surveyed all that my hands had done
    and what I had toiled to achieve,
everything was meaningless. (2:11)

Solomon concluded that life is short, work is empty, and we all end up dead!

Digging Deeper

✗ Swindoll, Charles. *Living on the Ragged Edge.* Waco, TX: Word, 1985.

An extended explanation of Ecclesiastes in a practical, pointed style. You will be challenged and helped by each chapter.

A Particular Perspective

What you have to remember as you read this book is that Solomon, by his own testimony, is writing from the perspective of a person living "under the sun." He has a strictly secular viewpoint. In his quest for satisfaction, Solomon never looked "above the sun" to find help, and

Ecclesiastes 3:1-2

**There is a time for everything,
and a season for every activity under heaven:
a time to be born and a time to die,
a time to plant and a time to uproot.**

so life on a purely horizontal level seemed hopelessly meaningless. Because he left God out of the picture, nothing on earth satisfied— and it never will satisfy. All the Madison Avenue promises of pleasure and excitement crumble into emptiness. Satisfaction and joy in life under the sun come from a relationship with the Lord God who reigns above the sun.

Solomon finally learned that! He returned to the Lord and found the fulfillment he was seeking, but he had paid a terrible price. His years of searching brought him back to the very God he had walked away from in the first place. His concluding advice was simple.

> Even if you live a long time, don't take a single day for granted. Take delight in each light-filled hour. (11:8 THE MESSAGE)

> Honor and enjoy your Creator while you're still young, Before the years take their toll and your vigor wanes. (12:1 THE MESSAGE)

The Teacher's final word is this:

> Fear God. Do what he tells you. (12:13 THE MESSAGE)

Walking the Walk

1. As you read Ecclesiastes, keep a list of the paths you have pursued to find fulfillment—money, sex, adventure, knowledge, career advancement. What satisfaction has each path brought? What price have you paid to follow each path? Your personal thoughts are the beginning of your own version of Ecclesiastes!

2. What do you want to accomplish in life? Be honest as you analyze your goals. How does a desire to please and obey God fit into the goals you are reaching for? Ask your spouse or a friend to help you refine your life objectives so that God is honored. Otherwise, you will come to the end of your life with the same sense of hopeless despair that overwhelmed Solomon.

Song of Songs

➤ Sit back and enjoy a remarkable love story!
➤ Discover God's attitude toward human sexuality.
➤ Rekindle the romantic flame in your own love relationship.

The Song of Songs is a beautiful ballad about the joys and pleasures of romantic love between a man and a woman. So what's it doing in the Bible?

The God who made us male and female provides us with specific instructions on how we can respond to each other as men and women. God used Solomon, a great and wise king of Israel, to write a marriage manual guaranteed to spark romantic fire in your love relationship.

The author of this "song for lovers" was most likely Solomon himself. The opening line of the book reads, "Solomon's Song of Songs." Solomon wrote more than a thousand songs (according to 1 Kings 4:32), but this one was at the top of the charts, a song above all other songs. Solomon probably wrote this ballad as a young man in the first bloom of love. Many other marriages would follow for him, but this was the first courtship and marriage. Perhaps the relationship described here was the fullest and most secure love that Solomon ever knew.

Key Characters

Groom: called "my lover" by his bride; probably King Solomon himself

Bride: Solomon's unnamed wife; called "my darling" by the groom

Chorus: a group of women who speak occasionally to add insight or information

We aren't told his fiancée's name. In 6:13 she is called "Shulammite"—a feminized form of Solomon's own name. He calls her "my darling"; she calls him "my lover."

Can We Read This in Church?

The book is a dialogue between Solomon and his bride. Occasionally a chorus of women, ladies of the court, chimes in to provide information or to issue a warning. The lovers talk about their passions, their dreams, their bodies, and their sexuality.

The book, in fact, has made a lot of people very nervous! God could have used medical terms to convey his plan for human sexuality—or the street slang we hear in a locker room. Instead, God moved Solomon to express these wonderful, powerful emotions in the language of poetry. But even his poetry is sensual and erotic.

Religious people down through the centuries have struggled with accepting a book about romantic love in the Bible. Some of them have been so embarrassed that they have covered up the normal meaning of Solomon's song by interpreting it as an allegory about God's love for Israel or Christ's love for the church.

One example will show you how absurd their interpretations can become. The woman in the love relationship says in chapter 1, verse 13: "My lover is to me a sachet of myrrh resting between my breasts." Pretty hot stuff for a Sunday sermon!

 **HELP FILE**

A SONG BY ANY OTHER NAME . . .

Most modern versions of the Bible call this book "The Song of Songs" or simply "The Song." That is the title the book gives itself in the first verse. You will also see the book referred to as "The Song of Solomon." Older Catholic Bibles title the book "The Canticles of Solomon." Canticle is the Latin word for "song" and comes from the Latin Vulgate version of the Bible used for centuries in the Catholic Church. Regardless of the title, the book stands alone in Scripture. There's no other book in the Bible quite like this one!

The first line of the book can also mean "a song *about* Solomon" or "a song *for* Solomon," so someone else could have written it as a tribute to Solomon or as an expression of Solomon's teaching. Usually the phrase is taken to mean "a song *by* Solomon."

This book should be rated PG-30, since the Jewish elders would not let anyone read Song of Songs until the person had reached the age of thirty.

God's name is never mentioned in the book.

Points 2 Remember

- [x] The Song of Songs is a poetic conversation between a lover and his beloved that traces the development of their romance from courtship through marriage and beyond.

- [x] The metaphors (word pictures) that are used in the poem are designed to evoke certain emotions. The key question to ask as you read them is, What feeling does this metaphor prompt in me?

- [x] Physical love and affection in marriage are gifts from God and are to be enjoyed to the fullest.

- [x] The cultivation of a growing romance requires personal involvement and time spent together. A deepening relationship doesn't happen by accident!

Jewish rabbis argued that, since the book pictures God's love for Israel, her statement refers to God's presence dwelling between two angels over the ark of the covenant (a piece of furniture in Israel's worship center). Some Christian teachers, looking for images of Jesus' love for the church, conclude that her statement refers to Jesus (the sachet of myrrh) being born between the writing of the Old Testament and the writing of the New Testament (her two breasts)!

The best understanding of the book, however, comes when we simply read what Solomon wrote. Two lovers express their deepest love in romantic, poetic words—words designed to stir the embers of affection in our love relationships.

Mixing It Up with Metaphors

Here's a sweet thought to try out on your wife or girlfriend: "Your hair is like a flock of goats descending from Mount Gilead." If you have had a close encounter with a goat recently, it's not a particularly romantic experience! Or how about: "Your nose is like the tower of Lebanon." Your significant other will probably have some words to describe you too—and "Romeo" won't be one of them.

All through the book Solomon and his bride praise each other with metaphors (word pictures) designed to evoke certain emotions, certain feelings. We do the same thing. On a cold winter night, wrapped in a blanket, sitting in front of a nice fire, we say, "I'm snug as a bug in a rug." Now, most of us aren't too crazy about bugs in our rugs! But the metaphor is designed to communicate how we feel. We feel warm and secure.

So the key to the metaphors in the Song of Songs is to ask, What feeling is prompted by this image? When Solomon says that his beloved's hair is like a flock of goats descending from Mount Gilead, we should imagine ourselves standing at a distance as a flock of black Palestinian goats cascade down a sand-colored hillside in the golden sunset. The peacefulness around us and the flowing movement of the flock are captivating, almost hypnotic—and that's the point. Solomon was captivated, playfully entangled, by his lover's dark, flowing hair.

Singing Solomon's Song

Solomon's love song is meant to be experienced more than analyzed, but we can see a pattern unfolding in this relationship as we work our way through the book.

Courtship (Song of Songs 1–3)

The first three chapters of the Song describe the courtship stage—romantic love before marriage. We are allowed to listen to the day-dreams of the bride-to-be (1:2–4) as she thinks about the night she will at last be married to the man she loves so much. The first words out of Solomon's mouth to his bride are words of compliment and praise—and she responds with gentle words of love back to him (1:9–10, 15–16). I wonder what it would do in my marriage if I tried to speak words of affection first, before my complaints or attacks. The early chapters of the Song picture a growing, God-honoring love between a man and a woman headed for marriage.

DiggiNG DeEpeR

✗   Gledhill, Tom. *The Message of the Song of Songs: The Lyrics of Love.* The Bible Speaks Today series. Downers Grove, IL: InterVarsity Press, 1994.

A detailed explanation of the book. Gledhill interprets the Song as "an extended love-poem."

Song of Songs 8:7

Many waters cannot quench love;
    rivers cannot wash it away.
If one were to give
    all the wealth of his house for love
    it would be utterly scorned.

The Wedding Night (Song of Songs 4)

Finally the big day arrived—and when the ceremony was over and the relatives were gone, the newlyweds were alone for the first time as husband and wife. In her nervousness, the bride said very little. Solomon, however, spoke tender words of love and appreciation as he took her into his arms.

As far as I can tell, God himself spoke in chapter 5, verse 1, and breathed his own blessing on their sexual union. Even God spoke in metaphors—the picture of a great feast of pleasure and joy. "Eat, O friends, and drink; drink your fill, O lovers."

Those who think God takes a prudish view of human sexuality need to take a fresh look at Solomon's Song! God designed us to be sexual beings. The greatest sexual fulfillment comes within the safe, God-ordained boundaries of marriage—and within those boundaries, sexuality is to be enjoyed to the fullest.

A Romantic Marriage (Song of Songs 5–8)

The rest of the book describes the growth of this couple's love after the wedding. One key to their ongoing pleasure in their marriage was the tenderness and honor they displayed toward each other. I think a lot of married couples lose that sense of honor. We joke at each other's expense. We easily jab or criticize or embarrass our mates. In God's ideal, however, we hear both husband and wife speak to each other in soft words. Even when there was a misunderstanding, this couple tried to work it out with compassion and forgiveness (see examples in 5:2–8 and 6:1–3).

Wrapping It Up

What poor lovers we have become! Physical love is an art that cannot develop without time and careful cultivation. If we ignore it, romantic love will dissolve. No amount of Bible study or Christian activity will ever replace the security and warmth of a growing marriage.

Solomon and his bride cultivated their love by spending time together. On one occasion the bride said:

> "Let's take a drive out in the country.
> We'll spend a night in that bed-and-breakfast we like so well.
> In the morning we'll walk out in the fields.
> We'll see if the daisies are in bloom
>> and if the pomegranate trees have blossomed." (7:11–12, my paraphrase)

Do you really think she cared if the pomegranates had blossomed? No way! That was just an excuse for time alone, time away from the responsibilities of home and job and even church. And you thought God wasn't concerned about something so ordinary! But he is concerned—concerned about *your* marriage.

We have time for our careers and time for overtime at work. We have time for sports and hobbies and yard work. What priority do we put on the development of our most significant human relationship, the life we share with our mate? If you want to be proud of some accomplishment in your life, don't let it be the purchase of a new house or a promotion in the company. Be proud of a growing, deepening, overflowing romantic adventure with the mate God has given you.

Walking the Walk

1. Plan a romantic evening for you and your spouse or sweetheart. Maybe a picnic in the park (or on the living room rug). If you are the male half of the relationship, read Song of Songs 4:1–7 to your beloved. (You may want to explain what you're doing so that she doesn't burst out laughing! Or rewrite the lines to reflect modern metaphors and emotions.) If you are the female half, read Song of Songs 5:10–16 to your lover.

2. Write a love letter to your spouse and put it where he or she will come upon it in the course of the day. Why do we stop being romantic when kids and diapers and *Monday Night Football* come along?

3. Put this book aside and invite your spouse into the bedroom for a romantic rendezvous. Take the initiative to light (or relight) the fire of romance in your marriage.

4. If you are dating someone, work on cultivating habits of honor and tenderness in your relationship. Do something this week out of the ordinary to show the person you love how much he or she really means to you.

GOOD LESSONS FROM A BAD EXAMPLE

A college student in the Bible survey course I teach was indignant. We were talking about the Song of Songs and Solomon's exaltation of human love. "Solomon had seven hundred wives and three hundred other women in his harem. Why should we listen to what *he* says about the beauty of married love? He was certainly no model husband!"

She had a good point. Solomon in his later years did take on more wives. Many of them were non-Israelite women (usually married to seal political treaties with other nations). He also had hundreds of concubines—women whose main function was to satisfy the king's sexual desires. If Solomon really believed that God's ideal was one man and one woman committed faithfully to each other, why did he live such a promiscuous life?

Some possible answers:

1. Solomon probably wrote this book early in his life before his slide into polygamy and sexual obsession. God gave Solomon great wisdom, and Solomon wrote the Song to convey that wisdom to us.

2. God never approved of Solomon's multiplication of wives. The Bible makes it clear that Solomon's obsession with sexual activity turned his heart away from the Lord (see, for example, 1 Kings 11:3–6).

3. The fact that Solomon departed from what God desired in his life does not necessarily disqualify him from writing about how we should live before God. If I teach my children that outbursts of anger are wrong and then later have an angry outburst myself, does that mean my teaching was faulty?

Solomon was a wise man, but like us he didn't always follow the wisest path. In his later years he strayed far from the Lord in his search for satisfaction only to discover that true fulfillment is found in obedience to God.

Part 6

PROPHETS

The Old Testament prophets changed people's lives—and they are still changing lives! Unfortunately, most of us don't know these men and women very well. They don't write easy, breezy stories. We've been intimidated by their weird visions or put off by their harsh words. When we read their words, we find ourselves called up short. After a session with the prophets, we never again see ourselves or our society or our God in the same way. We come away changed.

God's Press Conference

The prophets were men and women who spoke for someone else. That is a crucial fact to remember as you read these books. The prophets did not come to God's people with their own message. They spoke God's message—God's Word in God's words!

We see something similar almost every day. The men and women of the press gather in a room at the White House for a press briefing. The president doesn't show up for these daily sessions very often. Usually he sends his press secretary, his spokesperson to the media. When the press secretary reads a statement or answers a question, the people listening realize that the words reflect the thoughts and policies of the president, not the opinions of the spokesperson. The press secretary who gives personal opinion instead of presidential policy doesn't last long.

The prophets spoke for the Lord. Hundreds of times in their books you will read phrases like: "This is what the LORD says" or "The word of the LORD came to [the prophet]" or "Listen to the word of the LORD." Sometimes the prophets were so consumed by the message that God seemed to speak directly through them—"You have departed, O Israel, from *me!*"

What's a Prophet to Do?

The prophets had three basic responsibilities:

Most important, the prophets were preachers. They spoke to the people—kings and slaves alike—and to the problems of their own day. We still feel the sting of their words because the problems haven't changed much—and neither have the people. Even when they were threatened with punishment or death because of their words, the prophets had to speak.

Second, God spoke through the prophets to predict the future. Some of their predictions were fulfilled soon after the prediction; others were fulfilled hundreds of years later; still others are yet to be fulfilled.

Third, the prophets warned God's people of coming judgment and begged them to return to the Lord in full obedience and love. The prophets constantly reminded the people of Israel and Judah of the promises they had made as a nation to the Lord—and the promises God had made to them. God had promised blessing if they remained faithful to him and catastrophe if they followed the false gods of the nations around them.

Prophets had been part of God's program since Moses led Israel out of slavery in Egypt. Moses and his sister, Miriam, were both called prophets. After Israel settled in the land of God's promise, Deborah and Samuel spoke for God. In the days of David's reign, men like Nathan and Gad were God's voice.

Prophets emerged most strongly after the division of the nation of Israel. Many spoke to the people of Israel in the north or the people of Judah in the south. Some prophets spoke to or about other nations. A couple of prophets spoke God's message to the Jews in Babylon during the time of exile. None of them had it easy.

From Major to Minor

Seventeen books of the prophets occupy the final third of the Old Testament. The first five are called *major prophets;* the remaining twelve are called *minor prophets.* Those titles have nothing to do with the importance of the writers; they have everything to do with the length of their writings. Isaiah, Jeremiah, Ezekiel, and Daniel wrote long books. (Lamentations is short, but since Jeremiah wrote it, we include it with the "major" books.) The books of the minor prophets are much shorter.

You will not find these prophetic books pleasant—challenging, disturbing, piercingly honest, but not pleasant. The prophets make us angry because they pull away our masks and expose the selfishness and hypocrisy in our hearts. The prophets bring us comfort because they show us what is really going on behind the chaos of our world. The prophets make it difficult to continue leading a sloppy life.

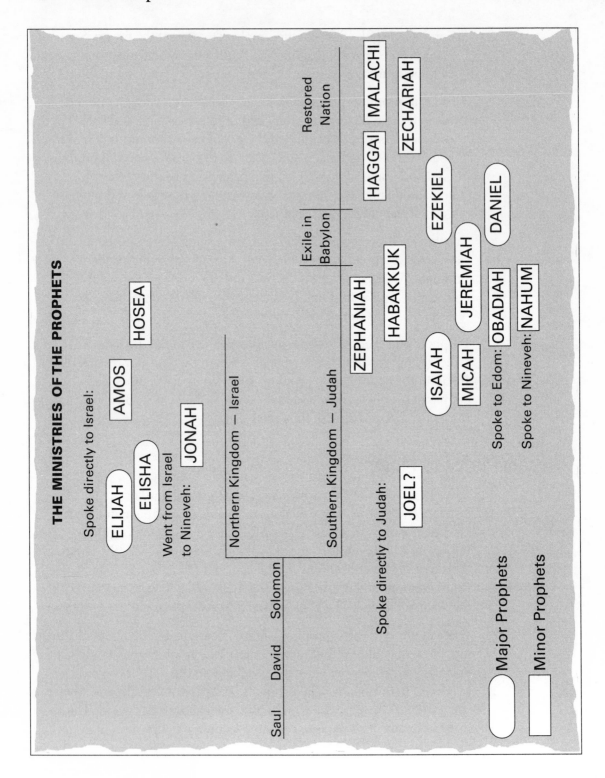

THE MINISTRIES OF THE PROPHETS

Saul   David   Solomon

Spoke directly to Israel:

ELIJAH   AMOS   HOSEA

ELISHA

Went from Israel
to Nineveh: JONAH

Northern Kingdom — Israel

Southern Kingdom — Judah

Spoke directly to Judah:

JOEL?

ZEPHANIAH   HABAKKUK

ISAIAH   EZEKIEL

MICAH   JEREMIAH

Spoke to Edom: OBADIAH   DANIEL

Spoke to Nineveh: NAHUM

Exile in
Babylon

Restored
Nation

HAGGAI   MALACHI

ZECHARIAH

Major Prophets

Minor Prophets

Isaiah

➤ Get caught up in vivid predictions of judgment and glory.

➤ Stand next to Isaiah as he has a dramatic vision of God.

➤ Find out what Isaiah wrote about Jesus—seven hundred years before Jesus was born!

Isaiah is considered by both Jews and Christians to be the greatest of the biblical prophets. What Elvis is to rock and roll, what Einstein is to modern science, Isaiah is among God's prophets.

Isaiah's Times

Isaiah's ministry spanned the reigns of five kings in the southern kingdom of Judah. He had the longest ministry of any prophet except Daniel. According to chapter 6 of his book, Isaiah's call to be God's spokesman came in the year King Uzziah died (739 B.C.). Uzziah was one of Judah's good kings, as was Jotham, his son and successor to the throne. They were followed by Ahaz, an evil, ungodly king. Then came Hezekiah, probably the king most faithful to God up to that point. Isaiah had his greatest impact during the years of Hezekiah's leadership. As far as we know, Isaiah lived a few years into the reign of the next king, Manasseh (until around 681 B.C.). Manasseh was the vilest of the Judean kings. A Jewish tradition claims that Manasseh executed Isaiah by having him cut apart with a saw!

The rising world power during Isaiah's lifetime was Assyria. To the northeast of Israel and Judah, the Assyrian Empire became larger and more

Key Characters

Isaiah: a prophet who spoke God's message—in good times and in bad

Hezekiah: king in Judah who listened to Isaiah's advice—most of the time

Seraphs: magnificent angels who surround God's throne (Isaiah 6:1–7)

The Servant of the Lord: a title Isaiah gives to the promised Messiah

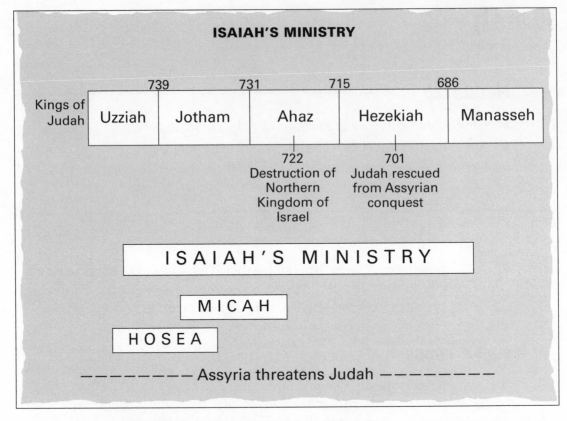

powerful with each new conquest. Ultimately, it was Assyria that crushed the northern kingdom of Israel in 722 B.C. Isaiah was alive to witness the devastation. Assyria would have swallowed Judah too if God had not miraculously intervened to cripple the Assyrian army. One of God's angels killed 185,000 Assyrians in one night! In the morning, what was left of the Assyrian army packed up and went home. (The story is in 2 Kings 19:35–36 and Isaiah 37:36–37.) Assyria continued to threaten Judah after that but never conquered Judah.

Isaiah's Life

We know more personal stuff about Isaiah than any other prophet. He was the son of Amoz (not to be confused with the prophet Amos), and he was probably one of the "royals" in Judah. Isaiah was married to a prophetess (8:3)—no name recorded for her—and they had two sons with incredible names—Shear-Jashub and Maher-Shalal-Hash-Baz! (I'm not kidding! The names appear in Isaiah 7:3 and 8:1, 3. Look them up!)

SPIRITUAL GENE POOL

Isn't it interesting that a godly father (Uzziah) produced a godly son (Jotham) who produced an evil son (Ahaz) from whom came one of Judah's godliest kings (Hezekiah) who fathered the worst of Judah's kings (Manasseh)! You just never know how your kids will turn out....

Isaiah was the official historian for King Uzziah and King Hezekiah. He was highly trained as a scribe and had wide experience as an advisor to kings. His book is written in impressive Hebrew. Every word is packed with meaning; every phrase is brilliantly polished.

Isaiah was also a very practical man. He spoke to people living in a shaky, uncertain world. Any day could bring the crisis of captivity or war—or downsizing or disability or a stock market crash. He challenged people in crisis to look to God alone for security. In a world falling apart, the only certainty could be found in an unfailing God.

Isaiah's Book

Isaiah's collected writings can be viewed as a Bible in miniature. Isaiah's prophecy has sixty-six chapters just like the Bible has sixty-six books. There are two major sections of Isaiah just like we have two sections of the Bible. The first division of Isaiah contains thirty-nine chapters exactly like the Old Testament contains thirty-nine books. The twenty-seven chapters of the second division of Isaiah parallel the twenty-seven books

HELP FILE

ONE OF THE BIBLE'S TOP TEN

Isaiah's name *(i-**zay**-ah)* means "The Lord is salvation."

Isaiah has been called the "Saint Paul of the Old Testament" because, like the apostle Paul in the New Testament, he explains how God in grace will rescue sinful humanity through the death of the Servant of the Lord, Jesus.

Isaiah is quoted in the New Testament more than any other Old Testament book. The prophet is mentioned by name twenty-one times. Isaiah's prophecy about the suffering of the Messiah (52:13–53:12) is quoted or alluded to eighty-five times in the New Testament.

ONE ISAIAH OR TWO — OR THREE?!

Because of the dramatic shift in mood and subject between chapters 1–39 and chapters 40–66 in Isaiah, some scholars have suggested separate authors for the two sections—the "original" Isaiah who wrote chapters 1–39 and a "deutero-Isaiah" or second Isaiah who lived later and who wrote chapters 40–66. Some even find a "third Isaiah" in the final chapters of the book.

Evangelical scholars have argued very convincingly for the unity of the book's authorship. Several verbal and literary parallels can be found that connect the two sections. For example, God is called "the Holy One of Israel" twenty-six times in the book, twelve times in chapters 1–39 and fourteen times in chapters 40–66. Outside of Isaiah's prophecy the title occurs only six times. The writers of the New Testament consistently refer to both sections as the work of one author, Isaiah the prophet.

Those who find two authors in Isaiah point to the Assyrian background for chapters 1–39 and the Babylonian background for chapters 40–66. (Babylon was an empire that arose later in history and overthrew Assyria.) But Babylon is mentioned twice as often in chapters 1–39 as in chapters 40–66. The only shift is a shift in perspective. In the first section of his book, the prophet focuses on the *present* crisis under Assyria's threat. In the second part of his book, Isaiah focuses on the *future* judgment of Judah that God will bring through the Babylonians.

of the New Testament. The first section of Isaiah covers the rebellion and sinfulness of God's people the same way the Old Testament records Israel's failure to follow the Lord. The second section of Isaiah opens with the announcement of God's promised deliverer and it ends with a description of the new heavens and new earth. The same themes are mirrored in the New Testament, which opens with the arrival of the Messiah and ends with the new heavens and new earth of eternity.

Isaiah's Message

God's Judgment (Isaiah 1–35)

Isaiah's book opens with a message aimed at his own people in Judah. Judah was filled with moral decay and spiritual disease. God had been a compassionate and generous Father, but his people had rebelled against him. God graciously invited them to repent and return to him as their only hope of avoiding his judgment.

Points 2 Remember

☑ Isaiah spoke God's message to the nation of Judah for more than fifty years. He warned the people of God's coming judgment but also assured them of God's control over world events.

☑ Isaiah predicted enough about God's promised Messiah to construct a fairly complete picture of Jesus, who was born in Bethlehem seven hundred years later.

☑ God called Isaiah to be a prophet by giving him a vision of the Lord exalted over all the universe (Isaiah 6).

☑ Isaiah spoke to people who were under a constant threat of conquest by Assyria. He pointed them to an unfailing God as their only security.

The account of Isaiah's vision of the Lord and his call to be God's prophet is one of the best-known passages in the Old Testament (chapter 6). As Isaiah stood in God's temple, he saw the Lord on his throne governing his universe. It was at this time that God set Isaiah apart as his servant and spokesman.

Chapters 7–12 are sometimes called the book of Immanuel (an Old Testament title for God's promised Messiah; in Hebrew it means "God with us"). These chapters repeatedly talk about the coming Messiah and the blessings of the Messiah's reign as king.

Judah was not the only nation God would hold accountable. Isaiah next spoke a series of judgment messages against eleven nations surrounding Judah: Babylon, Assyria, Philistia, Moab, Damascus (or Syria), Ethiopia, Egypt, Babylon (again), Edom, Arabia, Jerusalem (Judah), and Tyre (chapters 13–23). The first section of the book ends with a picture of the universal suffering that the world and the people of Israel will experience before they see God's dramatic intervention to bring human history to an end.

Historical Interlude (Isaiah 36–39)

These four chapters give us Isaiah's perspective on the Assyrian invasion of Judah that took place in 701 B.C. God was using Assyria to turn the hearts of the people of Judah back to the Lord. Isaiah also predicted the future Babylonian invasion of Judah that would not come until after Isaiah had died. Judah had managed to escape captivity under Assyria (chapters 36–37), but they would not escape the coming Babylonian conquest (chapters 38–39).

DOWNLOAD

Isaiah 53:4 – 6

Surely he took up our infirmities
   and carried our sorrows,
yet we considered him stricken by God,
   smitten by him, and afflicted.
But he was pierced for our transgressions,
   he was crushed for our iniquities;
the punishment that brought us peace was upon him,
   and by his wounds we are healed.
We all, like sheep, have gone astray,
   each of us has turned to his own way;
and the LORD has laid on him
   the iniquity of us all.

God's Comfort (Isaiah 40 – 66)

After he pronounced God's judgment, Isaiah began to tell his people about God's promises of future blessing and restoration. God's judgment was certain, but his anger would not last forever. Judah's hope rested on the power of God to keep his Word (chapters 40–48).

Isaiah also predicted that God would send a Deliverer, a Messiah who would suffer for the sins of God's people (chapters 49–57). At first God's Messiah would be rejected and killed, but ultimately he would be exalted and would usher in a kingdom of peace and justice. All who would trust in God's Redeemer would be delivered (chapters 58–66). Isaiah's predictions were fulfilled centuries later when Jesus came first as God's sacrifice for sin and then promised to return as the conquering King.

FOOtpRiNts in the SanD

One of the most well-known of the Dead Sea Scrolls is a complete scroll of the book of Isaiah. The Dead Sea Scrolls are a collection of biblical, religious, and social documents discovered in caves near the Dead Sea beginning in 1947.

Walking the Walk

1. Isaiah had an incredible grasp of the awesome character of God. As you read his prophecy, write down the various aspects of God's character that you find. Use the list in your own worship of God or in prayer as you give God praise for his greatness and his goodness. Allow your expanding understanding of God's splendor and majesty to increase your trust in him.

2. Evaluate your personal impact on people who are in crisis situations. What advice and direction do you give people? Do you point them to the latest self-help books—or do you point them to a powerful God and his promises to those who trust in him? Where do *you* turn first for help when you find yourself in difficult circumstances?

3. If you aren't prepared to tackle the entire book of Isaiah, at least acquaint yourself with the key passages of his prophecy.
   Isaiah 1—God's judgment on his people and his gracious call to repentance
   Isaiah 6—Isaiah's transforming vision of the Lord and his willingness to speak for God in his society
   Isaiah 40—God's promised comfort for his people
   Isaiah 52–53—The suffering Servant of the Lord

Digging Deeper

✗ Motyer, J. Alec. *The Prophecy of Isaiah: An Introduction and Commentary.* Downers Grove, IL: InterVarsity Press, 1993.

A detailed study of Isaiah's prophecy.

✗ Wiersbe, Warren. *His Name Is Wonderful.* Wheaton, IL: Tyndale, 1984.

A devotional look at Jesus as he is pictured in Isaiah.

JESUS IN ISAIAH

I remember where I was when I heard that President John F. Kennedy had been assassinated. My ninth-grade typing class was interrupted by the squeal of the public address system, and our principal choked out the words that brought the school and the nation to a standstill. "I am very sad to have to tell you that the president was shot today in Dallas, Texas. We have just heard that the president, President Kennedy, is dead."

That event marked our nation's history and the memory of an entire generation. But suppose we had a document that had been around for seven hundred years before 1963—a document written in the 1200s—that predicted the time when a great leader of a new land would ride in a carriage moved without horses. That leader (according to this document) would be killed by a metal ball hurled at his head, and his death would bring worldwide sorrow. We would hold that document in awe! But just such a prediction would fade in comparison to the detailed prophecies that are recorded in the Old Testament about a Deliverer who would come to the people of Israel.

Seven hundred years before Jesus was born, Isaiah was writing about him. He told us so much in his prophecy about Jesus that we can almost construct a fifth gospel just from Isaiah's predictions. Prophecies given in the Old Testament about God's promised Deliverer are called *messianic* prophecies. The word *Messiah* in Hebrew means "anointed one." In Greek the word is "Christ," a title repeatedly given to Jesus in the New Testament. Jesus is the Christ, the promised Messiah, the Anointed One of God.

Here are the key prophecies in Isaiah that were (or will be) fulfilled in the birth, life, death, resurrection, and future reign of Jesus.

His Birth

7:14—Born of a virgin; quoted in Matthew 1:22–23

9:6—Both God and man

For to us a child is born,
    to us a son is given,
        and the government will be on
            his shoulders.
And he will be called
    Wonderful Counselor, Mighty God,
    Everlasting Father, Prince of
    Peace.

9:7—Descended from David

He will reign on David's throne
    and over his kingdom.

His Youth

7:15; 53:2

A Prophet Would Announce His
    Coming

40:3—Quoted in Matthew 3:3;
    Mark 1:3; Luke 3:4; John 1:23
    in relation to John the Baptist

His Message of Deliverance

61:1–2—Quoted in Luke 4:18–19

His Miracles of Healing and Power

35:5–6; 61:1—Alluded to in
Matthew 11:5

53:4—Quoted in Matthew 8:17

His Relationship to God the Father

8:17—Quoted in Hebrews 2:13

42:1, 6; 49:1–3; 50:4–5; 61:10

His Rejection by His Own People

6:9–10—Quoted in Matthew
13:14–15; Mark 4:12; Luke
8:10; John 12:40

28:16—Quoted in Romans 9:33

29:10—Quoted in Romans 11:8

29:13—Quoted in Matthew 15:8–9;
Mark 7:6–7

53:1—Quoted in John 12:38

His Inclusion of Non-Jews in God's
Program

9:1–2—Quoted in Matthew 4:15–16

11:10—Quoted in Romans 15:12

42:6

49:6—Quoted in Acts 13:47

His Compassionate Nature

42:1–4—Quoted in Matthew
12:18–21

54:13—Quoted in John 6:45

His Suffering and Death for the Sins of Others

50:6; 52:14

53:1–10—Verse 9 is quoted in
1 Peter 2:22

53:12—Quoted in Luke 22:37

His Exaltation to the Highest Place

52:13

See, my servant will act wisely;
he will be raised and lifted up
and highly exalted.

53:10–12

55:3—Quoted in Acts 13:34

His Reign Forever as King

9:7; 11:3–5; 24:21–23

45:23—Quoted in Romans 14:11

59:16–21—Verses 20–21 quoted in
Romans 11:26–27

For more information on Old Testament messianic prophecy, see:

Kaiser, Walter, Jr. *The Messiah in the Old Testament.* Grand Rapids: Zondervan, 1995.

Smith, James. *What the Bible Teaches About the Promised Messiah.* Nashville: Thomas Nelson, 1993.

Other Old Testament prophets who spoke about the Messiah: Micah, Zechariah, Daniel.

Jeremiah

➤ What do you say to people who just won't listen?

➤ Watch as Jeremiah's predictions come true.

➤ Learn how God deals with our stubborn streaks.

Jeremiah was the undertaker of the Old Testament, the hospice worker in whose care the nation of Judah spent its dying days. Jeremiah witnessed the moral decay and ultimately the death of the nation of Judah under the boot of a conquering army. He felt powerless to stem the tide of his nation's departure from God. All he could do was stand up and announce the coming judgment and then go home and cry.

Jeremiah's book is not one to which you can turn for a positive, uplifting message. He didn't say much about the glorious days of the Messiah's future kingdom. Jeremiah was too busy bandaging the wounds of a population infected with a deadly moral plague to reflect on the glory of a future day. His message was a combination of terror and tears, warning and weeping. If you are already sad or depressed when you start the book, you won't get far before you turn away.

Key Characters

Jeremiah: a man who spoke God's message to people in crisis

Baruch: Jeremiah's scribe (secretary) who wrote out the prophet's words (Jeremiah 36:4)

Nebuchadnezzar: Babylonian general/emperor who led the attack against Jerusalem

A Job Nobody Wants

Jeremiah shouldn't have been surprised at the difficulty of his work and the unresponsiveness of his audience. God had told him what to expect. When God first called Jeremiah as his spokesman, King Josiah was on the throne of Judah. The nation of Judah was all that was left of the clans descended from Abraham, Isaac, and Jacob. The northern clans of Israel had been carried away decades earlier and scattered throughout the vast Assyrian Empire (722 B.C.). Now a new world power, Babylon, had reduced Judah to a tiny slice of land.

Josiah was a godly king and, at the time, things seemed to be going pretty well in Judah. Since Josiah had torn down the idol altars and pagan worship centers that once had filled the land, the worship of God was in full swing and the temple was full on the Sabbath. (You can read the story of Josiah's reign in 2 Kings 22:1–23:30 and in 2 Chronicles 34–35. Jeremiah was called by God in the thirteenth year of Josiah's reign [627 B.C.], which was also the first year of the spiritual renewal that swept through Judah under Josiah.) Unfortunately, the spiritual revival led by King Josiah didn't last very long. The nation slid back into the old way of disobedience to God just a few years after Josiah's death. God's judgment came when the armies of Babylon marched through Jerusalem's streets.

Jeremiah must have been pretty surprised to hear God's voice. God began by telling Jeremiah how long God had been watching him.

> "Before I formed you in the womb I knew you,
>> before you were born I set you apart;
>> I appointed you as a prophet to the nations." (1:5)

Jeremiah knew that the job of a prophet was a difficult, thankless job. He said to God, "I don't know how to speak very eloquently; I am only a child!" Probably Jeremiah was at least twenty years old—hardly a child—but it was the best thing he could come up with. God wouldn't take no for an answer, however. What God said next should have given Jeremiah a clue about what this call to a prophetic ministry involved.

> "You must go to everyone I send you to and say whatever I command you. Do not be afraid of them, for I am with you and will rescue you. . . .

> Today I have made you a fortified city, an iron pillar and a bronze wall to stand against the whole land—against the kings of Judah, its officials, its priests and the people of the land. They will fight against you but will not overcome you, for I am with you and will rescue you." (1:7, 18–19)

If I had been listening to God, I would have said to myself, "Let's see. Who will be against me? The king, the officials, the priests and the

QUICK VIEW

An Outline and Key Passages in Jeremiah

A. Jeremiah's Call (1)

B. Jeremiah's Preaching to Judah (2–45)

    1. From King Josiah to the first conquest by Babylon (2–20)

      a. Life is serious (16)

      b. A trip to the potter's house (18–19)

    2. From Josiah's successors to the captivity (21–45)

      a. God's new covenant (30–31)

      b. Jeremiah in a muddy pit (37–38)

C. Jeremiah's Proclamations to Other Nations (46–51)

    1. Babylon's ultimate destruction (50–51)

D. Historical Postscript (52) [probably added by Baruch, Jeremiah's secretary, or by the compiler of the book]. This chapter is almost identical to 2 Kings 24:18–25:30.

people. And who will be on my side? The Lord and . . . that's it!" Jeremiah had to face the people of Judah with the announcement of disaster and no one would stand with him—except the Lord. If you think that made Jeremiah's job easy, think about where you work or go to school. How easy is it to stand alone for what is right? God certainly stands with us when we defend his truth, but the attacks or ridicule of people around us are still hard to take.

God even gave Jeremiah a job description. "Your ministry," God said, will be "to uproot and tear down, to destroy and overthrow, to build and to plant" (1:10). Two-thirds of Jeremiah's ministry would be negative; only one-third would be positive. Jeremiah preached very few sermons that left people smiling. Most of the time people left his presence under the crushing weight of guilt or else raging mad.

Jeremiah wished at times that he could pick a new career path. Who wouldn't? On one occasion he wished for a place out in the wilderness,

DOWNLOAD

Jeremiah 29:11–13

"For I know the plans I have for you," declares the LORD, "plans to prosper you and not to harm you, plans to give you hope and a future. Then you will call upon me and come and pray to me, and I will listen to you. You will seek me and find me when you seek me with all your heart."

Points 2 Remember

☑ Jeremiah was a prophet who warned Judah of God's coming judgment through the Babylonians. He spoke to kings and to common people with forceful power and then went home to weep over their hardness of heart.

☑ When we willfully ignore God's Word, we will always have to pay a price.

☑ The person who speaks boldly for God in the marketplace develops that courage by spending time alone with God in humility and tears.

a hunting lodge where no one could find him (9:2). He wanted a little rest, a few minutes of peace and quiet, without people breathing down his neck. Another time Jeremiah decided that he just wouldn't speak anymore. If God wanted the message delivered, let him find someone else. But when Jeremiah kept his mouth shut, God's words became fire in his bones (20:9). He had to speak or be consumed!

So Why Read It?

Who wants to read a book as depressing as this one? Maybe that's why we don't hear many sermons preached from the book of Jeremiah. Unfortunately, many people turn away from Jeremiah before they discover the power of what God is saying through this man. We think his message is depressing when God intends it as demanding. We think it's about long ago and far away, when in fact God wants to use this book to challenge us to think carefully and seriously about our own lives and our own nation. Jeremiah does not advocate a "feel-good" approach to life, but a "do-right" approach!

Because our day is so much like Jeremiah's day, we need to listen closely to what he has to say. The destruction of the nation of Judah by the armies of Babylon came because of a spiritual decline. The people of Judah claimed to love God with their lips, but they refused to obey him with their lives. They sang "He is Lord" at church, but their hearts were far from God. Jeremiah stood before an outwardly religious but inwardly bankrupt nation, and he spoke God's Word.

If you look around, you find the same conditions today. Our society has the trappings of religion, but there is very little devotion to God. Every city, suburb, and village is filled with churches; the airwaves are crowded with preachers. We've come up with slick new techniques to attract people to our meetings, but most of the time it is a reflection of our effort and not God's power. There was no lack of priests or prophets in Jeremiah's day, but when it came to speaking God's truth, Jeremiah often stood alone.

"Babylon Is Coming! Give Up!"

God even told Jeremiah what he was to tell the people. He didn't have to hunt around for a juicy sermon!

> "From the north disaster will be poured out on all who live in the land. I am about to summon all the peoples of the northern kingdoms," declares the LORD.

> "Their kings will come and set up their thrones
>   in the entrance of the gates of Jerusalem;
>   they will come against all her surrounding walls

HELP FILE

A LONG BOOK

Jeremiah was a priest by birth (a descendant of Moses' brother, Aaron; priests served in the temple in Jerusalem); he was a prophet by God's commission.

Jeremiah's book is a collection of prophecies spoken at different times in his life. The prophecies are not in chronological order, but dates can be approximated by the kings who are named or by the events described.

This is the second longest book of the Bible. (Psalms is the longest.)

Jeremiah was a contemporary of the prophet Habakkuk. Ezekiel prophesied in Babylon during the last years of Jeremiah's ministry in Judah. Jeremiah refers to the prophet Micah by name (26:18). Later Daniel referred to Jeremiah and used Jeremiah's prophecy to predict that Judah's captivity in Babylon would end after seventy years (Jeremiah 25:11–12; 29:10; Daniel 9:2).

The Old Testament mentions eight other men named Jeremiah, including two others in this book (35:3; 52:1).

> and against all the towns of Judah.
> I will pronounce my judgments on my people
> because of their wickedness in forsaking me,
> in burning incense to other gods
> and in worshiping what their hands have made." (1:14–16)

No one living in Jeremiah's day could misinterpret who the northern kingdoms were. The Babylonian Empire crouched north of Judah like a tiger ready to pounce. Every time Jeremiah preached he said essentially the same thing: Babylon will come and destroy us as a nation.

Jeremiah gave an interesting conclusion to his sermons too. He stood before kings, government bureaucrats, the local ministerial association, corporate executives, and the homeless standing in line for a hot meal and said:

"This is what the LORD says:

'Whoever stays in this city [Jerusalem] will die by the sword, famine or plague, but whoever goes over to the Babylonians will live. He will escape with his life; he will live.' And this is what the LORD says: 'This city will certainly be handed over to the army of the kings of Babylon, who will capture it.'" (38:2–3)

Saying something like that would make you very popular in the middle of a war! Imagine telling people to give up, put down their weapons, surrender to the enemy, and abandon the cause.

Some of the people living in Judah thought that God would never allow Jerusalem to be taken. After all, the temple stood in Jerusalem. David the great king had reigned in Jerusalem. God's honor (it seemed) was at stake. A century earlier God had wiped out an Assyrian army waiting to invade Jerusalem (2 Kings 19:35–36). Why wouldn't God do the same thing to a bunch of Babylonians?

Jeremiah had a response to people who thought that way:

> "This is what the LORD says: . . . Even if you were to defeat the entire Babylonian army that is attacking you and only wounded men were left in their tents, they would come out and burn this city down." (37:9–10)

Needless to say, Jeremiah was not chosen "man of the year" by the local chamber of commerce. He was hated, hunted, thrown in a pit, imprisoned, attacked but, worst of all, ignored. As he prophesied, Nebuchadnezzar, the Babylonian ruler, swept down on Jerusalem and destroyed the

DiGGinG DeEpeR

✗ Feinberg, Charles. "Jeremiah." *The Expositor's Bible Commentary*. Vol. 6. Grand Rapids: Zondervan, 1986.

A detailed study and a very reliable interpretation of Jeremiah's book.

✗ Kidner, Derek. *The Message of Jeremiah*. The Bible Speaks Today series. Downers Grove, IL: InterVarsity Press, 1987.

A section-by-section survey of the prophecy of Jeremiah; a helpful guide.

✗ Peterson, Eugene. *Run with the Horses: The Quest for Life at Its Best*. Downers Grove, IL: InterVarsity Press, 1983.

An excellent biographical study of Jeremiah, filled with plenty of challenges about our own lives.

city. The walls were pulled down, the temple was burned to the ground, and the few people who survived were marched off to Babylon in chains.

God kept his promises! He had promised judgment if the people would not turn back to him with full commitment. So when the people refused to return to the Lord, judgment came. The survivors stumbling over the hard miles to Babylon could only mumble, "Jeremiah was right! If only we had believed God's Word. If only we had turned in repentance to the Lord. If only. . . . If only. . . ."

Walking the Walk

1.   If a prophet like Jeremiah came on the scene in our nation's capital, what would he find about our society to praise? What would he condemn? How do you think our national leaders would respond to him?

2.   Think about a time when you needed someone to have a corrective influence in your life. Who tried to "set you straight"? What was your reaction to that person's correction?

3.   As you read Jeremiah's book, look for insights into the personality and character of this man. Keep a "personality profile" in your journal or on a notecard. Identify one or two qualities you find in Jeremiah that you want to cultivate in your own life.

Rescuing a Few

God kept his promise of judgment—but what about his other promises? What about the promises he had made long before to Abraham and David, telling them that Israel would be his people forever? Had God forgotten what he said earlier? Was he so angry that his promises of blessing were easily ignored?

In spite of what appeared to be God's crushing of his people, God was also preserving a remnant—a few were being rescued. They were in chains; some were already in Babylon from earlier deportations; but they were alive. In Babylon the people of Judah prospered. They built homes, grew crops, started businesses, and tried to make a new future for themselves. In time the tiny remnant of God's people grew strong again.

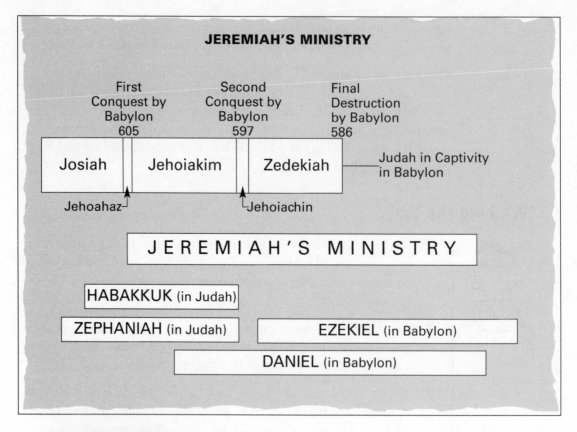

Standing Alone

In public Jeremiah was an unbending, powerful voice for God. He proclaimed God's message whether it was popular or not. He was exactly what God said he would be—a pillar of iron. But when Jeremiah got home, in his bedroom, on his knees, he was the tenderest of men. When Jeremiah saw the people of Judah continue in disobedience to the Lord, his heart was broken.

> Oh, that my head were a spring of water
>   and my eyes a fountain of tears!
> I would weep day and night
>   for the slain of my people. (9:1)

Jeremiah's life had to be incredibly lonely. His family was embarrassed by him, and his friends all abandoned him. God told Jeremiah, "Your brothers, your own family—even they have betrayed you" (12:6). Jeremiah didn't even have a wife to help him. God came to Jeremiah and said, "You must not marry and have sons or daughters in this place" (16:1). The prophet's single life was an object lesson to the people that sons and daughters born in Jerusalem would die when the sword of judgment fell.

I come away from Jeremiah impressed with the value of a sensitive heart toward God. In fifty years of hard, fruitless labor, without one convert, Jeremiah never allowed his heart to become hard. When Jerusalem fell and his people were chained together like animals to be led away, Jeremiah did not say, "See, I told you so!" Instead, he wept.

We shouldn't be surprised that six hundred years later when Jesus came on the scene and people saw how he was moved with compassion for them, some identified Jesus as another Jeremiah.

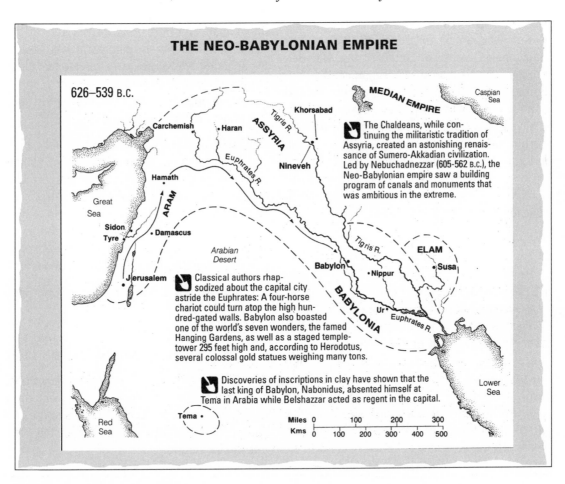

THE NEO-BABYLONIAN EMPIRE

626–539 B.C.

MEDIAN EMPIRE

The Chaldeans, while continuing the militaristic tradition of Assyria, created an astonishing renaissance of Sumero-Akkadian civilization. Led by Nebuchadnezzar (605-562 B.C.), the Neo-Babylonian empire saw a building program of canals and monuments that was ambitious in the extreme.

Classical authors rhapsodized about the capital city astride the Euphrates: A four-horse chariot could turn atop the high hundred-gated walls. Babylon also boasted one of the world's seven wonders, the famed Hanging Gardens, as well as a staged temple-tower 295 feet high and, according to Herodotus, several colossal gold statues weighing many tons.

Discoveries of inscriptions in clay have shown that the last king of Babylon, Nabonidus, absented himself at Tema in Arabia while Belshazzar acted as regent in the capital.

PEOPLE of the BiBLE

THE BABYLONIANS

The area of the Fertile Crescent between the Tigris and Euphrates rivers (in modern-day Iraq) was the home to several powerful ancient empires. The first empire to have direct impact on the people of Israel was the Assyrian Empire (745–626 B.C.; see p. 252 for more on the Assyrians). The Assyrians were the ones who conquered the northern division of the Israelite kingdom in 722 B.C. and scattered the Israelites throughout the vast Assyrian territory.

When Assyrian power began to decline, the Babylonians who lived south of the Assyrian heartland rose up against Assyrian control. The Babylonians had a long history of power and control in the region, and they deeply resented the cruel oversight of the Assyrians. The Babylonians were not content simply with their own independence. They wanted the Assyrian Empire destroyed—and they did it! They chased the Assyrian army into the farthest reaches of the Middle East.

Then the Babylonians proceeded to reconquer all the territory previously held by Assyria and more. They ruled the largest empire that part of the world had ever seen. Their empire, however, lasted less than a hundred years. In 539 B.C. stronger armies from the east swept over the Babylonian Empire. The new rulers were a coalition of the Medes (who lived north and east of Babylon) and the Persians (who lived east of Babylon). They would be the new kids on the block until Alexander the Great swept in from the west two hundred years later.

The religion of the Babylonians consisted of the worship of many gods in a confusing arrangement of names and relationships. The main deities were Bel (also called Marduk) and his wife, Ishtar. Other gods were Ea (lord of the deep water), Sin (the moon god), and Anu (god of the heavens). Babylonian gods were sexual beings who married, raised families, and were vulnerable to injury and even death. Human beings were created to relieve the gods of the burden of physical labor and to care for the gods through sacrifice and ritual.

Babylonian literature was composed in the Akkadian language and had wide influence in the ancient Middle East. Creation stories, Flood stories, wisdom literature, and historical chronicles have been recovered and translated from Babylonian texts.

The Babylonian Empire had its most direct effect on the Israelite people when the nation of Judah was conquered by King Nebuchadnezzar. Ultimately, thousands of Judahites were taken into exile in Babylon. A few returned to the Jewish homeland after the captivity was ended, but a large Jewish population remained and prospered around Babylon for hundreds of years.

For more on the Babylonians, check your local library:

Harry W. F. Saggs, *The Greatness That Was Babylon*, rev. ed. (New York: St. Martin's, 1991).

The Epic of Gilgamesh is a well-known hero story that includes an account of a great flood. Gilgamesh is from the Old Babylonian era (18th century B.C.). It was still around in the Neo-Babylonian period.

Lamentations

➤ Find out how people feel when they lose everything.

➤ Listen as God weeps for his disobedient people.

The book of Lamentations is a series of five "laments," or poems of grief, that Jeremiah wrote as he looked over the destroyed city of Jerusalem. It's a book filled with terror, loneliness, and tears. But if all you see is Jeremiah crying in this book, you have missed the point. Jeremiah's tears are a reflection of God's tears. God grieves over the disobedience of his children. Even when God brings correction to his own people, when the inevitable consequences of rebellion fall, God's heart is broken.

This book is in the Bible for another reason. It's here as a warning sign, surrounded by flashing lights. We all come to decisions in life that are like a fork in the road. One direction is our own way; the other direction is God's way—but God's way is uphill! More effort, greater sacrifice, and deeper commitment are required on God's path. Our own way, on the other hand, looks easier and more logical. But there is an end to our own path called consequences. The book of Lamentations stands at the fork in the road and says, "Stop! Listen to my words. The end of God's road is blessing; the end of your own way is bitterness." Maybe that's why this book is one of the least read books of Scripture—and maybe that's why some of our lives are in such a mess.

The Weeping Prophet

Nowhere in the book is Jeremiah the prophet named as the author, but there are several parallels between Jeremiah's prophecies and the poems in Lamentations. Furthermore, Jeremiah was an eyewitness of the destruction of the city of Jerusalem by the Babylonian army. He saw it all! The vividness and passion that pervade the book are indications of Jeremiah's authorship.

Jeremiah had warned the people in Jerusalem for years that God was going to bring crushing judgment on them if they did not repent and turn back to the Lord. Just as God promised, the Babylonian army under Nebuchadnezzar swept down on this rebellious nation and crushed them. God used a pagan nation as the instrument of his judgment on a people who would not listen, and now everything they held dear was gone. Their houses were destroyed, their children were slaughtered, their temple was burned, and their city was a pile of rubble. Jeremiah was left to kick through the rubble. As he walked over the streets filled with bodies and broken possessions, he cried—and God in heaven wept along with him.

In a temporary lean-to made out of pieces of wood and a few old sheets, Jeremiah sat down and wrote a journal called "Sobbings"— known to us as Lamentations.

Hearing the Voices

In each chapter the prophet adopted a different perspective, or "voice." In chapter 1 the city of Jerusalem seems to speak.

> How deserted lies the city,
> once so full of people! . . .

> Bitterly she weeps at night,
> tears are upon her cheeks. . . .

> Jerusalem has sinned greatly
> and so has become unclean. . . .
> she herself groans
> and turns away. (1:1, 2, 8)

DiggiNG DeEpeR

✗ Harrison, R. K. *Jeremiah and Lamentations.* Tyndale Old Testament Commentary series. Downers Grove, IL: InterVarsity Press, 1973.

A commentary on each section of the book.

☑ Lamentations is a series of poems expressing grief over the destruction of Jerusalem—and over the consequences that come from disobedience to God.

☑ When you make life decisions, be sure to look at the end result of each option. The path that seems best may not be the path that honors God. Lamentations reminds us that disobedience always brings disaster.

☑ God's faithfulness never fails. Each new day is a reminder of the limitless depths of his love and compassion.

In chapter 2 the Lord is the focus of Jeremiah's cry.

> How the LORD has covered the Daughter of Zion
>   with the cloud of his anger!
> He has hurled down the splendor of Israel
>   from heaven to earth. . . .

> The LORD determined to tear down
>   the wall around the Daughter of Zion. (2:1, 8)

God is pictured in some pretty shocking images in this chapter.

> Like an enemy he has strung his bow;
>   his right hand is ready.
> Like a foe he has slain
>   all who were pleasing to the eye. . . .

> The LORD is like an enemy. (2:4–5)

God in mercy warned Jerusalem about the inevitable consequences of their disobedience to him. He pleaded with them to return to him, and they refused. Now the Lord had become their enemy. The Babylonian army simply carried out the judgment God had determined.

Jeremiah was the "voice" of chapter 3. He spoke of God's judgment from a very personal perspective.

> I am the man who has seen affliction. (3:1)

In spite of Jeremiah's obedience to God, he tasted the same bitter judgment as the people who had ignored God. Sometimes we are caught in the backwash of the failure and disobedience of others! Jeremiah was willing to identify himself with his sinful congregation.

> Let us examine our ways and test them,
>   and let us return to the LORD.

SOBBING IN THE SYNAGOGUE

Orthodox Jews read the entire book of Lamentations out loud on the ninth day of the Jewish month of Ab, the traditional date of the destruction of the temple in 586 B.C. The day also commemorates the destruction of the second temple by the armies of Rome in A.D. 70. Some Jews living (or visiting) in Israel also read the book every week at the Western Wall, the last remnants of the temple foundation. The area is known as the "Wailing Wall" because Jews go there to express their sorrow over the destruction of their temple and to pray for a restoration of Israel's glory.

Lamentations is also read as part of the traditional Roman Catholic liturgy during the last three days of Holy Week (the week leading up to Easter Sunday). Christians have seen the suffering of Jesus prefigured in Jeremiah's sorrows. One of the best-known verses from Lamentations is applied by Christians to the abandonment Jesus must have experienced when he was crucified.

> "Is it nothing to you, all you who
> pass by?
> Look around and see.
> Is any suffering like my suffering
> that was inflicted on me,
> that the LORD brought on me
> in the day of his fierce anger?"
> (1:12)

Let us lift up our hearts and our hands
   to God in heaven, and say:
"We have sinned and rebelled
   and you have not forgiven." (3:40–42)

In chapter 4 the homes, possessions, and children of the people seem to speak. What was once a source of pride now lies destroyed.

How the gold has lost its luster. . . .
The children beg for bread. . . .
Those killed by the sword are better off
   than those who die of famine. (4:1, 4, 9)

The last poem in the book echoes the cries of the captives as they are marched off to Babylon in chains. They turned now to the Lord, but it was too late.

Remember, O LORD, what has happened to us;
    look, and see our disgrace. . . .
Joy is gone from our hearts;
    our dancing has turned to mourning.
The crown has fallen from our head.
    Woe to us, for we have sinned! (5:1, 15–16)

HELP FiLE

AN ACROSTIC POEM

Four of the five poems that make up Lamentations (chapters 1–4) have a very interesting structure. In the original Hebrew text, each line or each verse begins with a different Hebrew letter in the order of the Hebrew alphabet. Since there are twenty-two letters in the Hebrew alphabet, chapter 1, for example, has twenty-two verses. A poem structured according to the letters of the alphabet is called an "acrostic" poem. Chapters 2 and 4 are structured the same way—the twenty-two letters of the alphabet begin the twenty-two verses of each chapter.

Chapter 3 is a little different. It is still an acrostic poem, but three lines are given to each letter of the alphabet—verses 1, 2, and 3 all begin with the first letter in the Hebrew alphabet, the next three verses with the second letter, and so on. Twenty-two letters multiplied by three lines each gives a total of sixty-six

verses. Even though the poems are filled with strong passion, the structure shows that they were carefully and skillfully woven together. The unique structure was the author's way of demonstrating that he had exhausted all the possible ways of expressing his grief.

Chapter 5 also has twenty-two verses, but it is not an acrostic.

In the Hebrew Bible, Lamentations is found in the section the Jews call the "Writings"; it is located between the books of Ruth and Ecclesiastes.

Other laments can be found in the Psalms (Psalms 44, 80, and 88, for example), in the prophecies of Isaiah (10:1–4; 22:1–13) and Malachi (2:10–16), and even in the cry of Jesus over his rejection by his own people (Matthew 23:37–39). Lamentations is the only biblical book composed totally of laments.

God's Great Faithfulness

In spite of Judah's failure and in the middle of dreadful consequences, God's grace continued to reach out to those who had
turned away from him. In the middle of chapter 3, at the depths of
Jeremiah's own despair, we find some of the most wonderful
promises in Scripture.

> Yet this I call to mind
>   and therefore I have hope:
>
> Because of the LORD's great love we are not consumed,
>   for his compassions never fail.
> They are new every morning;
>   great is your faithfulness. . . .
>
> The LORD is good to those whose hope is in him,
>   to the one who seeks him. . . .
> Though he brings grief, he will show compassion,
>   so great is his unfailing love. (3:21–23, 25, 32)

At the lowest point in his life, Jeremiah focused on truth about God
that he had learned long before. Since God's character never
changes, Jeremiah's confident hope was that ultimately God would
bring good to his people out of incredible tragedy. That's the way
God is! He can take the worst disaster and our greatest failures and
bring good from them. But he waits until we return to him with a
broken heart and a spirit ready to follow him fully. The consequences
of our disobedience may still flood over us, but we are not alone. Our
loving Father followed us as we walked away, and now he holds on to
us through the storm.

Walking the Walk

1. As you read the book of Lamentations, keep in mind the perspective, or voice, of each chapter. Look for images or pictures of God that may give you a different view of his character. (Some of the images may make you a little uncomfortable!)

2. Carve out some time for quiet reflection on your own life. Are there specific areas of disobedience to God in your daily routine or in a relationship or even in your thought life? What temptations are you most vulnerable to follow? What steps can you take to strengthen areas of weakness?

3. Write out the promises of God's compassion from Lamentations 3 (especially verses 21–23, 25, and 32) and put them where they will be a reminder of God's unfailing love. Put a copy in the place where you tend to doubt God's love and care for you—on the dashboard of your car, next to your bed, inside your checkbook.

Ezekiel

— **Heads Up** —

➤ Get ready for some weird visions!
➤ Find out what God was saying to his captive people in Babylon.
➤ Come face-to-face with a prophet who came face-to-face with God.

Ezekiel was a fascinating man who wrote a fascinating book filled with strange visions. Ezekiel was a powerful preacher, a creative communicator, and a man carried away in visions of God. He seems a little eccentric, but he is worth the time and effort to get to know. Ezekiel, like no other prophet, saw deeply into God's character. When reading his book, we get a glimpse into the awesome majesty of the Lord.

The Horrible History

Ezekiel was born in Judah into a family of priests. At age twenty he began the ten-year training period required of priests of the Lord. He looked forward to the day when he would serve in the temple, leading God's people in worship. But Ezekiel's graduation never came. In 597 B.C., when Ezekiel was twenty-five years old, he was taken as an exile to Babylon.

Key Characters

Ezekiel: a *priest* who was taken as a *prisoner* to Babylon and who was then chosen to be a *prophet* of God

Nebuchadnezzar: Babylonian general/emperor who attacked and finally destroyed the city of Jerusalem

There were three deportations of Jews to Babylon. The first was in 605 B.C. when King Nebuchadnezzar, the Babylonian emperor, first brought Judah under Babylonian control. All Nebuchadnezzar took was a pledge of loyalty from the king, some gold and silver to replenish his treasury, and a handful of young men from the royal families of Judah. Daniel was one of the men taken to Babylon on that occasion. The plan was to train these men in the ways of Babylon and then to send them back as rulers over their own people.

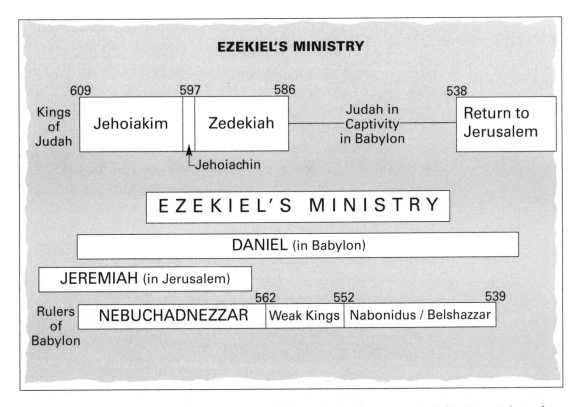

EZEKIEL'S MINISTRY

| Kings of Judah | 609 Jehoiakim | 597 Zedekiah | 586 Judah in Captivity in Babylon | 538 Return to Jerusalem |

Jehoiachin

E Z E K I E L ' S   M I N I S T R Y

DANIEL (in Babylon)

JEREMIAH (in Jerusalem)

| Rulers of Babylon | NEBUCHADNEZZAR | 562 Weak Kings | 552 Nabonidus / Belshazzar | 539 |

A few years after the initial conquest, however, Judah's King Jehoiachin rebelled against Babylonian authority. The armies of Nebuchadnezzar came to Jerusalem a second time, and the toll was heavier. Ten thousand Jews, all the prominent political and religious leaders and their families, were marched off to Babylon. King Jehoiachin was taken too, and his uncle, Zedekiah, was appointed king in his place. Among the ten thousand captives was a family of priests that included Ezekiel. His last glimpse of the temple was over his shoulder as he started the seven-hundred-mile walk to the place of exile.

The final blow to Jerusalem came in 586 B.C. Rebellion raised its fist once more in Judah, but this time Nebuchadnezzar had no pity. God's prophet Jeremiah recorded the final disaster in the poems of Lamentations.

When Ezekiel and the others reached Babylon, they were settled in an area south of the capital city on an irrigation canal called the Kebar River. They had to build homes, cultivate the land for food, and work to survive. Some of the Jews found it hard to settle in. They were confident that God would miraculously defeat the Babylonians and allow them to return to Jerusalem. They waited—but no deliverance came. Months stretched into years, and the city of the exiles became home.

Five long years after his deportation, God called Ezekiel to be a prophet. Ezekiel was thirty years old, the exact age when a priest entered into temple ministry. But Ezekiel never had that opportunity. Still, God gave him the privilege—and the burden—of speaking God's message. While Daniel spoke to the Babylonian rulers in the palace and Jeremiah spoke to the people still in Jerusalem, Ezekiel spoke to the exiles who sat waiting for a miracle of deliverance.

"Hear the Word of the LORD"

God's appointment of Ezekiel came through a vision and a voice. As Ezekiel looked out over the Babylonian plain one day, he saw a powerful windstorm sweeping down from the north. At least it looked like a storm. Actually it was an unfolding vision of the chariot throne of God carried by mighty angels and surrounded by brilliant light. Ezekiel could hardly find words to describe what he saw.

> This was the appearance of the likeness of the glory of the LORD. (1:28)

HELP FILE

A MAN OF PARABLES

Ezekiel, along with the other exiles from Judah, lived in a place called Tel Abib by the Kebar River (or canal), about fifty miles southeast of the modern-day city of Babylon in Iraq (1:1; 3:15).

Ezekiel (like the prophets Jeremiah and Zechariah) was both a priest (by birth) and a prophet (by God's appointment).

Ezekiel used parables or extended allegories much like Jesus in the New Testament. Ezekiel's seven parables:

A fruitless vine (15:1–8)
The adopted infant girl who becomes a prostitute (16)
Two eagles (17:1–21)
A tender branch (17:22–24)
The lioness and her cubs (19:1–9)
Two immoral sisters (23)
The cooking pot (24:1–14)

A shrine survives in Iraq at a place called al-Kifl, not far from the ruins of the ancient city of Babylon, which is tradiionally identified as the tomb of Ezekiel.

Ezekiel's response when confronted with the awesome majesty of God was to fall on his face. Then he heard God's voice: "Son of man [God's favorite description of Ezekiel], stand up on your feet and I will speak to you" (2:1).

God's commission was sobering. This would not be a cushy job!

> "Son of man, I am sending you to the Israelites, to a rebellious nation that has rebelled against me; they and their fathers have been in revolt against me to this very day. The people to whom I am sending you are obstinate and stubborn. Say to them, 'This is what the Sovereign LORD says.' And whether they listen or fail to listen—for they are a rebellious house—they will know that a prophet has been among them. And you, son of man, do not be afraid of them or their words. Do not be afraid, though briers and thorns are all around you and you live among scorpions. Do not be afraid of what they say or terrified by them, though they are a rebellious house. You must speak my words to them, whether they listen or fail to listen, for they are rebellious." (2:3–7)

"Speak to the People"

Ezekiel communicated God's message to the exiles in Babylon in several ways. Most of the time he simply spoke God's word. God made Ezekiel as hard and as stubborn in speaking the message as the people were in resisting the message. He never backed down; he never retreated.

Ezekiel also communicated to his people through symbolic actions—an early example of a drama ministry! On one occasion God told Ezekiel to take a brick, draw an outline of the city of Jerusalem on it, then crawl across the ground and attack it (4:1–3). What the prophet did was a "sign" to the people. When they said, "Ezekiel, what are you doing?" he said, "God will allow the city of Jerusalem to be attacked and destroyed. Give up your false hopes of miraculous protection."

On another day Ezekiel stood in the center of the marketplace and shaved his head and his beard. (Imagine doing that during lunch hour on Wall Street!) Using a scale,

ESSENTIAL READING

The glory of the Lord (1)
Ezekiel's call from God (2:1–3:15)
An allegory of God's unfaithful people (16)
God's diagnosis of a crumbling society (22)
The restoration of Israel (36)
Valley of dry bones (37:1–14)

Points 2 Remember

☑ Ezekiel spoke God's message to the Jewish exiles in Babylon before, during, and after the destruction of Jerusalem by the armies of Nebuchadnezzar in 586 B.C.

☑ Ezekiel had a profound awareness of the awesome character and glorious majesty of God. He also had a very sharp sense of the importance of human responsibility before God. A person's choice or a nation's choice to serve God or to ignore God will be respected, but the consequences of that decision will stand.

☑ God still seeks courageous people who will speak his truth whether the people around them will listen or not.

Ezekiel divided the shaved hair into thirds—one-third he set on fire, one-third he chopped up with a sword, and one third he threw into the wind. Then he picked up a few stray hairs and tied them in his robe. When people watching him asked, "What now, Ezekiel? Why are you doing this?" Ezekiel responded, "God will destroy Jerusalem. A third of the people will die from sickness or famine inside the walls; another third will die by the sword outside the walls; and the remaining third will be scattered to the wind. But a few, a remnant, will be preserved by God's power alone" (see 5:1–17).

Ezekiel's personal life was a vehicle for God's message too. If you think being a prophet of God was easy or glamorous, imagine yourself in this situation.

The word of the LORD came to me: "Son of man, with one blow I am about to take away from you the delight of your eyes. Yet do not lament or weep or shed any tears. Groan quietly; do not mourn for the dead. Keep your turban fastened and your sandals on your feet; do not cover the lower part of your face or eat the customary food of mourners."

So I spoke to the people in the morning, and in the evening my wife died. The next morning I did as I had been commanded. (24:15–18)

God allowed Ezekiel's wife to die! The next day Ezekiel went about his business as usual. Friends and neighbors said, "Ezekiel, have you lost it? You should be crying. You should be down at the funeral home." Ezekiel looked into their shocked faces and said, "God will allow Jerusalem and the temple to be destroyed, and you won't even know it is happening. Your sons and daughters left behind in Jerusalem will die, and you won't mourn. But when the tragic news finally makes its way to us, you will know that God is the Sovereign LORD. He is in control of his world, and he does what he purposes to do" (see 24:20–24).

"This Is What the Sovereign LORD Says"

Ezekiel's book centers on the final attack and ultimate destruction of the city of Jerusalem. He had one message before the city was attacked, another message during the actual siege, and a final message after the city fell.

Before the Attack (Ezekiel 1 – 24; 592 – 586 B.C.)

Jerusalem was crushed in 586 B.C.—eleven years after Ezekiel came to Babylon and six years after his ministry began. His message for six years to the exiles was "Jerusalem will fall." He said it, he acted it out, he did everything he could to convince the exiles of the certainty of God's judgment.

The exiles in Babylon were saying exactly what the people back in Judah were saying to the prophet Jeremiah. They thought it would never happen. They were convinced that God would never let his temple fall into the hands of outsiders. In fact, they were persuaded that God would soon bring all the exiles back to Jerusalem and that Judah's golden age of glory would return! But Ezekiel kept saying, "No, God will crush the city, and the Babylonians will be his instrument to do it."

Digging Deeper

✗ Craigie, Peter. *Ezekiel*. Daily Study Bible series. Philadelphia: Westminster, 1983.

One of the best study guides in this series. A reliable and helpful explanation of Ezekiel's book.

✗ Taylor, John. *Ezekiel*. Tyndale Old Testament Commentary series. Downers Grove, IL: InterVarsity Press, 1969.

A good tool for understanding a difficult biblical book.

As for the temple, God had given Ezekiel a vision showing him that God had removed his presence and special protection from the temple (chapters 8–11). Because the people had abandoned the Lord, the Lord now abandoned them. The temple was just an empty building.

During the Siege (Ezekiel 33; 586 B.C.)

For the months that the city of Jerusalem was surrounded by the Babylonian army, Ezekiel did not speak about Judah or the condition of the exiles. He spoke instead against the nations surrounding Judah—Ammon, Moab, Edom, Philistia, Tyre, and Egypt. God's judgment would also fall on them for their injustice and deliberate rejection of the true God.

After the Destruction (Ezekiel 33–48; 586–570 B.C.)

On the day the Jews in Babylon heard of the final collapse and destruction of Jerusalem, Ezekiel's message changed (33:21). He packed away his sermons on God's judgment and began to preach a new message of God's restoration. The people of Judah would finally turn back to the Lord in sorrow for their rebellion, and God in grace would restore his people.

That is the meaning behind one of Ezekiel's most famous visions—the vision of the valley of dry bones (chapter 37). God showed Ezekiel a vast valley filled with bleached bones. In the vision the bones reassembled and stood! They were then covered with human flesh and armed like a powerful army. There was just one problem. The bodies had no life. So God blew his own breath, his own Spirit, over the bodies and they came to life. God's scattered, shattered people would be regathered in the same way—by God's power alone.

In the eyes of the nations around them, the people of Judah were totally insignificant—far from home, few in number, and powerless. But God would not forget his people or his promises. The people would return to Jerusalem, and some day a great and glorious King, the Lord himself, would rule over a magnificent kingdom embracing the whole world. Ezekiel's book closes with a detailed description of the Lord's temple as it will appear and function in the future kingdom (chapters 40–48). The glory of the Lord will fill that temple forever (43:4–7).

Walking the Walk

1. As you read Ezekiel's book, try to grasp the majesty and overwhelming power of his visions. Imagine yourself standing in Ezekiel's place and seeing what he saw! Think about specific ways you can instill a new sense of awe in your worship of God. Have we reduced God (in our minds and hearts) to a convenient, manageable size—or do we occasionally find ourselves humbled by his transcendent glory?

2. Ezekiel was a committed, creative communicator. He was willing to break out of traditional patterns in order to reach people with God's message. Look carefully at the opportunities you have to share God's truth. Perhaps it is with your children or as a Bible study leader. Develop one or two new techniques or approaches you can use to help others grasp God's message.

3. If you have been disobedient to God in some area of your life, you may feel as spiritually "dry" as the bones in Ezekiel's vision. Ask God to breathe new life and energy into you!

Daniel

➤ Learn how to stand for what's right when the pressure is on.

➤ Discover the secrets of a long, impacting career.

➤ See into the future to the day of God's kingdom!

Daniel is best known for spending a night in a lions' den—and living to tell about it! But Daniel was far more than a lion tamer. He spoke God's message to the world leaders of his day. He knew what it was like to be at the top of the heap; he also knew what it was like to be ignored. He was a man given the highest honors by the world around him and at the same time a man who maintained his integrity through a long and productive life. Daniel interpreted dreams, spoke with angels, and wrote history before it happened.

Key Characters

Daniel: a young man from Judah to whom God gave the ability to interpret dreams and see into the future

Shadrach, Meshach, and Abednego: Daniel's three friends who survived being thrown alive into a fire (Daniel 3)

Nebuchadnezzar: Babylonian emperor; God humbled him by allowing him to lose his mind for seven years (Daniel 4)

Belshazzar: Nebuchadnezzar's grandson who literally saw the handwriting on the wall (Daniel 5)

Darius the Mede: Persian ruler who inadvertently condemned Daniel to be thrown in a lions' den (Daniel 6)

When I Was a Young Man

Daniel was born in Judah but barely graduated from middle school before he was taken to the city of Babylon. King Nebuchadnezzar and the Babylonian armies were expanding their empire to the west, and tiny Judah was swallowed up almost without resistance. The Babylonians were fairly gracious as conquerors go, and they only took a few young men from Judah's most prominent families. They were the brightest and the best. One of them, Daniel, was about fifteen years old.

The Babylonians did everything they could to change these men from narrow-minded Judahites who worshiped the Lord God into sophisticated Babylonians who worshiped the victorious gods of Babylon. They took Daniel seven hundred

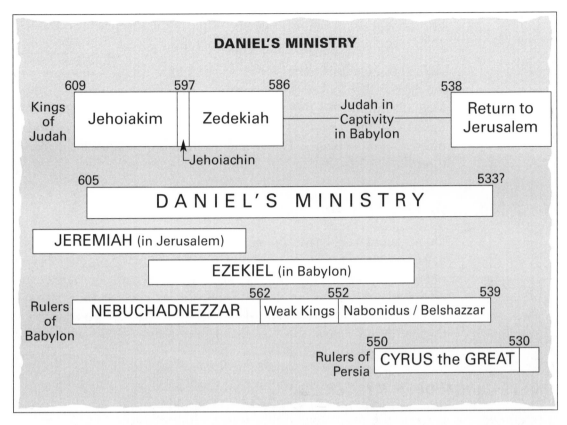

DANIEL'S MINISTRY

miles from his family and his religious community. They changed his name from Daniel (which means "God is my Judge") to Belteshazzar ("May Bel [a Babylonian god] preserve the king"). Instead of Hebrew Daniel learned to speak Akkadian. Instead of the law of God, Daniel studied the science, religion, and politics of Babylon.

It is interesting that Daniel never protested his name change or his enrollment in a pagan university or being forced to learn a new language. The crisis for Daniel came with the first meal. Undoubtedly the buffet table that first evening was spread with several foods that God's people were not allowed to eat. But there was a bigger problem than the pork chops and fried shrimp (two foods prohibited in the Old Testament under the law of Moses). The animals killed for the king's household were first offered as sacrifices to the idols of pagan gods. Daniel was convinced that if he ate the meat on the palace table, he would be participating in idolatry—and it was the continuing sin of idolatry that had brought God's judgment on his people in the first place! So Daniel, politely and with a wise alternative plan, refused to eat.

He and three of this friends asked to be given vegetables and water for ten days. If they looked thinner or sicker than those who ate the king's food, they would join them at the banquet table. If not, they could continue to eat the vegetarian plate each day. In the end, of course, God blessed their obedience. Daniel and his friends graduated at the top of their class (1:18–20).

A Mountain Out of a Molehill

I'm not sure I would have approached this situation like Daniel did. Most of us would have tried to impeach the officials who took away our religious rights or demeaned our cultural heritage. We would have demanded equal classroom time for instruction from textbooks that promoted our value system. But what was served on the dinner table or what had been done to the food ahead of time would have been of very little significance.

REVEALING HIDDEN MYSTERIES

The second half of the book of Daniel is often described as "apocalyptic" literature. The word means "unfolding" or "revealing" (from the Greek word *apokalypto*). Daniel unfolds or reveals the hidden plan of God for the future and predicts God's final triumph over the powers of evil. Apocalyptic literature also focuses on the end of time and often includes references to angels and the resurrection. Other Old Testament writers used apocalyptic elements (Isaiah 24–27; Joel; Zechariah 9–14). The longest and best-known biblical apocalypse is the New Testament book of Revelation.

In the period between the close of the Old Testament (about 400 B.C.) and the opening of the New Testament, apocalyptic literature flourished among the Jews, particularly in times of persecution or oppression. This style of literature focused on the climactic clash between good and evil and the final victory of God and of his faithful people.

We can find the same comfort from God's truth in difficult times. We may not be able to understand every detail of Daniel's prophecies or the visions in Revelation, but the overall message is very clear. God has not forgotten us! He is not sitting in heaven hoping everything will work out somehow. God is in control, and he will accomplish exactly what he desires and plans. Remember that when life comes crashing in on you!

Points 2 Remember

☑ Daniel was a spokesman for God during Judah's exile in Babylon. Daniel rose to prominence in the pagan government of Babylon and later of Persia but maintained his integrity and loyalty to God.

☑ Daniel is a model of how to survive in a society that pressures us to compromise God's truth. Daniel's highest priority was his commitment to God.

☑ Daniel received visions about Israel's future and wrote very detailed prophecies about the future of God's people.

☑ God is sovereign (the word means "in control") over human kingdoms and human affairs. He uses even wicked people to accomplish what he desires.

Daniel saw it differently. Eating food forbidden by God's law or participating in idolatry were direct violations of God's written Word—and Daniel had decided long before that first meal in Babylon that loyalty to God and obedience to God's Word would be the bedrock of his life. "Daniel resolved not to defile himself" (1:8).

Here was a fifteen-year-old boy faced with unbelievable pressure to conform to a Babylonian lifestyle, and he determined to stand true to God no matter what the cost! That's still what it takes to stand for God in a society that couldn't care less about God. That's still what it takes to stand against the world's pressure and the enemy's attacks. It takes a decision, a commitment, a settled conviction before God to live in obedience to God regardless of the cost. The path of obedience is not easy. Maintaining our integrity is incredibly hard at times. Any commitment to obedience in any area of life will be tested. But that is the challenge Daniel and Daniel's book puts before us. Where will we stand when the pressure to compromise is on—with the majority or with the few, who like Daniel, are determined to obey the Lord?

Daniel 4:17

"The Most High is sovereign over the kingdoms of men and gives them to anyone he wishes."

DownLoad

Exploring Daniel's Book

The book of Daniel divides into two sections. Chapters 1–6 are primarily biographical; chapters 7–12 are primarily prophetic. In the first section we read a summary of Daniel's life; in the second we read a record of Daniel's visions.

In chapters 1–6 you will find some of the best-known Bible stories: Daniel interpreted King Nebuchadnezzar's dream (chapter 2), Daniel's three friends survived the fiery furnace (chapter 3), a finger wrote on the palace wall predicting Babylon's downfall (chapter 5), and God protected Daniel in a den of lions (chapter 6).

Daniel lived during a time of great upheaval for the people of Judah. God performed several powerful miracles during Daniel's life to demonstrate his care and protection over his people even when they were captives far from their homeland. These events also show us that God rules over all the kingdoms of the world. It may seem to us at times that evil people have gained the upper hand, but God is the one in control. We can rest confidently in his authority and power.

The second part of Daniel's book is tougher sledding than the first part. A series of visions and prophetic messages are recorded that predict

Digging Deeper

✗ Peel, William. *Living in the Lions' Den Without Being Eaten*. Colorado Springs, CO: NavPress, 1994.

A practical explanation of Daniel's experiences and their application to life today. Focuses on Daniel 1–6.

✗ Wood, Leon. *A Commentary on Daniel*. Eugene, OR: Wipf & Stock, 1998 (reprint).

A detailed guide through Daniel's prophecies.

If you want to study the book of Daniel on your own, pick up:

✗ Connelly, Douglas. *Daniel: Spiritual Living in a Secular World*. LifeGuide Bible Study series. Downers Grove, IL: InterVarsity Press, 1984.

Daniel is one of my personal favorites!

what will happen to God's people over the next four hundred years. Most of the prophecies have been fulfilled, so they read like ancient history. But remember that they were written long before those events actually took place. Some of the prophecies have yet to be fulfilled. Daniel tells us a lot, for example, about the rise of a powerful evil ruler in the future and about the ultimate victory of God's anointed king.

Key Passages in Daniel 7 - 12

Earthly beasts and a heavenly conqueror (7:1–14)

Daniel's prayer of confession (9:1–19)

Daniel's prophecy of seventy "sevens" (9:20–27)

A future evil ruler (11:36–45)

The resurrection (12:1–4)

HELP FiLe

A LONG PUBLIC LIFE

Daniel's ministry stretched over more than seventy years — from 605 B.C. (the date of his exile to Babylon) until at least 533 B.C. (the latest date attested to in his book; 10:1). He had the longest public ministry of any prophet.

The first chapter of Daniel's book is written in Hebrew. The next six chapters are written in a related language called Aramaic. Aramaic was more widely spoken in Daniel's day, and since those chapters deal primarily with events and prophecies related to non-Jews, Aramaic was the appropriate language. The last five chapters of Daniel are directed primarily toward the Jews and are written in Hebrew.

Ezekiel, another prophet in exile in Babylon, referred to Daniel as a man whose wisdom and obedience to God put him in a class with Noah and Job (Ezekiel 14:14, 20).

No sin is recorded in Scripture in regard to Daniel. That doesn't mean he never sinned, but rather that he dealt with his personal sin quickly.

The book of Daniel is not included among the prophets in the Hebrew Bible; it is found in the section called the "Writings."

The Power of One Life

If you take the time to compare chapter 1 of Daniel with chapter 6, some fascinating facts emerge. The first chapter of Daniel describes our hero as a young man in his mid-teens; the sixth chapter describes him at the other end of his life in his mid-eighties. In both chapters the same character traits are evident. In both situations Daniel obeyed God at great personal risk. In both encounters Daniel committed himself to loyalty to God and to a life of integrity. Daniel survived more than seventy years in the ups and downs of a secular society because he made a decision as a young man to live his life to please the Lord first of all. It's never too early to make a decision like that—or too late!

You and I will seldom get what we deserve from the world around us, but God *always* rewards integrity. Daniel never became so tied to his position or to political power or to corporate influence that it made him compromise his loyalty to the one who reigned in his life as Lord.

Walking the Walk

1. As you read Daniel, think about your own culture and society. In what ways does our secular world seek to break down the commitment and integrity of good people? How have you had your integrity tested—and what was the outcome of each test?

2. Keep a record of specific lessons you can learn from Daniel and his friends about guarding your personal commitment to the Lord. Cultivate the qualities in your life that helped them survive in a pressurized secular culture.

3. What aspects of God's character are most prominent in Daniel's book? Do those character traits produce a sense of security and stability in your life or a sense of insecurity? Why?

4. If your enemies examined your personal life and your professional/work life, would they find something you would not be proud of? Could the leaders of your church or your Christian friends look through your desk or personal belongings or favorite Internet sites without finding things you might be ashamed for them to see? Integrity is not just a quality that should mark our public life. Integrity is also what we are when we are all alone.

A PICTURE OF THE FUTURE OR PIOUS FICTION?

Scholars who study the book of Daniel disagree over when the book was written. If Daniel lived at the time of Judah's exile to Babylon as he claims, he told his people what would happen to them over the next four hundred years with amazing accuracy. He predicted, for example, the rise of three great empires after Babylon's eventual collapse—and three great empires emerged as rulers over the Jews: the Persians, the Greeks, and the Romans. Daniel described the sweeping victories of Alexander the Great and the division of Alexander's empire. He even told how two Greek kings, one in Syria and one in Egypt, would fight over the Jewish homeland.

Because his prophecies were so detailed and so accurate, some scholars have concluded that the book of Daniel was actually written *after* all those events had taken place. The usual explanation is that in about 165 B.C. (450 years after Daniel was supposedly taken to Babylon) a Jew living in Palestine wanted to write a book to encourage the Jews living under the oppression of a Greek king named Antiochus Epiphanes. This king had conquered the area of Judah and had put a halt to Israel's public worship. The author of the book of Daniel simply portrayed himself as a godly man living four hundred years earlier. He told of great miracles of God's deliverance and retold the story of the Jews as if it were laid out by Daniel ahead of time. In the prophecy the wicked king, Antiochus, is destroyed, and God's kingdom ultimately replaces the evil kingdoms of this world.

According to this view, "Daniel" probably never existed. He was a heroic character created by the writer as the vehicle to tell the stories and to speak the prophecies of the book. The first readers of the book would have known that the story was fiction but would have been encouraged in difficult days by these accounts of God's power and deliverance.

Other students of Daniel's book have drawn a very different conclusion. They believe the evidence points out that a man named Daniel really existed and really lived in Babylon at the time of the exile. The accuracy of the predictions in Daniel's book comes from God's ability to know future events and to reveal those events to his prophets. Jesus believed that Daniel really existed, for he referred to "the prophet Daniel" in Matthew 24:15, and he quoted Daniel's prophecy (Daniel 7:13) as an accurate portrayal of events related to his future return to earth in glory (Mark 14:62).

THE MINOR PROPHETS

Prophet	Historical Setting		A Message to Us Today
Hosea	Before 722	Israel	God's love doesn't let go
Joel	Uncertain	Locust Plague	God restores the years destroyed by our faithlessness
Amos	765–755	Israel	God uses even the most unlikely people
Obadiah	After 586	Edom	God has the final say
Jonah	Before 750	Nineveh	We should rejoice in God's compassion and mercy to others
Micah	Before 700	Israel/Judah	God is faithful to fulfill his promises
Nahum	Before 612	Nineveh	God is a God of justice and holy anger as well as a God of love
Habakkuk	605	Rise of Babylon	Don't lose faith in the greatness and goodness of God
Zephaniah	639–629	Josiah's reforms	The God who judges can also restore
Haggai	520	New era	We should live as if God is in charge and not us
Zechariah	520	New era	There are no mistakes in God's plan
Malachi	430–410	Apathy	God holds us accountable for what we do and don't do

Hosea

➤ Read the unusual story of how a prophet's wife becomes a prostitute.

➤ Be moved by God's love for his unfaithful people.

➤ Find out how your deepest hurts can be transformed into a message of hope.

Hosea was asked by God to enter a marriage God knew would shatter. The prophet's life was a visible expression of the pain God felt when his people abandoned him for the false gods of the nations around them. But after all the tears and humiliation were over, God asked Hosea to do something so incredible we still stand amazed at it today.

Hosea's work as a prophet began with an extraordinary command from the Lord.

> When the LORD began to speak through Hosea, the LORD said to him, "Go, take to yourself an adulterous wife and children of unfaithfulness." (1:2)

Key Characters

Hosea: God's spokesman to Israel and Judah

Gomer: Hosea's unfaithful wife

Jezreel, Lo-Ruhamah, and Lo-Ammi: Gomer's children to whom God gave names that expressed his discipline of his own people; Jezreel means "God will scatter," Lo-Ruhamah means "no mercy," and Lo-Ammi means "not my people."

That command has been understood in several ways. Some students of Hosea believe that the prophet was to marry a woman who was already a prostitute. Other interpreters think that God simply had Hosea choose a woman from the immoral society of Israel in general. I am convinced that God asked Hosea to marry a woman who was not at that time a prostitute but who had a bent toward immorality. Hosea married a woman who in the future would embrace a lifestyle of adultery.

Hosea obeyed God's command. He married Gomer, and at first things went well. They had a happy home, and in time they had a child. "[Gomer] conceived and bore him a son" (1:3).

225

☑ Hosea spoke to Israel and to Judah about their spiritual departure from the Lord. As the last prophet before the northern kingdom's conquest by Assyria in 722 B.C., Hosea pleaded with his people to return to the Lord for deliverance.

☑ Hosea's marriage to an unfaithful wife pictured Israel's unfaithfulness to God. Hosea's continued love and restoration of his wife was a dramatic portrayal of God's unchanging love for Israel and his ultimate restoration of his people.

☑ God can take the scars of our lives and transform them by his love into a message of hope for the wounded people around us.

The first child was Hosea's. But soon after the birth of that son, things in Hosea's home began to change. Gomer began to leave in the afternoon or in the evening. Her talk, her looks, her clothes were different than before.

Gomer became pregnant again, but Hosea probably was not the father. Things continued to deteriorate in the marriage until Gomer no longer tried to hide her activities with other men. She gave birth to another child who was not Hosea's—and then she left. Gomer had many lovers who would pay a good price for an hour or two of her attention. Over the months and years that followed, Hosea would occasionally see Gomer on the streets or coming out of the bars. Her beauty quickly began to harden and fade. At first men sought her out, but in a few months she was the one propositioning men. Eventually Gomer simply disappeared into the underworld of the ancient city.

An Unfaithful People

Why would God put a man as faithful as Hosea through an experience like that? God tells us why in his first words to the prophet. Hosea was to marry a woman bent toward immorality "because the land is guilty of the vilest adultery in departing from the LORD" (1:2). Hosea's marriage was to be a picture of God's marriage to unfaithful Israel. God married Israel, and Israel abandoned him. They went after other gods; they committed spiritual adultery. God knows what it's like to go through the pain of a broken marriage!

Hosea came on the scene almost two hundred years after Solomon's kingdom had split in two. Hosea lived in the northern kingdom of Israel, but he spoke to both Israel in the north and Judah in the south. Both kingdoms had become strong militarily—and both kingdoms had begun to look to larger nations for political alliances. They no longer trusted in the Lord for their defense. They trusted in Egypt or in the rising Assyrian Empire for protection against their enemies. In God's eyes that was political adultery.

The people of Israel and Judah had also become spiritually corrupt. Worship centers to false gods dotted the cities and rural villages. In the minds of the people, the Lord was simply one god among many. They had become very tolerant—so tolerant that they accepted anything! Hosea spoke to his nation in the strong language of confrontation.

> Hear the word of the LORD, you Israelites,
>   because the LORD has a charge to bring
>   against you who live in the land:
> "There is no faithfulness, no love,
>   no acknowledgment of God in the land.
> There is only cursing, lying and murder,

HELP FILE

HOSEA

According to the kings listed in the first verse of the book, Hosea's ministry lasted for at least thirty years from the end of the reign of Jeroboam II in the northern kingdom of Israel (782–753 B.C.) to the early part of the reign of Hezekiah in the southern kingdom of Judah (728–687 B.C.). The majority of the prophecies in the book were spoken before the conquest of Israel by Assyria in 722 B.C.

Hosea may have fled to the southern kingdom of Judah before Israel's fall to Assyria. Many believing Israelites found refuge there (2 Chronicles 30:1–9). Hosea probably completed his writing in the south—and added some of God's warnings to the nation of Judah!

Both Hosea and the prophet Isaiah use the picture of a husband and wife to portray God's relationship to Israel (Isaiah 54:5; Hosea 2:19). In the New Testament, Christians are pictured as the bride of Jesus Christ (Ephesians 5:25–27).

> stealing and adultery;
> they break all bounds,
>   and bloodshed follows bloodshed. . . .
>
> "They will eat but not have enough;
>   they will engage in prostitution but not increase,
> because they have deserted the LORD
>   to give themselves to prostitution,
> to old wine and new,
>   which take away the understanding of my people.
> They consult a wooden idol
>   and are answered by a stick of wood.
> A spirit of prostitution leads them astray;
>   they are unfaithful to their God. . . .
> Therefore your daughters turn to prostitution
>   and your daughters-in-law to adultery." (4:1–2, 10–13)

Corruption, drunkenness, idolatry, and immorality were rampant in Israel—and Judah wasn't far behind. Men went to the pagan temples to hire prostitutes for their indulgence and found their own daughters there selling their bodies. That is the picture to keep in mind as you read Hosea's book. The prophet's marriage to an unfaithful wife is an object lesson in the unfaithfulness of God's people and the overcoming love of God.

QUICK VIEW

A. An Unfaithful Wife Loved by a Faithful Husband (1–3)

B. An Unfaithful Nation Loved by a Faithful God (4–14)
   1. The Lord's accusation (4:1–5:7)
   2. The Lord's judgment (5:8–10:15)
   3. The Lord's love (11–14)

Love Her Again

Most of us can only imagine the pain Hosea went through. Surviving the unfaithfulness of a spouse would be hard enough, but here was a man who had to live with the fact that his wife had sold herself to men repeatedly, day after day. Living with that reality, however, was not nearly as hard as doing what God told Hosea to do next.

SLAVERY IN ANCIENT ISRAEL

The Old Testament law permitted slavery. Non-Israelites could be held as slaves but were to be treated compassionately. If a slave owner mistreated or injured a slave, the slave was to be set free. An Israelite could not hold another Israelite in permanent slavery. God built provisions into the law that set slaves free on a regular basis.

The most common reason for slavery in Israel was indebtedness. If a man's debt was impossible to pay, he could sell himself (or his wife or his children) into slavery. Six years was the maximum time an Israelite could be enslaved for debt. Two other factors could also intervene: (1) a relative could pay off a man's debt and redeem him and his family from slavery or (2) he could be set free when the Year of Jubilee was celebrated (once every fifty years, during the Year of Jubilee, all Israelite slaves were set free).

Hosea's wife had abandoned her husband and could no longer earn a living as a prostitute. Her only recourse was to sell herself into slavery—until the one person she had hurt most intervened to set her free.

The main Old Testament passages on slavery are Exodus 21:2–11; Leviticus 25:39–55; and Deuteronomy 15:12–18.

> The LORD said to me, "Go, show your love to your wife again, though she is loved by another and is an adulteress. Love her as the LORD loves the Israelites, though they turn to other gods. . . ."
>
> So I bought her for fifteen shekels of silver and about a homer and a lethek of barley. (3:1–2)

Hosea did not just go out on the street and find Gomer. He went down to the back alley where worn-out women were auctioned off as slaves, and he purchased his own wife. He bought her back, took her home, and loved her again.

Hosea did that to show Israel something of the depth of the love of God. God had married Israel as a young virgin and, for a while, Israel had been faithful to God. But gradually Israel had turned away. The people of God's love had followed other gods, other lovers. Their moral strength rotted away until they found themselves in slavery. Assyria was ready to sweep down and clamp Israel in chains.

What about God in all of this? Would he cast Israel aside? That was what they deserved! To our amazement God continued to love his people with a love that refused to let them go. The day will come when God in love will buy back his people Israel and will restore them to a place of honor.

> For the Israelites will live many days without king or prince, without sacrifice or sacred stones, without ephod or idol. Afterward the Israelites will return and seek the LORD their God and David their king. They will come trembling to the LORD and to his blessings in the last days. (3:4–5)

In Love He Redeemed Us

Before we shake our heads at Israel's unfaithfulness, we need to think about ourselves. We were lost; we were headed our own way; in fact, we were up for sale in the slave market of sin—and this same God loved us. He came and paid the price of our release. He paid a price not in silver and grain but the price of his own Son. God took unlovely, wayward, unfaithful people like us and made us his own dear children. Human thought can't understand love like that. Human words can't fully explain it either. But the human heart embraces God's love, and we find ourselves transformed by its power.

Digging Deeper

✗ Kidner, Derek. *The Message of Hosea: Love to the Loveless.* The Bible Speaks Today series. Downers Grove, IL: InterVarsity Press, 1981.

A reliable guide through Hosea with good application of Hosea's message to our lives today.

Walking the Walk

1. As you read Hosea, you may sense that you are like the nation of Israel. You were found by God and loved by God, but you have begun to walk away from your love and obedience to God. Compromise, areas of disobedience, sinful entanglements have pulled you away from your commitment to the Lord. If you turn back to the Lord in repentance and obedience, you will find that God will graciously restore you. His love for you has never wavered.

2. On the other hand, you may feel like Hosea. You have been wounded or wronged by your mate or by a friend. The greatest temptation in that situation is to pull back in anger and bitterness or revenge. Hosea, however, took the deepest hurt of his life and made it a message of hope to the scarred and hurting people around him. God can do the same in your life! He can surround you with his love and then release you to have a ministry to those around you who are hurting.

3. Hosea's story prompts a response in us of deep humility and gratitude to God for his great love for us. Spend some time in worship to the Lord and express the thankfulness you feel in your heart to him. Act out your gratitude by obeying what God tells you to do.

Joel

— **Heads Up** —

➤ "The locusts are coming!"
➤ Listen to a man whose job was to make comfortable people uncomfortable.
➤ Explore the future day of the Lord.

God spoke to the prophet Joel at a time of crisis in Israel. The land had been invaded by a massive army—not of soldiers but of insects. Millions of locusts had blackened the sky and then stripped the earth of its vegetation. The resulting plague was so widespread and devastating that every aspect of the nation's life was threatened. Economic, political, social, even religious life ground to a halt.

God told Joel that these insects were agents of the Lord carrying out the work of judgment on a disobedient nation. The plague was designed by God to get his people to wake up. That is still Joel's message to God's people! Sometimes God uses calamity to communicate with his people. What you are going through right now in your life or in your home may be God knocking at the door, trying to get your attention.

Afflicting the Comfortable

The people to whom Joel spoke had not sunk into the deep moral decay that sometimes characterized the nation of Israel. When Joel looked out at his society, he saw complacency, not corruption. The people had taken their eyes off the Lord and had begun to focus only on themselves. Their equivalent of new toys, the hottest investments, a bigger screen television had become their consuming pursuits.

God sent the locusts to a nation steeped in comfort and spiritual apathy. As destructive as they were, the locusts were really the instruments of God's love. He loved his people too much to let them continue in their carelessness. The locusts were also just a small taste of the crushing

Points 2 Remember

☑ Joel was a prophet of God who spoke to God's people in a crisis. The invasion of locusts was not just a piece of bad luck; the insects were the agents of the Lord to get Israel's attention.

☑ Calamity and hardship teach us dramatic truths about God that we can learn in no other way.

☑ When God restores the person who has gone through difficulty, he does it abundantly. He repays the years eaten by the "locusts" of failure and disobedience with forgiveness and new opportunities.

judgment that would come if they simply continued on in the same direction.

The situation with many of God's people today is exactly the same. Christians are not corrupt, just complacent and comfortable. We are consumed by our rush for more of the things we already have. God may send calamity into our lives for exactly the same reason he sent the locusts to Israel—to get us to listen to his voice. The tragedy is that often we don't listen even when God's correction comes.

Lessons Learned from a Locust Plague

Joel points out several lessons that God wanted his people to learn as they tried to scrape together enough food each day to survive. He wanted them to learn, first of all, that material blessings are a gift from the Lord. He prospers us so we will thank him, not so we will greedily try to get even more. Joel called the people and the religious leaders to repent and to make a radical change in their lives.

> Declare a holy fast;
>   call a sacred assembly.
> Summon the elders
>   and all who live in the land
> to the house of the LORD your God,
>   and cry out to the LORD. (1:14)

Repentance from the people would be met with an outpouring of mercy from God. That's a second lesson Joel wanted his people to learn. God is not sitting in heaven with a club. God is eager to forgive.

"Even now," declares the LORD,
"return to me with all your heart,
with fasting and weeping and mourning."
Rend your heart
and not your garments.
Return to the LORD your God,
for he is gracious and compassionate,
slow to anger and abounding in love,
and he relents from sending calamity. (2:12–13)

That description of God's character is repeated at least nine times in the Old Testament. God wants us to remember it when things around us collapse.

The Day of the Lord

Joel's main message to his people stretched far beyond the days of the locust plague to a day yet to come. Joel said, "If you thought the locust invasion was devastating, wait until you hear about the day of the Lord. The invading army on *that* day will be powerful angels of the Lord!"

HELP FILE

A FAMILIAR NAME

Fourteen different people in the Old Testament have the name Joel (which means "the Lord is God"). The prophet Joel is mentioned only in his own book and in the New Testament book of Acts (Acts 2:16).

The book contains no historical reference point like the reign of a king or a particular battle. Some scholars date the book in the ninth century B.C. (about the time of Judah's King Joash [835–796]); others date it as late as the sixth century B.C., after the time of the exile in Babylon. Joel's message is timeless and is not seriously affected by the date of its original writing.

Joel spoke of beating plowshares into swords in preparation for a great battle (3:10); Isaiah reversed the imagery ("they will beat their swords into plowshares") as a picture of peace in God's kingdom (Isaiah 2:4).

BUGS IN THE BIBLE

The book of Joel is not the only place in the Bible where insects play a prominent role. Three of the plagues God brought on the Egyptians to secure the release of Israel from slavery involved swarms of insects— gnats (Exodus 8:16–19), biting flies (Exodus 8:20–32), and locusts (Exodus 10:3–15). God may have sent hornets into areas of Canaan to drive out the inhabitants ahead of the people of Israel (Deuteronomy 7:20; Joshua 24:12). When a vine grew up to shelter the prophet Jonah, God sent a worm (or caterpillar) to cut the vine down and to reveal the shallow self-centeredness of his prophet (Jonah 4:7). The New Testament prophet John the Baptist relied on insects for his "wilderness diet" of locusts and honey (Matthew 3:4). In the book of Revelation evil creatures (perhaps evil angels) are pictured as a swarm of locusts who torment humanity before Jesus' return to earth (Revelation 9:3–11).

Blow the trumpet in Zion;
　　sound the alarm on my holy hill.
Let all who live in the land tremble,
　　for the day of the LORD is coming.
It is close at hand—
　　a day of darkness and gloom,
　　a day of clouds and blackness.
Like dawn spreading across the mountains
　　a large and mighty army comes,
such as never was of old
　　nor ever will be in ages to come.

Before them fire devours,
　　behind them a flame blazes.
Before them the land is like the garden of Eden,
　　behind them, a desert waste—
　　nothing escapes them. . . .

Before them the earth shakes,
　　the sky trembles,
the sun and moon are darkened,
　　and the stars no longer shine.
The LORD thunders
　　at the head of his army;

his forces are beyond number,
    and mighty are those who obey his command.
The day of the Lord is great;
    it is dreadful.
    Who can endure it? (2:1–3, 10–11)

"The day of the Lord" is a term often used in the Old Testament to refer to a time when God powerfully visits his people or his world. It is used most often to refer to the final period of God's program, the wrap-up of human history. The prophets saw that day coming. It would be an era marked by devastating judgment on one hand and by incredible blessing on the other. The people of Jerusalem and Judah to whom Joel spoke thought they would get all the blessing and the nations around them would get all the judgment. Joel shakes them awake by announcing that judgment will come on unfaithful Judah as well!

God will bless some—those who follow the Lord in obedience. They will inherit a magnificent kingdom of peace and justice.

The Lord will roar from Zion
    and thunder from Jerusalem;
    the earth and the sky will tremble.
But the Lord will be a refuge for his people,
    a stronghold for the people of Israel. (3:16)

DiggiNG DeEpeR

✗ Hubbard, David Allan. "Joel." *Joel and Amos.* Tyndale Old Testament Commentary series. Downers Grove, IL: InterVarsity Press, 1989.

An excellent detailed explanation of Joel's book.

"I Will Repay You"

The lingering lesson from the locust plague comes to us as one of the greatest promises of hope found in the Bible.

"I will repay you for the years the locusts have eaten. . . .
You will have plenty to eat, until you are full,
    and you will praise the name of the Lord your God,
    who has worked wonders for you;

> never again will my people be shamed.
> Then you will know that I am in Israel,
>   that I am the LORD your God,
>   and that there is no other." (2:25–27)

When we return to the Lord from our complacency and disobedience, he not only receives us in mercy, he also restores the years destroyed by our faithlessness. As far as we know, the people of Joel's day repented and were spared further chastening. What happens in our lives depends on the decision we make today.

Walking the Walk

1. Review the last year of your life and think about any times of difficulty or pain. Did you consider at the time that God may have been using the difficulty to speak to you? How did you respond to the painful experience?

2. How can you communicate Joel's message to a friend who is going through a devastating experience? If you have a friend in that situation, ask God for wisdom to know the right time and to have the right words to speak to him or her.

3. Analyze your personal goals and desires. Are they focused first of all on honoring the Lord—or are they focused on your own comfort and advancement? Take the time to reformulate your goals to give the Lord the primary place, and then begin to pursue these new goals with the same (or greater) enthusiasm.

Amos

➤ Find out what God thinks of a society that focuses only on money.

➤ See that you don't have to have a theology degree to call a nation back to God.

➤ Face up to what God wants *you* to do for him.

While Amos was watching a flock of sheep, God called him to be a prophet. His resumé I was not very impressive, but he had a heart that burned with loyalty toward God.

Amos had not gone to theological seminary or Bible college. He was heavy into agriculture. He was a shepherd (1:1) and a caretaker of sycamore fig trees (7:14). It may have been his specialized skill of nurturing commercially valuable fig trees that drew Amos out of the country life in Judah and into the surrounding nations. As he carried out his work, Amos observed the injustice and idolatry that permeated the cultures around him. His conscience was stung as he saw the prosperity of his own people and the accompanying lack of obedience to the Lord.

Amos even may have prayed as he worked that God would do something to bring his people back to a life of faith and commitment to the law. God finally did do something, but it wasn't what Amos expected. God made him part of the answer to his own prayer! The Lord took this man from his flocks and his fig trees and thrust him out with a message of warning to people standing on the brink of judgment.

Key Characters

Amos: a shepherd, fig farmer—and prophet of God

Amaziah: a false priest who tried to chase Amos out of town (Amos 7:10–17)

The Farmer Prophet

We don't know anything about Amos's family because he is not mentioned anywhere else in the Bible. He had a relatively short prophetic career (765–755 B.C.) and then dropped out of sight. Amos came from the town of Tekoa, a village

Points 2 Remember

☑ Amos was a shepherd and fig farmer who became an outspoken defender of personal integrity and social justice.

☑ Amos lived in Judah but proclaimed God's word to all the nations around and especially to Judah's northern sister nation, Israel.

☑ God is far more interested in the purity and obedience of our hearts than he is in the academic and professional credentials on our resumés.

about ten miles south of Jerusalem, that could be considered back country—like rural North Dakota—not the kind of place you would expect to find a prophet. But God seems to prefer to use people who don't have much of a claim to prominence in the world's eyes. The Lord scans hearts, not credentials. In Amos's heart he found loyalty—and enough courage to be God's spokesman.

Even though Amos lived in the southern kingdom of Judah, most of his work was carried out in the northern kingdom of Israel. He walked into the prosperous urban centers, found his way to the largest churches, and stood in front of the leaders of the most influential denominations. When he was asked about his religious degrees and ministerial credentials, Amos said, "The LORD took me from my farming operation and said, 'Go, prophesy.' So—hear the word of the LORD!" (7:15–16, my paraphrase).

The Lord Roars

Amos's message was developed and delivered in three ways—through his burdens, his sermons, and his visions.

Burdens (Amos 1–2)

In the first section of his book, Amos presented his heavy messages ("burdens") to the nations all around him: to Syria, Philistia, Phoenicia, Edom, Ammon, and Moab, and finally to God's own people in Judah and in Israel. Every message of judgment was preceded by this phrase: "For three transgressions . . . and for four." Amos exposed the sin and injustice of each nation in turn. It was as if he were in court arraigning criminals for trial. He told about the deportations of Israelites by the Philistines and their sale as slaves (1:6). He revealed how the Ammonites had ripped open pregnant women in Gilead (1:13). Three sins of this magnitude were enough to bring God's judgment; the fourth pushed these nations over the edge.

The people of Israel and Judah probably applauded the judgment of God on the nations around them, but their joy turned to shock when they heard their own names mentioned in the same breath. Among Judah's many sins was that they had "rejected the law of the LORD" and had "been led astray by false gods" (2:4). On Israel's rap sheet were the sins of selling the needy for a pair of hot new footwear and trampling over the poor to gain financial advantage (2:6–7).

God would bring down the fire of his judgment on each of these nations. If he didn't, if he let them keep on sinning against him, his holy character would be compromised.

Walking the Walk

1. After reading chapters 1 and 2 of Amos, compose a message that Amos might deliver to our society and our nation. What specific issues disturb your conscience? What steps can you take to address those issues in our culture?

2. Examine the excuses you have used for not defending justice and truth in your workplace or even among your friends. How far are you willing to go to stand for what is right before God?

Sermons (Amos 3 – 6)

The next four chapters of Amos's book give us a summary of what the prophet said to the people of Israel during his ministry. Each message began with the phrase "Hear this word" (3:1; 4:1; 5:1). Amos reminded Israel of how often God had chastened them. He had withheld rain; he had struck their crops with mildew and locusts; he had even allowed enemies to defeat them in battle—but nothing had turned them back to him. Five times in chapter 4 the Lord says, "Yet you have not returned to me" (4:6, 8, 9, 10, 11). Every act of discipline broke over their hardened hearts, but their hearts were never broken.

Some of the people piously sat in church and said, "Won't it be wonderful when the Lord brings this old world to an end and we enter God's glorious kingdom?" God punctured that religious daydream by informing them that the day of the Lord would not bring them the blessing they thought it would.

> Woe to you who long
>   for the day of the LORD!
> Why do you long for the day of the LORD?
>   That day will be darkness, not light.
> It will be as though a man fled from a lion
>   only to meet a bear,
> as though he entered his house
>   and rested his hand on the wall
>   only to have a snake bite him. (5:18–19)

God rejected their religious activity and exuberant worship because just before they had come to church, they had oppressed good people and trampled on the poor.

Visions (Amos 7 - 9)

The last section of Amos's book contains six visions from the Lord. Amos saw a swarm of locusts headed toward Israel, but when he prayed, the Lord turned the judgment away (7:1–3). The same thing happened with the threat of a devastating fire sweeping over the land. Amos pleaded with God, and the Lord relented (7:4–6). Then God

HELP FILE

THE BURDEN-BEARER

Amos's name means "burden-bearer." He carried the heavy responsibility of delivering God's message to a hostile audience.

In Amos's book social justice is as important as personal integrity. Following God on Sunday produces a concern for our culture and a change in our corporation on Monday.

Amos was a contemporary of Hosea and Jonah, both prophets in Israel.

DoWNlOAd

Amos 4:12

"Prepare to meet your God."

showed Amos a plumb line, a device used to check the straight lines of a building or wall. In God's hand the plumb line was used to check the moral integrity of a nation. Israel and her religious leaders had fallen far from God's standard (7:7–17). The remaining visions of a basket of ripe fruit (8), the Lord standing at the altar (9:1–10), and the Lord restoring the ruined nation (9:11–15) spoke of the certainty of God's judgment and the ultimate intervention of God's grace.

God Still Speaks

As you have read the book of Amos, maybe you have realized that God has a message for you to speak, a burden for you to carry. Don't allow the limitations or excuses of the past to keep you from becoming an obedient servant of the Lord. Amos proved that some of God's most useful servants emerge from obscure places and rugged circumstances. Your background, your family, your past failures are not what determines your usefulness to God. Amos was so obscure that his parents were not even mentioned, and neither was Amos referred to again outside his own book. Nevertheless, he stood as a powerful voice for right and justice in his own society.

DiggiNG DeEpeR

✗   Motyer, J. A. *The Message of Amos: The Day of the Lion.* The Bible Speaks Today series. Downers Grove, IL: InterVarsity Press, 1974.

One of the best explanations of Amos with plenty of pointed application to contemporary society and life.

TOOL TIME

Bible Dictionaries

Next to a good study Bible, the best tool to help you understand the Bible is a Bible dictionary. You will find virtually every Bible name, place, and topic listed in alphabetical order. It will even help you pronounce those difficult names. Some of the articles are long (big subjects, key people); some articles are very brief.

As you read the Bible, if you come to a person or significant location or a nation's name that is unfamiliar, usually a note in your study Bible will give you a limited amount of explanation and background. If that note satisfies your interest and allows you to keep reading with understanding, fine. If the study Bible note just makes you want to find out more, pick up your Bible dictionary and plunge in. One article may send you to two or three other articles for an even fuller explanation. You can pursue a topic as far as your interest takes you.

The information about the Assyrians on the previous page, for example, was drawn from several of the Bible dictionaries on my shelves. Because the Assyrians play such a large role in the drama of the Old Testament, you will find a fairly lengthy article covering their history, religion, and culture.

Which One Should I Buy?

There are dozens of Bible dictionaries on the market. Some are multivolume sets; most are one volume. A few suggestions will help you make a good choice:

Take enough time in the bookstore to read several articles in each dictionary. You might want to take two or three biblical subjects or names in with you and look at the articles on those subjects in each dictionary. Check out the maps and charts. Are they clear or confusing? Buy the dictionary you find most helpful. If a bookstore has only one or two in stock, visit some other stores before you buy.

Be sure that the dictionary was written and published within the past twenty years. Some older dictionaries have been hidden behind modern covers, but the information is very outdated.

Be willing to invest some serious money in this tool. It will repay you with years of information and insight.

Ask people you trust which Bible dictionary they use. Your pastor or Bible study leader can give you some direction, but the final choice, of course, is yours.

Here are a few good ones to consider:

New Bible Dictionary, edited by I. H. Marshall and others. 3d ed. Downers Grove, IL: InterVarsity Press, 1996.
A handy, one-volume dictionary. Not spectacular to look at but packed with solid information.

The Illustrated Bible Dictionary. Downers Grove, IL: InterVarsity Press, 1998.
This is the *New Bible Dictionary* with color charts, maps, and photos added. Bigger print than the single volume too.

The New International Bible Dictionary, edited by J. D. Douglas and Merrill Tenney. Grand Rapids: Zondervan, 1987.

The NIV Study Bible Basic Library CD-ROM contains, along with other features, the *NIV Compact Dictionary of the Bible* (Grand Rapids: Zondervan).

Obadiah

── Heads Up ──

➤ Check out this short book with its pointed message.

➤ Discover what happens when a family feud gets out of hand.

➤ Beware: If you are a proud person, this book will hurt!

The name Obadiah is just that to many Bible readers—just a name. But in the shortest book in the Old Testament, Obadiah delivered a shocking message to some people who thought they were better than other people. They sat around and smirked at the misfortune of others, and Obadiah let them have it.

We know almost nothing about the man who wrote this biblical pamphlet. At least twelve men in the Old Testament have the name Obadiah. It means "servant of the Lord." We know the prophet's name; we know he had a vision; we know he wrote it down—and that's about all we know about him.

Key Characters

Obadiah: God's spokesman

Jacob: Abraham's grandson, Isaac's son; God changed Jacob's name to Israel, and the entire nation descended from his sons

Edom: the nation descended from Esau, Jacob's twin brother; Jacob cheated Esau out of their father's blessing

Two Brothers

We do know, however, something about the situation that prompted Obadiah to write his book. The background is a family feud. Back in the book of Genesis we read the story of the great father of the people of Israel, Abraham. Abraham had a son named Isaac who had twin sons, Esau and Jacob. Isaac's wife, Rebekah, knew there was a problem when the two sons wrestled inside her before they were even born! (You can read the story in Genesis 25:21–34.) Their struggle continued through childhood and adulthood and only calmed down when one of them left town.

Points 2 Remember

☑ Obadiah wrote a short essay announcing God's judgment on the people of Edom because they rejoiced over Jerusalem's destruction.

☑ God takes note of "Edomites" in every generation and deals severely with their proud spirits.

Esau's descendants were called Edomites. Jacob's descendants were called Israelites. For centuries each nation burned with hatred toward the other. The Edomites lived in a rugged mountainous region southeast of Judah. They built incredible fortresses and homes in the caves and cliffs of the area. They thought they were invincible. But in the days of the great kings David and Solomon, Edom was defeated by Israel and was forced to pay tribute to their hated cousins. Occasionally they rebelled, but Israel was larger and stronger. Israelite lordship grated on the Edomites.

Three hundred years after David and Solomon died, the Babylonian army smashed the remnants of Jacob's descendants. In 586 B.C. King Nebuchadnezzar and his troops burned the temple, pulled down the walls of Jerusalem, and marched the people into captivity.

On that day of calamity for Jacob's family, Esau's family had a party. The Edomites applauded as the Babylonians carted off the wealth of Jerusalem. After the Babylonians were gone, the Edomites came in and scavenged what was left. Some of Jacob's people tried to escape the Babylonian slaughter and were cut down by Edomites happy to see them die. Then the family of Esau ran back to their mountain stronghold and smugly congratulated themselves on how secure they were. What happened to the people of Jerusalem would never happen to them.

What Goes Around, Comes Around

The Edomites seriously underestimated the Lord God of Israel. Plastered on the posts and walls of the marketplaces of Edom the next morning was a one-page handbill written by an obscure prophet of God. Cold chills ran down the Edomites' backs as they read Obadiah's words.

> "The pride of your heart has deceived you,
>   you who live in the clefts of the rocks

and make your home on the heights,
you who say to yourself,
    'Who can bring me down to the ground?'
Though you soar like the eagle
    and make your nest among the stars,
        from there I will bring you down,"
                    declares the LORD. (verses 3–4)

The Coming Invasion (Obadiah 1 – 9)

The first message Obadiah wanted to get across to the Edomites was that God would see to it that they would find themselves in the same situation that the people of Judah had been in. The day would come when the nations around them would break through their defenses and reduce them to rubble. The scenes they laughed over during Jerusalem's destruction would be replayed in their own streets.

The Betrayal of Jacob's Family (Obadiah 10 – 11)

Obadiah justified the coming judgment on Edom by reminding them of their pride and violence against the people of Jerusalem. The Edomites had helped the enemy destroy their own relatives.

Helpless in the Day of the Lord (Obadiah 15 – 21)

As dreadful as the invasion of the surrounding nations would be, Edom would face an even greater judgment when they stood before the Lord. In that day no one from Edom will survive to enjoy the blessing

DiggiNG DeEpeR

✗   Finley, Thomas. "Obadiah." *Joel, Obadiah and Micah.* Everyman's Bible Commentary series. Chicago: Moody Press, 1996.

Finley does a superb job of helping us understand the setting and meaning of Obadiah's little book.

of God's kingdom. The family of Jacob will be delivered from judgment. The glory of the Lord will shine from Jerusalem. But Edom will be like the ashes left from a prairie fire.

> "The day of the LORD is near
>   for all nations.
> As you have done, it will be done to you;
>   your deeds will return upon your own head." (verse 15)

Walking the Walk

1. Evaluate your attitude toward your friends and coworkers. When you hear of someone's failure or firing, what is your first response? It's easy to feel good when other people, especially people we don't particularly like, get what's coming to them. We might even want to join in the attack. But Obadiah reminds us that God sets himself against the proud and conceited.

2. Map out a strategy to respond with genuine encouragement and help to someone who is struggling with failure or loss. If you know someone in that situation, even an enemy, put the strategy into action.

3. How can you respond to the person who can't wait to spread the latest gossip and to gloat over the difficulties of other people? What if you work with a person like that? What if you are married to a person like that?

Jonah

➤ Marvel at the story of a man who is swallowed by a giant fish—and lives to tell about it!

➤ Find out why Jonah got mad when his ministry succeeded.

➤ Listen to God's response to people who fail in a big way.

Everything and everyone in Jonah's story obeys God—except the prophet himself. A pounding storm, a colossal fish, and a tiny caterpillar all move at God's command. The people who hear God's message turn away from their evil ways. But Jonah tries to run from God's call.

Jonah was a prophet of the Lord in the northern kingdom of Israel during the reign of Jeroboam II (794–753 B.C.). Jonah liked his job and even gained some respect from Israel's king (2 Kings 14:25). It was God's call to an international ministry that Jonah couldn't handle. While Israel was growing strong and expanding its borders under Jeroboam II, a far greater power was rising to the northeast. Assyria was on the move, pushing toward Israel. The Lord told Jonah to get up and go to Nineveh, the capital city of Assyria, and deliver a message of God's approaching judgment.

Jonah got up, but he headed in the opposite direction. Nineveh was east of Israel; Jonah booked passage on the first ship headed west, as far west as a person could go—to Tarshish in Spain. Before you condemn Jonah, think about what God had asked Jonah to do. He wanted his prophet to go into enemy territory, to the main political and military center, and announce to the people of Assyria that the God of Israel was giving them six weeks to repent. They had to change their evil, violent ways within forty days or Nineveh would be toast. Maybe you would like to accept God's call to North Korea or to Iran's most radical revolutionaries. Jonah didn't run away because he didn't like the climate in Nineveh or because it was a long trip. He ran because God was calling him to go to the enemies of God's people.

Jonah paid his fare, went into his cabin, and fell asleep. A few hours from Israel's shore, however, God sent a storm unlike anything these sailors had seen before. In panic they woke Jonah and asked him to pray. Jonah knew right away that the storm was God's chastening hand. At Jonah's insistence, the sailors threw him overboard, and the storm subsided. They thought it was the end of Jonah, but God had other plans.

The God of the Second Chance

When Jonah hit the water of the Mediterranean Sea and began to sink, God was ready. God had prepared a great fish to swallow Jonah. But if all you see when you read this book is a fish, you have missed the point. Even Jonah is just a minor character in the story! Jonah's book is a book about God. Jonah's name appears eighteen times in the text, but

HELP FILE

WAS JONAH FOR REAL?

Some students of the Bible believe that the story of Jonah is an allegory or parable designed to speak to the narrow nationalistic spirit of Old Testament Israel. They believe that the writer of the book took Jonah's name from the historical record of 2 Kings 14:25 and built a fictional story around him. The "message" of the parable was that the God of Israel would rescue and deliver any person (even an Assyrian!) who truly turned from evil and believed in God. Some base their interpretation on the literary form of the book; others do not think the miraculous elements (the storm, the great fish) reflect true events.

Other students of Scripture believe that the book is an actual account of historical events. God is clearly powerful enough to prepare a great fish and to keep Jonah alive in the fish. The book is certainly written as a historical narrative using the names of real people and real cities and indications of time and distance in the real world. Jesus referred several times to Jonah, to his experience in the fish, and to his preaching in Nineveh (see, e.g., Matthew 12:39–40; 16:4; Luke 11:29–32). The evidence points to Jonah's book as an account of real events.

Jonah 2:2

"In my distress I called to the LORD,
   and he answered me.
From the depths of the grave I called for help.
   And you listened to my cry."

God's name appears thirty-nine times. Above the roar of the storm and the cry of the sailors and even the prayer of Jonah, stands God. The theme of the book of Jonah is the overwhelming greatness and inescapable grace of God.

In the stomach of the fish, Jonah began to pray. He didn't pray when God's call first came. He didn't pray when he boarded the ship to run away. He didn't even pray when the sailors were afraid and begged him to pray. But when God moved in and surrounded him, Jonah was willing to pray—and God said, "Jonah is finally ready to obey." So the fish vomited Jonah up on dry land.

As Jonah stood on the shore, one question hammered away at his soul. "Will God use me again? I'm a failure, a runaway. What happens now?" As Jonah struggled, an amazing thing happened. "The word of the LORD came to Jonah a second time" (3:1). God could have banished Jonah forever, but Jonah's God is a God of grace. He's the God of the second chance, the third chance, the hundredth chance! Whatever has invaded your life, whatever failures you wrestle with, God comes to you with restoring grace.

Digging Deeper

✗ Alexander, T. Desmond. "Jonah" in *Obadiah, Jonah, Micah.* Tyndale Old Testament commentary series. Downers Grove, IL: InterVarsity Press, 1988.

A short but helpful study of Jonah's story.

Seeing As God Sees

Jonah went to Nineveh and saw one of the greatest revivals in history. He preached God's message, and the whole population repented! But Jonah was angry. He went outside the city and sat down to watch God destroy Nineveh. When it didn't happen, Jonah began to pout. He said, "I *knew* this

Points 2 Remember

- ☑ Jonah was a prophet who tried to run from God's call, but God restored him and used him to warn the people of Nineveh.

- ☑ Jonah spoke God's message but had to learn to love the people to whom he spoke.

- ☑ God always comes to us in grace, even in our failures and disobedience. He is the God of another chance.

would happen! I knew God would save these Assyrian dogs!"

We suddenly see Jonah's real problem. Jonah tried to run away from God's call because he didn't want God to spare the people of Nineveh. He wanted them to be destroyed. He knew God would move the people to turn from their evil and seek God because that is what God is like. God is full of compassion and mercy. Jonah, however, wanted nothing to do with it. He couldn't stomach sharing heaven with a bunch of mobster Assyrians.

God revealed Jonah's prejudice by allowing a vine to grow up to shade Jonah from the hot sun—and then by sending a caterpillar to cut the vine at the root and cause it to wither. When Jonah complained, God pointed out that Jonah was more concerned with his own comfort than he was with an entire city of people who needed to hear the message of God's love and forgiveness.

That's where Jonah's book reaches out and grabs us. What do we see as we look around us? What concerns press heaviest on our hearts? Do we see our part of the world as God sees it, or does everything focus on what *we* want and what *we* need? I come to the end of Jonah's story and have to admit that I am usually far more upset about some minor inconvenience in my life than I am about my own lack of obedience to God or my neighbor's hard-hearted attitude toward the Lord. I am more interested in financing some new toy than I am about supporting a missionary so that he or she can spread the message of God's love. I am often critical and complacent when God desires to see compassion and commitment. We aren't told what happened to Jonah. The people of Nineveh repented; I wonder if Jonah ever did.

Walking the Walk

1. Read the book of Jonah even if you think you know the story. Unfortunately, we usually end the story when Jonah gets out of the fish, but God had more to say. As you read notice how Jonah's attitudes change as the events unfold. What did Jonah learn about God's character in the course of the book?

2. When you think about telling people about Jesus Christ, who would you choose to talk to first? Would you go first to an enemy or a friend?

3. When you imagine what heaven will be like, do you picture it inhabited only by people identical to yourself, people of the same ethnic background speaking the same language, raised in the same culture? What steps can you take to broaden your perspective on the composition of God's people?

PEOPLE of the BiBLE

THE ASSYRIANS

The fertile plain between the Tigris and Euphrates rivers (in present-day Iraq) was the home of the ancient Assyrians. The Assyrian Empire was the first great empire to march across the pages of the Bible. Assyria was strongest during the three hundred years that spanned the division of the kingdom in Israel (900–612 B.C.). The Assyrian armies conquered the northern kingdom of Israel in 722 B.C. and scattered the Israelites throughout their vast empire. They were also the ones who harassed and attacked the southern kingdom of Judah and forced the Judean kings to pay tribute money. The Assyrians were the people who heard Jonah preach and who (for one generation at least) vowed to obey the Lord God of Israel.

The Assyrians believed in many gods and embodied their gods in statues and carvings. The main god was Il; he was surrounded by a trio of cosmic deities, Sin (god of the moon), Shamash (god of the sun), and Ishtar (goddess of the planets). Thousands of Assyrian clay tablets have survived and give us details of the political, religious, and social aspects of their culture.

The Assyrian Empire first touched the people of Israel when ten small nations (including Israel) joined forces to try to stop Assyria's westward expansion. (Shalmaneser III ruled Assyria at the time.) Ahab, the king of Israel at the time, supplied 2,000 chariots and 14,000 soldiers for the battle. The ten-king coalition failed, and Israel ended up paying tribute to the Assyrians. (We learn about this coalition from Assyrian records; the battle is not recorded in the Bible.)

Other significant Assyrian kings:

Tiglath-Pileser III (744–727 B.C.) is mentioned in 2 Kings 15:29; 16:7–10; he is also called by his throne name, Pul, in 2 Kings 15:19 and 1 Chronicles 5:26. He brought the northern kingdom of Israel into the Assyrian Empire as a vassal (dependent) state.

Shalmaneser V (726–722 B.C.) with the help of his brother and successor, Sargon II (722–705 B.C.), surrounded and conquered Israel after Israel's King Hoshea foolishly refused to pay his taxes (2 Kings 17:3–6).

Sennacherib (705–681 B.C.) tried to conquer the southern kingdom of Judah but was turned away by God's intervention (2 Kings 18–19; 2 Chronicles 32; Isaiah 36–37). Sennacherib also made the city of Nineveh the permanent capital of Assyria.

The Assyrian Empire came to an end when the Babylonians rose up in revolt against their former rulers. The Babylonians destroyed Nineveh in 612 B.C. and chased the remnants of the Assyrian army into the mountains.

The Assyrians were a fierce, violent people. Their policy was to deport captive peoples and to scatter them into other regions of the empire. Conquered rulers were crushed, tortured, or forced to watch as their children were slaughtered. In their final defeat the Assyrians experienced only a taste of the suffering and destruction they had inflicted on others for hundreds of years.

For more information about the Assyrians, check out H. W. F. Saggs, *The Might That Was Assyria* (London: Sidgwick and Jackson, 1984), at your local library.

Micah

➤ See how God uses a man from an obscure place to preach a powerful message.

➤ Examine the consequences of mistreating the poor and disadvantaged.

➤ Find out what Micah had to say about Jesus—seven centuries before Jesus was born!

If he were living on earth today, Micah would probably operate a free medical clinic or a women's shelter. He was concerned for the overlooked and ignored people in his society, and he was called by God to speak against those in high places who were exploiting the poor. Micah still speaks with stunning power to the church of the affluent living in the land of plenty.

Micah lived in the southern kingdom of Judah in a quiet little town twenty miles southwest of Jerusalem. Micah may have been out of the mainstream politically, but he was no hayseed preacher. He was fully aware of what was happening in his world, in his nation, and in people's hearts.

Key Characters

Micah: a prophet from rural Judah who was courageous enough to take on the nation's corrupt political and religious leaders

Jotham, Ahaz, and Hezekiah: the three Judean kings who ruled during Micah's ministry

Micah prophesied during the reigns of three kings of Judah. The first was Jotham, who reigned from 750–732 B.C. Jotham was basically a good king, but his obedience to God was only so-so. Jotham was succeeded by a wicked son, Ahaz, who allied himself with the rising Assyrian Empire. It was during his reign (736–732 B.C.) that Assyria conquered and deported the people in the northern kingdom of Israel. The third king Micah knew was Hezekiah (716–687 B.C.), a godly man who withstood the Assyrian onslaught with God's help and who saved Judah from disaster.

Points 2 Remember

- ☑ Micah was a prophet in Judah who spoke boldly against injustice and the oppression of the defenseless.

- ☑ Micah served in a quiet, out-of-the-spotlight place but still sensed the power and presence of God.

- ☑ Micah warned of God's judgment, but he also spoke some of the most grace-filled words in the Bible.

The prophet lived and spoke during difficult, uncertain years for Judah. Assyria was a ravaging beast, smashing one nation after another. The common people were harassed by armies, ripped off by the rich, and oppressed by greedy politicians. The poor, the defenseless, the elderly, and the recently laid-off were victims of relentless exploitation. In that context Micah raised a voice for God.

Living As If People Mattered

As you read the book of Micah, you will move back and forth between judgment and hope. In the early chapters Micah speaks to both Israel (called "Samaria," after their capital city) and Judah (or "Jerusalem"). In the later chapters Israel is gone and only Judah remains. Israel experienced the judgment and captivity Micah predicted, and Judah would soon follow if they didn't turn back to the Lord.

A Dreadful Day of Judgment (Micah 1:1–3:12)

Micah preached like a prosecuting attorney as he dragged his own people into court and leveled one indictment after another at them. God himself was the witness against the people of Israel and Judah (1:2); the sentence passed on them was disaster and conquest (1:8–16).

God's severe judgment would come for several reasons. It would come because the wealthy were exploiting the poor. The law of God made it very clear that society was to care for the poor and the helpless, but these slumlords and sweatshop owners were far too busy to check their actions against God's standard of behavior. They would lie awake at night planning the next day's foreclosures and rip-off schemes.

> Woe to those who plan iniquity,
>   to those who plot evil on their beds!

At morning's light they carry it out
because it is in their power to do it. (2:1)

Political leaders in Judah's kingdom were to model compassion and honesty—but the leaders in Micah's day found it easier to tyrannize people. That was another reason for God's judgment.

"Listen, you leaders of Jacob,
you rulers of the house of Israel.
Should you not know justice,
you who hate good and love evil;
who tear the skin from my people
and the flesh from their bones;
who eat my people's flesh,
strip off their skin
and break their bones in pieces;
who chop them up like meat for the pan,
like flesh for the pot?" (3:1–3)

The worst problem was not in the central bank or the halls of government; the worst problem stood behind the pulpits of the land. The religious leaders were not courageous proclaimers of truth but deceivers of the people.

This is what the LORD says:

"As for the prophets

HELP FILE

OVERSHADOWED

Micah's ministry in Judah was overlapped (and probably overshadowed) by the ministry of Isaiah. Isaiah was the scholar, the poet, preaching to large crowds in Jerusalem. Micah, on the other hand, plodded along in relative obscurity in a small town.

Micah's name is really a question. It's a shortened form of Micaiah, which means "Who is like the LORD?"

Micah appears elsewhere in the Bible only when quoted in the book of Jeremiah (26:18) and in the gospel of Matthew (2:6).

THE MESSIAH IN MICAH

As part of his stirring description of Israel's glorious future kingdom, the prophet also paints a picture of the coming King, the promised Deliverer. There are some interesting contrasts in Micah's portrait, however. At one point Micah says:

> They will strike Israel's ruler
>   on the cheek with a rod.

> "But you, Bethlehem Ephrathah,
>   though you are small among the
>   clans of Judah,
> out of you will come for me
>   one who will be ruler over Israel,
> whose origins are from of old,
>   from ancient times." (5:1–2)

But in the next breath Micah says:

> He will stand and shepherd his flock
>   in the strength of the LORD,
>   in the majesty of the name of the
>   LORD his God.
> And they will live securely, for then
>   his greatness

> will reach to the ends of the earth.
> And he will be their peace. (5:4–5)

These two passages illustrate what the Old Testament prophets knew about the Messiah who is revealed in the New Testament as Jesus Christ. No clear distinction was made between the time of Jesus' first coming in humility and suffering (born as a baby in Bethlehem, struck on the cheek with a rod) and the time of Jesus' future second coming in power and glory (rules over the earth in power and peace). The Old Testament writers did not see two comings of the Messiah, just one. It was like looking at two mountain peaks from far away. They look like they are right next to each other or even part of one mountain. But when you get close, you see the long valley between the two peaks. From the perspective of the New Testament, we see the long time period between Jesus' first coming two thousand years ago and his still future return in glory.

> who lead my people astray,
>   if one feeds them,
>   they proclaim 'peace';
>   if he does not,
>   they prepare to wage war against him." (3:5)

Micah didn't mince any words. His concern was not political correctness; his burden was to warn his people before it was too late.

A Glorious Day of Triumph (Micah 4:1 – 5:15)

Micah moves in these chapters from the nation's failure to God's faithfulness. In spite of Judah's sin and the judgment God would bring, the Lord would not forget his promises to them.

> In the last days
>
> the mountain of the LORD's temple will be established
>   as chief among the mountains;
> it will be raised above the hills,
>   and peoples will stream to it.
>
> Many nations will come and say,
>
> "Come, let us go up to the mountain of the LORD,
>   to the house of the God of Jacob.
> He will teach us his ways,
>   so that we may walk in his paths."
> The law will go out from Zion,
>   the word of the LORD from Jerusalem. . . .
>
> "In that day," declares the LORD,
>
> "I will gather the lame;
>   I will assemble the exiles
>   and those I have brought to grief.

DiGGinG DeEpeR

✗ Grant, George. *The Micah Mandate.* Chicago: Moody Press, 1995.

The author explores the practical implications of Micah 6:8 for today. A very challenging book!

✗ Waltke, Bruce. "Micah." *Obadiah, Jonah, Micah.* Tyndale Old Testament Commentary series. Downers Grove, IL: InterVarsity Press, 1988.

A concise explanation of Micah's book with good insights into the historical background.

> I will make the lame a remnant,
>> those driven away a strong nation.
> The LORD will rule over them in Mount Zion
>> from that day and forever." (4:1–2, 6–7)

A Dark Day of Conflict (Micah 6:1 – 7:10)

In a sudden reversal from his earlier writing, Micah turned from the glorious future to the dreadful present. He reminded his listeners of God's care and protection in the past and contrasted their continued disobedience and rebellion against the Lord.

A Brilliant Day of Comfort (Micah 7:11 – 20)

Micah closed his book with a message of God's grace and forgiveness.

> Who is a God like you,
>> who pardons sin and forgives the transgression
>> of the remnant of his inheritance?
> You do not stay angry forever
>> but delight to show mercy.
> You will again have compassion on us;
>> you will tread our sins underfoot
>> and hurl all our iniquities into the depths of the sea. (7:18–19)

DoWNLoAd

Micah 6:8

> **What does the LORD require of you?**
> **To act justly and to love mercy**
>> **and to walk humbly with your God.**

Walking the Walk

1. Living a life that pleases God is not complicated; it's simple. (I didn't say *easy;* I said simple.) What does God require? To do what is right, to love justice and mercy, and to walk humbly in his presence. We are the ones who make the Christian life a complicated set of rules and rituals. The Bible focuses on the basics! You may want to memorize Micah 6:8—or write it on a card for your wallet or dashboard or workstation.

2. Micah painted a powerful picture of God's forgiveness. He pardons sin (7:18); he treads our sins under his feet (7:19); he hurls our failures into the depths of the sea (7:19). Do you live like a forgiven person? Or do you keep reminding God of sins he has already forgiven—and forgotten? How does God's forgiveness of you affect how you forgive other people?

3. Do you know someone—maybe someone in your church—who holds a strong commitment to justice? That person may be involved in social or political programs to address problems in our culture. Take the person to lunch and ask why and how he or she got started in a personal pursuit of justice. The conversation may prompt a new passion in your own life.

Nahum

➤ Watch as God brings a reign of terror to an end.

➤ Explore aspects of God's character that you may find hard to accept.

➤ Discover what God says to a nation that turns away from him.

God had already sent one prophet to the city of Nineveh. When Jonah spoke his message of impending judgment, the people of Nineveh turned from their evil ways. They believed God's word, and the city was spared. The people who heard Jonah, however, never passed God's warning to the next generation, and it was soon forgotten. Nineveh's sin multiplied. The people who populated this Assyrian capital were once more bent on military conquest and oppression. The Assyrian army had crushed the northern kingdom of Israel just one generation after Jonah's ministry. Judah had escaped conquest that time. But now the tiny nation of Judah, the last remnant of the family of Abraham, Isaac, and Jacob, was next on Assyria's hit list.

At that point of crisis, God raised up another prophet, a prophet who spoke one message and then dropped out of sight. Like the thrust of a dagger, Nahum announced the doom of the great city of Nineveh. Within forty years every prediction from Nahum's lips came true.

World Boxing Federation: God vs. Assyria!

When Nahum spoke, Assyria was at the height of its power, and the empire cov-

Points 2 Remember

☑ Nahum predicted God's judgment on the cruel Assyrians. Within forty years of Nahum's message, the city of Nineveh had been destroyed.

☑ Nahum also spoke a message of comfort to God's people in Judah and to all who felt Assyria's cruelty.

☑ Human injustice and savagery did not end with the fall of Nineveh; neither did God's judgment on those who are guilty of such cruelty.

ered most of southwest Asia. The Assyrians were brutal, cruel people. State portraits usually depicted their kings gloating over horrible punishments carried out on conquered people. The Assyrian annals (which still survive) record horrible atrocities: captives were boiled in tar, conquered kings were skinned alive, children were killed for sport. The Assyrians were proud of their cruelty. Some historians trace the practice of crucifixion to the Assyrians. Not exactly the kind of people you want to invite over for a Super Bowl party!

Nineveh was both proud and powerful. Thus, Nahum's announcements of Nineveh's destruction must have sounded pathetic at first. But in 612 B.C. destruction came. The new boys on the block, a rapidly rising Babylonian Empire, emerged to Nineveh's south and east. The Babylonian army smashed through Nineveh's defenses and flattened the city. They destroyed it so completely that for more than two thousand years no one even knew where it was. Nineveh is still just a haunt for archaeologists. God's judgment came, and it was final.

God's Dark Side

Nahum, like several other prophets, had amazing insight into God's character. He made it clear that Nineveh would not be destroyed simply by military strategy or the strength of a human army. Nahum pointed

HELP FILE

FULL OF COMFORT

Nahum *(nay-hum)* means "full of comfort." His message was a comfort to the oppressed people of Judah but certainly not to the oppressing Assyrians!

Nahum calls himself an "Elkoshite" in verse 1. No one knows for sure where Elkosh was. Some scholars think it was the original name of the city on the shore of the Sea of Galilee later called Capernaum because Capernaum means "city of Nahum." Other traditions place the tomb of Nahum not far from the ancient city of Nineveh. The claim is that Nahum's ancestors were captives deported into the Assyrian Empire when the northern kingdom of Israel was conquered in 722 B.C. If that is true, Nahum wrote his prophecy right on Nineveh's doorstep and then sent it to the people of Judah.

DownLoad

Nahum 1:7

The LORD is good,
 a refuge in times of trouble.
He cares for those who trust in him.

instead to a powerful God, standing in the shadows of history, raising up one nation and throwing down another. Some people don't like the God they meet in Nahum. We like to read that he is a God of power and good (1:3, 7), but what about this portrait of our heavenly Father:

> The LORD is a jealous and avenging God;
> the LORD takes vengeance and is filled with wrath.
> The LORD takes vengeance on his foes
> and maintains his wrath against his enemies. . . .
> Who can withstand his indignation?
> Who can endure his fierce anger?
> His wrath is poured out like fire;
> the rocks are shattered before him. (1:2, 6)

Most of us have a very narrow view of God. We have tried to create him in our image—or at least we've given him the qualities we like in God. Nahum shows us some aspects of the character of God with which we struggle. It helps to remember that all of God's character is perfect. His anger against sin and his judgment against those who do evil are as perfect as his mercy or his grace. God is a God of love, but he is also a God of justice and holy anger.

The word that best summarizes Nahum's picture of God's character is the word *awesome*. God is the one who inspires reverence and wonder. Nahum expects that we will take the Lord seriously. Nineveh forgot who God was, and in the end there was no escape.

DigginG DeEpeR

✗ Kohlenberger, John R. III. "Nahum." *Jonah and Nahum.* Everyman's Bible Commentary series. Chicago: Moody Press, 1984.

A short but well-done explanation of Nahum's book.

FOOtpRiNts in the SanD

Over the centuries skeptics and critics of the Bible were quick to point out that Nineveh was nowhere to be found. Then a French diplomat named Paul Botta began to uncover artifacts on an ancient site called Khorsabad (located today in Iraq) in 1843. Botta claimed it was Nineveh, but it turned out not to be.

Unwilling to let the French gain the upper hand in the scramble for antiquities, the British sent their own agent to the area. By 1847 Austen Layard had made two spectacular finds—the Assyrian city of Nimrud and the long-lost city of Nineveh. Probably the most remarkable discovery Layard made was the palace of King Sennacherib, who ruled Assyria from 704 to 681 B.C. The palace was made up of seventy-one rooms, including a magnificent library, and twenty-seven massive gateways, each flanked by stone bulls, lions, or sphinxes. Many of the treasures were transported to the stately halls of the British Museum.

Nahum's book is short, pointed, and fatal. He didn't drag out his message. He just spoke God's word and then sat down to wait for the news of Nineveh's fall.

Walking the Walk

1. As you read chapter 1 of Nahum, make a simple chart and list God's attitudes toward the wicked and his attitudes toward those who trust in him. Which aspect in each category do you tend to leave out of your portrait of God? How can you begin to paint each one into your view of God?

2. Evaluate how seriously you take God's Word. When you discover a principle in the Bible that is not operative in your life, do you shrug it off or do you come to terms with it?

Habakkuk

➤ Meet a man with a strange name who asked God some tough questions.
➤ Find out answers to such questions as, "Why doesn't God do something about the evil in our world?"
➤ Learn how to trust God when your world collapses.

Habakkuk didn't fit the mold of a prophet. Maybe he never did fit in very well; maybe it was that name of his! Not one word of Habakkuk's book was addressed directly to the people of his day. Instead, he recorded a series of conversations with God. Habakkuk asked God some very difficult questions—questions we might not have enough courage to ask.

Why do bad things happen to good people?

Why does it seem that good things happen to bad people in our world?

Why does it seem that God is absent or asleep when evil is strongest?

Where was God when Jews were being slaughtered during the Holocaust?

Where is God when life seems unjust and unfair?

Who's in Charge Here?

You can't understand Habakkuk's questions—or God's answers—unless you catch a glimpse of the days in which he lived. By the time of Habakkuk's ministry (about 605 B.C.), the northern kingdom of Israel had been gone for a hundred years. Judah, the southern kingdom (now the only kingdom of the Jews) had continued on. In time, a godly king named Josiah came to Judah's throne. He led a return to the Lord and a removal of foreign idols unlike anything Judah had seen for three hundred years. (You can read about Josiah's reforms in 2 Chronicles 34.)

Points 2 Remember

☑ Habakkuk was a prophet in Judah who let people listen in on his conversations with God.

☑ The evidence of faith is not when we are silent about our doubts, but when we are sure of God. Habakkuk still struggled with God's ways, but he knew that ultimately God would do what was right.

☑ Habakkuk shows us that God permits evil in our world. God may even use evil people to accomplish his purposes. Eventually, however, God will judge evil and triumph over it.

But Josiah died, and his son, Jehoiakim, became king. Jehoiakim was ungodly, and soon Judah returned to the idols and the obscene worship connected with them.

Meanwhile, several hundred miles away a new empire was stirring. The Assyrians had held sway for 150 years, but now the Babylonians (or "Chaldeans") were on the move. The Babylonians had learned how to be cruel by living under the Assyrian boot for so long.

Enter Habakkuk—a godly man, aware of his culture and in touch with his world. He saw the disobedience and sin of Judah and the rising power of Babylon, and he wondered where God was in all of it. How could God stand back and let his own people become so corrupt? How could God let people as cruel as the Babylonians rise to world power? If there really was a God out there, why didn't he do something?

What makes Habakkuk so practical is that Habakkuk asks our questions. We look at some corrupt, evil aspect of our society and say, "How can God let this go on?" We see abused children, or famine-stricken refugees, or dying babies and we ask, "Why does a good God let this happen?" Brutal dictators rise to power and we wonder, "Why doesn't God bring them down?" Habakkuk's problems are our problems. As we read his journal, God moves in with some answers.

The Prophet's Problems (Habakkuk 1–2)

Habakkuk asked God two questions. The first was: How can God allow Judah's sinfulness to continue?

How long, O LORD, must I call for help,

but you do not listen? . . .
Why do you tolerate wrong? (1:2–3)

God answered Habakkuk's question—but not with a direct answer. He told the prophet that he *was* doing something about Judah's sin. He was bringing a whip of discipline on his own people.

"Look at the nations and watch—
and be utterly amazed. . . .
I am raising up the Babylonians,
that ruthless and impetuous people." (1:5–6)

The conversation went like this:

Habakkuk: "God, what are you doing about the sin of the people of Judah?"

God: "You won't believe me if I tell you!"

Habakkuk: "Yes, I will. Tell me."

God: "I'm raising up the Babylonians to strike my own people."

Habakkuk: "I can't believe it!"

That was Habakkuk's second problem. "Wait, Lord! Why would you use the Babylonians of all people?"

Your eyes are too pure to look on evil;
you cannot tolerate wrong. . . .
Why are you silent while the wicked
swallow up those more righteous than themselves? (1:13)

Digging Deeper

✗ Baker, David. "Habakkuk." *Nahum, Habakkuk, Zephaniah.* Tyndale Old Testament Commentary series. Downers Grove, IL: InterVarsity Press, 1988.

An excellent concise treatment of Habakkuk and his message.

Habakkuk says, "Lord, the Babylonians are more wicked than we are! How can you use them to punish us?" That's like recruiting police officers down at the local jail!

God's answer was not exactly what Habakkuk wanted to hear. God told the prophet that he knew all about the wickedness of Babylon. He would use Babylon to discipline Judah but then, in God's own time, he would smash Babylon because they dared to touch his chosen people. Five times God pronounced "woe" on the people of Babylon (2:6, 9, 12, 15, 19). God ended by issuing a command.

> "The LORD is in his holy temple;
>   let all the earth be silent before him." (2:20)

God is not sitting on the edge of his chair nervously hoping things will work out on earth. He is in the place of control and power.

Habakkuk (and all of us who struggle with the presence and power of evil) are called to live by faith—to put our trust and confidence in God and in his control over human history.

> "The righteous will live by his faith." (2:4)

That verse is such a powerful perspective on what it takes to survive in an evil world that it is quoted three times in the New Testament as the

HELP FILE

AN OBSCURE PROPHET

Habakkuk *(ha-**back**-uk)* means "to embrace" or "to wrestle." That's what Habakkuk did—he wrestled with deep problems and hard questions.

We are told less about Habakkuk than almost any other prophet. Nothing is said about his parents, clan, or hometown.

Habakkuk was a contemporary of the prophets Zephaniah and Jeremiah.

One of the best-known Dead Sea Scrolls is a commentary on the book of Habakkuk. The Dead Sea Scrolls were Jewish religious documents collected about the time of Jesus and hidden in caves near the Dead Sea just before the Roman destruction of Palestine in A.D. 70.

governing principle of the Christian life (Romans 1:17; Galatians 3:11; Hebrews 10:38–39).

The Prophet's Prayer (Habakkuk 3)

When Habakkuk grasped the greatness of God and his majestic rule over creation, he responded with a passionate prayer, a hymn of confident trust in God's goodness regardless of our circumstances.

> Though the fig tree does not bud
> and there are no grapes on the vines,
> though the olive crop fails
> and the fields produce no food,
> though there are no sheep in the pen
> and no cattle in the stalls,
> yet I will rejoice in the LORD,
> I will be joyful in God my Savior.
>
> The Sovereign LORD is my strength. (3:17–19)

When we live by faith, we aren't worried about the things that go on in our world. We may be concerned and even motivated to action against evil, but we don't lose our faith in the greatness or the goodness of God.

Walking the Walk

1. What moral evil or social injustice bothers you most? How have you explained its existence up until now? Does Habakkuk's struggle help you understand the presence of evil—or does his book raise more questions?

2. Think over any troubling questions you have about God, the Bible, or how God works in our world. What avenues have you explored to resolve or answer those questions? Remember that God *can* answer all our questions but *may choose* to answer only a few. God will listen and will bring assurance to us, but he won't always explain himself. The issue we have to wrestle with is whether we will continue to trust him even when some of our questions remain unanswered.

Zephaniah

Heads Up

> ➤ Judgment day is coming!
> ➤ Learn why God is the only safe hiding place.
> ➤ Find out how God gets our attention when we don't want to listen.

My dad was a preacher—which made my brothers and me preacher's kids. When we were acting up in church, we always knew Dad's final warning. If we were talking or horsing around, we would first get "the stare." That was usually enough. Further disruption brought the snap of his fingers or a rap on the pulpit. A second warning was always followed by a close encounter of the worst kind after the service! One Sunday my dad had to stop his sermon and verbally correct his chattering son. Fortunately, it was my brother!

Points 2 Remember

☑ Zephaniah spoke to the people of Judah to warn them of approaching judgment from God.

☑ Woven into Zephaniah's strong words is the promise of grace, a small door of escape, a shelter from the blast of God's anger for those who in humble faith put their trust in the Lord.

☑ God will gently warn us only for a while. When we refuse to respond, he will turn up the volume!

Zephaniah spoke God's final warning to the people of Judah. He called them to turn back to God and to fully follow his law, but he also let them know that, as a nation, they had gone too far. You will find echoes of several other prophets in Zephaniah—warnings from Amos, Isaiah, and Joel. That's not because Zephaniah couldn't come up with new stuff; it's because his message was a summary of all the prophets who had come before him.

Zephaniah spoke during the early years of King Josiah of Judah (639–629 B.C. are likely dates for Zephaniah's ministry). Josiah would lead one of the great spiritual revivals in Judah's history, although it wouldn't last much beyond

Josiah's death. Zephaniah's preaching may have been a factor in Josiah's willingness to follow the Lord and in the nation's willingness to return to obedience to God. But as fervent as the nation's commitment was for a while, Zephaniah knew that it wouldn't last. He called the people of Judah to prepare for a much greater judgment than conquest by some earthly army. His call was to get ready to face the Lord God himself.

> "I will sweep away everything
>   from the face of the earth,"
>   declares the LORD.
> "I will sweep away both men and animals;
>   I will sweep away the birds of the air
>   and the fish of the sea.
> The wicked will have only heaps of rubble
>   when I cut off man from the face of the earth,"
>   declares the LORD. (1:2–3)

Focusing on Essentials

Zephaniah focuses our attention on two basic themes. As he stepped up to the pulpit, Zephaniah delivered his first theme like a fist in the stomach: Judgment day is coming! Zephaniah called the time of God's judgment "the day of the LORD." That phrase was used repeatedly by the prophets to refer to a day of God's coming to his people, a visitation for blessing or for judgment. In Zephaniah's mind, God would visit

Digging Deeper

✗ Allen, Ronald B. *A Shelter in the Fury*. Portland, OR: Multnomah, 1986.

An exploration of Zephaniah laced with plenty of practical application for today.

his people soon with a crushing blow from the Babylonian army. But another day of the Lord will follow, an awesome day affecting the whole earth, the day when God will reign in glory over his whole creation. That fateful day will begin with sweeping judgment.

> "The great day of the LORD is near—
>   near and coming quickly.
> Listen! The cry on the day of the LORD will be bitter,
>   the shouting of the warrior there.
> That day will be a day of wrath,
>   a day of distress and anguish,
> a day of trouble and ruin,
>   a day of darkness and gloom,
>   a day of clouds and blackness. . . .
> I will bring distress on the people
>   and they will walk like blind men,
>   because they have sinned against the LORD. . . .
> In the fire of his jealousy
>   the whole world will be consumed,
> for he will make a sudden end
>   of all who live in the earth." (1:14–15, 17–18)

Everyone will face the sweeping judgment of God on that future day. The false gods of the new age won't deliver anyone from God's evaluation. Wealth, position, and political power will all be meaningless. Zephaniah

HELP FILE

THE HIDING PLACE

The name Zephaniah _(zef-a-**nigh**-ah)_ means "hidden by the LORD" — a theme Zephaniah expands in his book as he pictures God as a hiding place.

In the first verse Zephaniah gives us his family history. It's the longest genealogy given of any prophet, and it may indicate that he was a person of some importance in Judah. The "Hezekiah" in his ancestry was probably King Hezekiah, who reigned in Judah seventy years earlier. His great-great-grandfather, Hezekiah, and Josiah, the king under whom Zephaniah lived, were both faithful to the Lord.

said that the unfaithful in Judah and the unbelieving in the nations around Judah will all meet the same end. They will be swept away.

The only place of safety in the day of the Lord is under the protection of the one doing the judging. The hiding place is in the Lord himself. That's the other theme woven into Zephaniah's book.

> Gather together, gather together,
>   O shameful nation,
> before the appointed time arrives
>   and that day sweeps on like chaff,
> before the fierce anger of the LORD comes upon you,
>   before the day of the LORD's wrath comes upon you.
> Seek the LORD, all you humble of the land,
>   you who do what he commands.
> Seek righteousness, seek humility;
>   perhaps you will be sheltered
> on the day of the LORD's anger. (2:1–3)

Those who take refuge in the Lord will not be swept away. They will find themselves surrounded by the joy and glory of God's kingdom.

> "I will leave within [Jerusalem]
>   the meek and humble
> who trust in the name of the LORD." (3:12)

In troubled times, we can be secure in the protective care of our God.

> "The LORD your God is with you,
>   he is mighty to save.
> He will take great delight in you,
>   he will quiet you with his love,
>   he will rejoice over you with singing." (3:17)

Zephaniah's promise of a shelter in the Almighty for those who trust in him is not just for those who lived in the past or those who will face God's judgment in the future. We can know the same security while resting in a hospital bed or standing in line at the unemployment office or weeping next to a fresh grave. There is nothing more fearful than facing the judgment of God. There is nothing more comforting than being sheltered securely in the love and power of God in the middle of overwhelming trouble.

Walking the Walk

1. If Zephaniah were writing today, on what examples of unfaithfulness among God's people would he focus? Do you sense God warning our nation or his people today?

2. Think about areas of your own life that you have been prompted by God to change. It could be a relationship that you have neglected or a personal habit that is wrong or an area of integrity that has been compromised. How often has God prodded you to change that specific aspect of your walk with him? What are the dangers of ignoring God's conviction in your heart? Outline specific steps you can take to become obedient to God's desire in your life.

Haggai

➤ Take a look at your priorities—from God's perspective.

➤ Listen to God's message to people on the career fast-track.

If you look around the next time you go to church, I think you will have to admit that as a whole the Christian community is out of shape—not physically, but spiritually. Most of us qualify as spiritual couch potatoes. We aren't persecuted very much, but we aren't taken very seriously either. There are a lot of churches and a lot of Christians; we just aren't doing much to impact the lives of the people around us. The engine is running, but we are in "neutral"—or "park"!

Now suppose a man or woman came on the scene who spoke with such power and authority that the whole Christian community was raised out of its comfortable slumber and was drawn to new levels of commitment and influence. God would use this person in such a way that we would begin to share the message of Christ with other people on a consistent basis. Our marriages and homes would be renewed. What if one person created such a hunger in us for God's truth that we couldn't be satisfied with just an occasional dip into the Scriptures? If God would send a person like that to us, we would be talking about it for months; we'd reap the fruit of that ministry for years.

It might surprise you to know that God did send a person like that to his people in the Old Testament. Unfortunately, we don't hear much about this man for a couple of reasons. First, he had a weird name—Haggai (*hag-eye*; the only person with that name in the whole Bible). Second, he wasn't one of the "big guns." Isaiah wrote sixty-six chapters of Scripture; Haggai wrote only two! His little tract isn't read much, but it still packs a powerful message.

Key Characters

Haggai: God's spokesman who urged the Jews to rebuild the temple

Zechariah: Haggai's fellow prophet

Zerubbabel: political leader of the Jewish community in Jerusalem

Joshua: the high priest and religious leader in Jerusalem

A Half-Built House

Jeremiah, Habakkuk, and Zephaniah said that the people of Judah would be conquered and taken captive by the armies of the Babylonian Empire. Everything those prophets predicted came true. The Babylonians came three times to Judah, and each time the price was heavier. Finally, in 586 B.C. the city of Jerusalem was destroyed and the people were led away in chains.

The people of Judah hated being taken to Babylon, but once they were there it wasn't so bad. The Babylonians let them live as a community and gave them land to farm. The Judahites (or, as they now were called, Jews) began to prosper. They prospered so much that fifty years later, when a new world empire came on the scene, the Jews were solidly entrenched in Babylon. The new rulers, the Persians, said that any captives of Babylon who wanted to return to their native soil could. But Jerusalem was a barren, ruined city. The farms of Judea hadn't been worked for fifty years. Why go back? Any normal person would have stayed in Babylon—unless his heart burned to see God's temple, the center of the Lord's worship, rebuilt. Out of a Jewish population in Babylon of almost two million people, only 50,000—less than 3 percent—returned to Jerusalem.

The first thing the people did was clear away the rubble from the area where Solomon's glorious temple had stood. They marked out a new

HELP FiLE

HAGGAI

Haggai's four messages were delivered during a four-month period in 520 B.C., the second year of the Persian ruler Darius Hystaspes, or Darius the Great.

Haggai was joined in his ministry by the prophet Zechariah.

Zerubbabel and Joshua mentioned in Haggai's book were the leaders of the return of exiles from Babylon. Joshua was the religious leader; Zerubbabel was the civil leader.

Haggai 2:6 is quoted in the New Testament in Hebrews 12:26. Haggai is also quoted or mentioned in some books of the Apocrypha (Ecclesiasticus 49:10–11; 1 Esdras 6:1; 7:3; 2 Esdras 1:40).

Points 2 Remember

☑ Haggai spoke to the Jews who had returned from captivity in Babylon and urged them to complete God's temple.

☑ Delay in doing what God commands or desires is really just disobedience. Slow obedience is *no* obedience.

☑ God will keep punching holes in our purses until we get our priorities right.

foundation and put up an altar so they could once again offer sacrifices to God. They couldn't sacrifice in Babylon; *this* was the place God had promised to bless.

But then more practical matters became the priority. The people needed houses to live in. They needed shops and laundromats and strip malls. So they began to clear the stones and broken timbers from the rest of the city. God's temple, however, remained neglected. They still offered sacrifices on the Sabbath and probably had a committee to investigate the feasibility of rebuilding the temple, but nothing much was done.

Gradually spiritual complacency settled over these fervent pioneers of faith. Other concerns, legitimate but lesser concerns, sapped their zeal. God got his hour or two each week, but the rest of the time he was the farthest thing from their minds. They had businesses to run and kids to take to soccer and careers to pursue. God, they thought, certainly understood. For sixteen years weeds covered the temple's foundation. The people had convinced themselves that if they first made themselves prosperous and satisfied their own needs, they would then be in a better position to meet their obligations to the Lord.

Consider Your Ways

Then one day—August 29, 520 B.C., to be exact—a man stood up in the marketplace of Jerusalem and began to speak. He was Haggai, a neighbor to some of the people conducting business that day. Haggai, of all people, said, "Friends, the word of the Lord has come to me. I have a message from God."

"Is it a time for you yourselves to be living in your paneled houses, while this house [God's temple] remains a ruin?"

Now this is what the LORD Almighty says: "Give careful thought to your ways." (1:4–5)

That was Haggai's theme—"Consider your ways!" He repeated similar warnings three more times in his little book (1:7; 2:15; 2:18).

Haggai stood up in a society like ours where people were busy, where people had to work hard to make ends meet. He spoke at a time when people wanted to do less not more. Haggai looked busy people right in the eye and said, "Give careful thought to your priorities in life." Haggai is not calling us to launch a new building program for our church. He is challenging us to evaluate our lives in the light of God's direction and biblical priorities.

The people in Haggai's day worked hard to have it all, yet they never seemed to get ahead.

"You have planted much, but have harvested little. You eat, but never have enough. You drink, but never have your fill. You put on clothes, but are not warm. You earn wages, only to put them in a purse with holes in it. . . .

"You expected much, but see, it turned out to be little. What you brought home, I blew away. Why?" declares the LORD Almighty. "Because of my house, which remains a ruin, while each of you is busy with his own house." (1:6, 9)

Digging Deeper

✗ Baldwin, Joyce. "Haggai." *Haggai, Zechariah, Malachi.* Tyndale Old Testament Commentary series. Downers Grove, IL: InterVarsity Press, 1972.

Baldwin gives excellent historical background and pointed explanation of Haggai's message.

✗ Wolf, Herbert. "Haggai." *Haggai and Malachi: Rededication and Renewal.* Everyman's Bible Commentary series. Chicago: Moody Press, 1976.

A concise, readable commentary.

TO BE PRECISE

Haggai stamps his book with very precise dates—and because the Babylonians and Persians kept such good historical records, we can pin them down to exact days. You may want to jot these in the margin of your Bible:

Haggai 1:1—August 29, 520 B.C.

Haggai 1:15—September 21, 520 B.C.

Haggai 2:1—October 17, 520 B.C.

Haggai 2:10, 20—December 18, 520 B.C.

What the people of Jerusalem didn't realize was that God was the one "blowing away" the bank account! He did it with the hope that they would get frustrated enough to say, "What are we really after anyway?" That may explain why some things in our lives never get straightened out! We give a nod of acquaintance to the Lord, but his Word doesn't make much of a difference in our lives.

We have all heard someone say, "Make Jesus Lord of your life." That is incorrect! We don't *make* Jesus the Lord of our lives; he *is* the Lord. We just live like he is or we live like we are.

A Success Story

Most Old Testament prophets were either ignored or attacked. Amazingly, Haggai had success! The people of Jerusalem responded to Haggai's message with joyful obedience. The work on the temple resumed, and Haggai's messages turned from challenge to encouragement. He even gave the people some glimpses of the future of this house of worship.

> "I will fill this house with glory," says the LORD Almighty. "The silver is mine and the gold is mine," declares the LORD Almighty. "The glory of this present house will be greater than the glory of the former house," says the LORD Almighty. "And in this place I will grant peace," declares the LORD Almighty. (2:7–9)

In Solomon's temple ("the former house") God's presence was shown by a bright cloud that filled the sanctuary (1 Kings 8:10–11). Five hundred years after Haggai's temple was completed, Jesus would enter it. When Jesus came to this earthly temple, God's presence was seen in the visible form of his own Son.

Walking the Walk

1. Take a few minutes to write down the five most important priorities in your life—not the priorities you want to have, and not the ones you think you should have, but the ones you really have. Ask yourself, What is most important to me? What is next in importance? The way to tell is to look at how much thought, energy, commitment, and resources you devote to each priority. If you say your family is a high priority but your hobby receives more of your time and attention than your kids, you need to hear Haggai's message—"Give careful thought to your ways."

2. Ask your spouse or a trusted friend to write out what they perceive your priorities to be. Spend some time talking over the list. God may use a "spokesman" (like he used Haggai) to tap you on the shoulder and show you where some rebuilding needs to be done.

3. Now make a list of what you believe God's priorities are for your life. How do the other two lists compare? How motivated are you to bring your list into line with God's list? Who can help you be more accountable for maintaining the right priorities?

Zechariah

Heads Up

➤ Meet a man who encounters angels and has strange visions.

➤ Find out what God is doing when he seems far away and unconcerned.

➤ Get the facts about God's promised King and his fabulous kingdom.

Zechariah was a visionary among the prophets. One fantastic night he saw eight visions, and he wrote them down for our amazement! Zechariah spoke to God's people after they had returned from years of captivity in Babylon. At first he teamed up with the prophet Haggai to challenge the people to complete the rebuilding of God's temple, but Zechariah's ministry went beyond just a great building program. He saw God's future kingdom when a more glorious sight than the temple would fill Jerusalem. In that future day God's people will see a powerful King reigning in majesty, ruling the whole earth.

Zechariah came to people who lived every day in depressing circumstances, and he gave them God's perspective on their situation. He took the long view of things. He lifted people's eyes beyond the tedious work of everyday life and gave them a glimpse of their incredible future.

Key Characters

Zechariah: a Jewish priest and God's prophet who returned from exile in Babylon and prompted his people to finish building God's temple

Haggai: Zechariah's fellow prophet

Darius: Persian king during Zechariah's ministry

What a Dump!

If you had walked into the city of Jerusalem in Zechariah's day, you would not have been very impressed. Eighty-five years earlier the city had been leveled by the Babylonian army. The temple had been burned, and the massive stones of the walls had been pushed into the ravines around the city. You would have been greeted by piles of trash! For fifty years after its destruction, no one had lived in Jerusalem. It was just a giant landfill! Then some new rulers took over. The

Persians allowed the Jews living as captives in Babylon to go home, but only 50,000 had the courage to return.

They cleared away the debris covering the temple area and started to rebuild God's house—but other things became more urgent. The people began to build their own houses and stores and restaurants. It took Haggai's prodding to get the people to return to the project they had started with such enthusiasm. One of the priests of Jerusalem, a man named Zechariah, soon joined Haggai.

A person walking into Jerusalem in 520 B.C. when Zechariah's ministry began would not have been very impressed with Jerusalem—nor with the God of Jerusalem! The people gathered on the Sabbath and heard wonderful promises written by prophets who had lived long before. Those prophets said that God would ultimately establish a magnificent kingdom of justice and purity and that God's anointed King would reign in Jerusalem and over the whole world. The people heard those promises but, as they looked around, must have had a hard time believing them.

Zechariah's job was to remind the people of Jerusalem that God had not forgotten his promises. Regardless of what things looked like out on the street, God was still in control. He was working out every detail of his plan even when it seemed like nothing much changed from day to day or year to year. Zechariah announced that the glorious kingdom and the global rule of a glorious King would still come. Isaiah and Hosea and Amos had not been misled. God would keep his promises.

HELP FiLe

PROPHET AND PRIEST

More than thirty people in the Bible have the name Zechariah.

Like Jeremiah and Ezekiel, Zechariah was also a priest.

Zechariah is mentioned by name three times outside his own book (Ezra 5:1; 6:14; Nehemiah 12:16).

The book of Zechariah is the longest of the minor prophets.

ZECHARIAH'S NIGHT VISIONS

Vision 1 (1:7–17)	A horseman is seen standing in a grove of myrtle trees with red, brown, and white horses. God will restore his people.
Vision 2 (1:18–21)	Four horns and four craftsmen appear. Israel's oppressors will be judged.
Vision 3 (2:1–13)	A man with a measuring line, an angelic architect, draws the plans for a fully restored city. God will protect and rebuild Jerusalem.
Vision 4 (3:1–10)	Joshua, the main priest of Israel, is cleansed by God and restored to his place as the leader of Israel's worship. Israel's religious leaders will be cleansed.
Vision 5 (4:1–14)	Zerubbabel, the civil leader of Jerusalem, is shown to be under God's hand of blessing. God's Spirit empowers God's leaders.
Vision 6 (5:1–4)	A flying scroll appears. Individuals will be cleansed from defilement.
Vision 7 (5:5–11)	A woman in a basket is carried away to Babylon. National sin will be removed.
Vision 8 (6:1–8)	Four chariots patrol the earth. God will judge the nations who have oppressed his people.

A New Voice

Zechariah's book divides into three parts: pictures, problems, and predictions. It's not a book to breeze through—or skip over! Some of it is extremely difficult, and most of it is a little weird, but you come away impressed in a new way with the majesty of God, who knows the future because he planned it all.

Points 2 Remember

- ☑ Zechariah spoke to God's people who had returned from exile in Babylon. He urged them to look beyond the difficulty of the present to the unwavering faithfulness of God.

- ☑ Zechariah's name means "the Lord remembers," and his message is that God will remember (and keep) all his promises to his people.

- ☑ In God's plan there are no mistakes.

Pictures (Zechariah 1 – 6)

After a short introduction, Zechariah recorded a series of eight visions that he had one after another on the same night. Zechariah even stamped them with a precise date—February 15, 520 B.C. A chart of the visions and each one's key message is on the facing page.

Problems (Zechariah 7 – 8)

For seventy years the Jews had observed certain days of the year with fasting (not eating) and mourning. These grief days commemorated the destruction of Jerusalem under the Babylonians. Some Jewish leaders came to Zechariah to ask if they should continue such grim observances. In anticipation of the new age coming, God reversed the days of fasting to days of feasting.

Predictions (Zechariah 9 – 14)

Zechariah concluded his book with two long oracles, detailed descriptions of future events. The first oracle (chapters 9–11) discusses the judgment of God on the enemies of his people. The second oracle (chapters 12–14) looks forward to the day when God's kingdom will emerge in full glory. The people of Israel will turn to God in renewed faith. The nations of the world will stream to Jerusalem to worship the great King.

God Still Moves

We come away from Zechariah's book dazzled by spectacular visions and encounters with angels. But we also come away with a renewed sense of God's active involvement in human history. Our world is moving toward a goal. We aren't just a speck of cosmic dust spinning into oblivion. God has a purpose in all that he does.

The day will come when we will see that God's good plan has never been frustrated. We'll see then how every piece fits into place—every sorrow, every loss, every joy. But God doesn't want us to wait until eternity to believe that. He wants us to believe it now, in the struggle, in the sorrow, in the tedious work of life. In God's plan there are no mistakes. Everything he has promised, he will do.

Walking the Walk

1. What are your dreams for the future? What would you really like to accomplish or attain in life? What are your desires and dreams for eternity, for life beyond death? Does your anticipation of heaven prompt any change in your life today?

2. We find it hardest to believe in the goodness or power of God when we go through times of sorrow or loss or difficulty. What specific truths about God or promises from God can you glean from Zechariah's book that will help you face life's hard times with more faith?

DiGGiNG DeEpeR

✗ Baldwin, Joyce. "Zechariah." *Haggai, Zechariah, Malachi.* Tyndale Old Testament Commentary series. Downers Grove, IL: InterVarsity Press, 1972.

A well-written explanation of a difficult book.

JESUS IN ZECHARIAH

Zechariah had a lot to say about the coming Messiah, God's anointed King. The writers of the New Testament Gospels and the writer of the New Testament book of Revelation often appealed to Zechariah's predictions to confirm events during Jesus' ministry in the past or at Jesus' return in the future.

Jesus will be a priest *and* a king. Such a combination in one person was not possible in Israel (Zechariah 6:13).

Jesus will enter Jerusalem on a donkey colt (Zechariah 9:9; see Matthew 21:5 and John 12:15).

Jesus will be betrayed for thirty pieces of silver (Zechariah 11:12–13; see Matthew 26:14–15; 27:3–10).

Jesus' body (hands, feet, side) will be pierced (Zechariah 12:10; see John 19:34, 37).

Jesus as Israel's shepherd will be struck down, and his sheep (his disciples) will scatter (Zechariah 13:7; see Matthew 26:31 and Mark 14:27).

Jesus will return in glory to the Mount of Olives just outside Jerusalem (Zechariah 14:4–8).

The enemies of God's people will be destroyed by Jesus at his return (Zechariah 14:2–3; see Revelation 19:11–21).

Jesus will reign in splendor over the whole earth (Zechariah 9:10; 14:9, 16; see Revelation 20:4).

Zechariah's predictions about Jesus' first coming were totally accurate—which suggests that his predictions about Jesus' second coming will be just as accurate!

Malachi

Heads Up

➤ Listen to God's final word to his people in the Old Testament.

➤ Discover what God thinks of people who go through religious motions but have insincere hearts.

➤ Catch a glimpse of the day when evil and injustice will be removed from the earth forever.

The "point-counterpoint" approach to controversial issues can be seen every day on television. A Republican and a Democrat, an environmentalist and a logging worker, a liberal and a conservative face off on the issues. Points are raised only to be answered by the other side. That journalistic style makes some interesting television. It makes the book of Malachi interesting too! Malachi got people's attention in the very same way. He raised a problem, often with a sarcastic question, and then gave God's answer. After God spoke, there wasn't much rebuttal!

Malachi (**mal-e-kigh**) spoke one hundred years after the first wave of Jews had returned to Jerusalem from exile in Babylon in 536 B.C. Two later waves had brought more Jews back to their homeland—one group came back under Ezra's leadership in 458 B.C., and another came back under Nehemiah's leadership about 444 B.C. Each return had brought new enthusiasm and spiritual fervor to the Jerusalem community. By Malachi's day (430 to 410 B.C.), the temple of God had been rebuilt, the worship of God had been fully restored, and the walls of the city had been raised again after 150 years of decay and disgrace.

But as at other times in Israel's history, the zeal of a revival soon wore thin. The

DiggiNG DeEpeR

✗ Wolf, Herbert. "Malachi." *Haggai and Malachi: Rededication and Renewal.* Everyman's Bible Commentary series. Chicago: Moody Press, 1976.

A brief commentary, but well done.

people slipped into a lifestyle of complacency and greed. The priests of Israel were interested only in a paycheck and how many vacation days the new temple contract included. The return of the Jews from captivity and the restoration of Jerusalem were so miraculous, so unheard of in history, it's hard to believe that social decay and spiritual decline could have set in so fast, but it did. Only the clear, pointed voice of a prophet could shake the community out of its lethargy.

We don't know for sure if Malachi was the prophet's name or a title given to him by God. Malachi means "my messenger." Some early Jewish traditions claim that Ezra the priest was the one who spoke these words. The author gives us no ancestors, no birthplace, no personal information at all. What we do know is that he spoke by the authority of God. The phrase "says the LORD" occurs twenty times in a book of just four short chapters. In fact, God directly speaks forty-seven of the fifty-five verses in the book, the highest proportion of any prophetic book. Malachi was God's spokesman but simply acts as the moderator in the debate over right and wrong.

What Was the Question?

Six point-counterpoint issues are raised in Malachi's book. The priests or the people take one side; the Lord takes the other.

Dispute 1: Does God Love Israel? (1:1 – 5)

This passage sets the pattern for the rest of the issues.

First, God makes a declaration: *"I have loved you," says the LORD.*

Then comes the counterpoint, a question or sarcastic remark heard by Malachi on the streets of Jerusalem: *But you ask, "How have you loved us?"*

The third element in each episode is God's response: *"Was not Esau Jacob's brother?" the LORD says. "Yet I have loved [in the sense of 'chosen'] Jacob and Esau I have hated [or 'rejected'].*

God's love was shown by his protection and restoration of Jacob's descendants, the people of Israel. God had chosen Jacob's descendants not because they were good or obedient to God (often they weren't).

Points 2 Remember

☑ Malachi was the last Old Testament prophet. He spoke to people who had experienced great blessing from God but who had slipped into spiritual complacency.

☑ Malachi warned about the deadening consequences of taking God's blessing and spiritual privileges for granted. Those of us who enjoy the freedom to worship and to witness need to appreciate God's goodness, not presume upon it.

God had chosen to bless Israel simply because it was his desire to do so. His love was unconditional.

Esau's descendants, on the other hand, had not been chosen as God's people. The family of Esau, the Edomites, made a choice too. They lived like they didn't care about God's blessing. The prophet Obadiah had predicted that the Edomites would suffer God's judgment, and now Obadiah's predictions were coming true.

> "I have turned his mountains into a wasteland and left his inheritance to the desert jackals."

Edom may say, "Though we have been crushed, we will rebuild the ruins." But this is what the LORD Almighty says: "They may build, but I will demolish. They will be called the Wicked Land, a people always under the wrath of the LORD. You will see it with your own eyes and say, 'Great is the LORD—even beyond the borders of Israel!'" (1:3–5)

God's disputes with Israel didn't get any easier—or any nicer!

The Other Disputes

Dispute #2: Compromising Clergy Don't Honor God (1:6–2:9)

Dispute #3: Disobedient People Break God's Covenant (2:10–16)

Dispute #4: Where Is God's Justice? (2:17–3:5)

Dispute #5: Why Won't You Turn Back to God? (3:6–12)

Dispute #6: Harsh Words Against the Lord (3:13–4:3)

A Final Announcement (4:4–6)

The Storm Before the Silence

When Malachi laid down his pen, the curtain closed on the Old Testament prophets. He was the last voice from God in a line that stretched clear back to Moses. For over one thousand years God had come to his people with his word. Now God's direct voice fell silent for four hundred years. The people of Israel still had the Scriptures that had been written in the past. Some people came on the scene claiming to be prophets, but no authentic voice from God would be raised in Israel until John the Baptist would burst out of the wilderness and announce the Messiah's coming appearance.

Malachi was the only prophet to end his book on an abrupt note of judgment instead of a promise of hope and future glory. The last word of the Old Testament is "curse." When we come to the New Testament, we read this:

> All who rely on observing the law are under a curse.... Christ redeemed us from the curse of the law by becoming a curse for us, for it is written: "Cursed is everyone who is hung on a tree." He redeemed us in order that the blessing given to Abraham [the Jews] might come to the Gentiles [non-Jews] through Christ Jesus, so that by faith we might receive the promise of the Spirit." (Galatians 3:10, 13–14)

This last Old Testament prophet summarized all the prophets. They all made it clear that we are to take God seriously. These courageous men spoke harshly at times. They named sins and they named sinners. They pushed their fingers into the faces of people who had made promises to God and pointed out that they had not kept those promises. Their world was hard to deal with. They didn't just laugh off compromise and disobedience and injustice. The prophets make us stop long enough to take a hard look at our actions and our attitudes before a holy, awesome God.

Walking the Walk

1. Think about a time in your life when your love for God was at its fullest. What has happened to your zeal since then? If you are experiencing spiritual renewal in your life right now, what steps will you take to keep your enthusiasm from cooling off?

2. Have you had a "Malachi" in your life—a friend or pastor or parent who confronted you about something wrong in your conduct or in your attitude? How did you respond to that person's correction? Maybe you need to make a call or write a letter to thank that person for caring about you enough to confront you.

3. Record your overall impression of the prophets in your journal or notebook. Give some thought to how their message has changed how you view God, how you pray, how you look at evil in the world, how you view your future.

BETWEEN THE TESTAMENTS

Between Malachi, the last Old Testament book, and Matthew, the first New Testament book, all you see in most Bibles is a blank page. It's like four hundred years of time simply vanish!

The long stretch of time between the testaments has been called the four hundred "silent" years. From a human perspective, plenty of things happened during those four centuries. But God sent no prophets to his people over that entire span; his voice was "silent." God's people still had the written Word of God from Moses and the prophets, but no new message came for four hundred years.

Then something incredible happened. A man came from the Judean wilderness right up to the people living around Jerusalem. He claimed to speak for God, and he said that his mission was to prepare the way for God's promised Messiah. The man's name was John the Baptist. He was the first true prophet of God since Malachi.

The events of the "intertestamental" period are important because they shaped the world of the New Testament. When the Old Testament ended, the Persians were the overlords of the Jews living in Palestine. The Persian Empire was pushed aside by the amazing conquests of Alexander the Great. He added Palestine to his Greek empire in 332 B.C. By the time of Alexander's death in 323 B.C., the entire eastern Mediterranean was under Greek control. The Greek language and Greek culture flourished in Asia Minor (Turkey), Palestine, and Egypt.

Greek domination over the Jews continued for more than 150 years. In 166 B.C. the Jews threw off their Greek dictators. After a revolt led by Judas Maccabeus, Judah became an independent nation for almost a hundred years.

In 63 B.C. the expanding Roman Empire found an excuse to intervene in Palestine, and the whole region came under Roman authority. Much of the Old Testament focused on the region east of Palestine—Assyria, Babylon, and Persia. The New Testament world is west of Palestine—Asia Minor, Greece, and the city of Rome itself.

The political system of Judah (now called Judea), the religious system of Judaism, and the cultural world of Palestine had been dramatically changed during the four hundred years after Malachi, but one thing had not changed. God's people still longed for God's promised Deliverer to come.

Part 7

GOSPELS

The first four books of the New Testament tell the story of Jesus. They are called "gospels"—a word that means "good news." The New Testament writers used the word *gospel* several ways.

1. The word was used to describe the content of Jesus' preaching. "Jesus went into Galilee, proclaiming the good news of God. 'The time has come,' he said. 'The kingdom of God is near. Repent and believe the good news!'" (Mark 1:14–15). Jesus brought the message that God was about to do mighty works among his people. That was good news!

2. The word *gospel* was also used to describe the message the early Christians proclaimed—a message centered on the death and resurrection of Jesus. When the Christians explained why Jesus died and rose again, and when they called people to believe on Jesus as Lord and Savior, they were preaching a gospel—good news.

3. In time the word was used to refer to written accounts of Jesus' life, death on the cross, and resurrection. Many "gospels" were written, but only four were recognized by early Christians as fully trustworthy accounts. These four were included in the collection of books we call the New Testament. The titles *Matthew, Mark, Luke,* and *John* refer to the authors of the books and are shortened forms of the full titles: *The Gospel According to Matthew*, and so on.

The Gospels are not biographies of Jesus. They are accurate accounts of Jesus' life and death, but they were not written just to inform readers. The gospel writers wanted to do more than inform; they wanted their readers to come to believe in Jesus. They intended to convert us! So they carefully selected events, miracles, and teachings and then arranged them in such a way that we would be drawn to Jesus as Lord. You may read a biography of Thomas Jefferson or Nelson Mandela and be impressed or inspired by his courage or wisdom. But when you read a gospel, the author's goal is to bring you to believe in Jesus, to put your faith in him.

Us Four and No More

But why do we need *four* Gospels? Couldn't someone have written just one story and included everything?

The four gospels give us four different perspectives on Jesus. If you and three friends were to visit the Carnegie Museum in Pittsburgh, you all would see the same exhibits. But if all of you were asked to write about the experience, you would write from different perspectives. One account might focus attention on the fabulous gem and mineral display, another on the art collection. Each account would be accurate, but each would have its own unique emphasis.

The early Christians recognized that there was only one gospel story but that each gospel writer brought his own perspective to that story—and each had a particular audience in mind.

Matthew wrote his gospel to a Jewish audience. His goal was to present Jesus as the true King of Israel, the Redeemer God had promised to send.

Mark's emphasis was on Jesus as the Servant of the Father. Mark's primarily Roman audience wanted a man of action. As a result, Mark focused on what Jesus *did*, not so much on what Jesus *taught*.

Luke was gripped by the humanity and compassion of Jesus. Luke's Greek audience was moved by the tender side of Jesus as he healed the sick or gathered children in his arms.

 HELP FILE

THE SYNOPTIC GOSPELS

Mark was probably the first gospel written. Matthew and Luke were written next and John last.

The first three gospels are sometimes called "Synoptic Gospels." The word *synoptic* means "to see in the same way." Matthew, Mark, and Luke all incorporate similar features in their accounts of Jesus—parables, miracles, the same key events. John's gospel has a very different style.

Matthew and Luke borrow heavily from Mark's gospel. Matthew includes almost the entire gospel of Mark but arranges some events differently. About 30 percent of Matthew's gospel is found in no other gospel account. Luke has almost 50 percent original material, and 90 percent of John's gospel is not recorded in Matthew, Mark, or Luke.

John wrote his account to present Jesus as God. He wanted his message to be clear enough that anyone of any age could read it and be drawn to Jesus.

Some people get discouraged reading the New Testament because they think it is the same story told four times. If you look for the changes in focus and emphasis, however, you will realize that you are seeing one magnificent life from four fascinating viewpoints. But all four gospels have one purpose—to bring you to believe in Jesus as Savior and God. You are free to reject what they say, of course. You can ignore it, discount it, or say it was all made up by overzealous followers. What you can't do is escape the person you meet in the pages of these four books. We either push Jesus aside as irrelevant or we embrace him as Lord.

DiGGinG DeEpeR

For more information on the Gospels and how they were written, see:

✗ Flynn, Leslie. *The Four Faces of Jesus.* Grand Rapids: Kregel, 1993.

✗ Green, Joel. *How to Read the Gospels and Acts.* Downers Grove, IL: InterVarsity Press, 1987.

If you want to see how the gospel accounts compare with each other, look at a harmony of the Gospels. The four gospels are printed side by side for easy comparison.

✗ Pentecost, J. Dwight. *A Harmony of the Words and Works of Jesus Christ.* Grand Rapids: Zondervan, 1981.

The life and ministry of Jesus have filled countless books. Here's one good one:

✗ Stein, Robert. *Jesus the Messiah: A Survey of the Life of Christ.* Downers Grove, IL: InterVarsity Press, 1996.

Matthew

— Heads Up —

➤ Meet Jesus the King!
➤ Listen to Jesus' most famous sermon—and find out why it is still relevant.
➤ Read about a corrupt tax collector whose life was changed.

As Matthew sat down to write his account of Jesus, two objectives crowded his mind. Most of all he wanted to impress his readers with the majesty of Jesus. Jesus had invaded Matthew's life as a great King. Jesus had ushered in a whole new age. All the old loyalties had faded into insignificance. Matthew wanted his readers to finish his book by bowing their heads and hearts in loyalty to Jesus the King.

Matthew also wanted to reach his own people, the Jews, with the message about Jesus and had them in mind as he wrote his memories of Jesus. Matthew quoted the Jewish Scriptures more than any other gospel writer. At every turn Matthew anchored what Jesus said and did in the predictions of the Old Testament. He carefully focused on Jewish readers because he wanted his own family, his own people, to know the truth about who Jesus was.

Working for the IRS

Matthew was able to record the truth about Jesus because he had spent at least two years as one of Jesus' closest followers. The fact that Matthew was a follower of Jesus is pretty amazing when you realize what Matthew did in his "B.C." (before Christ) days. Matthew was a tax collector.

Key Characters

Jesus: Israel's promised King

Matthew: the author of this gospel; he was a Jewish tax collector who became one of Jesus' closest followers

Joseph: Jesus' adoptive father; Joseph was engaged to Mary when she became pregnant with a child; Joseph took Mary as his wife in obedience to God's direction

Magi: "wise men" from east of Palestine (Babylon or Persia) who came to Jerusalem looking for the new king of the Jews (Matthew 2)

Herod: the puppet king of Judea when Jesus was born; he had a reputation for violence and murder, so it isn't surprising that he tried to kill Jesus

Pontius Pilate: the Roman governor of Judea who condemned Jesus to death on a cross

Points 2 Remember

- ☑ Matthew wrote his gospel to present Jesus as the King. God's promise of a Redeemer was fulfilled in Jesus.

- ☑ Matthew was a close follower of Jesus and had seen Jesus' miracles and heard Jesus' teaching first-hand.

- ☑ The kingdom of heaven exists wherever Jesus reigns as King.

- ☑ When you pledge your allegiance to Jesus the King, your life will never be the same.

No one today feels very comfortable talking to an IRS agent, but in Jesus' day tax collectors were the lowest of the low. They did the dirty work for the Roman oppressors. The right to collect taxes was auctioned to the highest bidder, who then had to charge even higher taxes to make a living for himself. Tax collectors were vultures, squeezing poor people for every dime. Matthew was looked upon as a thief and a traitor to his own people.

But Jesus saw something more in Matthew. Jesus saw a man ready to exchange his loyalty to money for a new allegiance. Here's how Matthew tells his own story in the book he wrote.

As Jesus went on from there, he saw a man named Matthew sitting at the tax collector's booth. "Follow me," he told him, and Matthew got up and followed him. (9:9)

Most likely Matthew had heard Jesus preach several times before this dramatic encounter. And each time Matthew had been drawn closer to this intriguing leader. Perhaps in a private conversation Matthew had told Jesus that he was willing to leave his career and follow Jesus as a disciple. Then one day the call came. Matthew looked up from his account books and saw Jesus' face in the collection window. "Follow me," Jesus said, and Matthew left it all behind.

Matthew left his old job, but he couldn't leave his old friends. Most Jews wouldn't have anything to do with Matthew, so he hung out with other tax collectors. The religious people put tax collectors in the same heap with prostitutes and other "sinners." Matthew invited all his friends to his house for a big party—and in the middle of it all was Jesus. These were the very people Jesus had come to rescue! The uppity religious critics looked down their noses at the whole thing, but

Jesus didn't care. He had come as a spiritual doctor to people who were sick and were honest enough to admit it.

Matthew never recovered from his confrontation with Jesus. Nothing in his life was ever the same. Jesus had reached down to transform even a hated tax collector. A king like that was worthy of lifelong allegiance.

The Life and Times of King Jesus

Matthew alternates in his book between what Jesus *did* and what Jesus *taught*. He records at least twenty specific miracles and shows Jesus' absolute authority over disease, deformity, demons, and nature. He reports that Jesus stilled a storm with a single command and that Jesus caused sickness to leave people with just a touch or a word. Multitudes came to Jesus, and he healed them all.

Matthew also focuses on what Jesus said. About 60 percent of the book is a record of Jesus' words. The most well-known teaching passage in Matthew's gospel is found in chapters 5 through 7, Jesus' Sermon on

ONLY IN MATTHEW

Matthew gives us the genealogy of Joseph, Jesus' adopted father (1:1–17). He also writes the story of Jesus' birth from Joseph's perspective.

Only Matthew tells us about the visit of the magi (wise men) from the east (2:1–12).

Several of Jesus' parables appear only in Matthew: parables of the kingdom of God (13:24–30, 36–52), the parable of the unforgiving servant (18:21–35), the parable of the laborers in the vineyard (20:1–16), and the parable of the bridesmaids (25:1–13).

Matthew alone gives the account of Peter trying to walk on water (14:28–31) and Jesus' blessing of Peter after his confession that Jesus was the Christ (16:17–19).

Jesus' description of the last judgment is found only in Matthew (25:31–46).

In Matthew's account of Jesus' betrayal and death, Matthew adds the information about Judas' suicide (27:3–10) and about Pontius Pilate, the Roman governor, washing his hands to remove his guilt in the death of Jesus (27:24–25).

Jesus' commission to his followers to make disciples in every nation is recorded only in Matthew's gospel (28:16–20).

Matthew 5:13 – 14, 16

"You are the salt of the earth. . . .

"You are the light of the world. . . . let your light shine before men, that they may see your good deeds and praise your Father in heaven."

---

the Mount—so named because Jesus preached it on a hillside. If you read nothing else in Matthew, don't miss those chapters.

All through his gospel Matthew puts the spotlight on the new kingdom Jesus was ushering in. The Old Testament prophets had promised a future day of glory and majesty for Israel. God's kingdom would come, they said, when God's King arrived. Jesus was the promised Deliverer—the Messiah, the Anointed One who would reverse the devastation brought upon the human race by Adam's disobedience to God.

The crowds wanted Jesus to set up a political kingdom. But those who listened carefully to his words realized that the primary dimension of Jesus' reign was a commitment to obey the spiritual demands of the King. Jesus did not come to overthrow Rome, but to change the hearts of those who put their trust in him.

This new kingdom exists wherever Jesus reigns as King. Jesus reigns in the hearts of those who follow him. Jesus reigns in the Christian community. We participate in the kingdom of heaven when we pledge our allegiance to the King.

Matthew's gospel divides into four sections—and each section focuses on the King.

The King Arrives (Matthew 1–10)

Jesus' credentials were undeniable. He was "the son of David, the son of Abraham" (1:1). Those two ancestors were essential links for anyone claiming to be king in Israel. They were also names that would grab the full attention of any Jewish reader. Jesus was born, worshiped, baptized, and tested—and then his ministry began. Jesus explained what life was like in his kingdom (chapters 5–7) and demonstrated his authority over every realm of human struggle (chapters 8–10).

The King Attacked (Matthew 11 – 20)

These chapters record the growing opposition to Jesus and his message. The religious leaders became more vocal in their hatred. Jesus focused more and more on preparing his close followers for the task ahead.

The King Abandoned (Matthew 21 – 27)

In a final showdown, those who had rejected Jesus seemed to win. Jesus was arrested, beaten, and nailed to a cross to die.

The King Alive (Matthew 28)

The triumph, however, belonged to Jesus! He rose from the dead and showed himself to his followers. Matthew ends the book with Jesus still directing his followers, still in command as ruling King.

> "All authority in heaven and on earth has been given to me. Therefore go and make disciples of all nations, baptizing them in the name of the Father and of the Son and of the Holy Spirit, and teaching them to obey everything I have commanded you. And surely I am with you always, to the very end of the age." (28:18–20)

Living Under a New Ruler

So—who is the king in *your* life? Those of us who live in a democracy don't like that question. We want our voice to be heard and our vote to

DiGGinG DeEpeR

✗ France, R. T. *The Gospel According to Matthew.* Tyndale New Testament Commentary series. Grand Rapids: Eerdmans, 1985.

A detailed study but very readable.

✗ Wiersbe, Warren. *Be Loyal.* Colorado Springs, CO: Chariot Victor Press, 1980.

A brief but helpful survey of Matthew's book.

count. We want some say in how our lives are governed. But God's kingdom is not a democracy. It's an absolute monarchy. One king is on the throne, and he calls the shots!

The problem with every monarchy the world has ever seen is that the ruler seems to be so easily corrupted by wealth or power. Kings and queens and dictators and czars start oppressing people and arresting the opposition. They set up gulags or start persecutions. Money is squeezed from a reluctant population, and threats become the law.

None of that is a problem in God's kingdom, because we have the right person on the throne. He's not into oppression. He prefers liberation. If you think submitting to Jesus as Lord will put you under the burden of a long list of rules, you don't know the King! Jesus will set you free from bondage. He will let you be all you could ever dream of being. He is not a king who commands obedience and carries a big club to use on those who step out of line. He is a king who has already made the ultimate sacrifice of himself to rescue us from sin's power. He draws us in allegiance to him with his love, not his threats. Once you meet this King, your life will never be the same.

Walking the Walk

1. What does it take to be a good citizen of a nation? How do those qualities apply to citizens of God's kingdom?

2. Take fifteen minutes and read the Sermon on the Mount (Matthew 5–7) out loud. What part of the sermon do you find most difficult or unrealistic? What section is most comforting?

3. Think of one way in which you already show your allegiance to Jesus as King. What acts of loyalty could you add to it?

4. Who *is* the king of your life?

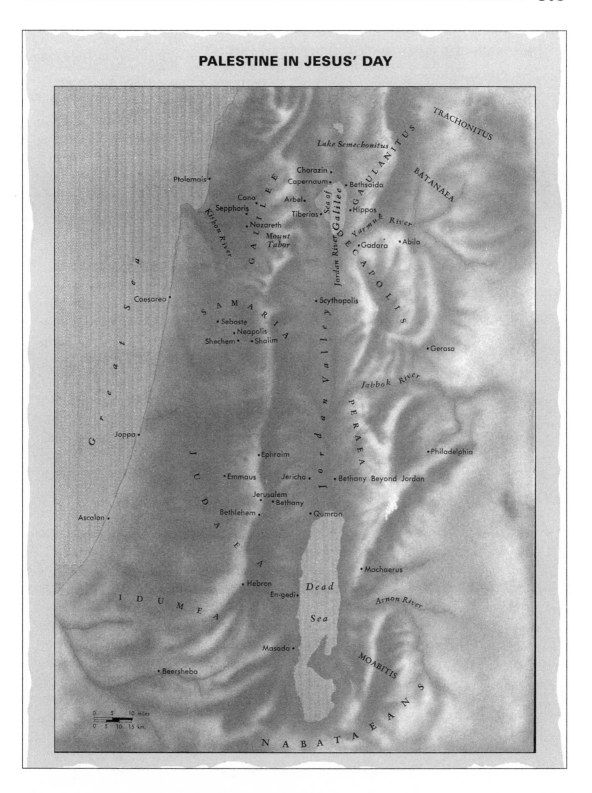

PALESTINE IN JESUS' DAY

JEWS AND JUDAISM IN THE NEW TESTAMENT

Jesus was a Jew. His whole ministry took place in a Jewish context. The Gospels will make more sense if you have a basic understanding of the Jewish world in which Jesus lived.

Politically the Jews in Judea lived under Roman authority. When Jesus was born, Herod the Great, a puppet king, ruled Judea. Later on, Roman governors were appointed to oversee the civil affairs. The Jews resented Roman rule and ultimately rebelled against it. In A.D. 70 the Roman armies smashed what was left of the Jewish state and destroyed the temple in Jerusalem.

Religiously the Jews in Judea looked to the temple as the focus of their worship. The people generally observed the law of Moses and offered the animal sacrifices required by the law. The *Sanhedrin* (or Council), a group of seventy religious leaders, governed the religious affairs of the Jews. Other important religious figures were the *high priest* (the most influential priest among all the priests who functioned in the temple) and *scribes* (scholars who devoted their lives to copying the text of the Old Testament). Jews living a distance away from the temple would gather for worship and instruction in a *synagogue*. No sacrifices could be offered in a synagogue, but prayers were said and the Hebrew Scriptures were read. Jews met for worship on the Sabbath, the seventh day of the week.

Religious Jews usually identified with one of the sects within Judaism.

The *Pharisees* were committed to a strict keeping of every detail of the law of Moses. Members of this group often came into conflict with Jesus. They accused Jesus of breaking God's law, of associating too closely with nonreligious people, and of claiming a unique relationship with God.

The *Sadducees* were the Jewish aristocrats. They cooperated with the Roman rulers and held positions of authority among the Jews. The Sadducees were also more liberal in their view of God's demands. They accepted only the first five books of the Old Testament as authoritative Scripture. They rejected any belief in life after death or a resurrection of the body. Most members of the Sanhedrin were Sadducees. They came into conflict with Jesus less often than the Pharisees but ultimately joined with them to condemn Jesus to death.

The *Zealots* opposed paying taxes to the Roman authorities and were intent on raising a rebellion against any outside rule over Judea.

The *Essenes* are not mentioned in the New Testament but were the fourth major sect of the Jews. The Essenes lived in separate communities and meticulously observed the purity laws of the Old Testament. The community that copied and hid the Dead Sea Scrolls near Qumran was probably an Essene community. John the Baptist may have had some association with the Essenes during his years in the wilderness.

Spiritually the Jews were looking for a Deliverer who would usher in a golden age—a return to the glory of David's great kingdom. God had promised throughout the Old Testament that he would send a Messiah, or Deliverer, to rule for-ever over his people. Roman tyranny over Palestine made that hope even stronger. The general expectation was that the Messiah would be a political/military leader who would overthrow the Romans. Jesus came offering a kingdom of truth and justice. Most of the Jews in Judea rejected his message.

HELP FILE

A GIFT OF GOD

The name Matthew means "gift of the Lord." In the gospels of Mark and Luke, Matthew is called by his Jewish name, Levi (Mark 2:14; Luke 5:27).

Matthew quotes from the Old Testament forty-four times in his gospel, more often than the other three gospel writers combined. He quotes from nineteen different Old Testament books and mentions fifteen Old Testament characters by name (not including nearly forty other names in the genealogy in chapter 1).

Not one direct word spoken by Matthew is recorded in any gospel, although he is named in all four gospels as one of the twelve close followers of Jesus.

According to historical accounts outside the New Testament, Matthew lived in Palestine several years after Jesus' return to heaven. He then went out as a missionary to Jewish people in Syria, Persia, and perhaps Ethiopia. The New Testament is silent on Matthew's later life.

Mark

➤ Get the story of Jesus for the Internet age—fast and to the point.

➤ Meet a man who failed but who still wrote a book of the Bible.

➤ Have your own encounter with Jesus!

Reading Mark's story of Jesus is like watching a fast-paced, action-packed video! Matthew, the writer of the first gospel, speaks to the thinkers among us—those who have the time and patience to study carefully. Mark's gospel appeals to the doers—to people who are busy, on the move, leading the charge in a high-powered world.

But don't expect Rambo to jump out of these pages—or Bill Gates or Michael Jordan. The hero of Mark's story is a servant. Mark paints a portrait of Jesus as the Servant of the Lord, the obedient Son of the Father, running to do whatever God desired.

You won't find the story of Jesus' birth in Mark—no stable in Bethlehem, no wise men, no shepherds. Mary and Joseph are hardly mentioned. There's no genealogy of Jesus either. No one really cares about the background or family tree of a servant. All we care about is what a servant is able to do. We want action—and that is precisely where Mark puts the emphasis. He tells us what Jesus *does*.

And we can barely keep up with Jesus! Mark fills his pages with phrases like "at once," "immediately," "just then," "without delay." He writes like the telemarketer who calls during dinner and talks so fast you can't get a word in edgewise. One sentence connects to the next; one story hooks into the next. Mark tells us urgently that this is important stuff and we had better listen.

Key Characters

Jesus: the miracle-working Servant of the Lord

Mark: the author of this gospel; an early Christian and a companion to Peter

Peter: one of Jesus' closest followers and the one who often took leadership among the disciples

John the Baptist: a prophet who announced the coming of Israel's promised Deliverer

DOwNLOAd

Mark 10:43 – 45

"Whoever wants to become great among you must be your servant, and whoever wants to be first must be slave of all. For even the Son of Man did not come to be served, but to serve, and to give his life as a ransom for many."

Mark is like a CNN reporter. He doesn't write; he reports. He wants us to feel as if we are right there on the scene, watching or participating in these incredible events. His gospel is a videotape of Jesus' ministry. We find ourselves breathlessly pulled along as Jesus, the Lord's Servant, rushes to do the Father's will.

"Friends, Romans, Countrymen, Lend Me Your Ears"

Mark wrote in his particular style because he wanted to grab the attention of a very specific audience. He was trying to penetrate his own culture. Mark's Jesus had to speak to the Romans, the masters of Mark's world.

You have to understand that the ancient Romans were not deeply intellectual. They were impressed with actions more than with ideas. While other people talked about conquering the world, the Romans did it. So when they were confronted with Jesus, the question they asked was, Why should I follow this man? Mark wanted the Roman readers to see Jesus as a man under orders—not from an emperor, but from the God of the universe.

The Romans were non-Jews, or Gentiles. They didn't have a background in the Old Testament Scriptures as the Jewish people did. The average Roman didn't care about fulfilled prophecy or Jewish customs or the law codes of Moses. Gentiles didn't understand all that. So Mark for the most part left it out. His focus was always on Jesus as a man who was powerful to act and powerful to save.

Mark also had a second audience in mind as he wrote. He wrote his gospel as a source of encouragement to the Roman Christians. These Christians were under intense persecution from Emperor Nero. Some Christians (perhaps the apostle Peter and the apostle Paul) had already

☑ Mark's gospel is a fast-paced, you-are-there account of Jesus' ministry, death, and resurrection.

☑ Jesus models servanthood. He never saw people in need as an interruption.

☑ Two appropriate responses surface as we read the book: to believe in Jesus as Redeemer and to follow Jesus as Lord. Any other response puts us on a path away from God's kingdom, not toward it.

been executed for their faith. The Christians needed to know that they weren't alone in their suffering; the one they worshiped as Lord had passed through his trials in victory. Since Jesus had gone to the cross, it was possible that they might be called to follow him there.

Mark's gospel is the gospel that best fits the twenty-first century. Modern Americans and Europeans and Japanese are very much like the Romans. We are out to conquer the world! We are driven to succeed. We want to see a gospel of action.

People in our culture don't have much religious or biblical background. We have to start with the basic facts—not intricate theology or church ritual—but a clear, straightforward presentation of Jesus. Men and women today want to know if Jesus can still calm life's storms, if he can still restore relationships, if he can still give purpose to life in an aimless, meaningless, hectic world. The Jesus we encounter in Mark's gospel can do all that and more!

Resumé of a Gospel Writer

Although Mark never mentioned himself by name in his book, the leaders of the early Christian community all agreed that this gospel was written by an associate of the apostle Peter whose name was Mark or John Mark. Mark got his start in Christian ministry a few years after Jesus' resurrection. He went with two Christian evangelists, Barnabas and Paul, as they preached about Jesus in cities where the message had not been heard before. Halfway through the trip, however, Mark went home. We aren't told why he left. Maybe he was discouraged or ill or homesick. Barnabas (his uncle) was disappointed, but Paul was unforgiving. A few years later, when Paul and Barnabas were getting ready

NAKED INTO THE NIGHT

Near the end of his book, Mark recorded an event that no other gospel writer said anything about. It happened in the Garden of Gethsemane as Jesus was being arrested:

A young man, wearing nothing but a linen garment, was following Jesus. When they seized him, he fled naked, leaving his garment behind. (Mark 14:51–52)

Many students of Mark's book believe the young man running naked from the scene was John Mark himself. Imagine trying to explain that to your mother when you got home!

for a second preaching trip, Barnabas said, "Let's take Mark again." Paul said, "No way!"—and the two friends went separate directions.

So, while Mark could list some impressive references on his spiritual resumé, he also had to add a big F for failure. If you have ever blown it, you can take heart. One of the people given the privilege of writing a book of the Bible had a life marked by failure.

But Mark's story didn't end with his failure and the argument that followed. Uncle Barnabas didn't give up on his young nephew. He mentored him and encouraged him until Mark became a strong Christian leader. Eventually Mark joined up with the apostle Peter. He carried Peter's bags and booked flights to the next meeting—and Mark probably heard Peter preach hundreds of times. He ended up in Rome with Peter and probably helped bury Peter after his execution.

Answering the Big Questions

Mark wrote his gospel to answer the big questions: Who is Jesus? Why did he die? Why should we care?

Who Is Jesus? (Mark 1–8)

The first half of the book focuses on Jesus' works. Jesus was a teacher, and we hear a few parables and a couple of short sermons, but most of the narrative tells us what Jesus did. He healed great crowds of people; he worked almost without rest. But Jesus was never too busy or too tired to focus his attention on one individual in need. Hurting people were never an interruption.

As we read this section of the story, our admiration for Jesus grows until we begin to ask ourselves the question Jesus finally asked his disciples: "Who do you say I am?" (Mark 8:27–29). Peter, the most outspoken of Jesus' followers, answered: "You are the Christ [Messiah]!" It's the same answer we have settled on as we have watched Jesus at work. Jesus is the King we've been waiting for, the Prophet who will bring us to God, the Master we will gladly follow.

Why Did Jesus Die? (Mark 9–16)

At that critical moment, Mark began to focus his reader's attention on the cross. Jesus the King would gain his kingdom by suffering and dying. Mark gave a lot of space to the last days of Jesus' earthly life: his betrayal by Judas, his trials, his agony on the cross. The point he wanted us to see is that Jesus' victory over death came at a great price—the torturous death on the cross. When the payment for human sin had been fully paid, God exalted his Servant to a place of incredible glory.

How Should I Respond?

Two themes that run through Mark's gospel are how we should respond to who Jesus is and how we should respond to what Jesus has

HELP FILE

AN EARLY ACCOUNT

One early Christian writer (Papias) says that Mark was the disciple of Simon Peter and that he wrote down a summary of Peter's preaching about Jesus that we can read today in the gospel of Mark.

Mark's gospel is some of the earliest New Testament writing. It may be the first record of Jesus' ministry and death

actually written down. Christians have loved and studied Mark's book for two thousand years. Mark's life and impact prove that we can never underestimate the power of God's forgiveness and grace to change a life.

If you want to read more about Mark's life on your own, look up Acts 12:25–13:5, 13; 15:36–40; and 1 Peter 5:13.

done on the cross. What surprises me is that most of the people in Mark's narrative rejected Jesus or ignored him. His own family misunderstood his mission; the crowd in his hometown was jealous of his wisdom; the religious leaders were antagonistic at best and murderous at worst. Even Jesus' own disciples betrayed him, disowned him, or abandoned him.

The people who were faithful to Jesus in Mark's story were the desperate—the hurting, the sick, the dying. They had nowhere else to go and no one else to whom they could turn. They cast themselves on Jesus and found all they needed and more!

Two responses seem to stand out as the responses God desires in those who read Mark's book. The first comes from a very minor character in the book, a Roman soldier whose name we don't even know. As he watched Jesus die he said, "Surely this man was the Son of God!" (Mark 15:39). Hopefully that was your response as you concluded your reading. The story of Jesus always forces a choice. Is he who he says he is? Will I believe in him or write him off?

The other appropriate response to Jesus comes in the first chapter of Mark. Jesus called some who knew him to follow him. The same

DiGGinG DeEpeR

✗ McKenna, David. *Mark*. The Communicator's Commentary. Waco, TX: Word, 1982.

A solid explanation of what Mark wrote, combined with practical insights and application for life today. A helpful guide.

✗ Garland, David. *Mark*. The NIV Application Commentary. Grand Rapids: Zondervan, 1996.

A more detailed study than McKenna's; very well done.

If you want to study the gospel of Mark on your own, work your way through the LifeGuide Bible Study on *Mark* written by Jim Hoover (Downers Grove, IL: InterVarsity Press, 1985). The guide is a reliable road map, and you get to enjoy the discovery of God's truth!

challenge is pressed on us as we read the story. If Jesus is the Son of God, how can I do less than follow him as Lord?

The lingering impact of Mark's gospel is not simply to pump us up to conquer our little slice of the world. Mark's story is designed to change us. Our presumptions and prejudices, attitudes and excuses are all punctured and put aside. The perceptions we have of Jesus and of our world are turned upside down. Jesus, the Servant, is really the Lord of all. The mark of success is not who has the most toys or who was able to climb to the top first. We succeed in God's kingdom by being the servant of all. The first is last. The one who saves his life is the one who gives that life away.

Walking the Walk

1. Try to carve out enough time to read through the gospel of Mark in one afternoon or evening. Let yourself be carried along by the power of the story. Write down some of your impressions when you finish. What do you remember most about Jesus from Mark's account?

2. Ask someone important to you—your spouse, your friend, your parents—what you can do to help him or her this week. If you aren't normally the "servant" in the relationship, make sure the person is sitting down when you volunteer! Do whatever that person asks with a willing spirit and don't look for praise or applause. You are following Jesus when you serve others.

3. Determine to look at the people around you differently. Focus on their needs and ask yourself how you can be an agent for good in their lives. An attitude like that may transform your marriage or your family life or your work environment beyond recognition!

TWELVE WHO FOLLOWED: JESUS' DISCIPLES

Early in his ministry Jesus asked twelve men to be his closest followers (disciples). Later Jesus commissioned these men to be his personal representatives (apostles). At first the men just spent time with Jesus. Gradually Jesus gave them responsibilities to tell people about him and even to do miracles in his name. The apostles were the leaders of the early church after Jesus returned to heaven (including Matthias, who was chosen to replace Judas—Acts 1:26). Their writings are recognized by Christians as Jesus' continuing message to his people. Paul of Tarsus was called as an apostle by Jesus in Acts 9—several years after Jesus had died on the cross, risen, and returned to heaven. Paul considered himself a fully authorized representative of Jesus (an apostle) but "one abnormally born" (1 Corinthians 15:8).

> **Simon Peter:** Leader and frequent spokesman for "the Twelve" (the original close followers of Jesus). Peter was married and lived in Capernaum. He denied Jesus three times but was later restored to Jesus' inner circle (John 21). He was the leader of the early church in Jerusalem. The books of 1 and 2 Peter were written by him. The gospel of Mark is a record of Peter's memories of Jesus. Tradition says that Peter was executed under Emperor Nero around A.D. 65 by being crucified upside down.
>
> **Andrew:** Brother of Peter. Both originally were fishermen and disciples of John the Baptist.

> **James:** Son of Zebedee, brother of John. James was one of the inner circle of Jesus' disciples with Peter and John. He was executed by Herod Agrippa I around A.D. 44 (Acts 12:1–2).
>
> **John:** Son of Zebedee, brother of James. John was Jesus' closest human friend and the one entrusted with the care of Jesus' mother, Mary. He wrote the gospel of John, the three letters of John, and the book of Revelation. Tradition says that he lived in Ephesus in Asia Minor in his old age and seems to be the only one of the Twelve to die of old age.
>
> **Philip:** One of Jesus' earliest followers along with Peter and Andrew.
>
> **Bartholomew:** Also called Nathanael (John 1:43–51).
>
> **Matthew:** Also called Levi. Matthew was a tax collector until Jesus called him to be his follower. Matthew wrote the gospel of Matthew. Later traditions describe his travels to Syria and Ethiopia, where he was martyred.
>
> **Thomas:** This disciple is best known for doubting the resurrection of Jesus until he personally saw and touched him (John 20:24–29; the origin of the phrase, "a doubting Thomas"). A fairly reliable tradition says that Thomas took the message of Jesus to India.
>
> **James (the younger one):** Very little is known about this disciple. He never speaks in the gospel record.

Judas: Also called Thaddaeus. His only recorded words appear in John 14:22.

Simon the Zealot: Before following Jesus, Simon was a member of a group of Jewish revolutionaries who were determined to overthrow Roman rule in Judea.

Judas Iscariot: The betrayer of Jesus. He was the treasurer of the group and a thief (John 12:4–6). Jesus knew early on that Judas would ultimately turn against him (John 6:70–71). Judas ended his life in suicide.

Lists of the Twelve: Matthew 10:2–4; Mark 3:16–19; Luke 6:13–16; Acts 1:13

Luke

➤ Read the book of a prominent doctor who wrote a religious best-seller!
➤ Explore a very personal, human portrait of Jesus.
➤ Learn what it means to be rescued by Jesus.

Luke's gospel is the closest thing we have to an "authorized biography" of Jesus. Luke was not an insider like Matthew or John. Luke hadn't seen Jesus' miracles or heard him teach or seen him after his resurrection from the dead. Luke had to rely on other sources for his story—written accounts, interviews with eyewitnesses, travel and observation through the land of Palestine. In the end Luke produced a carefully written, meticulously researched record of Jesus' life, death, and resurrection that is filled with details and human-interest stories. Luke takes us closer to Jesus the man than any of the other gospel writers.

Jesus' humanity is the focus of Luke's gospel. Luke presents Jesus as a man moved to compassion by human suffering, a man who enjoyed being around children. Jesus was not just God pretending to be human. He was a real human being, who came from heaven's glory to a stable and then to the dusty roads of Palestine—and finally to a bloody cross. Jesus lived in the real world with all its pain, sorrow, and disappointment. He knows from personal experience what human existence is all about.

Doctor Luke

Luke is the only Gentile (non-Jewish) New Testament writer. He most likely came to believe in Jesus through the preaching of the apostle Paul several years after Jesus had returned to heaven. Soon after Luke's conversion he began to accompany Paul on some travels. Paul needed Luke professionally and

Key Characters

Jesus: the Savior of the world, a man filled with compassion for hurting people

Luke: a non-Jewish Christian and companion of the apostle Paul; the author of the gospel of Luke and the book of Acts

Theophilus: the original recipient of Luke's story of Jesus

Mary: Jesus' mother; a virgin who conceived miraculously and gave birth to God the Son

personally. Luke was a physician, and he cared for Paul's physical needs. Luke was also a friend, and Paul often turned to him for encouragement and help in the work of spreading the message of Jesus.

At the end of Paul's third extensive preaching journey, Paul was arrested in Jerusalem after a riot started in the temple. The Jewish leaders accused Paul of stirring up rebellion among the people. For two years Paul sat in jail waiting for some resolution of his case. The indications we get from the book of Acts are that Luke was with Paul during that time. Luke had the opportunity to meet the other apostles and close followers of Jesus. He talked with people who had been healed by Jesus or had heard Jesus teach. As Luke listened to the stories, he began to write them down. Some of the accounts he had heard before, but some were new to him. He read other written records of Jesus' ministry including the newly written gospel of Mark. He walked the paths Jesus had walked. He stood on a boat in the Sea of Galilee and knelt in the Garden of Gethsemane where Jesus prayed. Finally, Luke sat down and put all the accounts together in a moving narrative of one powerfully significant life.

But Who Is Theophilus?

What prompted Luke to put it all together in one story was his burden for a friend. Luke dedicated his gospel to a man I wish we knew more about.

> Many have undertaken to draw up an account of the things that have been fulfilled among us, just as they were handed down to us by those who from the first were eyewitnesses and servants of the word. There-

FOOtPRiNts in the SanD

During a drought in 1986, the water level in the Sea of Galilee dropped. Two Israelis noticed the outline of a boat in the shoreline mud. It turned out to be a small fishing boat from the time of Jesus—maybe one like Jesus and his disciples were in on the night Jesus stilled the storm (Luke 8:22–25). The boat was twenty-seven feet long, eight feet wide, and five feet high. Fifteen passengers could ride in the boat as long as at least four were willing to row and one handled the helm.

Points 2 Remember

☑ Luke wrote his gospel to highlight Jesus' humanity.

☑ After careful research, Luke compiled the events from Jesus' life that would speak most powerfully to Gentile (non-Jewish) readers who were searching for spiritual fulfillment.

☑ The character and identity of Jesus gradually unfold in the book. We see him as a man, then as a great man, then as more than a man.

☑ There is no person Jesus cannot change, no boundary he will not cross to rescue someone in need.

fore, since I myself have carefully investigated everything from the beginning, it seemed good also to me to write an orderly account for you, most excellent Theophilus, so that you may know the certainty of the things you have been taught. (1:1–4)

We don't know who Theophilus was. His name *(thee-off-ill-us)* means "lover of God." Apparently he was a Gentile friend of Luke who had recently believed in Jesus and needed further instruction in the facts of Jesus' life—or he was someone Luke was trying to persuade to become a follower of Jesus. The title "most excellent" implies that Theophilus was a dignitary in the Roman government or among the leading citizens of a city.

What we learn from Luke's dedication of the book to Theophilus is that Luke wrote his gospel to speak to Gentiles— to the majority population of the Roman world. Luke was demonstrating the truth that the message of Jesus is not confined only to Israel or to any special race or class of people. God's love and acceptance are available to all who will believe in Jesus—not just males, but females too; and not just wealthy or influential females, but poor women, widows, and even prostitutes. Slaves can even get in on God's program. In fact, all the groups that society looks down on are welcome in God's kingdom—the poor, weak, disabled, homeless, even addicts and criminals. *Anyone* who believes finds a seat at the banquet table of God's forgiveness and grace.

A Long Journey But a Straight Road

Luke's gospel is the longest book in the New Testament, but it is a lot easier to follow than some of the shorter books. It divides into two parts with a dramatic turning point in the middle.

The Savior's Arrival (Luke 1:1 – 9:50)

In the first part of Luke's story, the Savior comes from heaven to earth. Luke had probably talked personally with Mary, Jesus' mother. As a result, we have all the details of Jesus' birth—the visit by an angel, the stable in Bethlehem where Jesus was born, the announcement to the shepherds that a Savior had arrived—a Savior *for them!*

Luke gradually introduces Jesus in various roles—as a teacher, as a healer, as the one with authority over demons. We see Jesus as a man, then as a great man, then as more than a man. Luke's presentation reaches a climax in chapter 9 when Jesus takes three of his followers (Peter, James, and John) up on a mountain and is "transfigured" before them—that is, the glory of Jesus' true identity as the Son of God was allowed to "shine through" his human body. This man was more than a healer or miracle-worker. He was God in visible form as a man.

The Savior's Departure (Luke 9:51 – 24:53)

Shortly after Jesus' transfiguration, the story takes a dramatic turn. Jesus begins to focus on the final aspect of his work on earth—his death on the cross, his resurrection, and his return to heaven.

> As the time approached for him to be taken up to heaven, Jesus resolutely set out for Jerusalem. (9:51)

In the chapters that follow, Jesus pours his heart into his disciples. He teaches them that following him as Lord and Master is not easy but that the rewards are eternal. Jesus also faces growing hostility from the reli-

DiggiNG DeEpeR

✗ Bock, Darrell. *Luke.* The NIV Application Commentary. Grand Rapids: Zondervan, 1996.

A very helpful explanation by an outstanding student of Luke's writings.

✗ Wilcox, Michael. *The Message of Luke's Gospel: Savior of the World.* The Bible Speaks Today series. Downers Grove, IL: InterVarsity Press, 1979.

A brief but well-written survey.

DOWNLOAD

Luke 19:10

"The Son of Man came to seek and to save what was lost."

gious leaders who feel threatened by his popularity. Finally, they coerce the Roman government into crucifying him. But even in the agony of his torturous death, Jesus displays compassion by forgiving the criminal on the cross next to his (23:39–43). The crucifixion was not the end, however. The tomb in which Jesus' friends buried him was empty three days later, and Jesus appeared several times to his followers. Luke ends his gospel with Jesus being taken up to heaven.

Searching

Most of us are just like the people Luke wanted to reach with his gospel. Most of us are Gentiles, not Jews. We come from a wide variety of cultural and ethnic backgrounds. We have very few needs, and most of us are pretty secure financially. Where we struggle is in our spirits. Life seems so empty at times, so pointless, and we wonder why we are here and what we are supposed to accomplish.

HELP FiLE

LUKE'S WRITINGS — PART 1

Luke is mentioned by name in three of Paul's letters (Colossians 4:14 — "our dear friend, Luke, the doctor"; 2 Timothy 4:11; Philemon 24).

Luke's gospel is the first volume of a two-part work. The book of Acts carries the story of Jesus and his followers beyond the resurrection through the spread of the gospel message to the entire Roman world.

Jesus calls himself the "Son of Man" twenty-four times in the gospel of Luke. This title points back to the Old Testa-

ment book of Daniel 7:13–14, which describes a divine being who is given authority over the nations of the world.

Matthew recorded Jesus' royal genealogy, his rightful inheritance of the throne of Israel through Jesus' adopted father, Joseph (Matthew 1:1–17). Luke, by contrast, most likely gave us Jesus' bloodline through Mary, his mother (Luke 3:23–38). Luke traced Jesus' ancestors back to Adam, the first human, to show Jesus' genuine link with the human race.

ONLY IN LUKE

Luke gives us the most complete coverage of Jesus' birth.

Only Luke (out of all the gospel writers) includes the details of John the Baptist's unusual birth (1:5–25, 57–80).

Only Luke tells of Mary's visit from the angel Gabriel (1:26–38), Mary's journey to see her relative Elizabeth (1:39–56), Jesus' birth in a stable, and the shepherds' visit (2:1–20).

Only Luke gives us the details of Jesus' circumcision and presentation to God in the temple (2:21–38). Jesus' visit to the temple at age twelve is recorded in no other gospel (2:41–52).

Luke is very careful to link events in the life of Jesus with political rulers and world events (see 2:1–3; 3:1–2).

Luke alone gives us some of Jesus' most vivid parables: the good Samaritan (10:25–37), the rich fool (12:13–21), the prodigal son (15:11–32), the scheming manager (16:1–13), and the rich man and Lazarus (16:19–31).

Only Luke records Jesus weeping over Jerusalem (19:41) and an angel coming to strengthen him in the Garden of Gethsemane (22:43).

Luke pictures Jesus in prayer more than any other gospel writer. At every major crisis, Jesus prayed.

Luke highlights Jesus' interest and attention toward women and children.

Luke alone tells the story of Jesus' appearance after his resurrection to two of his followers who were traveling to the town of Emmaus (24:13–35).

Maybe you have been turned off by a church or wounded by a Christian. Maybe you don't have any religious background. You might be a person who has tried several different religious traditions. What draws us to Jesus is an emptiness in our lives, a hole in our spirits that nothing seems to satisfy. You might feel like you've already blown it too badly to be accepted by God. You've convinced yourself that it's easier to live without him. But the hunger is still there, a hunger to know for sure that God is real and that he cares about you.

Luke's gospel is designed for people like us! We are introduced to a man who touches our lives at every level. He lived on earth two thousand years ago, yet we get the sense that he did it all just for us—for me. We also realize that there is no person that Jesus cannot reach and change, no boundary he won't cross if it means that one person is rescued forever from the penalty of sin and disobedience.

Jesus is, in fact, like the shepherd in the story he told (15:3–7). Ninety-nine of the shepherd's one hundred sheep made it safely into the barn for the night. Most of us would have been willing to take a 1 percent loss if it meant we wouldn't miss supper or *Monday Night Football*. This shepherd, however, determined to look until he found the missing sheep. He intended to do whatever it took to rescue that sheep and bring it safely home—and what the shepherd determined to do, he did. We cheer at the end of that story not because we love sheep so much, but because we feel like that sheep—lost, alone, and afraid. We cheer because we hope there's a Shepherd looking for us with the same commitment to our rescue. Luke's gospel points us to that Shepherd. His name is Jesus. And when Jesus rescues us, heaven explodes with joy!

Walking the Walk

1. Who is a Theophilus in your life—someone you can help bring either to faith in Jesus or to maturity as a Christian? Think of specific steps you can take to have a positive influence in that person's life.

2. Luke records four "songs" sung or spoken in praise of Jesus' coming to earth. Take the time to read each one and describe what you would have expected of Jesus if you had heard each one when it was first spoken—Mary's song (1:46–55), Zechariah's song (1:68–79), the angels' song (2:14), Simeon's song (2:29–32).

3. Jesus was moved with compassion to do what he could to help those in need who were right around him. What can you do today to be involved personally in helping an individual or family in need?

4. Who are the "outsiders" to your circle of friends or your church congregation? Work on developing a friendship with a person outside your economic, racial, or even religious "comfort zone." What concerns you most about doing that?

5. Would you live differently if Jesus had just been a courageous martyr and had not risen from the dead? How does his resurrection change your perspective on who Jesus was?

PARABLE ANYONE?

Luke records more of Jesus' parables than Matthew, Mark, or John. (According to *The NIV Study Bible,* Luke gives us twenty-eight parables; Matthew, twenty-three; Mark, nine; John, none!) A parable is a story that teaches spiritual truth. Parables are short, easy to remember—and potentially life-changing. The parables of Jesus had meaning on two levels. First, there was the story itself. Some of Jesus' listeners were entertained by the stories but never gave them much thought. Behind the simple story, however, was a deeper meaning. Sometimes the spiritual meaning was obvious. A few times Jesus interpreted the parable. At other times Jesus just told the story and left it up to his listeners to figure it out. As they thought about what Jesus had said and replayed the story over and over in their minds, suddenly a light went on! They understood what Jesus was trying to communicate—and saw it in very personal terms.

Probably the most famous parable recorded in Luke is the parable of the prodigal son (15:11–32). It's pretty clear that the runaway son pictures the person separated from God by disobedience and rebellion. The watching father in the story pictures God, who responds to those who return to him with grace and forgiveness. The person we usually ignore is the second son in the story, but he was the point of the whole parable! Jesus told the story to a bunch of religious people who were criticizing him for being so chummy with nonreligious "sinners." Jesus wanted these critics to know that God rejoiced over sinners who turned back to him. Jesus also wanted to point out the pious, self-righteous attitude of those who had stayed in the church all their lives and never committed the *big* sins. The attitude of the stay-at-home son needed to be changed as much as the behavior of the son who ran away. Jesus' critical listeners were not impressed.

To study some of Jesus' parables on your own, get John White's *Parables* in the LifeGuide Bible Study series (Downers Grove, IL: InterVarsity Press, 1985).

John

➤ Come face-to-face with God!
➤ Read a powerful account of Jesus' life written by his closest friend.
➤ Discover what Jesus said just before he died.

John wrote his gospel to convince his readers that Jesus is God. John doesn't tell us that until the end of the book, but he tips his hand dramatically in chapter 20:

> Jesus did many other miraculous signs in the presence of his disciples, which are not recorded in this book. But these are written that you may believe that Jesus is the Christ, the Son of God, and that by believing you may have life in his name. (20:30–31)

As John wrote, he very carefully selected events and encounters from Jesus' life that portray Jesus as God, the Lord of all. Jesus is always in control in John's gospel. Jesus' teaching, Jesus' miracles, Jesus' commanding presence in every situation conveyed one truth to John—Jesus is the eternal God who became fully human and lived here where we could see him.

John did not begin his gospel with Jesus' birth or a list of Jesus' ancestors. God has no beginning. John began with a ringing declaration.

In the beginning was the Word, and the Word was with God, and the Word was God. (1:1)

John's title for Jesus was "the Word." Jesus was the tangible expression of all that God is. Just as we explain our thoughts and feelings through words, the character and majesty of God were fully expressed in God's living Word, Jesus.

The Word became flesh and made his dwelling among us. We have seen his glory, the glory of

Key Characters

Jesus: God the Son, the Creator and source of life

John: the author of this gospel; one of Jesus' closest followers

The Word: John's title for Jesus in chapter 1

WITNESSES FOR THE DEFENSE

Seven different people in this book gave personal testimony to the fact that Jesus was God.

John the Baptist: "I have seen and I testify that this is the Son of God" (1:34).

Nathanael (a skeptic who became a follower): "Rabbi, you are the Son of God; you are the King of Israel" (1:49).

Peter (one of Jesus' closest friends): "We believe and know that you are the Holy One of God" (6:69).

Martha (a follower of Jesus): "I believe that you are the Christ, the Son of God, who was to come into the world" (11:27).

Thomas (a follower of Jesus who doubted that Jesus had risen from the dead): "My Lord and my God!" (20:28).

John (the author of the gospel): "Jesus is the Christ, the Son of God" (20:31).

Jesus himself: "I am God's Son" (10:36).

the One and Only, who came from the Father, full of grace and truth. (1:14)

Jesus became human, but he never ceased to be God. That's the point John makes all the way through his book. If you want to see God, John says, look at Jesus. If you want to hear God, listen to Jesus.

Meet the Author

John had plenty of opportunity to know and hear and talk with Jesus up close. The author of the fourth gospel was one of Jesus' closest companions. Out of all his followers, Jesus chose twelve to be with him as disciples. Within the group of twelve, three men—Peter, James, and John—were often asked by Jesus to go with him for times of prayer or to gain special insight. Within the inner circle of three, one man, John, was Jesus' dearest friend. John never refers to himself by name in his gospel. He is just "the disciple whom Jesus loved" (13:23; 19:26; 20:2; 21:7, 20). These are the memoirs of an intimate friend. Jesus had transformed John's life, and John wanted to pass that transforming message on to anyone willing to listen.

This was the last gospel to be written. The best evidence points to a date between A.D. 80 and 90 for its writing. The other three gospels (most likely) had been in circulation for several years. John wrote to add his unique perspective and to fill in some of the details not recorded by the other writers. There are no parables, for example, in John's gospel. The other gospels included plenty of them. On the flip side, John preserved several long speeches from Jesus that no other writer mentioned. The earlier gospels focused on Jesus and the crowds who followed him. John focused on the encounters Jesus had with individuals. John didn't include Jesus' anguish in the Garden of Gethsemane just before his arrest, because Matthew, Mark, and Luke gave that incident great coverage. Instead of simply repeating what had already been written, John gave us the intimate conversation Jesus had with his disciples that same night.

John wrote his gospel for a universal audience. He wanted everyone to know who Jesus was. Even today anyone can pick up John's book and understand its message. John wanted us to know that it was God in human flesh who astonished the people of his day with miracles and amazed them with his teaching. It was God who lived a perfect life and then allowed himself to be put to death on a cross for humanity's sins. It was God who three days after he died broke the chains of death and came out of the grave alive. Jesus was no ordinary religious teacher pointing people *to* God. Jesus was here *as* God, calling people to put their faith in him.

An Astonishing Book

The gospel of John begins with a poem or song that presents Jesus' majesty and power. The first eighteen verses set the tone for the rest of the book.

Digging Deeper

✗   Connelly, Douglas. *John: The Way to True Life.* LifeGuide Bible Study series. Downers Grove, IL: InterVarsity Press, 1990.

For those who want to study John on their own. You can do it!

✗   Milne, Bruce. *The Message of John: Here Is Your King.* The Bible Speaks Today series. Downers Grove, IL: InterVarsity Press, 1993.

An excellent explanation of John's message.

Jesus and the World (John 1:19-12:50)

In the first half of the gospel we are allowed to follow Jesus as he presents himself to the people of his day as the promised Messiah, God's Deliverer. John was particularly interested in certain miracles of Jesus and recorded seven of them. These miracles were not performed simply to alleviate human suffering or to meet human needs; John called them "signs." Like signs pointing to the right road, Jesus' miracles pointed to the truth of Jesus' claim to be the Son of God. Check them out for yourself:

1. Jesus changed water into wine (2:1–11).
2. Jesus healed a government official's son (4:43–54).
3. Jesus cured a sick man in Jerusalem (5:1–15).
4. Jesus fed five thousand people with a sack lunch (6:1–15).
5. Jesus walked on the surface of the water (6:16–21).
6. Jesus healed a man born blind (9:1–12).
7. Jesus raised his friend Lazarus from the dead (11:1–44).

These chapters also include some particularly powerful personal encounters with Jesus. Nicodemus, a Jewish leader, came to Jesus seeking more information about who Jesus was and about Jesus' miracles. Jesus responded by calling Nicodemus to be "born again" (3:1–21).

In chapter 4 Jesus really crossed some cultural lines. He talked with a woman (gender lines) who was a Samaritan (racial and religious lines) and who also was living in an immoral relationship with a man (moral lines). Jesus offered her "living water"—a life-changing relationship with him (4:4–42).

Some religious leaders brought a woman to Jesus. The woman had been caught in the act of adultery (so where was the man?). They wanted Jesus to agree that she should be stoned to death as the law of

DOWNLOAD

John 3:16

"For God so loved the world that he gave his one and only Son, that whoever believes in him shall not perish but have eternal life."

Moses required. That's when Jesus spoke his famous line: "If any one of you is without sin, let him be the first to throw a stone" (8:1–11).

Opposition to Jesus also rose to a fever pitch in these chapters. His enemies began to plot to kill him because "he was even calling God his own Father, making himself equal with God" (5:18). This section ends with Jesus declaring that the time of his death and final victory had come.

Jesus and His Friends (John 13:1 - 17:26)

In the hours before his arrest, Jesus gathered with his disciples in a banquet room built above the home of one of his followers. In this "upper room" Jesus tried to prepare his closest friends for the shock of his approaching death on the cross. In an act of humility, Jesus washed

BORN AGAIN?

People who claim to be "born again" actually take that phrase from the Bible. Jesus said to Nicodemus, a Jewish leader, "No one can see the kingdom of God unless he is born again" (John 3:3). Nicodemus thought Jesus was referring to a second *physical* birth when, in fact, Jesus was referring to a *spiritual* renewal. Our physical birth gave us physical life, but our spirits are dead toward God, unresponsive to his love. Spiritual birth gives us a whole new kind of life, eternal life, a life of friendship with God. We receive this new life by believing in Jesus as Savior. "Whoever believes in [Jesus] shall not perish but have eternal life" (3:16). Some people throw the term *born again* around pretty casually. In Jesus' mind, being born again had eternal significance.

John used the word *believe* ninety-eight times in the twenty-one chapters of his gospel. Belief has two crucial parts to it. First, it means accepting certain facts to be true. Before I can believe, I need reliable information, and I need to accept the information as true. The gospel of John presents reliable information about Jesus. You can accept the facts as true or reject those facts—or even ignore what John wrote. But simply acknowledging certain facts is not enough. Belief, genuine faith, includes a personal commitment to those facts. I rely on the facts to come true in my experience. Accepting the fact that Jesus is *the* Savior from sin's penalty is not enough. I must also acknowledge Jesus as *my* Savior. His death on the cross was for my sin. Christians use several terms to describe belief. We talk about *receiving* Christ or *accepting* Christ or *coming to* Christ in faith or *trusting* in Jesus as Savior. Those phrases all point back to John's simple word—*believe.*

ONLY IN JOHN

John is the only gospel writer to include the following accounts in his story of Jesus:

Jesus' first miracle: turning water into wine at a wedding in Cana (2:1–11)

The conversation between Jesus and Nicodemus, a Jewish leader (3:1–21)

Jesus' encounter with a woman of Samaria (4:4–26)

The miraculous healing of a man at the pool of Bethesda (5:1–15)

Jesus' healing of a man who had been born blind (9:1–41)

The raising of Lazarus from the dead (11:1–44)

Jesus washing his disciples' feet (13:1–17)

Jesus' final instructions and comfort to his disciples just before his arrest (14:1–16:33)

The prayer Jesus prayed to his Father on the way to the Garden of Gethsemane (17:1–26)

Jesus' appearance after his resurrection to "doubting Thomas" (20:24–29)

On the other hand, some of the material common in the other three gospels are not found at all in John's record.

No stories of Jesus' birth, baptism, or temptation in the wilderness

No parables

No miracles of power over evil spirits

No account of Jesus instituting the Last Supper, or Eucharist

The only miracle of Jesus reported in all four gospels was the miraculous feeding of five thousand from a boy's lunch! (Matthew 14:13–21; Mark 6:30–44; Luke 9:10–17; John 6:1–15).

the feet of his own disciples (13:1–17). Then Jesus exposed the treachery of Judas Iscariot, the disciple who had already cut a deal to betray him (13:18–30). After Judas left the room, Jesus had a long talk with the eleven disciples who remained. These chapters contain some of Jesus' most memorable and comforting words.

"Do not let your hearts be troubled. Trust in God; trust also in me. In my Father's house are many rooms; if it were not so, I would have told you. I am going there to prepare a place for you. And if I go and prepare a place for you, I will come back and take you to be with me that you also may be where I am." (14:1–3)

"I am the way and the truth and the life. No one comes to the Father except through me." (14:6)

P0ints 2 Remember

☑ John's gospel is an eyewitness account of Jesus' life, death, and resurrection written by Jesus' closest friend.

☑ John selected events and encounters that demonstrate Jesus' deity (the fact that Jesus was God). Jesus was the Word, the full expression of all that God is.

☑ John's message is clear. Those who reject Jesus are choosing a dead-end street. Those who receive Jesus are given real life—eternal life.

"Peace I leave with you; my peace I give you. I do not give to you as the world gives. Do not let your hearts be troubled and do not be afraid." (14:27)

"I am the vine; you are the branches. If a man remains in me and I in him, he will bear much fruit; apart from me you can do nothing." (15:5)

"My command is this: Love each other as I have loved you. Greater love has no one than this, that he lay down his life for his friends." (15:12–13)

Jesus also promised that when he left, someone else would come to help his followers. God the Father would send the Holy Spirit who would live in each believer in Jesus. Here's how Jesus said it:

"I will ask the Father, and he will give you another Counselor to be with you forever—the Spirit of truth. The world cannot accept him, because it neither sees him nor knows him. But you know him, for he lives with you and will be in you. I will not leave you as orphans." (14:16–18)

The section closes with Jesus' prayer to God the Father, asking him to reveal Jesus' glory and to protect his followers (17:1–26).

The rest of the New Testament simply unpacks the deep truths that Jesus taught in these few hours with his friends.

Jesus and His Victory (John 18:1 – 21:25)

In his closing chapters, John writes about Jesus' death on the cross and his resurrection to life. But even in the story of Jesus' arrest and trial and crucifixion, even in what for most of us would have been the most degrading experiences, Jesus was in control. When the soldiers came to arrest him, Jesus spoke just one phrase and they fell to the ground

(18:4–6). When the Roman governor, Pontius Pilate, pummeled Jesus with questions, Jesus said, "You would have no power over me if it were not given to you from above" (19:11). At the end of six hours on the cross, Jesus did not die as a powerless victim. He deliberately "gave up his spirit" (19:30). Three days later Jesus rose from the dead and presented himself alive to his followers.

Who Is This Man?

John reveals more in his book about who Jesus is than any other book in the New Testament. The first eighteen verses alone contain more descriptions of Jesus than any other passage in the Bible of the same length. Jesus is presented as:

- the Word (the full expression of who God is)
- the one who in the beginning was face-to-face with God the Father
- the one who is in himself God
- the Creator of all things
- light and life to every human being
- the rejected one and the received one
- the Word who became fully human
- the one and only Son of the Father
- the one full of grace and truth
- the one who made God known to us

You never find Jesus asking his disciples if people liked his teaching or if they were impressed with his miracles. Jesus asked, "Who do people say I am?" Jesus did not call people to embrace a set of religious rules

"I AM"

Jesus made seven powerful claims about himself in John's gospel. They all begin with the words, "I am."

"I am the bread of life" (6:35, 48).

"I am the light of the world" (8:12; 9:5).

"I am the gate" (10:7, 9).

"I am the good shepherd" (10:11, 14).

"I am the resurrection and the life" (11:25).

"I am the way and the truth and the life" (14:6).

"I am the true vine" (15:1).

or a code of moral ethics. He called people to put their trust in him, a person, the God-man.

John never recovered from his encounter with Jesus. If you have never personally believed in Jesus, the evidence about Jesus is clear. Jesus is the eternal God who came to earth to die as a sacrifice on the cross. He gives life to all who receive him. He is the way, the truth, and the life. His own testimony is that, if you reject him, you reject the only avenue of access to God. If you have trouble believing in Jesus, read the gospel of John. If you still have trouble, read it again!

If you already believe in Jesus, John's gospel is designed to give you fresh insight into who Jesus is—and to encourage you to renewed confidence in him as Savior and Lord and God. For John it came down to a struggle between light and darkness. Those who reject Jesus are choosing darkness. Those who receive him become children of God.

Walking the Walk

1. If someone came to your home or workplace tomorrow and made the same "I am" claims that Jesus made in John's gospel, what would you think of that person? Why do the same words sound so different coming from Jesus?

2. How would you characterize your own spiritual life right now? Is your relationship with the Lord: going well? in a rut? in need of attention? nonexistent? How will reading the gospel of John help?

3. If Jesus is "the bread of life," how are you relying on him for spiritual and emotional nourishment? If Jesus is "the good shepherd," how are you resting in his care and guidance?

4. Have you ever believed on Jesus as Savior? What hesitations or questions prevent you from believing? If you already believe, what sense of security does the teaching of John 3:16 bring to your mind?

Part 8

HISTORY

The story of the Bible is anchored firmly in space and time. Actual people, real places, and genuine events fill the pages of both the Old and New Testaments. The Christian faith is not based on myths or abstract philosophy. It is rooted in human history.

If the word *history* brings back memories of boring high school lectures filled with dry facts and obscure events, you are in for a surprise. The book of Acts will captivate your attention and interest like no other historical account. You will have a front-row seat to watch the beginning and growth of an amazing, world-changing revolution. We are still riding the wave that began way back then. You will find yourself wanting to read the next chapter of the book just to hear how the story ends. The book of Acts reads like a novel, but it's all true—and the story is still being written!

Acts

➤ So—what happened *after* Jesus went back to heaven?

➤ Feel the power of God's Spirit!

➤ Follow the spread of the message about Jesus to the whole world.

The book of Acts picks up the story of Jesus and his followers where the Gospels leave off. As the curtain opens, Jesus gives his final instructions to his disciples and ascends into heaven. Jesus challenges his followers to tell the whole world about what he has done, and then he leaves! How can eleven men—especially *these* eleven men—ever reach the whole world?

Key Characters

The Holy Spirit: God the Spirit who energizes Christians to carry out Jesus' final command

Peter: one of Jesus' closest followers and the leader of the early Christian community

Stephen: a Christian who made a courageous defense of Jesus and was stoned to death for it (Acts 7)

Paul (or Saul): he led the opposition to the Christians until Jesus appeared to him in a vision (Acts 9); he became Jesus' messenger to the Gentiles (non-Jews)

Barnabas: one of Paul's companions

Silas: another of Paul's associates

In the very next chapter of Acts, the power source arrived. God the Holy Spirit came upon Jesus' followers and gave them the courage to burst out upon their world with the life-changing message of Jesus' love. This book of the Bible is called "The Acts of the Apostles," but a better title might be the "The Acts of the Holy Spirit." God's powerful Spirit energized the Christian community, and they turned their society upside down.

Luke: Part Two

From the very first verses it is clear that the book of Acts is the second part of a two-part story.

In my former book, Theophilus, I wrote about all that Jesus began to do and to teach until the day he was taken up to heaven, after giving instructions through the Holy Spirit to the apostles he had chosen. (Acts 1:1–2)

A "former book" had already been written. That first book was about all that Jesus *began* to do and to teach. It covered the time from Jesus' coming to earth as a baby through his death and resurrection up to his return to heaven. The author's first account was obviously one of the four gospels. The Gospels told what Jesus *began* to do, but Jesus wasn't finished! Jesus went back to heaven, but just as he said he would, he sent the Holy Spirit to continue what he began. So a second account had to be written to carry on the story. In Acts the Christian community (called the church) was born. We see the church grow and develop. We see Christians boldly proclaiming the message that Jesus had risen from the dead. We see Christians persecuted and jailed and killed for their faith.

The book of Acts was originally given to a man named Theophilus. We don't know who he was, but his name gives us the clue we need to link the book of Acts with one of the Gospels. The third gospel in our New Testament began with a dedication of the book to a man named Theophilus, and we assume it's the same guy! So two books were written to give Theophilus an accurate overview of Jesus' life and ministry (volume 1) and then of the expansion of the Christian community throughout the Roman Empire (volume 2).

What we aren't told in Acts is who actually wrote this book. The overwhelming weight of evidence points to a man we know as Luke the physician. Luke was a committed Christian who frequently traveled with the apostle Paul on his preaching journeys. His association with Paul came through at times in his writing of Acts. In several sections of the book, the author switched from writing about Paul and his associ-

HELP FiLE

AN EDUCATED WRITER

Luke wrote in the polished style of an educated professional. He used over seven hundred Greek words not found anywhere else in the New Testament.

Luke included eighty geographical references and mentioned over one hundred people by name in the book of Acts. He was very precise in describing places and the titles of government officials. Archaeological evidence has confirmed Luke's accuracy over and over.

ates as "they" and "them" to writing about "we" and "us." In those sections, Luke himself was with Paul. (The "we" sections are 16:10–17; 20:6–21:18; 27:1–28:16.)

In Transition

One key fact to keep in mind as you read the book of Acts is that it is a transition book. It is the bridge between the Old Testament worship of God in Israel and the New Testament worship of God by Christians. When Acts opens, men and women are still under the law of Moses, they still worship in the temple in Jerusalem, they still operate under the old order of things. When Acts closes, Christians no longer keep the regulations of the law or offer animal sacrifices. They do not gather in the temple or in synagogues, but in assemblies called churches. How did that happen? How was that transition made? Acts will show us.

Acts also marks the transition from a Jewish focus to a whole world focus. When Acts opens, every follower of Jesus is a Jew. When Acts closes, dozens of communities filled with Jews and Gentiles (non-Jewish people) exist all over the Roman Empire. For 2,500 years God had focused his program on the descendants of Abraham. Now outsiders were getting in! Acts tells us how that happened.

A third transition in the book of Acts centers on geography. Everything in the Gospels took place in a very small territory on the far eastern frontier of the Roman Empire. When Acts opens, we are still in Jerusalem. By the end of the book, however, Jesus' followers are in Rome, the center of the empire and the springboard to everywhere else.

THOSE HATED "CHRISTIANS"

The followers of Jesus were first called "Christians" in the city of Antioch, but it wasn't a label they gave themselves. It came (most likely) from their enemies and seems to have been used as a religious slur. Followers of a certain leader were often identified by attaching -ian to the leader's name. Those who followed Christ and were committed to him as Lord were called "Christians." What started as a joke eventually was taken up by Jesus' followers themselves. By the second century they boldly proclaimed themselves to be "Christians." (The word Christian appears only three times in the Bible: Acts 11:26; 26:28; 1 Peter 4:16.)

Location, Location, Location

The whole story of Acts centers around geography. Jesus himself gave the best outline of the book in Acts 1:8:

> "You will receive power when the Holy Spirit comes on you; and you will be my witnesses in Jerusalem, and in all Judea and Samaria, and to the ends of the earth."

Jesus' empowered followers would bear witness to him first in Jerusalem, then in the larger regions of Judea and Samaria, and finally to the ends of the earth.

Established: Jerusalem (2 years) (Acts 1–7)

In this part of the book, the main emphasis is on the Jews living in Jerusalem as the church is established. The Holy Spirit swept over Jesus' followers on the Jewish feast day of Pentecost, fifty days after Jesus' resurrection from the dead (2:1–13). The apostles (Jesus' closest followers) began to proclaim a new message to the thousands of Jews gathered in the city.

Digging Deeper

✗   Marshall, I. Howard. *The Acts of the Apostles.* Tyndale New Testament Commentary series. Grand Rapids: Eerdmans, 1980.

A serious, reliable explanation of Acts.

✗   Stott, John. *The Spirit, the Church and the World: The Message of Acts.* Downers Grove, IL: InterVarsity Press, 1990.

One of the best guides to the book of Acts. The author explains what is happening in the book and what it means today.

If you want to read more about the history behind the New Testament, these books will help:

✗   Bruce, F. F. *New Testament History.* New York: Anchor Books, 1972.

✗   Guthrie, Donald. *The Apostles.* Grand Rapids: Zondervan, 1992.

✗   Niswonger, Richard. *New Testament History.* Grand Rapids: Zondervan, 1993.

WHEN WERE THEY WRITTEN?

Many of the letters of the New Testament were written during the time covered in Acts. Here are the best guesses we can make for when and where the following letters were written. You might want to pencil them in the margin of your Bible for future reference.

James: Written about A.D. 45 from Jerusalem—*Acts 12:24*

Galatians: Written about A.D. 48 from Antioch—*Acts 14:28*

1 Thessalonians: Written about A.D. 51 from Corinth—*Acts 18:5*

2 Thessalonians: Written a few months after 1 Thessalonians from Corinth—*Acts 18:11*

1 Corinthians: Written about A.D. 55 from Ephesus—*Acts 19:22*

2 Corinthians: Written a few months after 1 Corinthians from Ephesus—*Acts 20:1*

Romans: Written about A.D. 56 from Corinth—*Acts 20:3*

Ephesians, Colossians, Philippians, Philemon: Written during Paul's imprisonment about A.D. 60—*Acts 28:30–31*

"Men of Israel, listen to this: Jesus of Nazareth was a man accredited by God to you by miracles, wonders and signs, which God did among you through him, as you yourselves know. This man was handed over to you by God's set purpose and foreknowledge; and you, with the help of wicked men, put him to death by nailing him to the cross. But God raised him from the dead, freeing him from the agony of death, because it was impossible for death to keep its hold on him." (2:22–24)

Jesus' followers were speaking to the very people who seven weeks earlier had screamed for Jesus to be crucified. Some who heard the declaration of Jesus' resurrection were persuaded that Jesus really was God's promised Redeemer. They shouted, "What can we do?" Peter replied:

"Repent and be baptized, every one of you, in the name of Jesus Christ for the forgiveness of your sins." (2:38)

Three thousand Jews believed in Jesus that day, and the church was born. The church is not a building; the church is the assembled community of Christians. When Christians gather, whether it's in a magnificent cathedral or in a cave, they are the church. For two years the Christian community grew, but they stayed in Jerusalem. They stayed, that is, until opposition to this new message drove them out.

☑ The book of Acts picks up the story of Jesus and his followers where the Gospels end. Jesus ascended back to heaven but sent the Holy Spirit to empower the Christians to spread the message of Jesus the Savior.

☑ Two men are the focus of the story: Peter in chapters 1–12 and Paul in chapters 13–28.

☑ Acts is a transition book. God's program moves from a focus on Israel and the law to a focus on the world and the message of Jesus.

Enlarged: Judea and Samaria (12 years) (Acts 8–12)

The church that seemed secure in its beginning was suddenly scattered by persecution. The traditional religious leaders were opposed to the followers of Jesus, and many believers were forced to flee to other places to escape imprisonment. The Christians were scattered into the region around Jerusalem called Judea and Samaria (8:1). But as they went, they talked about Jesus, and soon, wherever Christians had settled, new churches sprang up. To the surprise of some of the apostles, Samaritan people began to believe in Jesus. An Ethiopian convert to Judaism heard the message of Jesus and became a believer. God even sent Peter to a non-Jew's house! Cornelius and his family heard the message, and they believed in Jesus. The Holy Spirit came upon them in his power and grace just as the Spirit had come upon the Jewish believers in Jesus (11:15–17). The Christians finally began to get the message that Jesus offered forgiveness and peace with God to *anyone* who would believe in him.

Even one of the Christians' fiercest persecutors was changed! A Jewish leader named Saul was determined to stop the Jesus movement. He imprisoned many Christians and even looked on with approval as Stephen, one of the Christian leaders, was stoned to death (8:1; 9:1–2). On his way to the city of Damascus to round up some Christians, Saul was confronted by Jesus in a vision (9:1–19). After his startling conversion, Saul became one of the most powerful preachers of the gospel.

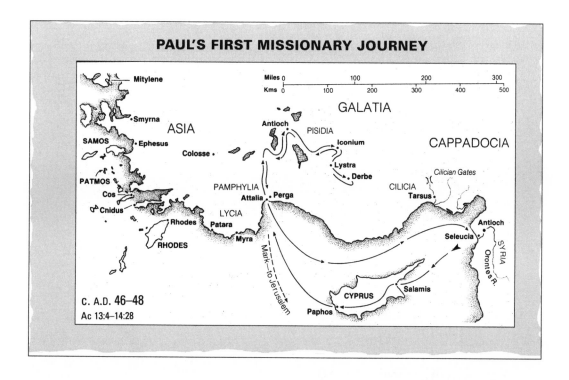

PAUL'S FIRST MISSIONARY JOURNEY

C. A.D. **46–48**
Ac 13:4–14:28

Expanded: The Ends of the Earth (15 years) (Acts 13 – 28)

In fact, it was Saul (or Paul) who was responsible for the next big leap in the spread of the gospel. The Holy Spirit spoke to the Christian leaders at Antioch and told them to send two men, Barnabas and Saul, on a journey to some areas where the message of Jesus had never been preached. They were sent out as missionaries, as men on a mission. They went to Cyprus and then into Asia Minor. In each city Saul and Barnabas saw people receive the message and believe in Jesus. Some of the converts were Jews, but more were Gentiles. Saul even pocketed his Jewish name and began to use his Roman name, Paul. When Barnabas and Paul returned to Antioch, the Christians were blown away by the news "[God] had opened the door of faith to the Gentiles" (14:27).

Other Christians weren't very happy about Paul's work among non-Jewish people. Shouldn't these new Christians be required to become Jews first and then followers of Jesus? The brain trust of the Christian community met in Jerusalem and decided that non-Jews were accepted into God's new program by faith in Jesus alone (15:1–21).

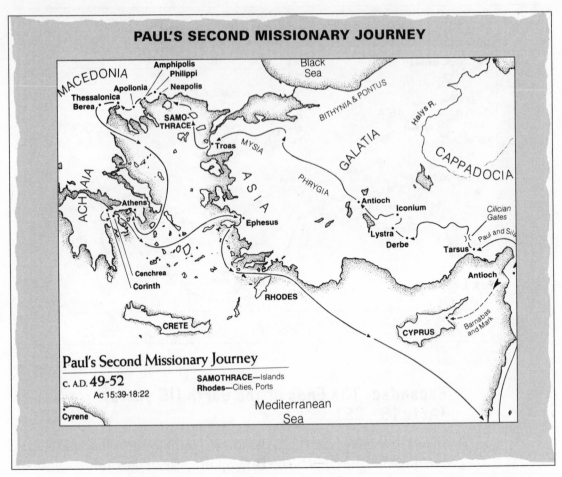

PAUL'S SECOND MISSIONARY JOURNEY

Paul's Second Missionary Journey

c. A.D. 49-52
Ac 15:39-18:22

SAMOTHRACE—Islands
Rhodes—Cities, Ports

Paul's second missionary journey (chapters 16–18) took him back to the churches in Galatia, but then God directed him to new territory. Paul and his friends (including Luke, the author) crossed over to Macedonia (modern-day Greece). In every city Paul preached the message of salvation through faith in Jesus Christ, and in almost every city Paul ended up in jail for his efforts!

Paul's third preaching journey (chapters 19–21) took him back to his fledgling congregations and gave him the opportunity to teach them more about following Jesus. The third journey ended in Jerusalem. When Paul entered the temple to worship, a riot started and Paul was put in prison again. For two years he waited for some resolution of the accusations against him, but nothing much happened. Finally, Paul appealed to Caesar, the Roman emperor, as a way out of the impasse.

PAUL'S THIRD MISSIONARY JOURNEY

Paul's Third
Missionary Journey Ac 18:23-21:17

c. A.D. **53-57**

CHIOS—ISLANDS
Rhodes—Cities, Ports

Mediterranean Sea

Miles 0   100   200   300
Kms 0 100 200 300 400 500

Because Paul was a Roman citizen, he had the right to appeal his case to the highest authority, to Emperor Nero. So, at government expense, Paul got a trip to Rome, the capital of the empire.

The book of Acts ends with Paul under house arrest in Rome waiting for his appearance before the emperor. Paul could receive guests, teach freely, and write letters. As an extra bonus, twenty-four hours a day Paul was chained to a Roman guard, one of Caesar's own personal bodyguards. Every six hours a new guard came and took the old guard's place, and every guard heard the message of Jesus the Savior. The gospel was making its way into the heart of the Roman Empire, into the household of Caesar himself.

Acts, Chapter 2000

The book of Acts is the only unfinished book of the Bible. Two thousand years later the "acts of God's Spirit" are still happening! In China, in eastern Europe, in Africa, in Brazil, in your neighborhood, God is still at work. Jesus began the wave by dying on the cross and rising again in power. The apostles continued the wave by taking the gospel to the world around them. Christians down through the centuries have moved the wave to every continent. God the Holy Spirit is writing another chapter of the book of Acts today as he continues to sweep over cities and communities and individual lives. Christians are still spreading the news of salvation in Jesus across the street and to the ends of the earth.

Walking the Walk

1. Where is your "Jerusalem," your area of activity and influence in the world? What effort have you made to tell the message of Jesus to people in your own community?

2. How can you expand your knowledge of what God is doing through the Christian community in other parts of the world? How can you personally be involved in the expansion of Christ's kingdom into unreached areas?

3. Try to trace the spiritual history of your family over the past three or four generations. Ask your parents and grandparents about their faith and what they remember of the faith commitments of their parents. How has your family's spiritual past influenced your spiritual present?

4. How would you explain to a friend what it means to become a Christian, a follower of Jesus Christ? Is there one person in your circle of friends who needs to hear that message? Ask God to give you the opportunity and courage to tell that friend about Jesus.

Bible Atlases

Some books of the Bible are rooted in or near specific places: cities, regions, rivers, or empires. The book of Acts, for example, is almost impossible to follow without a map of the Roman Empire. Paul's journeys just don't make much sense unless you see where he started and the stops he made and the route he took. Suddenly those long miles on foot or by sea become a reality.

Most study Bibles and reference Bibles include maps. They may be at the back or placed in the pages of the Bible where you need them. The maps in the previous chapter came from *The NIV Study Bible*. They are dropped in the pages of the book of Acts itself for handy reference.

A Bible atlas gives even more extensive maps with greater detail. Military campaigns in the Old Testament are displayed with the alignment and movement of armies. You can trace almost every path Jesus followed during his ministry in Palestine. In addition, an atlas usually has a section on the climate and landscape of biblical regions. An atlas anchors the action of the Bible in the real world.

When you decide to invest in a Bible atlas, look at several of them. Be sure the maps are easy to read. The text explaining the maps should be helpful, not confusing. If the bookstore you visit has only one or two atlases, check out other stores or even the public library for more options.

Some of the best atlases are:

The Zondervan NIV Atlas of the Bible. Edited by Carl G. Rasmussen. Grand Rapids: Zondervan, 1989.

A combination of history, geography, and maps that guides you through every period of biblical history.

The Macmillan Bible Atlas. Edited by Yohanan Aharoni and Michael Avi-Yonah. 3d ed. New York: Macmillan, 1997.
Excellent maps of every major battle, migration, and event in the Bible. The maps aren't very exciting to look at but are incredibly informative.

Electronic versions:

Logos Bible Atlas. Oak Harbor, WA: Logos Bible Research Systems.

The NIV Study Bible Basic Library CD-ROM contains, along with other features, full-color maps and photos of Bible lands. Grand Rapids: Zondervan.

Part 9

LETTERS

The last twenty-two books of the Bible are letters (the older term is *epistles*). Most of the letters were written to specific Christian communities or churches. Others were written to the entire Christian community. A few of the letters were written to individuals.

There are five known writers of the letters, and one writer who is unknown—the unnamed author of the letter to the Hebrews.

The apostle Paul wrote thirteen of the New Testament letters, more than half. Eighty-seven chapters came from his mind and heart. (The chapter divisions were added long after the New Testament was written, but I'm using them for a comparison of the writers.) Paul was converted to faith in Jesus Christ through a dramatic vision (Acts 9), and Jesus commissioned him to be an apostle, a personal representative of Jesus who spoke with Jesus' authority and wisdom.

The apostle John, who had been a follower of Jesus during Jesus' life, wrote three short letters (seven chapters total) and the much longer letter of Revelation.

The apostle Peter (another follower of Jesus we met in the Gospels) wrote two letters (8 chapters).

James, the half-brother of Jesus and a leader in the early church, wrote the earliest New Testament letter (5 chapters).

Jude, another half-brother of Jesus, wrote a one-chapter postcard about defending the faith when false teachers come around.

The letters these men wrote addressed specific people living in specific cities about specific problems. Only later were the letters collected into the New Testament. Christians recognized that these letters spoke to issues larger than immediate problems. These letters gave instruction to the whole Christian community about Christian belief and behavior.

WHO WROTE THE MOST?

Paul composed the greatest number of New Testament books but not the greatest volume of writing (13 books, 2,033 verses). The apostle John wrote a gospel, the book of Revelation, and three letters but only comes in third in the amount written (5 books, 1,414 verses). The most voluminous New Testament writer was Luke. His gospel and the book of Acts take up one-third of the New Testament (2 books, 2,158 verses).

Those of us reading the New Testament letters today are at a disadvantage in comparison to the original readers. We hear only one side of the conversation. We don't always know exactly what problems, questions, or circumstances prompted the writing of the letters. Sometimes we can recreate the setting pretty well. Other times we just have to piece it together the best we can.

The chapter and verse divisions in the letters help us find specific statements, but when reading the letters, the best approach is to ignore those divisions. If you received a letter from a friend, you wouldn't read one page every day until you finished. You would sit down and read it all the way through. Reading straight through each New Testament letter will help you sense the flow and power of what the author was trying to communicate.

The letters interpret the events of the Gospels. The Gospels told us that Jesus died and rose again. The letters tell us why those events are significant—and how we are to live in the light of those events. The letters instruct us, comfort us, challenge us, and at times expose things in our lives that aren't very pleasant. They push us along the road to Christian maturity.

LETTER WRITING, ANCIENT STYLE

The New Testament letters follow the customary style of the first century. Every child would have learned the proper form in school.

The letter began with the name of the writer. (So when did we start putting our name at the end?) The writer then sent greetings to those he was writing. Next came a section of thankfulness for the person(s) and for their help or encouragement to the writer. This section was dropped if it was a complaint letter!

The main body of the letter got to the heart of the matter. In most of Paul's letters the first part of the letter was instructional and the second part was practical—what he wanted his readers to *know* about the Christian faith and then what he wanted them to *do* as they lived out their faith.

Personal news and greetings came at the end of the letter, and the writer concluded with a word of farewell.

First-century writers couldn't have imagined e-mail or even regular "snail mail." Important letters were entrusted to a personal representative who hand-delivered the letter. The representative could also add any clarifications or additional information needed by the recipient.

Once a church received a letter from an apostle, the letter was publicly read and discussed by the whole community. The letter was then copied and circulated to other churches for their instruction and encouragement.

Romans

➤ Find out what Christians really believe.

➤ First get the bad news—then the best news!

➤ Learn how to try your hardest and still not get to heaven.

If Paul wrote the book of Romans today, he would probably be required to put a warning label on it: "Caution! Reading the contents may drastically alter your spiritual condition." For two thousand years, reformers, preachers, and religious activists along with lots of people just like us have been transformed by this book. It is sixteen chapters of spiritual dynamite. So read it at your own risk—and don't say you weren't warned!

Key Characters

Paul: a personal representative (apostle) of Jesus; the author of the letter

Abraham: the physical father of the Jews (Genesis 12:1–9); the spiritual father of all who believe on Jesus (Romans 4)

Adam: the first human being (Genesis 2:4–3:24), who along with Eve (the second human being) disobeyed God's command and separated themselves and all their descendants from God (Romans 5:12–19)

Phoebe: a female Christian leader who personally carried this letter to the Christian community in Rome (Romans 16:1–2)

Romans is a letter written by the apostle Paul to a group of Christians he had never met. They lived in a place where Paul had never been. Eventually Paul would end up in the city of Rome, but when he wrote this letter his visit was still a dream.

We don't know how the Christian community in Rome got started. Probably some of the Jews from Rome who were visiting Jerusalem when the church was born took the message of Jesus back home with them. (You can read the story in Acts 2. "Visitors from Rome" are mentioned in verse 10.) These Jewish Christians told other people about Jesus and his death and resurrection—and soon a church, a community of Christian believers, took root in the heart of the Roman Empire.

Paul had met some of the leaders of the Roman church as he traveled. Some of the Christians from churches Paul had established had gone to

Rome. Paul had links to the Roman church, but he had never had the opportunity to teach them the foundational truths of the Christian faith. Writing this letter gave Paul that opportunity—the chance to anchor their faith on bedrock truth. Paul said he wrote to them because it was his duty to proclaim "the gospel of God" (15:16). In its narrow sense, the "gospel" (or good news) is the message that Jesus died for human sin and rose again from the dead and that he will restore those who believe on him to friendship with God. In its broad sense (the way Paul uses the word in Romans 15:16), the "gospel" is the whole system of Christian belief.

That is what makes the book of Romans so powerful. It is the foundational document of the Christian faith. It is the Constitution, the Declaration of Independence, the Bill of Rights, and the Emancipation Proclamation in one document. If the rest of the New Testament were lost, every great truth of Christian belief could be drawn from Romans.

A Declaration of Faith

Romans is the most carefully organized of all of Paul's letters. He was a master teacher and systematically explained what it means to be a Christian. It didn't take Paul long to make his passion clear.

> I am not ashamed of the gospel, because it is the power of God for the salvation of everyone who believes. (1:16)

HELP FILE

ROMANS

Paul probably wrote the letter to the Romans from the city of Corinth in the winter of A.D. 56/57 (Acts 20:2–6). Paul didn't actually arrive in Rome until three years later (Acts 28:11–16).

The letter was dictated to a secretary named Tertius *(ter-she-us)* (16:22). It was carried to Rome by a Christian woman, Phoebe *(fee-bee)* (16:1–2).

Paul quoted more often from the Old Testament in Romans than in all his other twelve letters combined.

Romans was not the first New Testament letter Paul wrote, but it is placed first in the collection of Paul's letters because it is his longest and most foundational writing.

After a seventeen-verse introduction (1:1–17), Paul centered his explanation of the Christian faith around four themes.

Humanity's Problem (Romans 1:18 – 3:20)

Before we can appreciate Paul's stirring declaration of the *good* news of the gospel, we have to listen to some *bad* news. Paul first takes his readers into the courtroom of God. God the Judge sits behind the bench of justice. Paul stands as the prosecutor, calling all humanity before God.

Three groups await the verdict. The first to appear are those who have never heard the message about Jesus. What about people who worship idols or spirit gods? If they are sincere in their beliefs, shouldn't God accept them? Paul's answer is that even the most isolated people have enough truth about God available in the created world around them to make them accountable to God.

> For since the creation of the world God's invisible qualities—his eternal power and divine nature—have been clearly seen, being understood from what has been made, so that men are without excuse. (1:20)

What about moral people then? Don't good citizenship and charitable contributions count for anything? The problem is that even the moral person falls short of God's standard of perfection. A morally upright person will be the first to admit that he or she has failed often to do what is right. The best among us still struggle with a convicting conscience.

Being religious doesn't count for much either! A person may be very pious at church but be filled with evil thoughts or greedy motives. God doesn't look just at our outward religious actions; he looks at our hearts and minds. And what he sees inside is just as bad as what we see on the outside of the worst of people.

DoWNLOAd

Romans 8:38 – 39

For I am convinced that neither death nor life, neither angels nor demons, neither the present nor the future, nor any powers, neither height nor depth, nor anything else in all creation, will be able to separate us from the love of God that is in Christ Jesus our Lord.

Points 2 Remember

✓ Paul's letter to the Roman Christians is the Bible's fullest and plainest explanation of Christian belief.

✓ Romans clearly shows us our sinful condition before God and how Jesus has provided deliverance and salvation through his death on the cross.

✓ If all the rest of the New Testament were lost, every essential truth of the Christian faith could be drawn from Romans.

Paul's conclusion is that no one (including Paul himself) can claim to be good enough to gain God's approval. We all are spiritually bankrupt. None of us can earn a right standing with God by our own efforts or religious activity. Every human being stands condemned, because we all fall far short of God's standard for acceptance. He demands absolute moral perfection, not only in outward action, but also in inner motivation and thought. In ourselves, we have no standing with God; we wait to hear him sentence us to eternal separation from him.

God's Solution (Romans 3:21 – 8:39)

If Romans ended at verse 20 of chapter 3, we would have no hope of ever gaining acceptance and approval from God. But in the second section of Romans, God the Judge gets up from his seat, lays aside his robes of justice, and comes to earth to pay the penalty that we, the guilty ones, deserved. God was the one we had offended. God in his justice was perfectly right to sentence us to an eternity apart from him. But, to our amazement, God in his mercy and grace is willing to serve the sentence in our place!

> God demonstrates his own love for us in this: While we were still sinners, Christ died for us. (5:8)

Christ's death in our place satisfies every requirement and demand of God the Father. We receive a right standing before God not by our own efforts to be good (because we always fail at some point) and not by religious rituals (because rituals alone never please God). We receive God's acceptance by faith in Jesus alone.

> This righteousness [right standing] from God comes through faith in Jesus Christ to all who believe. (3:22)

When we believe in Jesus as Savior and Lord, when we accept the forgiveness and life that God offers us in Jesus Christ, we receive some amazing benefits.

"We have peace with God" (5:1). God is not angry with us. We are at peace.

We will be saved from God's hostility toward sin (5:9). God's wrath fell on Jesus as he died on the cross. It will never fall on those who believe.

We have been liberated from the power of sin and evil to control us (6:2, 6–7).

Even though we may still struggle with sinful actions or thoughts or desires, we have the power to overcome sin's demands (7:6–7; 8:9).

We have God's promise that we will never be condemned by God (8:1).

We have God's Spirit living in us to help us (8:15–16, 26).

We have God's promise that nothing will separate us from God's love (8:38–39).

This is one of the most thrilling and challenging sections of the Bible. If you are reading these chapters for the first time, you will find more promises than you can begin to absorb into your heart and mind. Those who have studied these passages for years continue to uncover wonderful truths.

DiGGinG DeEpeR

✗ Hughes, R. Kent. *Romans: Righteousness from Heaven*. Wheaton, IL: Crossway Books, 1991.

A series of practical sermons through Romans.

✗ Stott, John. *Romans: God's Good News for the World*. Downers Grove, IL: InterVarsity Press, 1994.

A classic study by a gifted teacher.

✗ Wiersbe, Warren. *Be Right*. Wheaton, IL: Victor Books, 1977.

A brief but helpful survey of Romans.

God's Honesty (Romans 9:1–11:36)

In the transition from chapter 8 to chapter 9 of Romans, Paul seems to veer off track. He has been talking about what it means to be a believer in Christ and about the benefits we receive from God—and now he switches into a long discussion about Israel! The point he makes is this: What about all the promises God made in the Old Testament to the people of Israel? If God hasn't kept those promises, how can we be sure he will keep the promises he makes to Christians in the New Testament? Paul argues that God *will* keep his promises to Israel. The people of Israel as a whole had rejected Jesus as God's Messiah—"not all the Israelites accepted the good news" (10:16). But God has not rejected Israel. God's focus today is on the church, which is made up of Jews and Gentiles (non-Jews). When God's program for the church is complete, God will again focus on the people of Israel.

Christian Accountability (Romans 12:1–16:27)

The last five chapters of Romans are the "so-what" section. It's great to know all this lofty teaching about salvation and Jesus, but how does it change my life? Paul tells us how. Pursuing a commitment to Jesus as the Lord of our lives begins by offering ourselves back to him. He was the ultimate sacrifice for me. Now, out of love for him, I offer myself back as a sacrifice to him.

> Therefore [in light of everything Paul had written in the first eleven chapters], I urge you, brothers, in view of God's mercy, to offer your bodies as living sacrifices, holy and pleasing to God—this is your spiritual act of worship. (12:1)

When you read that verse, it sounds like you have to put on a long robe, give away all your possessions, and move to a cave or monastery! But Paul is not talking about a career change. He's talking about a change in perspective. We are now living under a new Master. Sin, greed, pleasure, and desire used to be our masters, but not anymore. Our goal in life now is to please Jesus Christ—to please him as a lawyer, as a homemaker, as a parent, as a student. Wherever you are, in whatever arena you operate, you are called to follow Christ.

These chapters touch on issues we all need help with—relating to civil authority, getting along with other Christians, and responding to those who hate us or are intent on hurting us. Paul closes with a grocery list of greetings to a whole series of friends in the Roman church.

If you look at Romans simply as an ancient letter to an ancient church by a writer long dead, you will lose interest fast. But if you read it as a letter written to establish you in your faith and in your walk of obedience to God, you might find your life transformed.

Walking the Walk

1. Who taught you the basics about your job or a hobby or life in general? Who has been your mentor in the spiritual realm?

2. On a scale of 1 ("I am the center of everything") to 10 ("I consistently seek to obey Jesus in every area"), where would you rate yourself as a "living sacrifice" (Romans 12:1)? What would it take to move yourself one or two steps higher?

3. Explain how most people think they will gain God's approval and entrance into heaven. How does the book of Romans explain how we receive God's approval?

4. Reflect on one or two facts from Romans about Jesus or about salvation that impressed you the most. Are these facts real in your life and experience? Write a prayer or song to God expressing your gratitude for his grace and love to you—or tell a friend what God has done in your life!

THE BIG WORDS OF THE CHRISTIAN FAITH

You will encounter some long churchy-sounding words in Romans, but they are packed with important meaning. I've listed a few of them with their meanings.

Justified, justification

Terms from a Roman courtroom. Justification means that a judge declares a guilty person to be in the right because the penalty for his or her crime has been paid. When we believe in Jesus as our sacrifice, God (the Judge) declares us (who are guilty of sin) to be in right standing with him because someone else (Jesus) has paid the penalty we deserved.

> [We] are justified freely by his grace. (3:24)

> We have been justified through faith. (5:1)

Righteous, righteousness

To be in the right, to conform to God's will. We are sinners and so are in the *wrong* with God. When we put our faith in Jesus Christ, God gives us a new standing with him. We are in the right—not because we are good (we aren't), but because Jesus is good. God credits Jesus' perfect obedience to our account.

> A righteousness from God, apart from law, has been made known. (3:21)

> This righteousness from God comes through faith in Jesus Christ to all who believe. (3:22)

Redemption

A term from the slave market. We were slaves to sin—to our own desires and deeds that were not pleasing to God. Jesus paid the price for our freedom. His death on the cross released us from sin's grip.

> [We] are justified freely by his grace through the redemption that came by Christ Jesus. (3:24)

Atonement

A term from the system of animal sacrifices in the Old Testament. If a person disobeyed God's law, a sacrifice was required to restore the relationship between the sinner and God. Jesus was the final sacrifice for human sin. Through his death, the relationship with God is restored.

> God presented [Jesus] as a sacrifice of atonement. (3:25)

Reconciliation, reconciled

Jesus died to pay the penalty of our sin. God's anger against sin (his wrath) was absorbed by Jesus. God is now free to forgive us and restore us to friendship with him. Jesus took two enemies and made us friends.

> When we were God's enemies, we were reconciled to him through the death of his Son. (5:10)

Salvation, saved

By his death Jesus rescued us from the penalty and power of sin. God is absolutely pure and cannot look with approval on disobedience and evil. Since all of us have sinned and fallen short of God's standard, we all deserve the consequences of separation from God. Because Jesus paid our penalty, we can be restored to right standing with God. We have received salvation—deliverance from God's anger against sin and its consequences.

Since we have now been justified by his blood, how much more shall we be saved from God's wrath through him! (5:9)

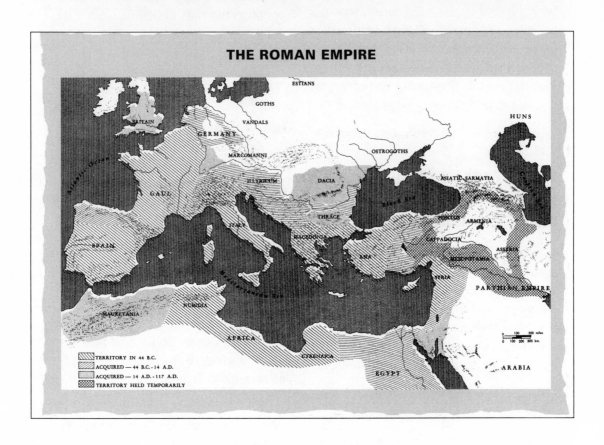

THE ROMAN EMPIRE

TERRITORY IN 44 B.C.
ACQUIRED — 44 B.C.-14 A.D.
ACQUIRED — 14 A.D.-117 A.D.
TERRITORY HELD TEMPORARILY

PEOPLE of the BiBLE

THE ROMANS

Jesus was born into a Roman world. The Roman Empire circled the Mediterranean Sea. What we call Europe, North Africa, and much of the Middle East was part of the largest political unit the world has ever seen.

According to Roman legend, the city of Rome was founded in 753 B.C. Around 500 B.C. the Roman Republic was formed. The Roman Senate and elected officials governed the city and its surrounding territory. Gradually the Roman armies conquered more and more territory. The Republic worked well for about four hundred years, until rebellion and political intrigue began to tear at the fabric of Roman society and power.

In 31 B.C. Julius Caesar's nephew, Octavian, emerged as the undisputed ruler of all of Rome's territory. Octavian, later called Augustus, kept the outward trappings of the Republic but was in fact the dictator. The era of the Roman Empire had begun. Caesar Augustus was still in power when Jesus was born.

Palestine had come under Roman jurisdiction in 63 B.C. when the armies under General Pompey used a political squabble as an excuse to invade Judea and conquer Jerusalem. Rome ruled through puppet kings and appointed bureaucrats from then on—and they ruled with an iron fist. In A.D. 66 the Jews of Judea rebelled against Roman rule. The revolt was crushed in A.D. 70 by the Roman general Titus. The temple was destroyed and thousands of Jews were slaughtered.

The universal language of the Roman Empire was Greek, not Latin. The apostle Paul could have entered virtually any city and preached the message about Jesus in Greek and he would have been understood. The Roman road system made travel easier and safer than it ever had been. The Roman "peace" (sustained by plenty of well-armed soldiers) provided an environment in which the gospel could spread quickly.

Later Roman emperors would persecute Christians, but the political umbrella of the empire was used by God to open the door of salvation to the whole world.

1 Corinthians

— Heads Up

➤ Discover what it's like in the middle of a church fight.
➤ Find out what God thinks about divorce—and dancing—and speaking in tongues!
➤ Get God's perspective on what true love really is.

The Christians at Corinth were a mess! They just couldn't seem to get their act straightened out. The apostle Paul was not only a spiritual father who had assisted at their spiritual birth (4:15); he was also their school teacher, standing over them to train them and help them outgrow their spiritual diapers (4:21). These Christians should have been spiritual adults, but they were still in the nursery.

Key Characters

Paul: a spokesman for Jesus to the Christian community; the founder of the church in Corinth

The Holy Spirit: the Third Person of the Trinity with God the Father and God the Son (Jesus); the Spirit lives in every Christian to guide and equip us for serving God

Peter: one of Jesus' original followers; some Christians at Corinth bragged about following Peter rather than Paul

Apollos: another early Christian teacher; some of the Corinthian Christians wanted to follow him rather than Paul or Peter

Part of the problem was the city where they lived. If ever there was a difficult place to be a Christian, it was Corinth. Corinth had a reputation for three things.

1. It was a fabulously wealthy city. Key trade routes by land and sea ran straight through Corinth, and one could make money fast.
2. Sports fans came regularly to Corinth for the athletic competitions held there. The Corinthian games were second only to the Olympic games in prestige and popularity.
3. Corinth was also notorious for its immorality. Above the city on a commanding hill stood the temple of Aphrodite, the Greek goddess of sexuality. Hundreds of prostitute priestesses fanned out through the city, selling their bodies as an act of religious worship. Corinth was the X-rated capital of the ancient world.

Along Came Paul

DoWNloAd

1 Corinthians 13:13

And now these three remain: faith, hope and love. But the greatest of these is love.

You could find just about anyone in Corinth—Greek adventurers, Roman bureaucrats, Jewish merchants, sailors, slaves, hucksters and prostitutes, pushers and politicians. Corinth had everything but a preacher! Paul walked into Corinth one day, and within a few months he saw a Christian community established in the heart of the most corrupt city in the Roman Empire.

Paul came to Corinth during his second extended preaching journey. He had been to other cities further north and had even preached in the great university center of Athens. I would have skipped Corinth as a lost cause, but Paul didn't. (You can read the story of Paul's stay in Corinth in Acts 18:1–18.) If love for Jesus could take root and grow in Corinth, it can grow anywhere.

As Paul and some of his friends worked and prayed and spoke about Jesus, slowly a community of believers—a church—was formed. It wasn't easy. Paul said he spoke the message even though he was full of fear and trembling (2:3). The opposition was so strong that Paul was ready to bail out after a few months of relentless persecution. Jesus had to appear to him in a vision and encourage him to stay in Corinth a while

HELP FiLE

TWO LETTERS

First and Second Corinthians are the first set of paired books in the New Testament. The title of the first letter is written 1 Corinthians (or I Corinthians), but it is referred to as "First Corinthians."

The city of Corinth was so notorious for its immorality that the people made up the word "to Corinthianize" to refer to drunkenness and sexual promiscuity. If someone said you had a "Corinthian" girlfriend or boyfriend, it was not a compliment!

Paul wrote the letters of 1 and 2 Thessalonians during his eighteen-month stay in Corinth (Acts 18:1–11).

Points 2 Remember

☑ Paul's first letter to the Corinthians was written to correct problems in the Christian community and to answer questions they had raised. Most of the issues discussed in the letter are still with us today.

☑ Paul's explanation of sacrificial love (chapter 13) and his examination of the resurrection (chapter 15) are the best-known sections of the letter.

longer. Paul stayed eighteen months in all (the years were A.D. 51–52) and then moved on. Shortly after, his second journey came to an end.

A couple of years later Paul got word of turmoil in Corinth. He had launched out on another journey and was met in Ephesus by a group of Christians from Corinth. They told Paul that there was trouble in the church.

My brothers, some from Chloe's household have informed me that there are quarrels among you. (1:11)

The Corinthian church was ready to blow apart! So Paul, under the guidance of God's Spirit, sat down and wrote a letter. He wrote it in A.D. 56, just four or five years after the church was established.

A Corinthian Guidebook

Paul's first letter to the Corinthian Christians is a book about problems. What makes it so practical is that we are still facing many of the same issues today.

Rebukes (1 Corinthians 1:10 – 6:20)

After a brief introduction (1:1–9), Paul issued a series of corrective instructions. He rebuked these Christians for their divisive attitude. Little, exclusive groups were forming in the church, and the people in one group were looking down their noses at the people in the other groups. Paul rebuked the whole community for their continued immaturity as Christians. He called them "mere infants in Christ" (3:1). They were tolerating open immorality among some of the Christians. It was such a scandal that even the non-Christians were shocked. To make matters worse, the Christians were suing each other in court!

Replies (1 Corinthians 7:1 – 16:4)

In the second half of the letter, Paul answered a list of questions that had been raised by the Corinthians. These issues are shockingly contemporary too!

What about marriage and divorce and remarriage? What does God think about what's going on in our homes? (Chapter 7)

What should we do about the questionable areas of life—the gray areas where the Bible is silent? In Paul's day the hot issue was eating meat that had first been offered to images of false gods. Today the issues that divide Christians are different, but the principles we can apply to those decisions remain the same. (Chapters 8–10)

What are the roles of men and women in church leadership? (Chapter 9)

Are the gifts of the Spirit still operating among Christians? Should we speak in tongues in church or not? (Chapters 12–14)

What about the future? Will our bodies be resurrected? Should we expect Jesus to return to earth some day? (Chapter 15)

The letter closes with personal greetings and a few final instructions. (Chapter 16)

Paul also did some serious teaching in the process of correcting the problems. He wrote a masterful explanation of how the message of the

DiGGinG DeEpeR

✗ Prior, David. *The Message of 1 Corinthians: Life in the Local Church.* The Bible Speaks Today series. Downers Grove, IL: InterVarsity Press, 1985.

Prior is a skillful guide through this book.

✗ Blomberg, Craig. *1 Corinthians.* The NIV Application Commentary. Grand Rapids: Zondervan, 1994.

A more in-depth study but filled with practical insights.

gospel works in people's lives (1:18–2:16). His examination of the resurrection of Jesus and of our future resurrection deserves careful reading (15:1–58). Paul's chapter on sacrificial love is a classic (13:1–13).

Walking the Walk

1. If Paul were writing a letter to the Christian community today, what issues would you want him to address? What rebukes would Paul issue to modern Christians?

2. Describe the view of "love" prevalent in our culture. How does it compare with the love Paul wrote about in chapter 13?

3. Paul makes it clear that the body of a Christian is a temple (or dwelling place) of God's Spirit (6:19–20). How can we "honor God" with our bodies? In what ways might we dishonor him? What specific changes should be made in *your* lifestyle to be obedient to God?

2 Corinthians

— Heads Up —

➤ Learn what the superpreacher Paul was really like.
➤ Find out how Paul handled a hostile takeover.
➤ Discover keys to success as a follower of Jesus—and they aren't what you expect!

The second letter of Paul to the Corinthian Christians gives us all some hope. In spite of the mess that Paul had to straighten out in 1 Corinthians, these Christians at last seemed to get with the program. Second Corinthians is the proof that we can have a lasting spiritual impact even when we've messed up big time.

Second Corinthians was written only a few months after the letter called First Corinthians, but in that short time the situation went from bad to worse to wonderful! Here's how things developed:

Paul wrote 1 Corinthians to deal with a host of problems—divisions in the church, immoral behavior among some of the Christians, and issues of hair length and speaking in tongues. Point by point, Paul tried to correct what was wrong.

Paul also sent Timothy, one of his associates, to Corinth. Paul thought Timothy's personal intervention might help. The news Timothy brought back was not good. Fights and factions persisted. To make matters worse, some false teachers had come to Corinth claiming to be true apostles of Jesus. Their real goal was to discredit Paul.

In an attempt to restore his relationship with these Christians, Paul made a quick visit to Corinth—and met with disaster. The insults were unbearable, and Paul returned to Ephesus. (Hints of this visit are found in 2 Corinthians 2:1; 12:14; 13:1–2.)

Key Characters

Paul: a true representative (apostle) of Jesus; a very human leader who struggled like we do

Titus: Paul's associate who was sent to check up on the situation in Corinth

LOST LETTERS

Some people are bothered by the fact that Paul refers in 2 Corinthians to a letter he wrote that we no longer have (2:4). But not everything the apostles wrote was prompted in their minds directly by God. Not everything they wrote had the authority of Scripture. Furthermore, we have references to other "lost" letters in the New Testament.

- After a church council at Jerusalem, the church leaders wrote a letter to all the groups of Christians, informing them of the decisions they had made. We have a brief summary of the letter in Acts 15:19–29 but not the letter itself.
- In Colossians 4:16 Paul mentions a letter to the Laodicean Christians that has not survived. Some scholars think Paul was talking about the letter to the Ephesian Christians that was supposed to be circulated to other churches in the region, including Laodicea.
- Paul points to a letter in 1 Corinthians 5:9 that he wrote to the Corinthians about the problem of immorality. He wrote the letter *before* he wrote the letter we call 1 Corinthians.
- And we could even mention that Jesus wrote on the ground once, but we have no record of what he wrote (John 8:6, 8).

Only the writings God wanted preserved for all generations of Christians were collected into the New Testament. Still, it would be fascinating to read these other letters too.

After that painful visit, Paul wrote a severe letter—a letter that was not included in our New Testament. Paul referred to this letter in 2 Corinthians 2:4: "For I wrote you out of great distress and anguish of heart and with many tears, not to grieve you but to let you know the depth of my love for you." Paul gave the letter to another associate, Titus, and sent him back to Corinth.

Then the waiting began. No word came for weeks, and Paul was convinced that the worst had happened. He was sure that Titus and his letter had been rejected and that the Christians had left the truth to follow false leaders. When he couldn't wait any longer, Paul left Ephesus and went to visit other churches, hoping to encounter Titus on his return trip.

The weeks of waiting were almost unbearable for Paul, but finally Titus came to him with great news. Paul's letter had caused deep sorrow and pain among the Christians, but it had also turned their hearts back to the Lord and back to Paul as God's true spokesman.

Paul wrote 2 Corinthians out of gratitude to God. He would visit the Corinthians again but this time with joy and anticipation.

Behind the Image

Maybe it was that new sense of security with these Christian friends that allowed Paul to open up so much in this letter. Paul is more vulnerable and personal in this letter than he is in any of his other letters. We don't just see the outside of the man—his travels, his writing—we are allowed to look into his heart.

If 2 Corinthians wasn't in the Bible, we would be tempted to think of Paul only as a great preacher, a supersaint, a man so far above us that we could never touch him. But in this book we see the human side of Paul—and he is *very* human. We see him struggling, and that encourages us when we struggle. We see Paul depressed, ready to quit, and his experience touches us on dark, difficult days. We see Paul disappointed with people and angry with himself and wrestling with God. We see him pacing the floor at 2:00 A.M. with tears streaming down his face. We get inside the plaster statue of the saint and find a man who knows what it feels like to have a broken heart.

We also discover that Paul had learned to triumph over the disappointments of life by clinging to an all-sufficient God. Second Corinthians will show us that when we are insufficient (which is most of the time), God is fully sufficient. When we are weak, God shows himself strong. When we collapse, God holds on. When we complain, God hears. When Paul reached the lowest point of his experience, when he "despaired even of life," he found solid ground.

Digging Deeper

✗ Wiersbe, Warren. *Be Encouraged.* Wheaton, IL: Victor Books, 1984.

A brief but practical guide through this challenging book.

✗ Barnett, Paul. *The Message of 2 Corinthians: Power in Weaknesses.* The Bible Speaks Today series. Downers Grove, IL: InterVarsity Press, 1988.

An in-depth study of 2 Corinthians.

Points 2 Remember

- ☑ Second Corinthians was written by Paul after a painful, insulting encounter with the Corinthians had been resolved.

- ☑ We learn more in this letter about the personal struggles and priorities of Paul the man than we learn in any of his other writings.

- ☑ We think broken things are of no value, but that is never true when God's grace is involved. He takes broken people and raises them to greatness.

But this happened that we might not rely on ourselves but on God, who raises the dead. He has delivered us from such a deadly peril, and he will deliver us. On him we have set our hope. (1:9–10)

Cutting a Path

The letter of 2 Corinthians falls into three main sections.

Personal Integrity (2 Corinthians 1–7)

In these chapters Paul explained his work and the passion that burned in his heart. His transparency is shocking.

This is our boast: Our conscience testifies that we have conducted ourselves in the world, and especially in our relations with you, in the holiness and sincerity that are from God. (1:12)

Unlike so many, we do not peddle the word of God for profit. On the contrary, in Christ we speak before God with sincerity, like men sent from God. (2:17)

We have renounced secret and shameful ways; we do not use deception, nor do we distort the word of God. On the contrary, by setting forth the truth plainly we commend ourselves to every man's conscience in the sight of God. (4:2)

We put no stumbling block in anyone's path, so that our ministry will not be discredited. Rather, as servants of God we commend ourselves in every way: in great endurance; in troubles, hardships and distresses; in beatings, imprisonments and riots; in hard work, sleepless nights and hunger; in purity, understanding, patience and kindness; in the Holy Spirit and in sincere love. (6:3–6)

Financial Policy (2 Corinthians 8 – 9)

Paul was not doing God's work for personal financial gain, but he still encouraged Christians to be generous in giving their money. Paul was collecting a gift for the poor, oppressed Christians in Jerusalem. As he urged the Corinthians to give, Paul laid out timeless principles for how we are to give our resources to God.

See that you also excel in this grace of giving.

I am not commanding you, but I want to test the sincerity of your love. . . . For you know the grace of our Lord Jesus Christ, that though he was rich, yet for your sakes he became poor, so that you through his poverty might become rich. (8:7–9)

Remember this: Whoever sows sparingly will also reap sparingly, and whoever sows generously will also reap generously. Each man should give what he has decided in his heart to give, not reluctantly or under compulsion, for God loves a cheerful giver. (9:6–7)

God-given Authority (2 Corinthians 10 – 13)

Unfortunately, a small minority of doubters still remained in Corinth. So, in the final section of the letter, Paul defended his authority as a true representative of Jesus Christ. The false teachers who *claimed* the same authority were servants of the enemy, not servants of Christ. Paul even wrote out his resumé! See if you are impressed.

Are they servants of Christ? (I am out of my mind to talk like this.) I am more. I have worked much harder, been in prison more frequently, been flogged more severely, and been exposed to death again and again. Five times I received from the Jews the forty lashes minus one. Three times I was beaten with rods, once I was stoned, three times I was shipwrecked, I spent a night and a day in the open sea, I have been constantly on the move. I have been in danger from rivers, in danger from bandits, in danger from my own countrymen, in danger from Gentiles; in danger in the city, in danger in the country, in danger at sea; and in danger from false brothers. I have labored and toiled and have often gone without sleep; I have known hunger and thirst and have often gone without food; I have been cold and naked. Besides everything else, I face daily the pressure of my concern for all the churches. Who is weak, and I do not feel weak? Who is led into sin, and I do not inwardly burn? (11:23–29)

Paul made it clear that he didn't just sit down with a career counselor one day and say, "I think I'd like to be an apostle!" He didn't choose the job. Jesus chose him! Those who think being an apostle is glamorous need a reality check—shipwrecks, beatings, stoning, and on top of everything else, a weight of concern for the Christians under his care.

Taking It Home

What you will learn from 2 Corinthians is that the character of Jesus is developed in us not through comfort and promotion but most often through brokenness and pain. If you are being broken or humbled in your life right now, God is working on you. We think broken things are to be tossed aside, but that is not true in God's program. God in his grace takes broken, weak people and fashions them into men and women of wisdom and influence.

Walking the Walk

1. Think about the people with whom you can be most open and vulnerable. Is there any person around whom you can be totally transparent? What fears do you have about that level of vulnerability?

2. What do you think Paul would say to Christian leaders today about their attitude toward financial appeals? What would Paul say to you about how willingly you give of your resources to further God's work and to help people who are in need?

3. Paul was not just another Christian giving his opinion on a subject. He was a uniquely chosen representative of Jesus. How does that affect how you read Paul's letters? Are they just ancient religious writings, or are they written with a higher level of authority behind them?

Galatians

> ➤ Discover how to "check out" the teaching of any Christian leader.
> ➤ You *are* free—now live like it!
> ➤ Have a life-changing encounter with God's Spirit.

Galatians is probably the very first New Testament letter Paul wrote. It is also his most passionate letter. Paul was fighting to protect some Christians he loved. He was also fighting to defend the truth of the message he preached. Paul wrote in blunt, direct words so that everyone who read the letter would know how strongly he felt. This is not a book to be read while you are drifting off to sleep. You need to be awake, standing up—and have your boxing gloves on!

Key Characters

Paul: a personal representative of Jesus and spokesman for God to the Christian communities

Peter: the leader of the original followers of Jesus; he is rebuked by Paul for separating himself from non-Jewish Christians (Galatians 2:11–21)

Sarah: Abraham's wife through whom Isaac was born

Hagar: Sarah's slave; Sarah asked Abraham to produce a child through Hagar when it seemed like she would not be able to bear a child; Hagar's child was named Ishmael

Paul had come to the Roman province of Galatia on his first preaching journey. He and his companion, Barnabas, had proclaimed the message of Jesus' death and resurrection in several Galatian cities, and some who heard the message had believed in Jesus. (Acts 13 and 14 tell us the story of Paul's experiences in these cities.) Small Christian communities called churches were formed in each city. The Christians gathered for prayer and worship and encouragement—and to be taught the basic beliefs of their new faith. Most of the Christians in Galatia were Gentiles (non-Jews). The ethnic background of those who came to hear Paul preach didn't matter, because Paul had learned that the message of Jesus' love was available to *all* who believe, not just to the people of Israel.

After Paul left Galatia, some Jews in the city of Jerusalem heard that Paul had been preaching

Galatians 4:4 – 7

But when the time had fully come, God sent his Son, born of a woman, born under law, to redeem those under law, that we might receive the full rights of sons. Because you are sons, God sent the Spirit of his Son into our hearts, the Spirit who calls out, "_Abba,_ Father." So you are no longer a slave, but a son; and since you are a son, God has made you also an heir.

his message in Gentile cities. It was bad enough that Paul had stirred up such controversy among the Jewish people over Jesus, but now he was telling Gentiles they could get in on God's program—disgusting, idol-kissing Gentiles! So these Jews went up to Galatia and said, "Look, Paul only told you part of the story. Believe in Jesus if you want to, but God is pleased by the law of Moses. We have a few rules for you to keep." These Jews were trying to persuade the Galatians that to be a good Christian you had to first be a good Jew.

And they were very persuasive! They would read verses from the Bible, making their viewpoint seem so clear. (Remember, the New Testament hadn't been written yet. The only Bible they had was what we now call the Old Testament.) The Christians in Galatia began to waver in their belief. When Paul had been there, he had sounded so convincing, but now they weren't sure. Paul had said that the Christian life was lived under the leadership of the Holy Spirit. These new teachers said that Christians were to live according to traditions and rules.

When Paul heard what was happening in Galatia he was livid! These teachers from Jerusalem were not simply creating trouble in the churches; they were changing the gospel, the truth about salvation in Jesus Christ.

What makes the book of Galatians so relevant today is that rule-keepers are still around. They knock on your door and come across the television cable and radio airwaves. Some even stand in church pulpits. Their message is the same as the false teachers of Paul's day. "Jesus is okay to start with," they will say. "But a _real_ Christian keeps our rules."

Points 2 Remember

☑ The letter to the Galatians is Paul's passionate defense of the message of God's grace against the twisted teaching of rigid rule-keepers.

☑ The teaching of any religious leader, denomination, or organization is to be measured against the teaching of the apostles as it is preserved in the New Testament. Any religious claim or experience not in agreement with biblical truth has to be carefully examined.

☑ Some things are worth fighting for—especially the truth of the Bible and Christians who are being led astray by false teaching.

One Step at a Time

The book of Galatians can be divided into three sections, each of which focuses on an issue that still needs to be addressed today.

Who Can We Believe? (Galatians 1–2)

The first two chapters center on the question of authority. The Galatian Christians were torn between two groups of teachers, each claiming to speak God's truth and yet contradicting each other. Who were they to believe? Paul claimed to be an apostle, an authorized representative of Jesus. But the Jewish teachers claimed to come from the mother church in Jerusalem. Both sides had good credentials. People in both groups seemed to be sincere and good. How were they to choose?

The situation is the same two thousand years later except, instead of two voices to choose between, we are bombarded by dozens of conflicting voices. Very persuasive men and women will appeal to a denomination or a particular church leader or a traditional teaching or even a vision from God to make powerful arguments for their position. They quote scholars and bishops and church creeds. They write books and position papers and say, "Read this! This is the latest version of truth from God!" And we say, "Who can we believe?"

In his opening line of the letter, Paul asserted his authority as an apostle of Jesus Christ. He was not a representative of the church, but a representative of Christ.

> Paul, an apostle—sent not from men nor by man, but by Jesus Christ and God the Father. (1:1)

Paul was amazed that the Galatian Christians had been drawn away from his teaching so quickly.

> I am astonished that you are so quickly deserting the one who called you by the grace of Christ and are turning to a different gospel— which is really no gospel at all. (1:6–7)

The point Paul makes in these chapters is that Christians are to test the teaching of a pastor or a denomination against the teaching of the apostles of Jesus Christ. The standard of Christian truth is what the apostles have written in the New Testament. Christian belief and behavior has to be based on the authority of the apostles' teaching, not on tradition or denominational position papers, not even on visions or messages supposedly from God or an angel.

How Can We Be Forgiven? (Galatians 3 - 4)

The second issue Paul addressed in Galatians was the question of salvation. How can a pure God forgive sinful people? The teachers from Jerusalem said, "When you keep the rules, God takes notice." Paul said, "Acceptance before God is possible only through the death of Jesus on the cross."

The Old Testament law has a very important function: It points out how often we fail! The law is a finger punching us in the chest and saying, "Look at how often you disobey God." The law's job is to condemn

Digging Deeper

> ✗ McKnight, Scot. *Galatians*. The NIV Application Commentary. Grand Rapids: Zondervan, 1995.
>
> A detailed, well-written exploration of Galatians.
>
> ✗ Stott, John. *The Message of Galatians: Only One Way*. The Bible Speaks Today series. Downers Grove, IL: InterVarsity Press, 1968.
>
> Excellent! A skilled teacher explains one of Paul's more challenging letters.

us. It pins us down until we are finally forced to say, "I can't keep all the rules, God. I have failed." That is when Jesus comes along and says, "I have paid the penalty for a lawbreaker like you. Believe in me, and I will set you free from the condemning accusation of the law."

> Christ redeemed us from the curse of the law by becoming a curse for us. (3:13)

Faith is simply admitting that we can't do anything about our failures and that we are trusting in what Jesus did for us to make the difference.

How Do We Behave As Christians? (Galatians 5–6)

Most Christian teachers will say that we are forgiven by faith in Jesus alone—but then some will add this: After we are forgiven and made new, we've got some rules to keep! Paul's declaration in the closing chapters of Galatians is that we are forgiven by grace, and we are to live in the freedom of God's grace. The Christian's behavior and decisions are not guided by a long list of human rules. The Christian is guided by the Holy Spirit who lives in us. Paul warned these Galatian Christians not to go back under a yoke of slavery by embracing rule-keeping as a way of life.

Our liberty in Christ is not a free pass to do whatever we want, however. We are free to obey God's Spirit. We are free to love and serve others as Jesus did. Living a life of sinful behavior grieves God's Spirit. The evidence that the Holy Spirit is operating in my life is that I display the character of Jesus—the "fruit" (evidence) of the Spirit.

> So I say, live by the Spirit, and you will not gratify the desires of the sinful nature. . . .
>
> The acts of the sinful nature are obvious: sexual immorality, impurity and debauchery; idolatry and witchcraft; hatred, discord, jealousy, fits of rage, selfish ambition, dissensions, factions and envy; drunkenness, orgies, and the like. I warn you, as I did before, that those who live like this will not inherit the kingdom of God.
>
> But the fruit of the Spirit is love, joy, peace, patience, kindness, goodness, faithfulness, gentleness and self-control. Against such things there is no law. (5:16, 19–23)

Be Free

Galatians can be summarized like this: You *are* free—now live like it! False teachers will try to twist God's truth. Well-meaning traditionalists will try to set you straight. Rule-keepers will condemn you because you ignore their lists. But stand firm in your freedom in Jesus Christ— freedom to fully follow the Spirit's leading, freedom to obey the apostles' teaching, freedom to love as Jesus loved.

Walking the Walk

1. You can read the whole letter of Galatians in less than twenty minutes. Try reading it out loud—and insert some of the passion Paul must have felt as he wrote the letter.

2. What are some of the Christian "rules" you have been exposed to? Are those rules in line with biblical instruction or not? How can you respond to someone who suggests you ought to be keeping more rules in your life?

3. What would you say to someone who thinks that keeping the Ten Commandments or living by the Golden Rule is enough to gain God's approval?

4. As you look over the list of qualities produced by the Holy Spirit (Galatians 5:22–23), which ones are most obvious in your daily routine? Which one definitely needs more cultivation?

Ephesians

➤ Discover your role in God's eternal plan.
➤ Find out how God wants you to relate to those around you.
➤ Learn the tactics of spiritual warfare.

Most of Paul's letters were written to solve specific *problems*. His letter to the Ephesian Christians, however, was designed to give them a new *perspective*. Paul wanted his readers to realize how rich they were because of their faith and loyalty to Jesus Christ. Your response may be, "Yeah, right. Where's my share of the wealth?"

If you believe in Jesus as Savior and Lord, you *are* rich! Your wealth is not measured in stock options or treasury bonds. The Christian holds the title to something even better. Every spiritual blessing is already ours because of Jesus. Here's a partial list of assets in your portfolio:

You were chosen by God before the universe existed.

You have been redeemed by Jesus' death from the power of sin.

You have been forgiven by God's grace of all the wrong in your life.

You have been adopted as God's own child.

You have grace and peace from God.

You have access to God's wisdom.

You are part of an eternal plan that God has committed himself to carry out.

All those riches, and I have only scanned the first ten verses of the book!

Key Characters

Paul: a traveling preacher who established Christian communities throughout the Roman Empire

Jews: the physical descendants of Abraham through his son Isaac and grandson Jacob

Gentiles: non-Jewish people; they did not receive God's law through Moses as the Jews did

Who Were These Rich People?

If you had visited the city of Ephesus in A.D. 60 (about the time this letter was written) and had gone to the Christian meeting on a Sunday, you would not have seen many wealthy people in the congregation. I'm sure there were a few from the upper economic class, but most of the Christians were merchants and tradespeople and even slaves. You would also have noticed that those social and economic distinctions didn't seem to matter much. Slaves and slave owners sat together and mingled freely. Those with money didn't parade it, and those without money were not intimidated.

The Christian community in Ephesus was strong. Paul himself had lived in the city for three years during his ministry, so these Christians were well taught. The congregation was guided by capable, mature leaders. This was not a church without problems, but they had learned how to resolve problems quickly.

Paul's letter to the Ephesian church is a summary of Paul's teaching on what it means to be "in Christ." When a person makes a decision to

HELP FILE

A PRISON LETTER

Ephesians is one of Paul's prison letters, written during his time under house arrest in Rome. (See Acts 28:16–31.) The other prison letters are Philippians, Colossians, and Philemon.

Ephesians is the least personal of Paul's letters. Only two names appear (other than names for God, Jesus, and the Holy Spirit): Paul (1:1; 3:1) and Tychicus (**titch**-*i-cuss*) (6:21).

The longest sentence in the Greek New Testament is Ephesians 1:3–14. We have broken it into several sentences in our English versions, but in Greek it's one very long sentence (202 words)!

Not one command or instruction appears in chapters 1–3. Paul simply declares what God has done. In chapters 4–6, the section describing how Christians are to live, thirty-five commands are listed!

The letters of Ephesians and Colossians have strong similarities: 78 of the 155 verses in Ephesians are repeated in Colossians with only slight variation.

PREPARE FOR BATTLE

In Ephesians 6:10–18 Paul used the imagery of war to give us an important perspective on the Christian life. The battle is between God's plan to rescue human beings from sin's power and all the forces that resist God's plan. We feel the struggle as Christians in our own minds and decision-making. The battle also rages in the world around us. Evil and perversion and injustice are pervasive—just watch the news!

God's enemy according to Paul is a whole cosmic system, visible and invisible, directed by an evil being called the devil. The devil's kingdom (as a weak imitation of God's kingdom) contains both angels and humans. Evil angels attack Christians and seek to defeat them in their obedience to God or in their witness to the world. Human beings promote evil too. Sometimes we do it intentionally, sometimes we simply fail to do what is good and right, sometimes we simply choose to remain ignorant of the evil and injustice around us.

Our protection in the battle is what Paul calls the "armor of God." Each piece of the soldier's equipment represents a spiritual resource at our disposal—like the chest covering of our right standing with God, the shield of confident faith, the sword of God's written Word.

Living as God's people in a dysfunctional, hostile world is not easy. It is, in fact, warfare. Our responsibility is to come up with strategies for defeating an already defeated enemy. Our general, Jesus, has been exalted above every power. We serve at his command and under his authority. Jesus gives us the protection we need and the power to fight. We just have to be courageous enough to take up spiritual arms against the enemy!

fully follow Jesus Christ, that person is placed *in* Christ—and it is in Christ that we discover the lavish riches of God's grace and love for us. The proof that we have become part of Christ is that we are given the Holy Spirit, who lives in every genuine believer.

> You also were included in Christ when you heard the word of truth, the gospel of your salvation. Having believed, you were marked in him with a seal, the promised Holy Spirit. (1:13)

Paul's prayer for those who read his letter was that they would begin to grasp the incredible spiritual wealth and awesome spiritual power available to those who believe in Christ.

Points 2 Remember

☑ Paul's letter to the Ephesians is a summary of what God has done to rescue us from the old life and to give us new life in Jesus Christ.

☑ We do not live differently in order to gain God's approval. We live a new life because we already received God's approval when we believed in Jesus.

☑ God will empower us to do anything he commands us to do.

☑ Christians are linked to each other as closely as parts of the same body. We are all members of God's household.

I pray also that the eyes of your heart may be enlightened in order that you may know the hope to which he has called you, the riches of his glorious inheritance in the saints, and his incomparably great power for us who believe. (1:18–19)

Surfing the Book

Ephesians, like several of Paul's letters, has two main parts. The first three chapters focus on what we believe; the last three chapters focus on how we live in light of what we believe.

Learning (Ephesians 1–3)

You won't find three chapters anywhere in the Bible packed with more life-changing ideas. Chapter 1 highlights who we are and what we possess as followers of Jesus Christ. These are the riches deposited in every Christian's spiritual bank account. It's worth the time to read your bank statement!

Chapter 2 explains what God has done for us and to us in Christ. We couldn't do anything for ourselves. We were "dead" toward God (2:1), but God made us alive in Christ. He raised us up from our spiritual graves and already sees us seated in heaven. Furthermore, God took two groups that were full of hostility and suspicion and put us together in one new living organism. Jews and Gentiles (non-Jews) were restored to friendship with God and then brought to peace with each other. Social and racial and economic distinctions dissolve among Christians because we are all "fellow citizens . . . and members of God's household" (2:19).

Chapter 3 of Ephesians carries Paul's thought one step further. He tells us what God intends to do through the church, through people committed to Jesus.

You and I don't do anything in the first three chapters of Ephesians. All we do is receive one wave after another of God's power and provision. That's exactly what Paul prayed would happen!

> I pray that you, being rooted and established in love, may have power, together with all the saints, to grasp how wide and long and high and deep is the love of Christ, and to know this love that surpasses knowledge—that you may be filled to the measure of all the fullness of God. (3:17–19)

We have to lie down and rest after we finish chapter 3—or at least take some deep breaths. It's a challenge to absorb so much truth, but it's even more of a challenge to live our lives in the light of that truth.

Living (Ephesians 4 – 6)

Christians don't work at living lives of integrity and obedience to God in order to gain God's approval. We live obediently because we already have God's approval. Paul calls us "to live a life worthy of the calling you have received" (4:1). These chapters are filled with practical instructions on how to live a life that honors Jesus—a life of unity with other Christians (4:1–16), a life of purity and love (4:17–5:21), a life of harmony in the home and workplace (5:22–6:9), and a life of victory over the attacks of the enemy (6:10–20).

A New Society

The book of Ephesians describes the new society God is building among his people. The foundation of this society is the death and

DoWNLOAd

Ephesians 2:8 – 9

For it is by grace you have been saved, through faith — and this not from yourselves, it is the gift of God — not by works, so that no one can boast.

resurrection of Jesus and the deliverance from sin's bondage that he purchased for us. Entrance into God's new society is by God's grace through faith in Jesus Christ. The energy source of the new order is the Holy Spirit who lives in us. The operations manual is the New Testament, where we learn how a changed person lives a changed life. The goal of the new society is to bring praise and honor to God the Father and to God the Son, Jesus Christ.

A society, however, is not made up of just one person. Christians are not only linked in a new way to God, but we are also linked in a new way to other Christians. Paul used several word pictures to make his point. We are "one new man" created from two divided groups (2:15). We are "one body" (2:16) directed by one "Head," Jesus Christ (4:15). We are one "building," a temple for God the Spirit (2:21). We are one "household," the family of God the Father (2:19).

Remember who you are in Christ when you go to work tomorrow. Live a life worthy of your high position. Remember how important those other Christians in your church or study group are. Make every effort to preserve the unity of the Spirit. Remember the spiritual resources available to you when the enemy tempts you to disobey God's instruction. Stand your ground.

> You were once darkness, but now you are light in the Lord. Live as children of light. (5:8)

Digging Deeper

✗ Rowland, Randy. *Get a Life . . . and a Faith That Works.* San Francisco: HarperSanFrancisco, 1992.

Practical, personal—delightful!

✗ Stott, John. *The Message of Ephesians: God's New Society.* The Bible Speaks Today series. Downers Grove, IL: InterVarsity Press, 1979.

One of the best explanations of this letter available.

Walking the Walk

1. Of all the things God has done for us listed in chapters 1–3, which one impresses you the most? Why?

2. Of all the commands issued by Paul in chapters 4–6, which one do you find most difficult to obey? Why?

3. How realistic is Paul's concept of the devil and powers of darkness (6:11–12) in our modern world? Would we be better off eliminating the idea of a personal devil, or Satan?

4. What aspects of your behavior distinguish you from people who are not followers of Jesus Christ? What areas need some work?

5. What kind of people would feel awkward or uneasy in your church? What can you do to remove those barriers in your church?

Philippians

➤ Read a joyful letter written from a jail cell!

➤ Get the facts about Jesus.

➤ Learn what's wrong with the attitude "Why pray when you can worry?"

Paul's letter to the Christians in the Greek city of Philippi (*fill-i-pie*) is an enthusiastic confirmation of their faith in Jesus and their progress toward spiritual maturity. These were people Paul loved and enjoyed being around. The story of how the Philippians became Christians is so remarkable that, if it wasn't in the Bible, we might not believe it!

It all started when Paul was in the middle of his second preaching journey. He had visited the people in Galatia who had believed on Jesus during his first journey, but then he hit a brick wall. Paul and his companions, Silas and Timothy, tried to break into new territory with the message of salvation, but every door seemed to close. They ended up on the northern edge of Asia Minor (modern Turkey) wondering what went wrong. That night God gave Paul a vision of a Greek man calling Paul to come over to Greece and help them learn about Jesus. The next day Paul and his friends boarded a boat headed toward the Greek mainland. One of the first cities they visited was Philippi.

There weren't enough Jews in Philippi to support a synagogue, but Paul found an outdoor Jewish worship service on the Sabbath day. Because he was a rabbi, Paul was invited to speak in the service. His message was about the Messiah, the Deliverer whom God had promised to send. Paul told his audience that the Messiah had come and

Key Characters

Paul: a personal representative of Jesus, founder of the church at Philippi and frequent prisoner

Timothy: Paul's most trusted companion

Epaphroditus: a messenger from the Philippian Christians to Paul (Philippians 2:25–30)

Euodia and Syntyche: two women in the Philippian church who found it easy to disagree with each other (Philippians 4:2–3)

A 90-SECOND GUIDE TO JESUS: WHO HE WAS AND WHAT HE DID

In Philippians 2:5–11 Paul wrote a powerful and poetic summary of who Jesus was and how we should see Jesus today.

> Your attitude should be the same as that of Christ Jesus:
>
> Who, being in very nature God,
>   did not consider equality with God
>   something to be grasped,
> but made himself nothing,
>   taking the very nature of a servant,
>   being made in human likeness.
> And being found in appearance as a man,
>   he humbled himself
>   and became obedient to death—
>   even death on a cross!
> Therefore God exalted him to the highest place
>   and gave him the name that is above every name,
> that at the name of Jesus every knee should bow,
>   in heaven and on earth and under the earth,
> and every tongue confess that Jesus Christ is Lord,
>   to the glory of God the Father.

Jesus is not a baby in the manger anymore—although that's the only way some people ever see him. Jesus is not a teacher wandering over the hills of Palestine. Jesus is not still on the cross—although some people want to keep him there. He's not in a tomb either! Jesus is exalted to the highest place. He is Lord over all!

that new life was available to all who would believe in him. One woman who heard the message of Jesus that day was not a Jew by birth. She had embraced the worship of the one true God, but she was a Gentile. As Paul preached that day, the Lord opened Lydia's heart to receive Jesus as God's Son and her Savior.

A few days later Paul and Silas passed through the marketplace, where a fortune-teller had set up a booth. A slave girl, dominated by an evil spirit, was owned by the fortune-teller and actually did the work of predicting people's futures. This girl took one look at Paul and began to shout, "These men are servants of the Most High God, who are telling you the way to be saved." At first Paul ignored her. What the girl said was true, but Paul wasn't exactly thrilled with the endorsement of an evil spirit. Finally, he commanded the evil spirit to leave the girl. The girl's owner wasn't very happy with the situation, however, because his source of income had vanished, so he had Paul and Silas beaten and thrown into prison.

The First Christian Concert

Paul and Silas were faithfully serving God, yet they ended up in jail! What would you have done in that situation? Paul and Silas began praying—and then singing. When they were done singing, God applauded, and an earthquake rocked the jail. The prisoners found themselves set free. The jailer had heard the singing too. He asked Paul how he could have the same joy they had demonstrated. He wanted to know how to be saved, set free from sin's power in his life. Paul's answer rocked the jailer's heart—"Believe in the Lord Jesus and you will be saved." Probably a few prisoners believed that night too.

The city magistrates ordered Paul and Silas to leave the city of Philippi. But before they left, I think they had a praise gathering with the newly formed church. Lydia, the sophisticated businesswoman, was there. The jailer was present with his family. Maybe a few ex-cons came—and maybe even the slave girl who had been delivered from the bondage of an evil spirit came. They were the charter members of the Philippian church! (By the way, these details about how the church was started are not in Paul's letter to the Philippians. They are found in Acts 16.)

Many years later Paul was under arrest again. This time he was in Rome waiting for the emperor to hear his case. Epaphroditus (*ee-paf-ro-die-tus*), a leader in the church at Philippi, came to Rome to bring money to Paul and to tell him how much his friends loved him. The letter Paul wrote back to the Christian community is our New Testament letter of Philippians.

These were people Paul loved with deep affection. When he remembered their faces, a smile came over Paul's face and joy filled his heart. His letter is an exploration of what it means to experience contentment and joy even in life's most difficult circumstances.

Exploring the Letter

As you read Philippians, several key themes emerge:

Paul's circumstances. Paul wanted these Christians to know what was happening in his life. He wanted to thank them for their support and regular gifts. Check out 1:12–30; 4:10–19.

Stress on unity. Paul also wrote to encourage these Christians to have the right attitude toward one another. Being part of a Christian community is not a game of put-downs and cut-downs. Humility and unity are the marks of genuine Christianity. For more, read 2:1–11; 4:2–5.

Warning about false teachers. Paul was concerned that false teachers would find inroads into the Christian community. He clearly separated himself from these "enemies of the cross of Christ" (3:18). The entire third chapter focuses on that problem.

Rejoicing. Paul's primary goal in this letter was to challenge the Christians to rejoice regardless of the circumstances around them. The Christian knows that God is at work in *every* circumstance of life to bring about what he desires and to sculpt us into men and women with the character of Jesus. We may not rejoice *for* every situation, but we can rejoice *in* it because we know that nothing is outside God's control. In each chapter Paul returned to the theme of Christian joy (1:3–6; 2:12–18, 25–30; 3:1; 4:4, 10–13).

Digging Deeper

✗ Swindoll, Charles. *Laugh Again: Experience Outrageous Joy.* Dallas: Word, 1991.

An engaging (and joyful!) study through Philippians.

✗ Thielman, Frank. *Philippians.* The NIV Application Commentary. Grand Rapids: Zondervan, 1995.

An in-depth study of this letter with insightful connections to life today.

Under the Circumstances

If there has ever been a time when we needed to reclaim a sense of joy, it's today. Watch the evening news or pick up a newspaper, listen to the music and watch the movies of our culture, talk to people you work with. For every joyful or encouraging word you hear, you will hear dozens of lines that express discouragement and despair. Paul in his letter to the Philippians is not advocating a silly, naive view of life around us. Paul was a realist. He knew human life at its most depraved and most difficult. But he also knew what it was like to have confident trust in God and to draw upon the resources of God's joy in the worst circumstances. What will impress your neighbors or coworkers most about your commitment to Jesus is not your church attendance or Bible study. What will make the greatest impact is when they see genuine joy flowing over your lips and your life.

The late Mother Teresa was asked what qualities were necessary to work in her mission to the unloved and dying in Calcutta. Without any hesitation she said two things were needed: the desire to work hard and a joyful attitude. Joy takes the grind out of life—in Calcutta or wherever you are.

DOWNLOAD

Philippians 4:6 – 7

Do not be anxious about anything, but in everything, by prayer and petition, with thanksgiving, present your requests to God. And the peace of God, which transcends all understanding, will guard your hearts and your minds in Christ Jesus.

Walking the Walk

1. Set your computer clock or wristwatch to alert you at the beginning of each hour for one day. Check your attitude when the alarm goes off. Are you most often angry? frustrated? impatient? tense? Did the alarm ever catch you laughing?

2. Review your list of relationships. Who are the joy givers on the list? Who are the joy stealers?

3. Think of people who believed in you and encouraged you in life's pursuits—a teacher, a parent, a friend. Take the time to write or call that person. Be prepared to thank them in specific detail for their investment in you.

4. Who are you helping to reach their potential in life? Write out some ways you can encourage your mate, your children, or a friend to reach toward their dream.

Colossians

— Heads Up —

➤ Jesus is Lord!
➤ Find out why Jesus is so important.
➤ Learn how to live like Jesus.

Colossians is a letter written by the apostle Paul to a group of Christians who were under attack. They lived and worked and worshiped in the city of Colosse on the western edge of Asia Minor (present-day Turkey). These Christians had come to believe in Jesus as Lord, but now they were under pressure to make some changes in their belief system—and everyone wanted a piece of them.

The people who still held to the worship of Greek and Roman gods and goddesses wanted the Christians to be more tolerant of other deities. Jesus was fine as long as they added the goddess Artemis (a great temple dedicated to Artemis was located in the nearby city of Ephesus) or some other deity to their list.

The rule-keepers in Colosse said that faith in Jesus Christ wasn't enough to gain God's approval. They had long lists of new rules and traditions for the Christians to follow. Most of the rules started with the word "don't": Don't eat this, don't drink that, don't do these things, don't violate our sacred days.

Key Characters

Paul: the author of the letter and a servant of Christ

Epaphras: representative of the Christian community in Colosse and friend to Paul

Tychicus: Paul's associate who carried this letter to the Colossian church (Colossians 4:7–9)

Other people were pressuring the Christians to accept what they claimed was new truth. They said that Paul and the other Christian leaders had not given the Christians the full story. In the view of these "know-it-alls" Jesus was a great person, but he was not God. Jesus was close to God and a lot like God, but he wasn't God himself. Their promise was that if the Christians would just open their minds a little to this new truth, they would be so much more fulfilled.

A different group of people in Colosse was telling the Christians that real fulfillment would come only through a dramatic experience. These people had seen visions and talked with angels. They had gone without food for days or lived in poverty for years. That was the way (they said) to find genuine joy.

Everyone wanted to add something to Jesus Christ—Jesus plus new gods, Jesus plus new rules, Jesus plus new truth, Jesus plus new experiences. The Christians were standing true to Christ, but they were starting to get a little shaky. They felt intimidated by these pressure groups. Maybe they really did need something new or something more. Maybe Christ wasn't enough.

Enter Paul

Paul would have loved to have gone to Colosse. He would have had the problem straightened out in no time. But Paul was in chains in Rome, under arrest, waiting for his trial before the emperor. He couldn't go to

HELP FILE

COLOSSIANS

The people living in Colosse (ko-**loss**-ee) were called Colossians (ko-**losh**-anz). The full title of this book is "The Letter of Paul to the Colossians." Obviously it was not written to all the people living in Colosse, but to the Christian community in that city.

Paul was probably not the person who first preached the message of Jesus in Colosse. More likely a man named Epaphras came from Ephesus (where Paul did preach) and started the church in

Colosse. Read Acts 19:8–10 for more background.

Epaphras later traveled to Rome to tell Paul what was happening in the church. He is mentioned in Colossians 1:7 and 4:12–13. Acts 28:16–31 tells us about Paul's imprisonment in Rome. Colossians was written about A.D. 60.

The New Testament books of Colossians, Ephesians, and Philemon were written about the same time.

Points 2 Remember

☑ Colossians presents Jesus Christ as the supreme Lord of all. Jesus is more than adequate to meet every spiritual and practical need of those who trust in him.

☑ Those who believe in Jesus are made new by God's power. The challenge of the Christian life is to live outwardly what God has made us inwardly.

Colosse personally, so he sat down and wrote a letter to the Colossian Christians—and the letter still speaks to us today. We are still surrounded by people who want to add something to Jesus! The rule-keepers are still with us telling us what "good Christians" should or should not do. Those who devalue Jesus are still around. They knock on our doors and try to tell us that Jesus is not God. Other voices want to make every path the path to God whether faith in Jesus is involved or not. So we still need to hear what Paul wrote so long ago.

Like most of Paul's letters, Colossians divides into two parts.

Teaching: Who Christ Is (Colossians 1–2)

First Paul focused on the supremacy of Jesus. The Colossian Christians did not have to apologize for Jesus. He is the supreme Lord. He is the exact, visible representation of all that God is. He is the Head of all things, the Creator of all things, the Conqueror of all things.

Jesus Christ is not some weak, minor deity seated somewhere with all the other gods. He is not just one more religious teacher who was revered by his followers but who was no different than all the other religious leaders of the world. Jesus is the Lord God who came to earth to rescue human beings from the eternal penalty of sin and who is now exalted in heaven.

All the groups pressuring the Colossian Christians wanted to add something to Jesus. Paul declared that the central message of the Christian faith is that we receive God's eternal approval through Jesus Christ plus *nothing*. We don't have to look anywhere else for spiritual truth. All we will ever need is found in Christ alone.

The question is still asked today: Who is Jesus? Lots of different answers are given, and it can seem confusing. The Bible's answer, however, is pretty clear.

He is the image of the invisible God. (1:15)

Jesus is the invisible God made visible.

For by him all things were created. (1:16)

Jesus was not created. He is the Creator.

Once you were alienated from God and were enemies in your minds because of your evil behavior. But now he has reconciled you by Christ's physical body through death to present you holy in his sight. (1:21–22)

We are restored to God's friendship because Jesus died on the cross for us.

Christ, in whom are hidden all the treasures of wisdom and knowledge. (2:2–3)

All genuine spiritual truth is connected to Jesus.

In Christ all the fullness of the Deity lives in bodily form. (2:9)

Jesus is God. When he became human, he did not stop being God.

Living: Christ in Us (Colossians 3 - 4)

Not only did the Colossian Christians need to get their facts straight about Jesus; they also needed to get some facts straight about themselves. When they believed in Jesus as Savior and Lord and committed themselves to follow him, everything about their lives changed—and that still happens today. The person who makes a faith commitment to Jesus is made new. The old person "dies" and a new person is raised to life. That is a fact. We *are* new men and women in Christ. The question we have to ask next is, Do I live like the new person I am, or am I still living like the old person I was before I believed in Christ?

DiggiNG DeEpeR

✗ Hughes, P. Kent. *Colossians and Philemon: The Supremacy of Christ.* Westchester, IL: Crossway Books, 1989.

An excellent series of practical studies through Colossians.

✗ Wiersbe, Warren. *Be Complete.* Wheaton, IL: Victor Books, 1981.

A clear, concise explanation of Colossians.

The Christian life is not a frustrating attempt to live by a long list of Christian rules. The Christian life flows from an inner change produced by God. In the second half of Colossians, Paul tells us how to live like the new people we are.

> Put to death, therefore, whatever belongs to your earthly nature: sexual immorality, impurity, lust, evil desires and greed, which is idolatry. Because of these, the wrath of God is coming. You used to walk in these ways, in the life you once lived. But now you must rid yourselves of all such things as these: anger, rage, malice, slander, and filthy language from your lips. Do not lie to each other, since you have taken off your old self with its practices and have put on the new self, which is being renewed in knowledge in the image of its Creator. (3:5–10)

The "new" person in Christ behaves differently than he or she did before Christ. The new person relates differently to other Christians (3:12–17). The new person has a new life at home (3:18–21) and at work (3:22–4:1). The new person even talks differently! The Christian prays to God and speaks with grace to those outside the faith (4:2–6).

If we believe in the Jesus of Colossians 1 and 2, we can't keep living the way we've always lived. If we have really committed ourselves to Jesus as Lord, our lives will change. Jesus is supreme, and Jesus is all we will ever need for spiritual fulfillment and peace with God. The goal today—and every day—is to live like that is true.

Walking the Walk

1. How has reading Colossians changed your view of Jesus?

2. What would you say to friends who want to experiment with alternative forms of spirituality?

3. How does your life measure up to Paul's portrait of:
    the Christian in church (3:12–17)?
    the Christian at home (3:18–21)?
    the Christian in the workplace (3:22–4:1)?

4. What one or two specific attitudes or actions that marked the old life can you begin to "put off"? What attitudes and actions of the new life will you "put on" in their place?

1 Thessalonians

— Heads Up —

➤ Find out what to do in tough times.

➤ Be reminded that Jesus is coming soon!

➤ Learn how to live until Jesus returns.

The apostle Paul wrote this letter to a group of Christians who were being persecuted for their faith in Jesus. Paul had been there when these people had believed in Jesus, and he had pulled them together as a community. But then he had been forced to leave. He had been their spiritual teacher, but he had to abandon them at the worst possible time.

Here's how events unfolded:

Paul visited the city of Thessalonica (in the northern area of Greece) on his second extensive preaching trip. Paul was accompanied by Silas and a young assistant named Timothy.

Thessalonica was a large city, and just as Paul expected, there was a Jewish synagogue. On the Sabbath, Paul and Silas went to the synagogue and began to tell people that the promised Messiah had come. Using the Old Testament Scriptures, they demonstrated how Jesus of Nazareth had fulfilled the promises about the coming Deliverer.

Key Characters

Paul: an apostle of Jesus and founder of the church at Thessalonica

Timothy: Paul's associate who visited the Thessalonians and reported back to Paul on their progress

The results were mixed. Some believed in Jesus, but many rejected the message. To make matters worse, most of the non-Jews who had been attracted to Judaism for its high ethical teaching were persuaded to follow Jesus. In the end, the new Christian community was barred from worshiping in the synagogue, and they began to meet in homes.

As Paul's congregation grew, the Jews who had not believed in Jesus became more and more

DOWNLOAD

1 Thessalonians 4:7

For God did not call us to be impure, but to live a holy life.

upset—to the point that a riot began! The Jews accused the Christians of stirring up a rebellion against Rome and acting contrary to Roman authority by following King Jesus instead of Caesar. The city officials forced the leader of the young Christian community to promise that Paul and Silas would leave town. (You can read the whole story in Acts 17:1–10.)

Paul, Silas, and Timothy moved on. They went to other Greek cities and eventually ended up in Corinth. From Corinth Paul wrote a letter to the Christians left behind in Thessalonica, and he sent Timothy back to hand deliver it to the church.

When Things Get Tough . . .

First Thessalonians is one of Paul's earliest letters. It was written to a young church out of Paul's deep concern and love.

The letter falls into two parts:

Looking Back (1 Thessalonians 1–3)

Paul first reminded these Christians about their dramatic conversion.

HELP FILE

A LONG NAME

The Thessalonian (thess-a-**low**-nee-an) letters are another set of paired books in the Bible. They are written as 1 Thessalonians and 2 Thessalonians (or I Thessalonians and II Thessalonians) but are referred to as "*First* Thessalonians" and "*Second* Thessalonians."

In Paul's day, Thessalonica (thess-a-low-**nigh**-ka) was the capital of the Roman province of Macedonia. It was located on the main road from Rome to the eastern part of the empire. Thessalonica was a "free city," which meant the citizens were exempt from most taxes! The city survives today as the Greek city of Salonika.

> Our gospel [Paul's message about Jesus] came to you not simply with words, but also with power, with the Holy Spirit and with deep conviction. . . . In spite of severe suffering, you welcomed the message with the joy given by the Holy Spirit. (1:5–6)

Paul had been with the Thessalonian Christians six to eight weeks at most. Apparently Paul's opponents had tried to use Paul's quick exit from the city as proof that he didn't really care about the Christians, but only his own safety. So Paul reaffirmed his love and reminded them of his sacrifice for their good.

> You know, brothers, that our visit to you was not a failure. . . . With the help of our God we dared to tell you his gospel in spite of strong opposition. . . . We loved you so much that we were delighted to share with you not only the gospel of God but our lives as well, because you had become so dear to us. (2:1, 2, 8)

Paul desperately wanted to return to Thessalonica but couldn't without endangering the whole community. He sent Timothy to encourage them and reassure them of Paul's love.

Looking Ahead (1 Thessalonians 4 - 5)

Paul couldn't bring himself to end his letter without instructing these Christians on some key points. First, he urged them to live to please God (4:1–12). Then he gave them important insight about what will

DigginG DeEpeR

✗ Stott, John. *The Gospel and the End of Time: The Message of 1 and 2 Thessalonians.* The Bible Speaks Today series. Downers Grove, IL: InterVarsity Press, 1991.

A reliable guide through these books by a highly respected teacher.

✗ Wiersbe, Warren. *Be Ready: 1 and 2 Thessalonians.* Wheaton, IL: Victor Books, 1979.

Brief but practical and easy to read.

Points 2 Remember

- ☑ Paul's first letter to the Thessalonian Christians was written to encourage and instruct them during a difficult time of opposition to their faith.

- ☑ Even though the letter is filled with commands, Paul was confident of their willing obedience because of the commitment of these Christians to fully follow Jesus.

happen when Jesus returns from heaven as he promised he would (4:13–5:11). Paul closed with a list of commands about a variety of things—and Paul knew these Christians would strive to obey everything he said. Some Christian communities had to be persuaded to obey with long arguments and passionate pleas. The Christians at Thessalonica were eager to the follow the Lord completely.

. . . The Tough Follow Jesus

The little letter of 1 Thessalonians takes only a few minutes to read, but it challenges us to a lifetime of committed living. Opposition will come; the enemy will throw all he can at us at times. That's when we find out whether our faith is real or not. That's the time to read this letter

RAPTURE WARNING: OCCUPANT MAY VANISH!

Each chapter of 1 Thessalonians ends with a statement about the return of Jesus from heaven (1:10; 2:19; 3:13; 4:13–17; 5:23). Before he ascended to heaven, Jesus promised his disciples that he would come back some day.

"In my Father's house are many rooms; if it were not so, I would have told you. I am going there to prepare a place for you. And if I go and prepare a place for you, I will come back and take you to be with me that you also may be where I am." (John 14:2–3)

Since the day Jesus left, his followers have looked for his return. In 1 Thessalonians 4:13–17, Paul explains what will happen to Christians at Jesus' return. That event is often called "the rapture" (even though that word is never used in the Bible). Christians who have died will be resurrected, and Christians still alive will be changed. They will be given new eternal bodies and will be "caught up" to meet Jesus in the air.

The Bible does not tell us when Jesus will come again. Instead, it urges us to be ready for his return at any time.

again. When persecution or ridicule or opposition presses down, that's when God calls us to hang in there. The message about Jesus is true. The promises God made will be fulfilled. Keep going, and keep trusting him.

Walking the Walk

1. Imagine that you, like Paul with the Thessalonian Christians, had only six to eight weeks to have a positive influence on your group of friends or your family. What would be the three most important principles you would want to communicate to them?

2. Since your influence really *is* limited by time, what steps can you take in the next six weeks to begin to have the influence you desire?

3. How do you typically respond to a command from the Bible? Do you think you are becoming more willing in your obedience to God or more reluctant?

2 Thessalonians

➤ Watch a group of Christians grow even under pressure.

➤ Learn how to respond to people who predict when Jesus will return.

➤ Discover the rule, "If you don't work, you don't eat!"

Paul wrote his second letter to the Thessalonian Christians just a few months after the first. Paul was still in Corinth, about two hundred miles south, and he was still under a restraining order that prohibited him from visiting Thessalonica. (A riot had started during Paul's previous visit.) The persecution against the Christians had worsened, and a new problem had cropped up. The Christians had received a report that claimed to be from Paul, but it contradicted some of the teaching Paul had already given them. In addition to opposition from the outside, these Christians now struggled with confusion inside the community. Paul wrote his second letter to set the record straight.

Encouragement (2 Thessalonians 1)

In his first letter Paul had urged the Thessalonian Christians to continue to pursue positive character traits, such as confident faith in God and enthusiastic love for one another. Every Christian traveler who visited Thessalonica confirmed that Paul's words had spurred the Christians to action.

Your faith is growing more and more, and the love every one of you has for each other is increasing. (1:3)

Paul encouraged them to be faithful to Jesus and to hold firmly to the Christian teaching they had received from Paul.

Key Characters

Paul: the founder of the Thessalonian church and a spokesman for Jesus

The man of lawlessness: Paul's title for a future evil ruler who will try to control the world (2 Thessalonians 2:1–12)

Points 2 Remember

☑ Paul wrote his second letter to the Thessalonian Christians to encourage them to stay faithful to Jesus and to correct misinformation they had received about God's final wrap-up of human history.

☑ Christians are looking for Jesus to return, but that doesn't excuse us from hard work or wise planning.

Instruction (2 Thessalonians 2)

The confusion in the church centered around the return of Jesus. Paul had already told them that Jesus would return to take Christians out of the world (1 Thessalonians 4:13–17). They also knew from Paul that Jesus' return would begin the final wrap-up of human history. Jesus' second coming would begin a time called "the day of the Lord."

The problem was that the Christians had heard or read some account, supposedly by or about Paul, that said the Christians were already in the day of the Lord. Had they missed Jesus' return? Had Paul been wrong in his teaching? Would Paul, like people today who "predict" Jesus' return, need to go back and correct what he had said before?

Paul assured the Thessalonian Christians that he had not changed his teaching. The report they had received had not been from Paul but from someone trying to deceive them. The wrap-up of human history had not begun. The day of the Lord would not begin until "the man of lawlessness" was revealed (2:3) and he exalted himself as God. In the end he would be overthrown by Jesus.

Requests (2 Thessalonians 3)

Some of the Christians had been so certain that Jesus would return soon that they had quit their jobs and were just sitting around waiting to go to heaven! Paul told them to go back to work. Paul was convinced

2 Thessalonians 2:16–17

May our Lord Jesus Christ himself and God our Father, who loved us and by his grace gave us eternal encouragement and good hope, encourage your hearts and strengthen you in every good deed and word.

DoWNLoAd

that Jesus could return at any moment, but he kept working to spread the message of salvation. He concluded his letter with a call to calm.

> Now may the Lord of peace himself give you peace at all times and in every way. (3:16)

Jesus Is Coming! August 8, 2010 . . .

People who think they know when Jesus will return are still around. They sell their books or build a web site or gather their followers on a hillside so they will be first in line to see Jesus. When their predictions don't come true, they write another book to explain their error and to set a new timetable for the end of time. Jesus had this to say about the time of his return:

> "No one knows about that day or hour, not even the angels in heaven, nor the Son, but only the Father. . . .

> "Therefore keep watch, because you do not know on what day your Lord will come." (Matthew 24:36, 42)

The next time someone claims to know when Jesus will come again, put the book back on the shelf, turn the channel on the television, or click off the web site and pick up the Bible!

Walking the Walk

1. How do you respond to the Bible's teaching that Jesus will come to earth again? With laughter? Fear? Expectation?

2. If you were convinced that Jesus would return in exactly one year, how would you prepare? How would your life change? Spend some time reflecting on the fact that the Bible says Jesus could return at any moment—and then begin to make the changes that will prepare you for that event.

3. What should our attitude be toward people who are genuinely in need? How should we respond to people who are just too lazy to work?

For "Digging Deeper" see the resources listed under 1 Thessalonians.

1 Timothy

➤ Get tips on how to be a great Christian leader.
➤ Look at what churches need to change—and what they should never change.
➤ Measure your church by God's yardstick.

Suppose a highly respected Christian leader would write a heartfelt letter to Christians everywhere about the following issues:

The roles of men and women in public worship

The relationship between the church and the state

How to pick church leaders who can be trusted

How much pastors should be paid

The responsibility of Christians with money toward those with none

What to do when older people put a strain on the family

Most of us would welcome any insight we could get on those issues! And a letter like that is exactly what we have in 1 Timothy. This instruction comes not just from a modern church leader, but from an apostle of Jesus Christ. He spoke with Jesus' authority to Christian communities everywhere.

The Truth, the Whole Truth, Nothing but the Truth

Paul's overriding concern in his first letter to Timothy was that the truth he had received from the Lord and had taught throughout his career would be faithfully guarded and handed on to others. Paul never entertained the view that all religious belief led to the same God. He, like Jesus and all the other New Testament writers, was convinced that God's truth had been communicated to humanity through Jesus, God's Son, and through the teaching of Jesus' apostles, which we have in the New Testament, God's Word.

Four individuals or groups of people interact in 1 Timothy. If you keep the groups and their relationship straight, it will go a long way toward helping you understand the letter.

Paul

The first key character is Paul himself. He called himself "an apostle of Christ Jesus by the command of God" (1:1). Paul wrote this letter sometime after the close of the book of Acts (the fifth book of the New Testament). Acts ended with Paul under house arrest in Rome waiting for a trial before the Roman emperor. Apparently Paul was given his freedom after that trial. According to some of the early Christian writers, Paul then went on another extensive missionary journey, perhaps even reaching Spain with the message of Jesus.

The churches Paul had established earlier in his career were now led by the next generation of Christian leaders. Timothy, for example, had been put in charge of the church in the city of Ephesus. Paul was concerned that the new generation of leaders would follow the truth that God had given to Paul and the other apostles. So Paul constantly called Timothy back to the teaching of the apostles as foundational truth for Christian belief.

False Teachers

False teachers had come along in Paul's footsteps. They were teaching a system of belief different from the one Paul had taught. They had wandered from the truth and abandoned the true message of Jesus

DiGGinG DeEpeR

✗ Fee, Gordon. *1 and 2 Timothy, Titus.* The New International Biblical Commentary. Peabody, MA: Hendrickson, 1988.

A reliable and interesting guide through all three letters.

✗ Stott, John. *Guard the Truth: The Message of 1 Timothy and Titus.* The Bible Speaks Today series. Downers Grove, IL: InterVarsity Press, 1996.

A masterful study of 1 Timothy and its implications for Christians today.

☑ First Timothy is a letter written by Paul to his friend Timothy, who was the leader of the Christian community in Ephesus. Paul instructed Timothy in how he should behave as a Christian leader and what kind of people he should appoint to leadership roles.

☑ Paul's concern was that the truth God had given to Paul and the other apostles would be protected and passed on to the next generation.

(1:6; 4:1). Paul was not particularly diplomatic when he confronted those who twisted and changed the truth of God. He was not inclined to broadmindedly see the beliefs of the false teachers simply as an alternative belief system to the Christian faith. He called them "hypocritical liars" (4:2) and their teaching "meaningless talk" and "godless myths" (1:6; 4:7).

Timothy

Timothy had joined Paul as a younger associate fairly early in Paul's career. (Timothy is first mentioned in Acts 16:1–3.) A close and enduring friendship developed between these two men. Paul repeatedly called Timothy his "son whom I love, who is faithful in the Lord" (1 Corinthians 4:17). Timothy knew Paul's mind and heart more closely than any of Paul's other associates. Paul had given Timothy several assignments over the years, but the assignment to stand against the false teachers in Ephesus was the most difficult of all.

Paul warned his young associate not to be drawn away by the false teachers. Instead, he was to study the Old Testament and the written teachings from Paul. Timothy was to guard the truth. In addition he was to live a life of honor and integrity before everyone, friend and enemy alike.

DoWNLoAd

1 Timothy 2:1 – 2

I urge, then, first of all, that requests, prayers, intercession and thanksgiving be made for everyone — for kings and all those in authority, that we may live peaceful and quiet lives in all godliness and holiness.

Command and teach these things. Don't let anyone look down on you because you are young, but set an example for the believers in speech, in life, in love, in faith and in purity. (4:11–12)

Church Leaders

Timothy's responsibility was to teach the things he had learned from Paul to faithful Christian leaders who would in turn teach the next generation. Paul was very specific about the qualifications of leaders in the Christian community. They were to exhibit consistent moral character and integrity, and they were to be loyal to the truth God had given through Paul. They were to be examples to the other Christians—not of perfect men and women, but of men and women committed to following Jesus fully.

We've Always Done It That Way

Every church has its own unique personality. Some Christian communities prefer formal, structured worship. Others prefer an expressive, open style of worship. It's interesting that in this whole letter on the church, Paul didn't say one word about what kind of buildings Christians are to meet in, what style of music is best, how often to have services, or whether Christian drama is appropriate. Paul focused on the essentials—guarding the truth, selecting church leaders who followed Christ, being obedient to God's Word. In the other areas, God has given us wonderful freedom.

God doesn't want us to use the church down the street as the measuring stick for our church; he wants us to use his truth. How committed are we to holding faithfully to what God has said through the writers of

HELP FILE

A POPULAR NAME

Timothy's name appears twenty-four times in the New Testament in twelve different books.

The two letters to Timothy are the sixth set of paired books in the Bible. The titles are written 1 Timothy and 2 Timothy (or I Timothy and II Timothy), but they are referred to as "*First* Timothy" and "*Second* Timothy."

DON'T STOP READING!

Paul's two letters to Timothy and his letter to Titus are sometimes called the "pastoral letters." Unfortunately, some people avoid these letters because they think only pastors or church leaders will find them interesting. The books, however, are filled with basic information about how Christian communities, called churches, are to function. If you are part of a church, these three letters are the operating manuals. When all else fails, read the directions!

the New Testament? It seems that we never change what should be changed to reach out to people around us with the message of Jesus' love. We hold on to our traditional ways as if they came from Jesus himself. But at the same time we easily ignore God's truth and end up altering what should never be changed—God's instructions to his people. The letter of 1 Timothy is a needed reminder of what is really important.

Walking the Walk

1. How would you respond to a friend who said that he or she had decided to follow the teachings of a cult or another religion rather than the Christian faith?

2. Some people have accused Christians of being elitist because we ask people to convert from other religions (or no religion) to faith in Jesus. Was Paul wrong to think that faith in Jesus is the only way to God?

3. As you read 1 Timothy, mark the areas of Paul's teaching that your church adheres to strongly. What aspects of 1 Timothy are followed less consistently by your church? What can you do to strengthen your church's obedience in those areas?

2 Timothy

── *Heads Up* ──────────────────────

➤ Be encouraged by a powerful letter from a condemned man.

➤ Learn what it means to be a friend.

➤ Take a look at the legacy you are leaving.

Paul's second letter to his friend and associate Timothy was the last New Testament letter Paul wrote. It may have been the last letter Paul ever wrote. Paul did not compose the letter in a comfortable motel room or in a friend's home. He wrote the letter from a prison in Rome. Paul was locked in a damp, cramped dungeon. Chains hung from his wrists and around his ankles. For long hours visitors were shut out and Paul sat all alone. The shadow of death stretched across Paul's path like at no other time in his ministry. In his desperate loneliness, Paul reached out to a trusted friend.

We can't be absolutely certain about the events that brought Paul to this prison cell, but this is probably how it went:

At the end of the book of Acts, Paul was under house arrest in Rome waiting for a trial before the Roman emperor.

Apparently Paul was released after his trial and resumed his preaching ministry. When Paul wrote the letters of First Timothy and Titus, he was obviously able to travel freely, because he mentions all the places he had been and intended to go.

Key Characters

Paul: a prisoner in Rome facing execution for his faith

Timothy: Paul's associate and dearest friend, a pastor in the city of Ephesus

In A.D. 64 a great fire swept through Rome. Historians today believe the emperor, Nero, arranged for the fire to be set, but the people rose up in such anger that Nero needed someone else to blame. Nero pointed the finger at the Christians. He said they were trying to bring about the end of the world in a judgment of fire.

Christians in Rome were rounded up, imprisoned, tortured, and killed in public arenas. Christianity was declared an illegal religion.

Within a year or so, the persecutions spread to the Roman provinces. Paul, who was recognized as one of the leaders of the Christian community, was arrested and sent to Rome again.

By the time Paul wrote 2 Timothy, he had already had a preliminary hearing (4:16–18) and was waiting for his final trial. He was almost certain that he would be condemned to death.

Some of Paul's friends had been able to care for him a little. Others had been sent out on other missions. At least one had abandoned Paul.

Out in the Christian churches, false teachers were using Paul's imprisonment as an opportunity to bring confusion and division into the congregations.

In the middle of depressing circumstances, Paul wrote to his closest friend. Paul realized that his own work was almost at an end. From a purely human perspective, the future of the Christian faith rested on second-generation leaders like Timothy. In this letter Paul passed the torch of Christian teaching to Timothy and to the faithful leaders Timothy himself would develop.

Second Timothy is an intensely personal letter. Paul remembers their early days together in God's work (1:3–5; 3:10–11). Paul applauded Timothy's unfailing allegiance—to the message of the gospel, to Paul as a mentor and friend, and to Timothy's own calling as a Christian leader.

DiggiNG DeEpeR

X   Stott, John. *The Message of Second Timothy: Guard the Gospel.* The Bible Speaks Today series. Downers Grove, IL: InterVarsity Press, 1973.

A powerful and challenging study through this letter.

Points 2 Remember

- ☑ Second Timothy was Paul's last New Testament letter. He wrote to encourage his friend Timothy to remain faithful to the truth about Jesus Christ that he had learned from Paul.

- ☑ In difficult days of loneliness or pain, we need a few loyal friends who will come to us and help us through the trial.

- ☑ Our responsibility to God's truth does not end when we learn it ourselves. We are to teach that truth to others.

False teachers were still a concern. Paul urged Timothy to "guard the good deposit" (1:14) of truth that Paul had invested in his life. He commanded Timothy to faithfully "preach the Word" (4:2) so the truth would be infused into the hearts and minds of God's people.

Come to Me

The primary purpose of Paul's letter was to ask Timothy to come to Rome (4:9). In his days of loneliness and difficulty, Paul didn't want crowds of people around him. He wanted a few select friends who would care for him and encourage him. Luke was already with Paul, and Mark was to be picked up on the way. But above anyone else, Paul needed Timothy's presence.

That's a good principle to remember when you have dark days of loneliness or pain. You don't need thirty people to come over for dinner! You need two or three close friends—and it's perfectly legitimate to name the ones you want. Give those friends a call and say, "Come. I need you to be with me."

One thing you won't find in this letter is any indication that Paul was afraid of his approaching death. He said:

2 Timothy 2:1 – 2

You then, my son, be strong in the grace that is in Christ Jesus. And the things you have heard me say in the presence of many witnesses entrust to reliable men who will also be qualified to teach others.

For I am already being poured out like a drink offering, and the time has come for my departure. I have fought the good fight, I have finished the race, I have kept the faith. Now there is in store for me the crown of righteousness, which the Lord, the righteous Judge, will award to me on that day—and not only to me, but also to all who have longed for his appearing. (4:6–8)

Early Christian historians tell us that Paul ultimately was sentenced to be executed by beheading. He was taken to a public execution spot outside the city of Rome, the executioner's sword flashed in the sun, and Paul stepped into the presence of Christ.

You don't need an outline to understand 2 Timothy. All you need is a sense of the situation Paul was in as he wrote it—and an open heart to listen to God speak to you through Paul's final words.

Walking the Walk

1. Read 2 Timothy as if you were receiving the last letter from a trusted friend or loving parent. Mark the verses that could be written to you as direction for your own spiritual growth.

2. What friends are on your "short list" of people you could call on in difficult or lonely circumstances? Are you ever courageous enough to tell them you are hurting emotionally or struggling spiritually? What can you do to develop a deeper relationship with those friends?

Titus

➤ Learn how to live a life that others want to follow.

➤ Find out how to make "home improvements."

➤ Discover how you can take your faith to work.

We know far less about Titus (*tie-tus*) than we know about Timothy—but what we do know is very significant. Titus became an associate of the apostle Paul very early in Paul's ministry. Titus is mentioned in Paul's letter to the Galatians and in his second letter to the Corinthians, but he never appears in the book of Acts. Titus was a Gentile, a non-Jew. Some of Paul's Jewish associates viewed Titus as an outsider. Yet when Paul preached the message of the gospel in Titus's hometown, Titus believed in Jesus. He was proof that the message of salvation in Jesus was available to anyone who believed.

Soon after Titus became a Christian, he began to work with Paul in spreading the gospel to other Gentiles. A close bond of friendship developed, and Titus became a personal representative of Paul. When a Christian community needed attention or encouragement and Paul was unable to go himself, he sent Titus.

Paul's letter to Titus was written to encourage and help Titus in the biggest task Paul had given him yet. It all happened something like this:

Key Characters

Paul: a personal representative of Jesus and mentor to Titus

Titus: Paul's associate and trusted representative; a Gentile (non-Jew)

As the book of Acts closed, Paul was in Rome under arrest, waiting for his trial before the emperor.

Apparently Paul was set free after his trial and he resumed his traveling and preaching ministry. Paul and Titus went to the Mediterranean island of Crete and went from city to city preaching about Jesus. In each city people believed in Jesus as Savior and Lord.

These fledgling Christian communities began to meet for worship and instruction, but without Paul or Titus, no one had been taught enough as a Christian to do much teaching of others. So Paul left Titus on Crete with the responsibility of mentoring leaders in each church.

After Paul left Crete and had time to reflect on the task Titus had been given, he sat down and wrote this letter.

From Raw Recruits to Committed Disciples

Titus's job wasn't going to be easy. The Cretan Christians had come out of an immoral way of living, and it would take a while to unlearn their old ways. They had received very little instruction in Christian beliefs or in how to live like Christ in the world. Titus would have to patiently guide them into the new lifestyle of a follower of Jesus.

To make matters worse, false teachers were already at work on these young Christians. In fact, some false teachers followed Paul around and preyed on immature converts.

Paul didn't expect Titus to do the whole job by himself, however. He wanted Titus to appoint Christian leaders (he called them "elders" in 1:5) in each congregation. These leaders would gradually assume more and more responsibility for the instruction and protection of the Christians under their care.

Paul's letter to Titus is focused on three critical areas of Christian living.

Church (Titus 1)

Paul began by reviewing the qualifications of those who were selected as church leaders. The leaders were to model Christian behavior and moral character before the whole community. Paul also warned Titus about the spiritual damage false teachers can bring to a church.

Home (Titus 2)

The work Titus was asked to do had a very practical side to it. Following Jesus as Lord meant living differently at home. Titus was responsible to instruct each group in the Christian community about how to function within the family setting.

Points 2 Remember

☑ Paul's letter to Titus is a summary of the instruction Titus was to give to the new Christians under his care.

☑ The letter focuses on practical ways to follow Jesus as Lord in the church, in family relationships, and in the community.

World (Titus 3)

Paul also wanted Titus to show these Christians that living in obedience to the Lord didn't end at the church door after the worship service on Sunday morning. They were to take their faith out into the streets and marketplace. Their conduct in their workplace or neighborhood would demonstrate the reality of the change Jesus had made in their lives.

Those who follow Jesus do not live differently in order to gain God's approval. We already received God's approval when we believed in Jesus. Christians live differently because we have been changed by God's power. Here's how Paul summarized that dramatic change:

> At one time we too were foolish, disobedient, deceived and enslaved by all kinds of passions and pleasures. We lived in malice and envy, being hated and hating one another. But when the kindness and love of God our Savior appeared, he saved us, not because of righteous things we had done, but because of his mercy. He saved us through the washing of rebirth and renewal by the Holy Spirit, whom he poured out on us generously through Jesus Christ our Savior. (3:3–6)

Digging Deeper

✗ Stott, John. *Guard the Truth: The Message of 1 Timothy and Titus.* The Bible Speaks Today series. Downers Grove, IL: InterVarsity Press, 1996.

Stott's explanation of the letter to Titus is superb!

Walking the Walk

1. Is there anything about your life in your school or workplace that marks you as a follower of Jesus?

2. Reflect on your behavior at home with your mate or family or roommate. Would someone watching you at home recognize that you are a Christian?

3. Of the four categories listed in Titus 2:1–8—older men, older women, younger women, young men—where would you place yourself? How well do you measure up to the do's and don'ts listed in your category? Which one can you start to work on this week?

Philemon

➤ Read about a runaway slave who comes home.

➤ Discover how God receives those who have been running from him.

➤ Learn that being a peacemaker means being a risk-taker.

Several short letters are tucked in the pages of the New Testament. These biblical "postcards" are personal notes—warm expressions of Christian commitment rather than long excursions into Christian teaching. The book of Philemon is a one-page letter from the apostle Paul to his friend Philemon (*fi-lee-mon*). The letter was delivered, not by one of Paul's associates, but by one of Philemon's runaway slaves.

Here's the plot of the story:

Paul and Philemon had become friends during one of Paul's preaching journeys. Paul had come to Ephesus in Asia Minor and had begun to proclaim the message of Jesus as Savior and Lord. Philemon lived in Colosse, a city near Ephesus. God saw to it that Philemon and Paul met. Philemon heard the message and believed in Jesus.

Key Characters

Paul: an apostle of Jesus Christ and friend to Philemon

Philemon: a wealthy Christian in Colosse who came to believe in Jesus under Paul's teaching

Onesimus: Philemon's slave who ran away but then returned as a Christian

Some time later one of Philemon's slaves, a man named Onesimus (*o-ness-i-muss*), decided to steal some money and run away. Slaves in the Roman Empire were not viewed as persons but as things, as objects to be bought and sold. When a runaway slave was caught, the letter *F* for *fugitivus* (fugitive) was branded on his forehead. Roman custom and law allowed a Roman master to execute a slave if he chose to do so.

Onesimus made his way to Rome to lose himself in the masses of the poor who crowded the capital of the empire.

Somehow Onesimus came in contact with Paul, who was under house arrest in Rome. Onesimus became a Christian, and Paul mentored him in his faith.

In time Paul decided to send Onesimus back to Philemon. He wrote this letter, put Onesimus on a ship, and the runaway slave returned to his master.

Put yourself in Philemon's place. After two years Onesimus shows up at your door. Your first response is anger, but he gives you a letter, damp from his nervous hands. You open it to read: "Paul, a prisoner of Christ Jesus . . . to Philemon, my dear friend."

Compelling Persuasion

Paul could have simply commanded Philemon to receive Onesimus back. After all, Paul was an official representative of Jesus. Instead, Paul appealed to Philemon as a friend and brother in Christ.

> Although in Christ I could be bold and order you to do what you ought to do, yet I appeal to you on the basis of love. (verses 8–9)

Points 2 Remember

☑ Paul wrote this letter to urge his friend Philemon to restore a runaway slave named Onesimus.

☑ Onesimus had become a Christian and was now to be received by Philemon as a brother in Christ.

☑ Just as Paul intervened to restore the relationship between Philemon and Onesimus, Jesus intervened to restore us to friendship with God the Father.

Paul asked Philemon to do two things: (1) Restore Onesimus to his former position in the household.

> Welcome him as you would welcome me. (verse 17)

(2) Receive Onesimus as a brother in Christ.

> No longer as a slave, but better than a slave, as a dear brother. (verse 16)

This is the New Testament's answer to the issue of slavery in the Roman Empire—not a political revolution, but a spiritual relationship. As Philemon took Onesimus back, it wasn't long until he recognized that he could not own a

Christian brother. Christian masters began to set their slaves free. They were not coerced by law but compelled by love.

The letter to Philemon is also a powerful illustration of Christ's rescue of those of us who were separated from God by our sin. Everyone of us was a fugitive running from the God who made us. Just as Paul intervened to restore Onesimus to Philemon, Jesus intervened to restore us to God. Jesus took the penalty we deserved. Because of Jesus' death on the cross, God is willing to receive and restore all who accept Christ's gift of forgiveness.

The Rest of the Story

We are never told in the Bible what happened to Onesimus and Philemon. We leave them standing on the doorstep reading Paul's letter. We do have some hints from other sources, however, about how the story ended. About forty years after the letter to Philemon was written, a well-known Christian teacher named Ignatius was arrested and sent to Rome to be executed for his belief in Jesus Christ. On his way to Rome, Ignatius wrote letters to groups of Christians to encourage them to stand firm in their faith. One letter was sent to the Christians at Ephesus, and in the letter Ignatius sent a greeting to the bishop (or leading pastor) of Ephesus. The bishop's name was Onesimus.

It is possible that Philemon ultimately set Onesimus the slave free and that he became a prominent Christian leader in the city of Ephesus. Quite an accomplishment for a runaway slave! But that's what Jesus can do. He's a specialist in changing lives.

DiGGinG DeEpeR

✗ Garland, David. "Philemon." *Colossians and Philemon*. The NIV Application Commentary series. Grand Rapids: Zondervan, 1998.

A thorough and interesting explanation of the book of Philemon.

Walking the Walk

1. Read the letter to Philemon as if you were the injured party in the situation. How do you think Philemon responded to Onesimus after reading Paul's note?

2. As you scroll through your family and friends, is there a broken or strained relationship you could help to restore? What steps as a third party could you take to bring two friends or family members back together?

3. What risks was Paul taking to write this letter? What are you willing to risk to be a peacemaker?

Hebrews

➤ Jesus is better and higher than anything or anyone else!

➤ Find out what Jesus is doing in heaven right now.

➤ Get some encouragement to keep going when you feel like quitting.

The book of Hebrews is a mystery. People refer to it as a letter—the letter to the Hebrews—but it's really not. Ancient letters began with a greeting and the author's name. Hebrews begins with a long sentence about how God spoke in the past and how he still speaks today. The book is more like a sermon than a letter.

No one knows for sure when or where this book was written. We don't know who the original audience was either, for the writer never identifies his readers. We assume that the first readers were Hebrew Christians (thus the title "Hebrews"), because the author warned them about abandoning their faith in Jesus and going back under the Old Testament law. He wrote a lot about the Jewish priests and the animal sacrifices, things Jewish people would understand.

Key Characters

Jesus: the fulfillment of all of God's promises; the Son of God

Moses: the human recipient of God's old covenant of the law

Aaron: Moses' brother; God appointed him to be the leading priest (high priest) for Israel

Melchizedek: a priest of God in Abraham's day (five hundred years before Moses and Aaron lived); Jesus is a priest like Melchizedek

We don't even know who wrote this book. Some people think they know. In fact, plenty of long, boring books have been written trying to prove who wrote it. The best suggestion comes from a third-century Christian leader named Origen, who said, "God only knows" who wrote Hebrews.

Jesus Is Better

There's no mystery about the point of the book of Hebrews, however. The book was written to demonstrate the superiority of Jesus over everything and everyone else. The very first sentence sets the stage. God spoke in the past in many dif-

DoWNLOAd

Hebrews 13:5

God has said,

"Never will I leave you;
  never will I forsake you."

ferent ways, but God has spoken supremely in his Son, Jesus Christ. Jesus is God's final word to humanity. Everything God wanted to say, he said in Jesus.

Maybe that's why the human author never signed his name to this book. He wanted the attention to be focused on Jesus. The author quoted about one hundred times from the Old Testament in his writing, but he never once identified the human writer of an Old Testament book by name. He wanted all of us who read his book to realize that when we listen to the Bible, we are listening to God. God still speaks through his Son and through his Book.

We can make a pretty reasonable guess about the Christians who first heard this book read. They were a group of Jewish people who had come to believe in Jesus as their Messiah and Lord. They had never seen Jesus, but they had believed in him. Their faith in Jesus had brought them hardship and painful confrontations. Their own families had rejected them, but these Christians found a new family within the group of believers. Then persecution began. Some of them lost their jobs because of their loyalty to Christ. Some lost their property or were imprisoned. No one had died for their faith yet, but it was only a matter of time.

The writer of Hebrews heard about the sufferings of his friends. He also heard that some of them had stopped meeting with other Christians. They were in danger of throwing off their faith in Jesus and returning to the safety of Judaism.

So What's the Point?

Most Christians today are not pressured to return to Judaism, but we are still in danger of drawing back from a full commitment to Jesus Christ. Our own desires and the attractions of a secular culture grow stronger and stronger. We want to follow Christ, but the cost seems to get higher all the time. We are happy to accept God's free gift of eternal life and forgiveness by believing in Jesus, but we don't want to go much further. It's too risky. Our society can tolerate a Christian. It has even become respectable to embrace a religious interest (as long as we

CHRISTIANS UNDER FIRE

Most students of the book of Hebrews believe that the Jewish Christians who first read or heard this message lived in Rome. The author referred to an earlier time of suffering (10:23–34). His description fits well into the hardships that Jewish Christians suffered under the Roman emperor Claudius in A.D. 49. The Roman historian Suetonius wrote that "there were riots in the Jewish quarter at the instigation of Chrestus. As a result, Claudius expelled the Jews from Rome." The name Chrestus is probably a corruption of Christos or Christ. The banishment of Jewish Christians from the synagogues created an explosive situation among the Jews. The emperor simply expelled them all.

As the author wrote Hebrews, fifteen years had passed. New persecution under Emperor Nero was looming. No Christian had been killed yet, but martyrdom would come soon enough (12:4). Nero blamed the Christians for a fire in Rome in A.D. 64. Nero probably hired thugs to set the fire, but he needed a scapegoat. Many Christians died in Nero's persecution including the apostles Peter and Paul.

Since Nero's day hundreds of thousands of Christians have died for their faith. What you may not realize is that the century in which most Christians were martyred was not the first or second century when Christians were thrown to lions in Roman arenas. More Christians died in the twentieth century for their faith than in any other century before, and the twenty-first century doesn't look like it will be much better.

keep it private). What our secular society doesn't like is a fully committed follower of Jesus Christ. We are challenged to be obedient to Jesus as Lord in every area of life, but we draw back when we see what it will cost. Our time, our resources, our career path will be under new leadership. Jesus will be in charge, not us! So we simply settle back into a comfortable sleep.

How to Find Yourself in This Book

Three groups of Christians are addressed in the book of Hebrews, and you are in one of these groups. The author moves back and forth from one group to the other, but he keeps coming back to you.

The first group is those who are *wavering*. The writer comes to those of us who have received Jesus as Savior but who are uninvolved and marginal in our commitment. He urges us to press on in our spiritual

Points 2 Remember

☑ Hebrews was written to Jewish Christians who were in danger of returning to Judaism rather than remaining faithful to their commitment to Jesus Christ.

☑ The author demonstrates the superiority of Jesus over everyone and everything else.

☑ We can run the race of life with endurance and courage. Many others have remained loyal to Christ in far worse circumstances. The key is to hold on to Jesus, who will always hold on to us.

quest. Here's an example of the author's challenge to the spiritual couch potato:

> Let us hold unswervingly to the hope we profess, for he who promised is faithful. And let us consider how we may spur one another on toward love and good deeds. (10:23–24)

If you are complacent in your Christian faith, the book of Hebrews will be like a stone in your shoe, pushing and poking into your life. God doesn't want you to settle back. He wants you to press on.

The second group addressed in the book is a group in danger. These are people who need a *warning*. These are second- or third-generation Christians who have grown up in church. They can rattle off Bible verses and say all the right words, but they have never made Mom and Dad's faith their own faith.

The book of Hebrews warns us that it is possible to know a lot about the Bible and to go through the motions of the Christian experience and still not have genuine, personal faith in Jesus. The book confronts us with some sobering words:

> Anyone who rejected the law of Moses died without mercy on the testimony of two or three witnesses. How much more severely do you think a man deserves to be punished who has trampled the Son of God [Jesus] under foot? . . . It is a dreadful thing to fall into the hands of the living God. (10:28–29, 31)

The final group the writer of Hebrews is concerned about are those who are *weary*. These are the people who are fully committed to Christ, but they are tired and discouraged. To them the book of Hebrews brings encouragement and refreshment.

So do not throw away your confidence; it will be richly rewarded. You need to persevere so that when you have done the will of God, you will receive what he has promised. (10:35–36)

How to Find Your Way Through This Book

Remember as you read that Hebrews focuses on the superiority of Jesus over everyone and everything else. Remember also that the author compares Jesus and what Jesus accomplished on the cross with the program of God under the *old* covenant. Prominent Old Testament people, rituals, and sacrifices reemerge in Hebrews.

Jesus: Supreme in Who He Is (Hebrews 1:1 – 7:28)

Jesus is superior to the prophets (1:1–3). God spoke through the prophets, but God's final "word" is his Son.

Jesus is superior to angels (1:4–2:18). Angels were God's messengers to bring the law to Moses on Mount Sinai, but God's new agreement was brought to us by his Son. Angels may be magnificent beings, but they fall down in worship before Jesus.

Jesus is superior to Moses (3:1–4:13). Moses, the greatest prophet of the Old Testament, was a faithful servant in God's household. Jesus is the only Son over God's household. Because the people Moses led out of captivity in Egypt disobeyed, they did not enter into the rest in the land God had promised. If we disregard God's message to us in his Son, we will never enter heaven's rest.

Jesus is superior to Aaron's family, the priests of Israel (4:14–7:28). God chose the descendants of Moses' brother, Aaron, to be priests in Israel. Jesus is a greater priest. Jesus was not a descendant of Aaron, but was a priest patterned after another priest, Melchizedek. (Melchizedek appears in Genesis 14:18–20, where Israel's ancestor Abraham paid tribute to him.) The priests in the line of Aaron offered only animals as a sacrifice. Jesus offered himself, the perfect substitute—human for human.

Jesus: Supreme in What He Did (Hebrews 8:1–10:39)

Jesus brought us into a better covenant (8:1–13). Even in the Old Testament, God promised a "new" covenant that would fulfill and surpass the old covenant of the law.

Jesus offered a better sacrifice (9:1–10:18). The animal sacrifices offered in Israel's tabernacle were not able to fully cleanse the worshiper's conscience from guilt over wrong. Jesus offered himself as the one great sacrifice for human sin. His death has cleansed us forever. The Old Testament priests offered sacrifices every day. Jesus offered one sacrifice on the cross, and it never has to be offered again.

Jesus made a way for us to draw near to God (10:19–39). We can come into God's presence confident that we will be accepted, because Jesus, our Priest forever, is at God's right hand.

Keep Pressing On (Hebrews 11:1–13:25)

The author calls up a long list of Bible heroes who faithfully followed God. If they remained loyal in difficult times, we can too.

> Let us fix our eyes on Jesus, the author and perfecter of our faith, who for the joy set before him endured the cross, scorning its shame, and sat down at the right hand of the throne of God. Consider him who endured such opposition from sinful men, so that you will not grow weary and lose heart. (12:2–3)

DiggiNG DeEpeR

✗ Lane, William. *Call to Commitment.* Nashville: Thomas Nelson, 1985.

The author does an outstanding job of summarizing the book of Hebrews.

Walking the Walk

1. If the author of Hebrews would have lunch with you this week, how would he evaluate your spiritual condition: in good shape? a little flabby but on the right course? too much junk food? call 911? What prescription for spiritual health would he give you?

2. In which of the three groups addressed in the book of Hebrews would you place yourself? How will you respond to God's challenge to you from this book?

3. Did reading Hebrews make you feel more or less secure in your relationship with Jesus? Why?

4. When (if ever) did you drift away from your commitment to Jesus Christ? Why did it happen? What brought you back?

5. Think of a friend who may be discouraged in his or her walk of faith. Based on what you've read in Hebrews, how can you encourage that friend?

James

➤ Read about a practical approach to the Christian life.

➤ Take a look at impressive examples of wise, compassionate living.

➤ Learn how to control your tongue.

One of the earliest writings in the New Testament is tucked in almost at the end. The book of James was written in the very-early days of the Christian story when most of Jesus' original followers were still alive. Most of the Christians were Jewish, and they still met in a Jewish synagogue, not a church. But people back then were just like people today. They had problems and struggles and difficult issues to face. Pride and jealousy had created tension in the Christian community. Some of the affluent were looking down on those who were poorer. Some of the Christians were self-righteous in their judgment of other Christians, while others were living a lifestyle that contradicted their claims to be followers of Jesus. Gossip was the main indoor sport for a few in the group. Something had to be done to get these Christians back on track.

Problems inside the group were matched by persecution from the outside. Most of these Christians had started out in the Jerusalem church under James' instruction, but persecution had scattered them to new areas. They were Christian refugees, pushed around because they believed in Jesus as Savior and Lord.

Key Characters

James: the author of the letter; the half-brother of Jesus

Elijah: an Old Testament prophet who asked God to withhold rain until Israel stopped worshiping idols (James 5:17–18)

One brave, respected Christian leader wrote a letter to this community of believers, and it was so powerful and practical that Christians everywhere wanted a copy. The letter was written by James.

James 1:5

If any of you lacks wisdom, he should ask God, who gives generously to all without finding fault, and it will be given to him.

Jimmy Who?

Three men named James play a significant role in the New Testament. Two of these men were among the original twelve disciples of Jesus— James the son of Zebedee (brother of John) and James the younger. Almost nothing is said about James the younger (or "Little James") in the New Testament, so he is not a likely candidate to be the well-known author of this book. James the son of Zebedee was executed for his faith by the ruler Herod Agrippa very early in the book of Acts (Acts 12:1–2). He *may* have written the book but probably not.

The best candidate is the third James, a half-brother of Jesus himself. The Bible teaches that Jesus was conceived in a virgin named Mary by the power of God. Even after Joseph married Mary, they had no sexual relationship until after Jesus was born (see Matthew 1:25). But then Joseph and Mary seem to have had a normal marriage, and from it came at least six more children. Four brothers are named in the Gospels (James, Joseph, Simon, and Judas; see Matthew 13:55–56). "Sisters" (at least two)

HELP FiLE

AN EARLY BOOK

Many scholars believe the book of James was written between A.D. 45 and 50, making it the first (or one of the first) books of the New Testament. Other early writings included Galatians (written by Paul around A.D. 49) and the gospel of Mark (probably written about A.D. 65).

Early church writers referred to James as "camel's knees" because of his devotion to prayer. In A.D. 62 (just thirty years after Jesus' death and resurrection), James was arraigned before the Jewish high priest and charged with breaking the law of Moses. While the Roman authorities looked the other way, James was taken to the high wall of the temple, thrown down, then stoned to death.

JAMES AND PAUL DUKE IT OUT

When you first read the book of James, it seems that he contradicts some things that Paul says in his letters. For example:

James: What good is it, my brothers, if a man claims to have faith but has no deeds? Can such faith save him? (James 2:14)

Paul: It is by grace you have been saved, through faith ... not by works, so that no one can boast. (Ephesians 2:8–9)

James: You see that a person is justified [made right with God] by what he does and not by faith alone. (James 2:24)

Paul: A man is not justified by observing the law, but by faith in Jesus Christ. (Galatians 2:16)

Well, which is it? Are we made right with God by faith alone or by faith plus good works? What seems at first glance to be a contradiction really isn't. Both James and Paul use the same words but with a different emphasis. Paul is making the point that we cannot earn acceptance with God by keeping a list of rules or doing good deeds. God receives us purely by his grace when we put our faith in Jesus.

On the other hand, James wants to make it clear that genuine faith always produces a changed life. To claim to have faith in Christ but never to act like a follower of Christ is a contradiction. Right actions and compassionate deeds are the evidence of authentic faith.

are mentioned but no names are given. Jesus' half-brothers (same mother) grew up with Jesus, but they did not believe in Jesus as the Messiah until after Jesus rose from the dead. Jesus specifically appeared to James (according to 1 Corinthians 15:7), and James believed that Jesus really was the Lord of all, God's promised Deliverer. In the early years of the Christian community in Jerusalem, James rose to a place of leadership and respect (for verification, read Acts 12:17; 15:13–21; Galatians 1:19; 2:9). When some of the Christian communities outside of Jerusalem began to have problems, this James stepped in with correction and wise advice.

Tough Love

The book of James reads like the "wisdom" books of the Old Testament (especially Proverbs). You will also find some striking similarities to the

Points 2 Remember

☑ James wrote a passionate, practical letter to Christians under pressure.

☑ Genuine faith will always produce the fruit of an obedient, compassionate life.

teaching of Jesus in the Gospels. His book is short, easy to read, even funny. (Check out his discussion of the human tongue in chapter 3.) The hard part is to live out the teaching of James. The central message of the book is that genuine faith in Jesus as Savior will be reflected in a life of obedience to Jesus as Lord. Like every other New Testament writer, James looked at faith as a fundamental requirement of the Christian life. Personal belief and commitment to Jesus Christ are the foundations upon which everything else rests. But a claim of faith alone is not enough. True faith always expresses itself in outward acts of obedience to God. Good deeds do not earn us a place in heaven, but good deeds are the proof that we have a genuine commitment to Jesus Christ.

Three things impress me about this book. First, James wrote a very personal letter. He wrote to people he loved, and they knew it. We can take a lot from someone who really cares. Second, James wrote a passionate letter. He was very direct. Best of all, James wrote a practical letter. He didn't traverse the Milky Way with long, lofty discussions. He wrote about the here and now. He confronted his readers with how to live every day. What he says may hurt, because it may uncover secrets in your life you thought were well hidden. But remember that it comes from a heart of love.

Digging Deeper

✗ Nystrom, David P. *James.* The NIV Application Commentary. Grand Rapids: Zondervan, 1997.

A helpful, in-depth study.

✗ Stulac, George. *James.* IVP New Testament Commentary series. Downers Grove, IL: InterVarsity Press, 1993.

A clearly written guide.

Walking the Walk

1. When you pray, do you want God to give you answers or wisdom? What's the difference? Which has God promised to give? (See James 1:5.)

2. Do you tend to evaluate a person's commitment to Jesus Christ by what that person believes or by how that person acts? What are the limitations of each approach? What is the value of each approach?

3. As you read the book of James, pick one key issue that the book raises that you need to work on in your life. Plot out some practical ways to bring your actions or attitude in that area in line with what James teaches.

1 Peter

➤ Read a letter to persecuted Christians.

➤ Find out why difficult times come into your life.

➤ Listen to a man who failed and was restored by God's grace.

The apostle Peter wrote this letter when it was tough to be a Christian. He wrote it because he was convinced that following Jesus would only get tougher as time went on. Thirty years had passed since Jesus had returned to heaven, and Christian communities had sprung to life in virtually every major city in the Roman Empire. As the churches grew, opposition grew. Jewish leaders who refused to accept Jesus as Israel's promised Messiah loudly criticized the Christians. Followers of the old gods of Rome or Greece or Persia viewed the message of Christianity as a threat to the established way of life in the empire. Political leaders and government bureaucrats looked at the Christians as troublemakers. Christians were barely tolerated in some cities and were openly persecuted in others. Suffering because of loyalty to Jesus became a universal experience.

Peter saw what was happening. He heard reports and read letters from persecuted friends. He was also perceptive enough to notice the dark clouds gathering on the horizon. The Roman emperor Nero had not made any moves against the Christians, but Peter knew that Nero could turn against any group at any moment. It was only a matter of time before Nero's brutal insanity would focus on the Christians.

Peter wrote this letter to Christians scattered throughout the Roman provinces in Asia Minor (modern-day Turkey). It's a letter just as relevant to Christians scattered throughout the world today. The book shows us how to survive in a world turned hostile and how to focus on the hope we have in Jesus instead of on the hopelessness of the situation around us.

Those of us who live in modern democracies haven't had to face much adversity or persecution, but Christians in other cultures turn again and again to 1 Peter for comfort and insight. If you can imagine living in a nation where Christianity is not the majority religion and where freedom of religion is unheard of, if you can imagine losing your job because of your faith or being imprisoned for owning a Bible, you will get a glimpse of what 1 Peter is all about. If you can't imagine those situations and you think it will never happen here, you are ignoring two thousand years of experience. Jesus was falsely condemned and brutally executed, and he warned his followers not to expect anything better.

You Have Mail!

Peter's letter is not about gloom and despair, however. Peter wrote to encourage Christians to deepen their trust in God in every situation of life but especially in times of trial or suffering. When days of difficulty, pain, or loss sweep over us, that is not the time to pull away from the Lord, but an opportunity to draw closer to him. Trials help us grow into mature Christians. Time on the anvil under the hammer blows of testing make us more effective channels of God's love and grace to others.

Peter built his book around two main themes.

Growing into Maturity (1:1 – 2:10)

Peter began his letter with a concise outline of what it means to be a Christian.

Christians are people who have been given a "new birth" (1:3).

HELP FILE

AN APOSTLE'S LETTERS

Peter's letters are another set of paired books in the Bible. The book titles are written 1 Peter and 2 Peter (or I Peter and II Peter) but are referred to as "*First* Peter" and "*Second* Peter."

Simon Peter was one of Jesus' closest followers and often took the role of the leader of the twelve disciples/apostles.

DOWNLOAd

1 Peter 5:6 – 7

Humble yourselves, therefore, under God's mighty hand, that he may lift you up in due time. Cast all your anxiety on him because he cares for you.

Christians have "a living hope through the resurrection of Jesus Christ from the dead" (1:3). We face whatever trials come with confidence in a living Savior who cares for us.

Christians have been promised "an inheritance that can never perish, spoil or fade" (1:4).

Christians may face trials and experience grief, but we have God's promise that the trials come to make us stronger in our faith (1:7).

Christians demonstrate their faith by living lives that are different from the lives of non-Christians. We obey God's truth and have sincere love for other Christians (1:22).

Christians crave the nourishment of God's Word (2:2).

Followers of Jesus "are a chosen people, a royal priesthood, a holy nation, a people belonging to God" (2:9).

Points 2 Remember

☑ Peter wrote this letter to encourage Christian friends to remain faithful to Jesus during times of difficulty and suffering.

☑ Trials may come in different ways and at unpredictable times, but God always uses them to make us stronger.

Surviving in Hostility (2:11 – 5:14)

After Peter explained all that God had done for Christians, he encouraged his readers to remain faithful to God even when their neighbors turned against them.

Dear friends, I urge you, as aliens and strangers in the world, to abstain from sinful desires, which war against your soul. Live such good lives among the pagans that, though they accuse you of doing wrong, they may see your good deeds and glorify God on the day he visits us. (2:11–12)

Peter then issued a whole series of commands designed to help Christians in any age survive in a hostile environment. These chapters tell us how to live Christ-honoring lives without being religious geeks. We may face such trials as injustice at work (2:18–20) or a mate who resists our efforts at spiritual growth (3:1–7). The Christian's example in every difficult situation is Jesus, who did not retaliate when he suffered, but committed himself and the situation to God (2:21–23). The trials God allows us to go through are painful now, but the investment of our endurance will bring an incredible return—strong, mature inner character.

And the God of all grace, who called you to his eternal glory in Christ, after you have suffered a little while, will himself restore you and make you strong, firm and steadfast. (5:10)

The Legacy of a Failure

Unfortunately, the first thing most of us remember about Peter is his failure. Peter boasted loud and long about his willingness to die for Jesus, but when crunch time came, Peter repeatedly denied even knowing Jesus. (Look at Mark 14:66–72.) It's unfortunate that an image of failure comes first to our minds when we hear Peter's name,

Digging Deeper

✗ Marshall, I. Howard. *1 Peter*. IVP New Testament Commentary series. Downers Grove, IL: InterVarsity Press, 1991.

An excellent explanation of Peter's letter and its application today.

✗ Swindoll, Charles. *Hope Again: When Life Hurts and Dreams Fade*. Dallas: Word, 1996.

A warm, practical guide through 1 Peter by a trusted pastor and teacher.

because Peter became a great leader in the early years of the Christian church and was a powerful witness to the resurrection of Jesus. He traveled widely, preaching the message of the gospel. In the end, most likely he was executed for his faith, crucified in Rome.

Peter's most enduring legacy, however, is the two letters he wrote to encourage Christians who were hurting. His first letter is short, clear, full of instructions, covered with tenderness and concern—and the Christians I know rarely read it. Maybe we have it too easy. Maybe it's because our commitment to Jesus isn't strong enough to arouse anyone's curiosity, much less opposition. Maybe we will read 1 Peter more when it gets tougher to follow Christ.

Walking the Walk

1. How do you normally respond to pain or struggle? Do you panic? Do you look for the easy way out? Do you set out to tell everyone about it? What have you learned from Peter's letter about facing trials?

2. If you were asked to tell a new believer in Jesus what to expect in the Christian life, what would you say? What resources have been most helpful in your experience of following Jesus?

3. Call to mind a friend or family member who is going through a tough time. Follow Peter's example and write a letter (or an e-mail) of encouragement to that person. Don't drift into giving him or her easy, pat answers; make the letter an expression of genuine concern.

2 Peter

➤ Discover the fate of false teachers.

➤ Read about the legacy Peter wanted to leave behind.

➤ Learn how to separate truth and error.

In his second letter the apostle Peter wrestled with his own mortality. He knew that he would soon face execution. He had been condemned because of his faith and because he was such a prominent leader in the Christian community. In Peter's own words: "I will soon put [the tent of this body] aside, as our Lord Jesus Christ has made clear to me" (1:14). Facing death has a way of clearing a person's mind and focusing attention on what is really important.

Key Characters

Simon Peter: the leader of Jesus' original disciples; an apostle and traveling preacher

Noah: a good man who survived the Flood in a giant ark (2 Peter 2:5; Genesis 6:9–9:17)

Lot: Abraham's nephew who was rescued before the cities of Sodom and Gomorrah were destroyed by God (2 Peter 2:7–8; Genesis 19:1–29)

Balaam: a wizard who was hired to curse the nation of Israel (2 Peter 2:15–16; Numbers 22–24)

What was really important to Peter was not his own survival. He didn't ask his Christian friends to pray for an angel to release him from his Roman jail cell (as had happened to Peter thirty years earlier in Acts 12). What pushed on Peter's heart were the Christians he would leave behind. Emperor Nero's persecution of Christians was in full swing—but the Christian community would survive persecution. Both Peter and the apostle Paul had been sentenced to death—but the church would survive the death of its leaders. The real threat to the communities under Peter's care came from false teachers. Evil men and women were infiltrating the church and attempting to lead Christians away from Christ. They championed a false message and dishonorable behavior. To make matters worse, some of the Christians were buying their books and attending their seminars!

Peter wrote his second letter to call the Christians back to a firm stand on the firm ground of God's truth.

> Dear friends, this is now my second letter to you. I have written both of them as reminders to stimulate you to wholesome thinking. (3:1)

Thinking . . .

Peter's goal was to plow up the fields of his readers' minds so they would remember his teaching as an apostle of Jesus and would reject the deceiving false teachers. Second Peter requires careful reading and serious thinking to understand. It's not a letter to just breeze through; it's to be examined with care. Peter didn't focus on the calming aspects of God's truth in this book. Instead, he tried to stir up his readers so they would come to grips with truth they had already heard but had yet to implement. They could no longer float and be pushed along by the strong current of false teaching. The time had come for action, for a defense of the truth.

Second Peter is very different from 1 Peter. You might be surprised by what Peter *doesn't* talk about in this second letter.

Nothing is said about Jesus' suffering on the cross—a subject mentioned in every chapter of 1 Peter.

No mention is made of Jesus' resurrection in 2 Peter.

The Holy Spirit is never mentioned either.

Peter included nothing about prayer, baptism, or the body of Christian believers, the church.

WARNINGS	The warnings of the letter were directed toward the false teachers who were ravaging the churches. The entire second chapter is a strong, blunt condemnation of these people in some of the boldest words in the Bible. These enemies of God's truth are called "arrogant" (2:10), "brute beasts" (2:12), and "blots and blemishes" (2:13). They have "eyes full of adultery" and are "experts in greed" (2:14), "springs without water" (2:17), and "slaves of depravity" (2:19).
REMINDERS	Peter also wanted to remind his readers of their blessings as the people of God. *[God's] divine power has given us everything we need for life and godliness. (1:3)* In contrast to the unruly behavior of the false teachers, Peter encouraged the Christians to pursue the character traits displayed by Jesus. *Make every effort to add to your faith goodness; and to goodness, knowledge; and to knowledge, self-control; and to self-control, perseverance; and to perseverance, godliness; and to godliness, brotherly kindness; and to brotherly kindness, love. (1:5–7)*
PROMISES	Peter also focused his readers on God's "very great and precious promises" (1:4) — solid anchors during difficult days. For example, when the Christians were ridiculed for their belief in the return of Jesus to earth, they were to hold fast to the promise from God that "the day of the Lord will come like a thief" (3:10). Christians "are looking forward to a new heaven and a new earth" (3:13).

What Peter did talk about in this letter falls under three themes (see the chart above). As you read the letter, you can easily mark each section as a warning, as a reminder, or as a promise from God.

You can read through the sixty-one verses of 2 Peter in five minutes and it won't mean much to you tomorrow. Or you can read 2 Peter slowly and carefully and think about each verse or section of verses. You can let Peter's words stimulate your mind and challenge your own grasp of

Digging Deeper

✗ Lucas, Dick, and Christopher Green. *The Message of 2 Peter and Jude: The Promise of His Coming*. The Bible Speaks Today series. Downers Grove, IL: InterVarsity Press, 1995.

A thoughtful guide through a very thought-provoking letter.

✗ Moo, Douglas J. *2 Peter, Jude*. The NIV Application Commentary. Grand Rapids: Zondervan, 1996.

An excellent explanation of 2 Peter with plenty of practical insight for today.

truth. You will leave the book more mature, more discerning, more prepared to stand your ground against people who want to lead you away from the truth God has given. Don't be carried away by the false teachers clamoring for your attention. Instead, follow Peter's advice:

Grow in the grace and knowledge of our Lord and Savior Jesus Christ. (3:18)

Walking the Walk

1. How do you respond to people who follow religious teaching that is not in agreement with the Bible?

2. How do you think Peter would respond to people who might come to his door or into a Christian meeting with teaching that is not in line with Scripture?

3. Is it possible to defend the Christian faith without being offensive? What qualities discussed in 2 Peter would you have to cultivate in order to defend your faith more boldly?

John's Letters

— **Heads Up** —

➤ Get back to the basics!

➤ Find out what to do when you do what's wrong.

➤ Examine some practical ways to deal with problems—and with problem people.

1 John

Church fights are not new. Even in the early decades of the Christian movement, division and church splits developed. One of Jesus' disciples, the apostle John, discovered that several of the churches under his care were in turmoil. The cause was hard to detect at first. Apparently some deceivers claiming to be followers of Christ had drifted into the small Christian communities. They had talked like Christians and looked like Christians, so the established Christians had been happy to welcome them into their congregations. But gradually their real motives began to surface.

These new church members began to question some of the teachings that John had given the Christians. They looked around at a corrupt, evil society and concluded that anything physical was impure. A pure God could not create an impure world, could he? The world, they concluded, had been created by evil demons, not by a good God. If the physical world was impure, physical bodies must be impure too. So how could the heavenly Christ inhabit an impure body? Their answer was that Jesus only appeared to be human. Jesus was God pretending to be a man.

When the Christians objected to this "new" teaching and used John's teaching as their authority, the false teachers said that John could not be trusted as a teacher. John had not had the special spiritual experiences with which they had been blessed. In response, John called them liars (2:4, 22; 4:20).

Wrong teaching always leads to wrong living. The false teachers also denied the reality of sin in a Christian's life. If our pure spirits are locked in evil bodies while we live on earth, we can't be held responsible for any wrong we do. "My body made me do it" was their theme. When the Christians kept resisting this new teaching, the false teachers formed their own group and dragged some of the less discerning Christians away with them.

A Father's Voice

John had a tender voice. The apostle Paul wrote his letters like a teacher, carefully arranging his arguments. James wrote as a pastor shepherding his flock. John wrote as a father. With a parent's concern, he penned a serious letter to his children. First John was a circular letter intended to be read by all the Christian communities in the area. It was also a corrective letter designed to anchor these Christians to the truth John had declared to them all along.

 **HELP FILE**

TRIPLET BOOKS

John's letters are the only triplet books in the Bible. They are written 1 John, 2 John, 3 John (or I John, II John, III John), but they are referred to as "*First* John, *Second* John, *Third* John."

No author is listed for 1 John. In 2 and 3 John the author calls himself "the elder." Parallels in thought and expression between the letters and the gospel of John along with significant testimony from early Christian writers have led most students of the Bible to name the apostle John as the author of these letters.

Early church historians suggest that John was the only apostle of Jesus to die from natural causes. The rest were killed for their faith. Late in life John resided in Ephesus in Asia Minor. The churches that first received this letter were probably in that area.

John's last two letters are the shortest books in the New Testament — postcards jotted on a single piece of paper.

Third John is the only New Testament book that does not use the names Jesus or Christ. John simply refers to "the Name" in verse 7.

1 John 2:1

My dear children, I write this to you so that you will not sin. But if anybody does sin, we have one who speaks to the Father in our defense—Jesus Christ, the Righteous One.

John's letter is marked by three outstanding characteristics.

Simple words. John used easy words like *love, light, darkness, sin, born, brother.* Repeatedly John called his readers "dear children" or "little children." He put the truth on a level everyone could understand.

Profound concepts. John's use of simple language does not mean that he had small ideas. Once you begin to think deeply about what John has said, you find no bottom, no limit to the implications of the truth. "God is love" is one of John's simplest statements (4:16), but who can grasp the depth of love embedded in the character and actions of God?

Dramatic contrasts. John liked to present his ideas as black or white—no gray, no shades of meaning, one way or the other.

> "Anyone who claims to be in the light but hates his brother is still in the darkness" (2:9). *My thought when I read that is: What if I hate my brother only once in a while? Do I lose my place in God's light?*
>
> "He who does what is right is righteous. . . . He who does what is sinful is of the devil" (3:7–8). *Uh, John—one question: I try to do what is right and usually I succeed. But if I fail, even once, am I out of the program?*

One of the keys to understanding this letter is to keep in mind that John normally refers to a person's *habitual* way of life. "No one who lives in [God] *keeps on* sinning" (3:6, my emphasis). Christians do sin, but if our habitual practice is to sin, that is proof that we have not received genuine life from God.

The Word of Life

John's first letter is almost impossible to outline. It's a letter from a parent! He talked about one theme, moved to two or three others, and then came back to his first theme. The best way to learn what is in the book is to read it—and then read it again. Look for John's key concepts:

WALKING IN GOD'S LIGHT	This is the message we have heard from him and declare to you: God is light; in him there is no darkness at all. If we claim to have fellowship with him yet walk in the darkness, we lie and do not live by the truth. But if we walk in the light, as he is in the light, we have fellowship with one another, and the blood of Jesus, his Son, purifies us from all sin. (1:5–7)
PRACTICING GOD'S TRUTH	No one who is born of God will continue to sin, because God's seed remains in him; he cannot go on sinning because he has been born of God. (3:9)
DEMONSTRATING GOD'S LOVE	This is how we know what love is: Jesus Christ laid down his life for us. And we ought to lay down our lives for our brothers. If anyone has material possessions and sees his brother in need but has no pity on him, how can the love of God be in him? Dear children, let us not love with words or tongue but with actions and in truth. (3:16–18)
RESTING IN GOD'S PROMISES	This is the testimony: God has given us eternal life, and this life is in his Son. He who has the Son has life; he who does not have the Son of God does not have life. I write these things to you who believe in the name of the Son of God so that you may know that you have eternal life. (5:11–13)

John was very concerned that the Christians under his care would learn to discern between truth and error. He urged them not to *trust* every

Points 2 Remember

☑ First John is a letter written to several congregations under John's direction. He warned the Christians not to be swept away by those claiming to have "new" truth from God.

☑ John wrote as a father to his children. Rather than arrange arguments, he wove important themes together.

☑ Christian belief is to be anchored to what God has spoken in the Bible. We evaluate every spiritual experience and teaching against the measuring stick of Scripture.

teacher claiming to be a Christian but to "*test* the spirits to see whether they are from God, because many false prophets have gone out into the world" (4:1, my emphasis). Love is an important element in the Christian community, but so is truth! In order to tell what is false, you have to have some standard of truth. God has given us his truth in the Bible. Any teaching or spiritual experience that does not measure up to God's truth is suspect. What was declared "from the beginning" should be the anchor for what we believe today.

2 John

John's second letter is a personal letter to one congregation. No names appear in the letter except those of God the Father and Jesus Christ, but we can piece things together pretty well. John as "the elder" addressed the letter to "the chosen lady and her children," probably a reference to an individual Christian community. The lady's "sister" is most likely a nearby church. John had warned all the churches in his first letter to be very cautious and discerning toward some teachers who did not hold to the apostle's teaching about who Jesus was. This particular church had read that letter, but they needed further instruction.

It was hard for first-century Christian leaders and missionaries to find places to stay as they traveled around the Roman world. When they could, they stayed with members of the local Christian community. The community John wrote to in 2 John had a wonderful reputation for hospitality and sacrificial love. John commended them for their love but urged them to use greater discernment toward those they welcomed into their homes and Christian meetings. Their love needed limits—the boundaries of God's truth.

Many deceivers, who do not acknowledge Jesus Christ as coming in the flesh, have gone out into the world.... If anyone comes to you and does not bring this teaching [about Jesus], do not take him into your house or welcome him. (verses 7, 10)

These are instructions to a church under siege. This certainly doesn't erase the commands of the New Testament to show gracious hospitality to strangers or to those in need. But if false teachers come into a community for the purpose of attacking clear biblical teaching, Christians are to turn away and refuse them access to the congregation. No one said standing for the truth of God was easy. Sometimes it takes incredible courage!

3 John

Some people never get it! The apostle John wrote his first letter to all the churches in his realm of influence to warn them about false teachers. Most of the troublemakers packed up, moved out, and formed their own communities. One leader of a small house church decided to oppose John, so John dashed off the shortest letter in the New Testament to try to hold things together until he could get there personally.

Three men stand out in 3 John:

Diotrephes (*die-ott-ra-feez*) loved to be in the spotlight. When the false teachers came into his church with their "new" truth, he welcomed them. When John wrote to warn the Christians about the false teachers, Diotrephes started a smear campaign against him. His tactics were brutal: malicious gossip about John and stubborn

DiggiNG DeEpeR

✗ Stott, John. *The Epistles of John.* Tyndale Bible Commentary series. Grand Rapids: Eerdmans, 1964.

Stott is creative and convincing.

✗ Thompson, Marianne Meye. *1–3 John.* IVP New Testament Commentary series. Downers Grove, IL: InterVarsity Press, 1992.

A careful, interesting study of John's letters.

refusal to allow any Christian teachers access to the congregation. Anyone who *did* welcome the true Christian teachers was kicked out of the church!

Gaius (***gay***-*us*) stood in opposition to Diotrephes, but he wasn't making much progress. John wrote 3 John to Gaius to encourage him to remain committed. Gaius had sheltered the traveling Christian teachers and had sent them on their way with money for their expenses (verse 6).

Demetrius (*de-**mee**-tree-us*) was John's associate who brought the letter to Gaius. John wanted Gaius to welcome Demetrius and introduce him to the other Christians.

People like Diotrephes are still around. They love a place of power in the Christian community, and they use that power to beat up other Christians. John's letter gives us a strategy to counteract that kind of power play. John could have just written off the situation as a lost cause, but he stayed in contact. He enlisted Gaius as an ally and sent Demetrius to strengthen the ranks of those who remained faithful to Christ. Confronting power-hungry people is no time for a "wait and see" or "run and hide" attitude. That's when you need courage—the courage that comes from standing for what is right.

Walking the Walk

1. Which is easier to do—"walk in love" or "walk in truth"? Which is more important? How can you keep a proper balance?

2. How would you respond to someone who says, "It really doesn't matter what you believe as long as you are sincere and loving"?

3. What insights have you gained from these letters that will help you confront someone who holds to the truth but who has an unloving attitude? How can you help someone who is very loving but not very discerning?

Jude

— Heads Up —

➤ Read Jude's colorful characterizations of false teachers.
➤ Get some direction for defending what you believe.

Most of us don't like to emphasize the negative. Some people seem to enjoy the negative outlook on life, but they aren't the type we like to be around very much. Maybe that's why the little book of Jude is so neglected. Jude doesn't say much about the wonderful blessings of God. Instead, he makes us sit up straight and listen to some things we'd rather not hear.

Or maybe we ignore Jude because cultivating discernment is hard work. Developing the ability to separate truth from error is not very appealing in a day when it is more fashionable to be gullible and inoffensive. When we hear religious teaching that contradicts biblical truth, we just shrug it off—or worse yet, we don't even realize the teaching is not in line with the Bible. We're bombarded by all kinds of messages claiming to be from God, and the popular mind-set is to tolerate everything. What's "true" for you may not be "true" for me—but that's okay! If Jude were around, he would write a serious letter to Christians today—just like the letter tucked away at the end of the New Testament.

Key Characters

Jude: the author of the letter; Jesus' half-brother

Michael: a powerful angel of God (Jude 9)

Cain: Adam and Eve's son who killed his brother Abel (Jude 11; Genesis 4:1–16)

Balaam: an Old Testament sorcerer hired to curse Israel (Jude 11; Numbers 22–24)

Korah: an Israelite who led a rebellion against Moses and Aaron (Jude 11; Numbers 16)

Enoch: one of the early (pre-Flood) followers of God (Jude 14; Genesis 5:18–24)

Hey, Jude

But who is this guy? We know Peter and John and Paul, even James. But Jude? Most likely, Jude was one of Jesus' half-brothers. The Bible teaches that Jesus was born of a virgin named Mary and that he had no human biological father.

Jude 24 - 25

To him who is able to keep you from falling and to present you before his glorious presence without fault and with great joy — to the only God our Savior be glory, majesty, power and authority, through Jesus Christ our Lord, before all ages, now and forevermore! Amen.

(Access Matthew 1:18–25 and Luke 1:26–38 for the details.) But after Jesus was born, Mary and Joseph had a normal marriage relationship. Four sons and at least two daughters were born into their home (Matthew 13:55–56; Mark 6:3). One of the sons was James, the author of the New Testament letter of James. Another of the boys was named (in Hebrew) Judah or (in Greek) Judas or (in English) Jude.

Jude sat down one day intending to write a few lines to some Christian friends about the positive blessings of salvation in Jesus Christ. He had the letter all mapped out in his mind. But as he began to write the first words of greeting, Jude was prompted by God to write on a different subject.

> Dear friends, although I was very eager to write to you about the salvation we share, I felt I had to write and urge you to contend for the faith that was once for all entrusted to the saints. For certain men whose condemnation was written about long ago have secretly slipped in among you. They are godless men, who change the grace of our God into a license for immorality and deny Jesus Christ our only Sovereign and Lord. (verses 3–4)

Jude's letter is a warning about false teachers who were infiltrating the Christian communities with perverted teaching. Apparently these

Di99inG DeEpeR

X   Lucas, Dick, and Christopher Green. *The Message of 2 Peter and Jude: The Promise of His Coming.* The Bible Speaks Today series. Downers Grove, IL: InterVarsity Press, 1995.

A detailed study with insights for "contending for the faith" today.

☑ Jude wrote his letter to warn Christians about false teachers and to urge them to defend the Christian faith.

☑ God has given us a body of truth (called "the faith") through the apostles and other New Testament writers. Christians have a responsibility, not only to believe that truth, but also to vigorously guard it from attack.

people were trying to convince the Christians that because they had been saved and forgiven by God's grace, they could now do whatever they wanted to do. Since the penalty for their sin was fully paid by Jesus on the cross, they could keep on living in sin and God wouldn't care. God's grace was a cover for immoral behavior!

Jude wrote to tell the Christians to stay away from these teachers. He pulled several illustrations from the Bible to show that God will judge the false teachers severely. His advice was: Don't be standing next to them when God's lightning strikes!

The Christians were not to be deceived by the false teaching either. They were to "build [themselves] up in [the] most holy faith" (verse 20). God's grace *does* cleanse us from all sin, but the proper response to grace is to love and serve the gracious Giver. Liberty in Christ is never a license to sinful, immoral behavior.

Defending the Faith

The Christian faith is not something up for grabs. It's not a position paper that can be divided up and voted on every few years. Jude says "the faith . . . was once for all entrusted to the saints [that is, to Christians]" (verse 3).

"The faith" is the truth that God has given to us in the Bible—truth about God himself, sin, salvation, eternity. That body of truth was given through the apostles, the authorized representatives of Jesus, and through other writers of Scripture called prophets. By the time the apostles and prophets moved off the scene, that truth had been fully received. We aren't looking today for new Scripture. Our responsibility as Christians is not to change God's truth, but to understand and defend God's truth. Unfortunately, some Christians will fight to the extreme to defend a favorite tradition or a certain style of worship music, but they aren't bothered at all when foundational truths of the Bible are questioned or abandoned. Jude's letter is a wake-up call to Christians to stand firm in God's truth.

Walking the Walk

1. Jesus commanded us not to judge one another (Matthew 7:1–5) and yet Jude wants us to judge those who claim to teach God's truth. How can we do both?

2. Do you tend to be too gullible or too suspicious? What are the dangers of each extreme when it comes to listening to religious teaching?

3. What advice would Jude give to a person today who is involved in a religious organization that does not teach biblical truth?

Revelation

— Heads Up —

➤ Preview the final wrap-up of human history.
➤ Be held spellbound by strange visions and cosmic battles.
➤ Find out what Jesus thinks of your church.
➤ Stand amazed as you see into the future.

If you like to read the last chapter of a book first so you know how the story ends, you will love the book of Revelation. It's the last chapter in God's story—and it's an incredible ending!

For some reason the book of Revelation frightens a lot of people. They open its pages and read about beasts and plagues and worldwide catastrophes and quickly find something else to read. Other people don't read anything in the Bible but Revelation. Every event in the headlines or in their lives is somehow linked to the end of time.

Key Characters

Jesus: God's Son; the same person who died on the cross and rose from the dead; he is now exalted in heaven

John: the author of the book; one of Jesus' original followers

The Lamb: another name for Jesus

The beast: a future ruler who opposes God

The false prophet: an associate of the beast who performs miracles designed to deceive the people of the earth

The dragon: Satan; the source of power behind the beast and false prophet (all three are mentioned together in Revelation 20:10)

A Few Provisions for the Journey

A few simple facts will keep us on track as we read this book.

What Is It?

The book of Revelation is actually a letter—a letter sent to a cluster of seven first-century Christian communities in Asia Minor (the nation of Turkey today). Within the larger letter are seven smaller letters, one to each church (chapters 2 and 3). Jesus himself talks to each congregation, and then the entire Christian community is given a glimpse into the future in the rest of the book.

The full title of the book is "The Revelation of Jesus Christ." The word *revelation* means "an unveiling." The book unveils truth about Jesus Christ. He is the focus of everything recorded in the book.

Who Wrote It?

The book was written by John (1:1, 4, 9; 22:8). He didn't tell us specifically *which* John he was, but from the earliest days of Christianity the book has been linked to John the apostle, the close friend and follower of Jesus, the author of the gospel of John. John was an old man when he wrote the book. He was in exile on Patmos, a prison island in the Aegean Sea off the western coast of Asia Minor. The Roman emperor Domitian was on the attack against the Christians, and he sent John into exile because John was such a respected Christian leader.

Why Was This Book Written in Such a Strange Way?

Most of Revelation is a record of what John "saw." God gave John a series of visions. Some are visions of heaven; some are visions of earth. The visions are filled with symbols and images—and most of the time we aren't told directly what the symbols mean. For example, in Revelation 5:6 John looked into heaven and saw a lamb standing in front of the throne of God. The lamb is obviously a symbol. In this case, the lamb is a symbol for Jesus. Later in the book (chapter 12) John saw an immense dragon. The dragon was a symbol, too, an image of Satan, the

HELP FILE

REVELATION

This book is sometimes called "The Apocalypse" (based on the Greek word translated "Revelation" in 1:1).

Specific numbers appear several times in Revelation—look especially for the numbers 7, 12, and 24.

The most common mistake people make in referring to the Bible is to call this book *Revelations*—but the name is singular, Revelation.

In the book of Revelation, John refers directly or indirectly to thirty-two different Old Testament books.

666: THE MARK OF THE BEAST

One of the best-known images from Revelation is the number 666. Rock groups and gang members have fully exploited its shock value. John used the number as a cryptic explanation of the Antichrist's name. This evil ruler, called "the beast" in Revelation 13, will require people to be permanently marked on the hand or forehead with his name or with the number of his name. Without the mark, no one will be able to buy or sell in the marketplace.

This ruler will also force everyone small and great, rich and poor, free and slave, to receive a mark on his right hand or on his forehead, so that no one can buy or sell unless he has the mark, which is the name of the beast or the number of his name.

This calls for wisdom. If anyone has insight, let him calculate the number of the beast, for it is man's number. His number is 666. (13:16–18)

For generations people have tried to link the number 666 with political leaders who were oppressive or who seemed to favor a world government. Almost every United States president over the past century has been identified by someone as the Antichrist. But no one has been right so far!

evil enemy of God. Satan is not a dragon, but the dragon pictured certain aspects of Satan's character.

So why confuse us with all the imagery? Why not just say, "I saw Satan at war with God's holy angels"? To John's first-century readers, the imagery was not nearly as strange as it is to us. Those Christians were far more familiar with the weird Old Testament visions of Daniel and Ezekiel than we are. Other books of end-of-the-world visions were circulating in those days too. They were not visions from God, but the use of imagery to convey a message was a familiar style of communication.

Another reason God used imagery so extensively in this book was to communicate his message more dramatically. We can talk about evil rulers in the abstract sense, but a video clip highlighting the faces of Hitler and Stalin and Pol Pot makes a direct emotional connection to our minds. John's description in Revelation 13 of a monster rising out of the sea as a picture of an evil oppressor of God's people brings the truth home with terrible reality. We remember the image far longer than a dry theological discussion of the nature of evil. John's language triggers our emotions as well as our minds.

But Is It Worth Reading?

I've actually heard some people say that they avoid reading Revelation because it is too confusing. I try to remind those people that we know how the story ends. God wins! And his victory is already secure and certain when the book opens. In addition, God specifically promises a blessing on the person who reads the book of Revelation.

> Blessed is the one who reads the words of this prophecy, and blessed are those who hear it and take to heart what is written in it. (1:3)

So what are you waiting for? This book will unveil the glory and majesty of Jesus like no other book of the Bible.

APOCALYPSE NOW!

The book of Revelation is sometimes called "The Apocalypse" (based on the Greek word translated "Revelation" in verse 1). Apocalyptic *(a-pok-a-**lip**-tik)* literature was very popular among the Jews in the centuries after the Old Testament was completed (400 B.C. through A.D. 200). In the book of Revelation, God used a popular writing style to communicate his message.

Characteristics of apocalyptic style:

- The central features are dreams or visions filled with symbolic creatures and events.
- Visions are recorded exactly as they are seen by the author.
- The visions are usually explained by a heavenly interpreter, such as an angel or God himself.
- The focus of the writing is on the future or the end of time.
- This literature was normally written during times when the readers were oppressed or persecuted.

A few principles will help you interpret the apocalyptic writing in the Bible (Revelation, Daniel, Zechariah):

- The visions were never meant to be explained to the smallest detail. What is most important is the main thrust.
- Try to follow the heavenly interpreter's explanation without adding to it or elaborating on it.
- Keep the focus on the final conclusion— God wins!

JUST DO IT!

If you have never read Revelation before (or if it has been awhile), pick up your Bible and read through the twenty-two chapters. Ignore the study notes and interpretive outlines for now and listen to the book itself. You won't understand it all (no one does!), but you will get a wonderful sense of the sweep and power of the book.

Making Sense

Christians have interpreted the book of Revelation in at least three ways. All Christians accept the book as part of God's truth, but they use different frameworks in an attempt to understand what the book means and what it means for us today.

Framework #1: The visions of Revelation do not link to actual historical events; rather, they picture the timeless battle between good and evil. In this view the "beast coming out of the sea" in Revelation 13, for example, is not a picture of an actual person in the past or in the future but a general symbol of evil rulers and oppressive governments in any age.

Framework #2: The visions of Revelation explain events that happened to the first-century Christians. Some Christians look at Revelation as a description of events limited to John's own time. They read it as a symbolic account of Rome's persecution of the Christian community. According to this view, John wrote to encourage the Christians to remain faithful to the Lord during the persecution. The "beast coming out of the sea" pictured the Roman emperor or even the entire official Roman Empire rising up in opposition to the followers of Christ.

Framework #3: The visions of Revelation explain events still in the future. Other Christians believe that the "beast coming out of the sea" represents an evil world leader who has yet to appear. According to this view, John saw events that will precede the final wrap-up of human history. God will bring severe judgment on the earth just before Jesus returns in glory and power to destroy every enemy.

Personally, I like parts of all three views! Overall, Revelation certainly shows us that God will ultimately triumph over evil and injustice (#1). John also wrote to encourage his fellow Christians during a time of persecution. His words gave them assurance of God's reign over the world even when his enemies seemed strong (#2). But the book claims to be a book of prophecy, explaining things yet to come. In that light, I take the view that the events described by John in Revelation 4–22 have yet to happen. John saw visions that represented real events that will someday actually unfold in human history (#3).

"I Saw Heaven Standing Open"

Revelation was outlined by Jesus himself as he commissioned John to write the book.

> "Write, therefore, what you have seen [Part 1], what is now [Part 2] and what will take place later [Part 3]." (1:19)

Part 1: "What You Have Seen" (Revelation 1)

The book opens with John's account of his exile on the island of Patmos and his vision of Jesus in his heavenly glory. John was Jesus' closest friend on earth, but when John saw Jesus on this occasion, he didn't run up, slap Jesus on the back, and say, "Jesus, it's good to see you!" Confronted with the majesty of Jesus, John fell at his feet.

Part 2: "What Is Now" (Revelation 2–3)

Next, Jesus addressed each of the seven churches. They not only read about themselves; they also read about each other. The seven Christian communities were actual churches in the late first century, but they also represent different churches where you live. In every city or

---

DoWNLoAd

Revelation 5:12

"Worthy is the Lamb, who was slain,
to receive power and wealth and wisdom and strength
and honor and glory and praise!"

Points 2 Remember

☑ The book of Revelation unveils Jesus Christ in his majesty and power.

☑ John saw the events leading up to Jesus' glorious return to earth.

☑ The images and symbols in the book represent real events and people.

☑ Christians agree on the fact of Jesus' ultimate return and final victory but differ on what framework to use to interpret Revelation.

☑ When it seems like evil and injustice are winning, remember that God's victory has already been made certain by Jesus' death on the cross and resurrection to life.

☑ God is in full control of our future!

region you can find at least one church like the church at Ephesus, the first church Jesus addressed. "Ephesian-type" Christians have a rich spiritual heritage, but they have lost the intense love of Jesus that marked their early years.

If Jesus were writing to most churches today, my personal opinion is that he would simply repeat what he said to the church at Laodicea (*lay-odd-i-see-a*):

"You say, 'I am rich; I have acquired wealth and do not need a thing.' But you do not realize that you are wretched, pitiful, poor, blind and naked." (3:17)

Part 3: "What Will Take Place Later" (Revelation 4 – 22)

The longest section of the book focuses on events leading up to Jesus' return to earth as conquering King. John was taken into heaven, and he saw God's throne room and Jesus empowered to reclaim the universe from the grip of sin and death (chapters 4–5). Chapters 6–19 track three waves of judgment that God will pour out on the world: As Jesus broke each of seven wax seals on a scroll, seven judgments were released (chapter 6); as seven angels blew seven trumpets, another wave of even more devastating plagues was unleashed (chapters 8–9); the final devastation of God's enemies came as seven angels poured seven bowls of wrath on the earth (chapters 15–16).

In between the waves of judgment, John inserted short interludes in which he explained certain events in more detail. Sometimes John jumped to an event still future. At other times he seemed to go back and fill in details of events already mentioned. For example, in the interlude between the trumpet judgments and the bowl judgments, John described Satan's expulsion from heaven (chapter 12), the rise of an evil world leader commonly called the Antichrist (chapter 13), and the final reward of 144,000 people that he had first mentioned back in Revelation 7 (chapter 14).

Just when it seemed the universe was ready to collapse under the weight of God's judgment, John saw Jesus return to earth as a great Conqueror.

> I saw heaven standing open and there before me was a white horse, whose rider is called Faithful and True. With justice he judges and makes war. His eyes are like blazing fire, and on his head are many crowns. He has a name written on him that no one knows but he himself. He is dressed in a robe dipped in blood, and his name is the Word of God. The armies of heaven were following him, riding on white horses and dressed in fine linen, white and clean. Out of his mouth comes a sharp sword with which to strike down the nations. "He will rule them with an iron scepter." He treads the winepress of the fury of the wrath of God Almighty. On his robe and on his thigh he has this name written:
>
> KING OF KINGS AND LORD OF LORDS. (19:11–16)

Revelation pictures human history coming to its fulfillment and conclusion as Jesus sets up an eternal kingdom of glory and justice. Those

Digging Deeper

Written from the perspective that the visions of Revelation focus primarily on events in the future:

✗ Walvoord, John. *The Revelation of Jesus Christ.* Chicago: Moody Press, 1989.

Written from the perspective that the visions of Revelation focus primarily on events in the early church:

✗ Wilcock, Michael. *The Message of Revelation: I Saw Heaven Opened.* The Bible Speaks Today series. Downers Grove, IL: InterVarsity Press, 1989.

who stood against God are separated from God's kingdom and condemned to a lake of fire. Those who faithfully followed Christ inherit a kingdom of unimagined splendor.

The Bible closes with one final invitation:

> Whoever is thirsty, let him come; and whoever wishes, let him take the free gift of the water of life. (22:17)

And one final promise. Jesus says:

> "Yes, I am coming soon." (22:20)

JESUS IN REVELATION

The book of Revelation comes from Jesus and centers on Jesus. Every title given to Jesus in the book displays a particular aspect of his character or power.

"The faithful witness" (1:5)
"The firstborn from the dead" (1:5)
"The ruler of the kings of the earth" (1:5)
"The Alpha and the Omega" (1:8; 21:6; 22:13)
"The First and the Last" (1:17; 2:8; 22:13)
"The Living One" (1:18)
"The Son of God" (2:18)
"The Amen" (3:14)
"The faithful and true witness" (3:14)
"The ruler of God's creation" (3:14)
"The Lion of the tribe of Judah" (5:5)
"The Root of David" (5:5)
"The Lamb" (twenty-nine times beginning at 5:8)
"Lord of lords and King of kings" (17:14; 19:16)
"Faithful and True" (19:11)
"The Word of God" (19:13)
"The Beginning and the End" (21:6; 22:13)
"The bright Morning Star" (22:16)
"The Lord Jesus" (22:20, 21)

Walking the Walk

1. If Jesus would write a letter to your church or religious community, what would he commend? What would he condemn? What counsel would he give you?

2. How does the Bible's picture of the future affect you: Make you fearful? Give you confidence? Make you smile because it's too weird to believe?

3. Should we take a stand against wrong and injustice and immoral behavior—or just wait for Jesus to come back and take care of it all? What issue in our culture deserves your involvement to change or correct?

4. What question about the future would you like answered? Why would you like to have that answer?

Acknowledgments

Several people gave significant help to the production of this book. Cindy Bunch-Hotaling encouraged me to pursue the idea when I was ready to give up. Tom Skaff, Judy Skaff, Steve Aikman, Eileen Unger, and Ron Radke were my resident "Blockheads" who read most or all of the chapters and gave me their evaluations. Rich Tesner helped me put together the original proposal with his graphic design expertise. Jack Kuhatschek, Jim Ruark, Laura Weller, and all the other people at Zondervan have guided the book flawlessly through the editorial and production process.

My deepest gratitude goes to my wonderfully supportive church family at Cross Church and to my wife, Karen, and my family. You make life incredibly good!